VEGETABLE TERATOLOGY

AN ACCOUNT OF THE PRINCIPAL DEVIATIONS FROM THE USUAL CONSTRUCTION OF PLANTS

BY MAXWELL T. MASTERS

INTRODUCTION.

Till within a comparatively recent period but little study was given to exceptional formations. They were considered as monsters to be shunned, as lawless deviations from the ordinary rule, unworthy the attention of botanists, or at best as objects of mere curiosity. By those whose notions of structure and conformation did not extend beyond the details necessary to distinguish one species from another, or to describe the salient features of a plant in technical language; whose acquaintance with botanical science might almost be said to consist in the conventional application of a number of arbitrary terms, or in the recollection of a number of names, teratology was regarded as a chaos whose meaningless confusion it were vain to attempt to render intelligible,—as a barren field not worth the labour of tillage.

The older botanists, it is true, often made them the basis of satirical allusions to the political or religious questions of the day, especially about the time of the Reformation, and the artists drew largely upon their polemical sympathies in their representations of these anomalies. Linnæus treated of them to some extent in his 'Philosophia,' but it is mainly to Angustin Pyramus De Candolle that the credit is due of calling attention to the importance of vegetable teratology. This[Pg xxii] great botanist, not only indirectly, but from his personal research into the nature of monstrosities, did more than any of his predecessors to rescue them from the utter disregard, or at best the contemptuous indifference, of the majority of botanists. De Candolle gave a special impetus to morphology in general by giving in his adhesion to the morphological hypotheses of Goethe. These were no mere figments of the poet's imagination, as they were to a large extent based on the actual investigation of normal and abnormal organisation by Goethe both alone, and also in conjunction with Batsch and Jaeger.

De Candolle's example was contagious. Scarcely a botanist of any eminence since his time but has contributed his quota to the records of vegetable teratology, in proof of which the names of Humboldt, Robert Brown, the De Jussieus, the Saint Hilaires, of Moquin-Tandon, of Lindley, and many others, not to mention botanists still living, may be cited. To students and amateurs the subject seems always to have presented special attractions, probably from the singularity of the appearances presented, and from the fact that in many cases the examination of individual instances of malformation can be carried on, to a large extent, without the lengthened or continuous investigation and critical comparative study required by other departments of botanical science. Be this as it may, teratology owes a very large number of its records to this class of observers.

While the number of scattered papers on vegetable teratology in various European languages is so great as to preclude the possibility of collating them all, there is no general treatise on the subject in the[Pg xxiii] English language, with the exception of Hopkirk's 'Flora Anomala,' a book now rarely met with, and withal very imperfect; and this notwithstanding that Robert Brown early lent his sanction to the doctrines of Goethe, and himself illustrated them by teratological observations. In France, besides important papers of Turpin, Geoffroy de Saint Hilaire, Brongniart, Kirschleger and others, to which frequent allusion is made in the following pages, there is the classic work of Moquin-Tandon, which was translated into German by Schauer. Germany has also given us the monographs of Batsch, Jæger, Rœper, Engelmann, Schimper, Braun, Fleischer, Wigand, and many others. Switzerland has furnished the treatises of the De Candolles, and of Cramer; Belgium, those of Morren, &c., all of which, as well as many others that might be mentioned, are, with the exception of Moquin-Tandon's 'Eléments,' to be considered as referring to limited portions only and not to the whole subject.[1]

In the compilation of the present volume great use has been made of the facts recorded in the works just cited, and especially in those of Moquin-Tandon, Engelmann, and Morren. A very large number of communications on teratological subjects in the various European scientific publications have also been laid under contribution. In most cases reference has been given to, and due acknowledgment made of, the sources whence information has been gathered. Should any such reference be omitted, the neglect must be attributed to inadvertence, not to design. In selecting[Pg xxiv] illustrations from the immense number of recorded facts, the principle followed has been to choose those which seemed either intrinsically the most important, or those which are recorded with the most care. In addition to these public sources of information, the author has availed himself of every opportunity that has offered itself of examining cases of unusual conformation in plants. For many such opportunities the author has to thank his friends and correspondents. Nor has he less reason to be grateful for the suggestions that they have made, and the information they have supplied. In particular the writer is desirous of acknowledging his obligations to the Society, under whose auspices this work is published, and to Mr. S. J. Salter, to whom the book in some degree owes its origin.

The drawings, where not otherwise stated, have been executed either from the author's own rough sketches, or from the actual specimens, by Mr. E. M. Williams. A large number of woodcuts have also been kindly placed at the disposal of the author by the proprietors of the 'Gardeners' Chronicle.'[2]

As it is impossible to frame any but a purely arbitrary[Pg xxv] definition of teratology or to trace the limits between variation and malformation, it may suffice to say that vegetable teratology comprises the history of the irregularities of growth and development in plants, and of the causes producing them. These irregularities differ from variations mainly in their wider deviation from the customary structure, in their more frequent and more obvious dependence on external causes rather than on inherent tendency, in their more sudden appearance, and lastly in their smaller liability to be transmitted by inheritance.

What may be termed normal morphology includes the study of the form, arrangement, size and other characteristic attributes of the several parts of plants, their internal structure, and the precise relation one form bears to another. In order the more thoroughly to investigate these matters it is necessary to consider the mode of growth, and specially the plan of evolution or development of each organ. This is the more needful owing to the common origin of things ultimately very different one from the other, and to the presence of organs which, in the adult state, are identical or nearly so in aspect, but which nevertheless are very unlike in the early stages of their existence.[3] Following Goethe, these changes in the course of development are sometimes called metamorphoses. In this way Agardh[4] admits three kinds of metamorphosis, which he characterises as: 1st. Successive metamorphoses, or those changes in the course of evolution which each individual organ undergoes in[Pg xxvi] its passage from the embryonic to the adult condition, or from the simple and incomplete to the complex and perfect. 2. Ascending metamorphoses, including those changes of form manifested in the same adult organism by the several parts of which it consists—those parts being typically identical or homologous, such as the parts of the flower, or, in animals, the vertebræ, &c. 3. Collateral metamorphoses, comprising those permutations of form and function manifested in homologous organs in the different groups of organisms, classes, orders, genera, species, &c.

Thus, in the first instance, we have a comparative examination of the form of each or any separate part of the same individual at different epochs in its life-history; in the second we have a similar comparison instituted between the several parts of the same organism which originally were identical in appearance, but which have in course of evolution altered in character. In the third form we have the comparative view not of one organ at different times, nor of the several parts of one organism, but of the constituent elements pertaining to those aggregates of individuals to which naturalists apply the terms classes, orders, &c.

In successive metamorphosis we have a measure of the amount of change and of the perfection of structure to which each separate organ attains.

In ascending metamorphosis we have a gauge of the extent of alteration that may take place in the several homologous organs under existing circumstances.

In collateral metamorphosis, in the same way, we have an illustration of the degree of change possible in aggregates of organisms under existing circumstances.

[Pg xxvii]

Now it is clear that from an investigation of all three classes just mentioned, we shall be able to gain an idea of those points which are common to all parts, to all individuals or to all aggregates, and those that are peculiar to some of them, and, by eliminating the one from the other, we shall arrive at conclusions which will be more or less generally accurate or applicable, according to the ability of the student and the extent to which the comparative analysis is earned. It is thus that morphologists have been enabled to frame types or standards of reference, and systematists to collocate the organisms they deal with into groups. These standards and groups are more or less artificial (none can be entirely natural) in proportion to the amount of knowledge possessed by their framers, and the use they make of it.

From this point of view teratological metamorphosis of all three kinds demands as much attention as that which is called normal. We can have no thorough knowledge of an organ, of an individual which is an aggregate of organs, or of an aggregate of individuals of whatever degree, unless we know approximately, at least, what are the limits of each. It is not possible to trace these limits accurately in the case of natural science, but the larger our knowledge and the wider our generalisations, the closer will be our approach to the truth.

The most satisfactory classification of malformations would be one founded upon the nature of the causes inducing the several changes. Thus, in all organised beings, there is a process of growth, mere increase in bulk as it were, and a process of evolution or metamorphosis,[Pg xxviii] in accordance with which certain parts assume a different form from the rest, in order the better to fit them for the performance of different offices. Should growth and development be uniform and regular, that is in accordance with what is habitual in any particular species, there is no monstrosity, but if either growth or development be in any way irregular, malformation results. Hence, theoretically, the best way of grouping cases of malformation would be according as they are the consequences of:—1st. Arrest of Growth; 2ndly. Excessive Growth; 3rdly. Arrest of Development; 4thly, of Excessive or Irregular Development.

In practice, however, there are so many objections to this plan that it has not been found practicable to carry it out. The inability arises to a great extent from our ignorance of what should be attributed to arrest of growth, what to excess of development, and so on. Moreover, a student with a malformed plant before him must necessarily ascertain in what way it is malformed before he can understand how it became so, and for this purpose any scheme that will enable him readily to detect the kind of monstrosity he is examining, even though it be confessedly artificial and imperfect will be better than a more philosophical arrangement which circumstances prevent him from employing.

The plan followed in this volume is a slight modification of that adopted by Moquin-Tandon, and with several additions. In it the aim is to place before the student certain salient and easily recognisable points by reference to which the desired information can readily be found. Under each subdivision will be found general explanatory remarks, illustrative details, and usually a summary of the more important facts[Pg xxix] and the inferences to be derived from them. Bibliographical references and lists of the plants most frequently affected with particular malformations are also given. In reference to both these points it must be remembered that absolute completeness is not aimed at; had such fullness of detail been possible of attainment it would have necessitated for its publication a much larger volume than the present.[5] It is hoped that both the lists of books and of plants are sufficiently full for all general purposes.[6]

In the enumeration of plants affected with various malformations the ! denotes that the writer has himself seen examples of the deviation in question in the particular plant named, while the prefix of the * indicates that the malformation occurs with special frequency in the particular plant to which the sign is attached.

Teratological alterations are rarely isolated phenomena, far more generally they are associated with other and often compensatory changes. Hence it is often necessary, in studying any given malformation, to refer to two or more subdivisions, and in this way a certain amount of repetition becomes unavoidable. The details[Pg xxx] of the several cases of malformation given in these pages are generally arranged according to their apparent degree of importance. Thus, in a case of prolification associated with multiplication of the petals, the former change is a greater deviation from the customary form than the latter, hence reference should be made, in the first instance, to the sections treating on prolification, and afterwards to those on multiplication. To facilitate such research, numerous cross references are supplied.

3

In the investigation of teratological phenomena constant reference must be made to the normal condition, and *vice versâ*, else neither the one nor the other can be thoroughly understood. It cannot, however, be overlooked that the form and arrangement called normal are often merely those which are the most common, while the abnormal or unusual arrangement is often more in consonance with that considered to be typical than the ordinary one. Thus, too, it is often found that the structural arrangements, which in one flower are normal, are in another abnormal, in so far that they are not usual in that particular instance.

For purposes of reference, a standard of comparison is required; and this standard, so long as its nature is not overlooked, may, indeed must be, to some extent, an arbitrary one. Thus in the phanerogamous plants there is assumed to exist, in all cases, an axis (stem, branches, roots, thalamus, &c.), bearing leaves and flowers. These latter consist of four whorls, calyx, corolla, stamens, and pistils, each whorl consisting of so many separate pieces in determinate position and numbers, and of regular proportionate size. A very close approach to such a flower occurs[Pg xxxi] normally in *Limnanthes* and *Crassula*, and, indeed, in a large proportion of all flowers in an early stage of development. To a standard type, such as just mentioned, all the varied forms that are met with, either in normal or abnormal morphology, may be referred by bearing in mind the different modifications and adaptations that the organs have to undergo in the course of their development. Some parts after a time may cease to grow, others may grow in an inordinate degree, and so on; and thus, great as may be the ultimate divergences from the assumed standard, they may all readily be explained by the operation, simply or conjointly, of some of the four principal causes of malformation before alluded to. The fact that so many and such varied changes can thus readily be explained is not only a matter of convenience, but may be taken as evidence that the standard of reference is not wholly arbitrary and artificial, but that it is a close approximation to the truth.

It has already been said that an arrangement like that here considered as typical is natural to some flowers in their adult state, and to a vast number in their immature condition. It would be no extravagant hypothesis to surmise that this was the primitive structure of the flower in the higher plants. Variations from it may have arisen in course of time, owing to the action of an inherent tendency to vary, or from external circumstances and varied requirements which may have induced corresponding adaptations, and which may have been transmitted in accordance with the principle of hereditary transmission. This hypothesis necessarily implies a prior simplicity of organisation, of which, indeed, there is sufficient proof; many cases[Pg xxxii] of malformation can thus be considered as so many reversions to the ancestral form.

Thus, teratology often serves as an aid in the study of morphology in general, and also in that of special groups of plants, and hence may even be of assistance in the determination of affinities. In any case the data supplied by teratology require to be used with caution and in conjunction with those derived from the study of development and from analogy. It is even possible that some malformations, especially when they acquire a permanent nature and become capable of reproducing themselves by seed, may be the starting-point of new species, as they assuredly are of new races, and between a race and a species he would be a bold man who would undertake to draw a hard and fast line.[7]

Discredit has been cast on teratology because it has been incautiously used. At one time it was made to prove almost everything; what wonder that by some, now-a-days, it is held to prove nothing. True the evidence it affords is sometimes negative, often conflicting, but it is so rather from imperfect interpretation than from any intrinsic worthlessness. If misused the fault lies with the disciple, not with Nature.

Teratology as a guide to the solution of morphological problems has been especially disparaged in contrast with organogeny, but unfairly so. There is no reason to exalt or to disparage either at the expense of the other. Both should receive the attention they demand. The study of development shows the primitive condition and gradual evolution of parts in any[Pg xxxiii] given individual or species; it carries us back some stages further in the history of particular organisms, but so also does teratology. Many cases of arrest of development show the mode of growth and evolution more distinctly, and with much greater ease to the observer, than does the investigation of the evolution of organs under natural circumstances. Organogeny by no means necessarily, or always, gives us an insight into the principles regulating the construction of flowers in general. It gives us no archetype except in those comparatively rare cases where primordial symmetry and regularity exist. When an explanation of the irregularity of development in these early stages of the plant's history is required, recourse must be had to the inferences and deductions drawn from teratological investigations and from the comparative study of allied forms precisely as in the case of adult flowers.

The study of development is of the highest importance in the examination of plants as individuals, but in regard to comparative anatomy and morphology, and specially in its relation to the study of vegetable homology it has no superiority over teratology. Those who hold the contrary opinion do so, apparently, because they overlook the fact that there is no distinction, save of degree, to be drawn between the laws regulating normal organisation, and those by which so-called abnormal formations are regulated.

It is sometimes said, and not wholly without truth, that teratology, as it stands at present, is little more than a record of facts, but in proportion as the laws that regulate normal growth are better understood, so will the knowledge of those that govern the so-called monstrous formations increase. Sufficient has[Pg xxxiv] been already said to prove that there is no intrinsic difference between the laws of growth in the two cases. As our knowledge increases we shall be enabled to ascertain approximately of what extent of variation a given form is capable, under given conditions, and to refer all formations now considered anomalous to a few well-defined forms. Already teratology has done much towards showing the erroneous nature of many morphological statements that still pass current in our text-books, though their fallacy has been demonstrated again and again. Thus organs are said to be fused which were never separate, disjunctions and separations are assigned to parts that were never joined, adhesions and cohesions are spoken of in cases where, from the nature of things, neither adhesion nor cohesion could have existed. Some organs are said to be atrophied which were never larger and more fully developed than they now are, and so on. So long as these expressions are used in a merely conventional sense and for purposes of artificial classification or convenience, well and good, but let us not delude ourselves that we are thus contributing to the philosophical study either of the conformation of plants or of the affinities existing between them. What hope is there that we shall ever gain clear conceptions as to the former, as long as we tie ourselves down to formulas which are the expressions of facts as they appear to be, rather than as they really are? What chance is there of our attaining to comprehensive and accurate views of the genealogy and affinities of plants as long as we are restricted by false notions as to the conformation and mutual relation of their parts?[8]

[Pg xxxv]

That teratology may serve the purposes of systematic botany to a greater extent than might at first be supposed becomes obvious from a consideration of such facts as are mentioned under the head of Peloria, while the presence of rudimentary organs, or the occasional appearance of additional parts, or other changes, may, and often do, afford a clue to the relationship existing between plants—a relationship that might otherwise be unsuspected. So, too, some of the alterations met with appear susceptible of no other explanations than that they are reversions to some pre-existing form, or, at any rate, that they are manifestations of a phase of the plant affected different from that which is habitual, and due, as it were, to a sort of allotropism.

The mutations and perversions of form, associated as they commonly are with corresponding changes of function, show the connection between teratology and physiology—a connection which is seen to be the more intimate when viewed in the light afforded by the writings and experiments of Gærtner, Sprengel, and St. Hilaire, and, in our own times, especially by the writings and experiments of Mr. Darwin, whose works on the 'Origin of Species,' and particularly on the 'Variation of Animals and Plants under Domestication' comprise so large a collection of facts for the[Pg xxxvi] use of students in most departments of biology. It will suffice to allude, in support of these statements, to the writings of Mr. Darwin on such subjects as rudimentary organs, the use or disuse of certain

5

parts according to circumstances, the frequently observed tendency of some flowers to become structurally unisexual, the liability of other flowers perfectly organised to become functionally imperfect, at least so far as any reciprocal action of the organs of the same flower is concerned, reversions, classification, general morphology, and other subjects handled at once with such comprehensive breadth and minute accuracy of detail by our great physiologist.

In the following pages alterations of function, unless attended by corresponding alterations of form, are either only incidentally alluded to, or are wholly passed over; such, for instance, as alterations in the period of flowering, in the duration of the several organs, and so forth.[9]Pathological changes, lesions caused by insect puncture or other causes, also find no place in this book, unless the changes are of such a character as to admit of definite comparison with normal conformation. Usually such changes are entirely heteromorphous, and, as it were, foreign to the natural organisation.

The practical applications of teratology deserve the attention of those cultivators who are concerned in the embellishment of our gardens and the supply[Pg xxxvii] of our tables. The florist lays down a certain arbitrary standard of perfection, and attempts to make flowers conform to that model. Whether it be in good taste or not to value all flowers, in proportion as they accord with an artificial and comparatively inelastic standard of this kind, we need not stop to enquire; suffice it to say, that taking the matter in its broadest sense, the aim of the florist is to produce large, symmetrical flowers, brightly and purely coloured, or if parti-coloured, the colours must be distinct, harmonious, or contrasted. When all this is done, the flower, in most instances, becomes 'monstrous' of the eyes in the botanist, though all the more interesting to the student of morphology on that account. In like manner the double flowers, the "breaks," the "sports" which the florist cultivates so anxiously, are all of them greater or less deviations from the ordinary form, while the broccolies, the cabbages, and many other products of our kitchen gardens and fields owe the estimation in which they are held entirely to those peculiarities which, by an unhappy application of words, are called monstrous by botanists. Grafting, layering, the "striking" of cuttings, the formation of adventitious roots and buds, processes on which the cultivator so greatly relies for the propagation and extension of his plants, are also matters with which teratology concerns itself. Again the difficulty experienced occasionally in getting vines, strawberries, &c., to set properly, may sometimes be accounted for by that inherent tendency which some plants possess of exchanging an hermaphrodite for a unisexual condition.

For reasons then of direct practical utility, no[Pg xxxviii] less than on purely scientific grounds, it is desirable to study these irregularities of growth, their nature, limits, and inducing causes; and to this end it is hoped the present work may, in some degree, contribute.

FOOTNOTES:

[1]An excellent summary of the history of Vegetable Teratology is given in Kirschleger's 'Essai historique de la Tératologie Végétale,' Strasburg, 1845.

[2]In some instances diagrams and formulæ are given in explanation of the conformation of monstrous flowers; in general these require no further explanation than is given in the text, unless it be to state that the horizontal line—is intended to indicate the cohesion of the parts over which it is placed, while the vertical line | signifies the adhesion of the organs by whose side it is placed. The formula

$$S \quad S \quad S \quad S \quad \text{-----------------------} \quad | \quad P \quad P \quad P \quad P \quad | \quad |$$
ST ST ST ST ST

shows that the sepals (S) are distinct, the petals (P) coherent, and the stamens (ST) adherent to the petals.

[3]Wolff was the first to call attention to the great importance of the study of development. He was followed by Turpin, Mirbel, Schleiden, Payer, and others, and its value is now fully recognised by botanists.

[4]Agardh, "Theoria Syst. Plant.," p. xxiii.

[5]In the memoirs of Hopkirk, Kirschleger, Cramer, Hallier, and others, malformations are arranged primarily according to the organs affected, an arrangement which has only convenience to justify it. It is hoped that the index and the headings to the

paragraphs in the present volume will suit the convenience of the reader as well as if the more artificial plan just alluded to had been adopted.

[6]Cryptogamous plants are only incidentally alluded to in these pages, owing to their wide difference in structure from flowering plants. Attention may, also, here be called to a paper of M. de Seynes in a recent number of the Bulletin of the Botanical Society of France, vol. xiv, p. 290, tab. 5 et 6, in which numerous cases of malformation among agarics are recorded. See also same publication, vol. iv, p. 744; vol. v, p. 211; vol. vi, p. 496.

[7]On this subject see a paper of M. Naudin in the 'Comptes Rendus,' 1867, t. 64, pp. 929–933.

[8]It is probable that many terms and expressions calculated to mislead in the way above mentioned are made use of in the following pages. The inconsistency manifested by their use may be excused on the ground of ignorance of the true structure, and by the circumstance that in many cases facts alone are recorded without an explanation of them being offered. Moreover, it is desirable to act in conformity with the usual practice of botanical writers, and not to change established terminology, even if suspected to convey false ideas, until the true condition of affairs be thoroughly well ascertained by organogenetic research or other means.

[9]A curious illustration of the latter class of alterations came under the writer's notice last summer (1868), and which he has reason to believe has not been previously recorded, viz. the persistence in an unwithered state of the petals at the base of the ripe fruit, in a strawberry. All the fruits on the particular plants alluded to were thus provided as it were with a white frill. Whether this be a constant occurrence in the particular variety is not known.

[Pg 1]

VEGETABLE TERATOLOGY.
BOOK I.
DEVIATIONS FROM THE ORDINARY ARRANGEMENT OF ORGANS.

As full details relating to the disposition or arrangement of the general organs of flowering plants are given in all the ordinary text-books, it is only necessary in this place to allude to the main facts at present known, and which serve as the standard of comparison with which all morphological changes are compared.

Even in the case of the roots, which appear to be very irregular in their ramification, it has been found that, in the first instance at least, the rootlets or fibrils are arranged in regular order one over another, in a certain determinate number of vertical ranks, generally either in two or in four, sometimes in three or in five series. This regularity of arrangement (Rhizotaxy), first carefully studied by M. Clos, is connected with the disposition of the fibro-vascular bundles in the body of the root. This primitive regularity is soon lost as the plant grows.

In the case of the leaves there are two principal[Pg 2] modes of arrangement, dependent, as it would seem, on their simultaneous or on their successive development; thus, if two leaves on opposite sides of the stem are developed at the same time, we have the arrangement called opposite; if there are more than two, the disposition is then called verticillate or whorled. On the other hand, if the leaves are developed in succession, one after the other, they are found to emerge from the stem in a spiral direction. In either case the leaves are arranged in a certain regular manner, according to what are called the laws of Phyllotaxis, which need not be entered into fully here; but in order the better to estimate the teratological changes which take place, it may be well to allude to the following circumstances relating to the alternation of parts. The effect of this alternation is such, that no two adjacent leaves stand directly over or in front one of the other, but a little to one side or a little higher up. Now, in the alternate arrangement the successive leaves of each spiral cycle alternate one with another till the coil is completed. For the sake of clearness this may be illustrated thus:—Suppose the spiral cycle to comprise five leaves, numbered 1, 2, 3, 4, 5, then 2 would intervene between 1 and 3, and so on, while the sixth leaf would be the commencement of a new series, and would be placed exactly over 1. This arrangement may be thus formularised:

6   7   8   9   10   1   2   3   4   5

7

In the verticillate or simultaneous arrangement of leaves the case is somewhat different. Let us suppose a whorl of eight leaves, surmounted by a similar whorl of eight. In such a case it will generally be found[Pg 3] that the whorls alternate one with another, as may be represented by this symbol:

9   10   11   12   13   14   15   16 1   2   3   4   5   6   7   8

The simplest illustration of this arrangement is seen in the case of decussate leaves, where those organs are placed in pairs, and the pairs cross one another at right angles. This may be expressed by the following symbol:

7   8   5   6   3   4   1   2

Thus, while in both the annular and the spiral modes of development the individual members of each complete series necessarily alternate one with another, in the former case the series themselves alternate, while in the successive arrangement they are placed directly one over the other. There are, of course, exceptions, but the rule is as has been stated, and the effect is to prevent one leaf from interfering with the development and growth of its neighbours.

In the case of the whorled or simultaneous arrangement the conditions of growth must be uniform on all sides, but in the successive or spiral disposition the conditions influencing growth act with unequal force, on different sides of the stem, at the same time. In the whorl there is an illustration of radiating symmetry, while in the spiral arrangement there is a transition to the bilateral symmetry. There are frequent passages from one to the other even under normal circumstances; thus, while the one arrangement[Pg 4] obtains in the ordinary leaves, the parts of the flower may be disposed according to the other method. In the annular disposition it generally happens that the rings are separated one from the other by the development of the stem between them, the internodes between the constituent leaves themselves of course being undeveloped; on the other hand, in the spiral or successive arrangement there is no such alternate growth and arrest of growth of the stem between the leaves, or between successive cycles, but the growth is, under favorable conditions, continuous—leaf is separated from leaf, and cycle from cycle, by the continually elongating stem. Thus, the two modes of growth correspond precisely with those observed in the case of definite and indefinite inflorescence respectively.

FIG. 1.—Diagram showing the arrangement of parts in a complete, regular, pentamerous flower: *s*, sepals; *p*, petals; *st*, stamens; *o*, ovaries.

The same arrangements, that are observed in the disposition of the leaves, apply equally well to the several parts of the flower; thus, in what is for convenience considered the typical flower, there is a calyx of five or more distinct sepals, equal in size, and arranged in a whorl, a corolla of a similar number of petals alternating with the sepals, five stamens placed in the same position with reference to the petals, and five carpels alternating with the stamens. Throughout this book this arrangement is taken as the standard of reference. Nevertheless the spiral order does occur in the floral leaves as well as in those of the stem; it often happens, especially when the organs are numerous, that they form spiral series;[Pg 5] and the same holds good very generally, when the parts of the flower are uneven in number, as in the very common quincuncial arrangement of the sepals, &c.

To these general remarks, intended to show the agreement between the disposition of the leaves of the stem and those of the flower, it is merely necessary to add that the arrangement of the placentas, as well as that of the ovules borne on them, is also definite, and takes place according to methods explained in all the text-books, and on which, therefore, it is not necessary to dilate in this place.

The branches of the stem or axis correspond for the most part in disposition with that of the leaves from the axils of which they originate, subject, however, to numerous disturbing causes, and to alterations from the usual or typical order brought about by the development of buds. These latter organs, as it seems, may be found in almost any situation, though their ordinary position is in the axil of a leaf or at the end of a stem or branch.

The points just mentioned are of primary importance in structural botany, and as such are seized on not only by the morphologist, but by the systematic botanist, who finds in them the characters by which he may separate one group from another. Thanks to the labours of those observers who have devoted their attention to that difficult but most important branch of study, organogeny, or the investigation of the development of the various organs, and to the researches of the students of comparative anatomy or morphology, the main principles regulating the arrangement and form of the organs of flowering plants seem to be fairly well[Pg 6]established, though in matters of detail much remains to be cleared up, even in such important points as the share which the axis takes in the construction of the flower and fruit, the nature of the placenta, the construction of the ovules, and other points.

The facts already known justify the adoption of a standard or typical arrangement as just mentioned. The intrinsic value of this type is shown by the facility with which all varieties of form or arrangement may be explained by reference to certain modifications of it. It must, however, be considered as an abstraction, and should be looked on in the light rather of a scaffolding, which enables us to see the building and its several parts, than of the edifice itself, but which latter, from our imperfect knowledge and limited powers, we could not see without some such assistance.

The typical form may be, hypothetically at least, considered as the primitive one transmitted by hereditary descent from generation to generation, and modified to suit the requirements of the individual, or in accordance with circumstances. If it be borne in mind that it is but an artificial contrivance, more or less true—a means to an end, and not the end itself—no harm will arise from its employment; and as knowledge increases, or as circumstances demand, the hypothetical type can be replaced by another more in accordance with the actual state of science.

Teratological changes in the arrangement of organs depend upon arrest of growth, as when parts usually spirally arranged remain verticillate, owing to the non-development of the internodes, or to excessive growth, or development; but in many instances it is[Pg 7] impossible, without studying the development of the malformed flower, to ascertain whether the altered arrangement is due to an excessive or to a diminished action. Practically, however, it is of comparatively little importance to know whether, say, the isolation of parts, that are usually combined together, is congenital (*i.e.* the result of an arrest of growth preventing their union), or whether it be due to a separation of parts primitively undivided; the effect remains the same, though the cause may have been very different.

The principal alterations to be mentioned under this head may therefore be conveniently arranged under the following categories:—Union, Independence, Displacement, Prolification, Heterotaxy, and Heterogamy.

[Pg 8]

PART I.
UNION OF ORGANS.

The union of parts, usually separate in their adult condition, is of very common occurrence as a malformation. The instances of its manifestation admit of being grouped under the heads of Cohesion, where parts of the same whorl, or of the same organ, are united together; and of Adhesion, where the union takes place between members of different whorls, or between two or more ordinarily wholly detached and distinct parts. In either case, the apparent union may be congenital (that is, the result of a primitive integrity or a lack of separation), or it may really consist in a coalition of parts originally distinct and separate. In practice it is not always easy to distinguish between these two different conditions. Indeed, in most cases it cannot be done without tracing the development of the flower throughout all its stages. It is needless to make more than a passing allusion to the frequency with which both congenital integrity or subsequent coalescence of organs exist under ordinary circumstances. Considered as a teratological phenomenon, union admits of being grouped into several subdivisions, such as Cohesion, Adhesion, Synanthy, Syncarpy, Synophty, &c. Each of these subdivisions will be separately treated, but it may be here said that, in all or any case, the degree of fusion may be very slight, or it may be so perfect that there may be a complete amalgamation of two or more parts, while to all outward appearance the organ may be single. The[Pg 9] column of Orchids may be referred to as an illustration under natural circumstances of the complete union of many usually distinct parts.

9

In the uncertainty that exists in many cases as to the real nature of the occurrence, it would be idle to attempt to explain the causes of fusions. It is clear, however, that an arrest of development will tend towards the maintenance of primordial integrity (congenital fusion), and that pressure will induce the coalition of organs primarily distinct.

CHAPTER I.
COHESION.

Following Augustin Pyranius De Candolle, botanists have applied the term cohesion to the coalescence of parts of the same organ or of members of the same whorl; for instance, to the union of the sepals in a gamosepalous calyx, or of the petals in a gamopetalous corolla. It may arise either from a union between organs originally distinct, or more frequently from a want of separation between parts, which under general circumstances become divided during their development. Nothing is more common as a normal occurrence, while viewed as a teratological phenomenon it is also very frequent. For the purposes of convenience it admits of subdivision into those cases wherein the union takes place between the branches of the same plant, or between the margins of the same leaf-organ, or between those of different members of the same whorl.

Cohesion between the axes of the same plant.—This cohesion may occur in various manners. Firstly. The branches of the main stem may become united one to the other. Secondly. Two or more stems become joined together.[Pg 10] Thirdly. The branches become united to the stem; or, lastly, the roots may become fused one with another.

FIG. 2—Cohesion of two branches in *Dipsacus sylvestris*.

The first of these is most commonly met with, doubtless owing to the number of the branches and the facilities for their union. An illustration of it is afforded by the figure (fig. 2), showing cohesion affecting the branches of a teazle (*Dipsacus sylvestris*). Union of the branches may be the result of an original cohesion of the buds, while in other cases the fusion does not take place until after development has proceeded to some extent. Of this latter kind illustrations are common where the branches are in close approximation; if the bark be removed by friction the two surfaces are very likely to become united (natural grafting). Such a union of the branches is very common in the ivy, the elder, the beech, and other plants. It may take place in various[Pg 11] directions, lengthwise, obliquely, or transversely, according to circumstances. This mode of union belongs, perhaps, rather to the domain of pathology than of teratology. Some of the instances that have been recorded of very large trees, such as the chestnut of Mount Ætna, are really cases where fusion has taken place between several of the branches, or suckers, thrown out from the same original stem.[10] The same process of grafting occurs sometimes in the roots, as in *Taxus baccata* mentioned by Moquin, and also in the aerial roots of many of the tropical climbing plants, such as *Clusia rosea*, &c.

FIG. 3.—Fasciation in Lettuce.

Fasciation.—In the preceding instances of union between the branches, &c., the actual number of the fused parts is not increased; but if it happen that an unusual number of buds be formed in close apposition, so that they are liable to be compressed during their growth, union is very likely to take place, the more so from the softness of the young tissues. In this way it is probable that what is termed fasciation is brought[Pg 12] about. This is one of the most common of all malformations, and seems to affect certain plants more frequently than others. In its simplest form it consists of a flat, ribbon-like expansion of the stem or branch; cylindrical below, the branches gradually lose their pristine form, and assume the flattened condition.

FIG. 4.—Fasciation in *Asparagus*.

FIG. 5.—Fasciated branch of *Pinus Pinaster*.

Very generally the surface is striated by the prominence of the woody fibres which, running parallel for a time, converge or diverge at the summit according to the shape of the branch. If the rate of growth be equal, or nearly so, on both sides, the stem retains its straight direction, but it more generally happens that the growth on one side is more rapid and more vigorous[Pg 13] than on the other, and hence arises that curvature of the fasciated branch so commonly met with, *e.g.* in the ash (*Fraxinus*), wherein it has been likened to a shepherd's crook. It is probable that almost any plant may present this change. It occurs alike in herbaceous and in woody plants, originating in the latter case while the branches are still soft. It may be remarked that, in the case of herbaceous plants, the fasciation always affects the principal stem, while, on the other hand, in the case of trees and shrubs the deformity occurs most frequently in the branches; thus, while in[Pg 14]the former it may be said that the whole of the stem is more or less affected, in the latter it is rare to see more than one or two branches of the same tree thus deformed. It is a common thing for the fasciated branch to divide at the summit into a number of subdivisions. These latter may be deformed like the parent branch, or they may resume the ordinary aspect of the twigs.

FIG. 6.—**Fasciation and spiral torsion in the stem of** *Asparagus*.
Sometimes the flattened stem is destitute of buds, at other times, these organs are scattered irregularly over its surface or are crowded together in a sort of[Pg 15] crest along the apex. When, as often happens, the deformity is accompanied with a twisting of the branch spirally, the buds may be placed irregularly, or in other cases along the free edge of the spiral curve. In a specimen of *Bupleurum falcatum* mentioned by Moquin the spiral arrangement of the leaves was replaced by a series of perfect whorls, each consisting of five, six, seven, or eight segments, and there was a flower-stalk in the axil of each leaf.

When flowers are borne on these fasciated stems they are generally altered in structure; sometimes the thalamus itself becomes more or less fasciated or flattened, and the different organs of the flower are arranged on an elliptical axis. A case of this nature is described by Schlechtendal ('Bot. Zeit.,' 1857, p. 880), in *Cytisus nigricans*, and M. Moquin-Tandon describes an instance in the vine in one flower of which sepals, petals, stamens, and ovary were abortive, while the receptacle was hypertrophied and fasciated, and bore on its surface a few adventitious buds.[11] The pedicels of *Streptocarpus Rexii* have also been observed in a fasciated state.[12]

It has been occasionally observed that the fasciated condition is hereditary; thus, Moquin relates that some seeds of a fasciated *Cirsium* reproduced the same condition in the seedlings,[13] while a similar tendency is inherited in the case of the cockscomb (*Celosia*).

With reference to the nature of the deformity in question there is a difference of opinion; while most authors consider it to be due to the causes before mentioned, Moquin was of opinion that fasciation was due to a flattening of a single stem or branch. Linnæus, on the other hand, considered such stems to be the result of the formation of an unusual number of buds, the shoots resulting from which became coherent as growth proceeded:—"*Fasciata dici solet planta cum plures caules connascuntur, ut unus ex plurimis instar fasciæ evadat*[Pg 16] *et compressus*" (Linn., 'Phil. Bot.,' 274). A similar opinion was held by J. D. Major in a singular book entitled 'De Plantâ, Monstrosa, Gottorpiensi,' Schleswig, 1665, wherein the stem of a *Chrysanthemum* is depicted in the fasciated condition.

FIG. 7.—**Fasciation in the scape of the Dandelion (***Leontodon Taraxacum***)**.
The striæ, which these stems almost invariably present, exhibit the lines of junction, and the spiral or other curvatures and contraction, which are so often met with, may be accounted for by the unequal growth of one portion of the stem as contrasted with that of another. Against this view Moquin cites the instances of one-stemmed plants, such as *Androsace maxima*, but, on the other hand, those herbaceous plants having usually but a single stem not unfrequently produce several which may remain distinct, but not uncommonly become united together. Prof. Hincks[14]cites cases of this kind[Pg 17] in *Primula vulgaris, Hieracium aureum*, and*Ranunculus bulbosus*. I have myself met with several cases of the kind in*Primula veris*, in the Polyanthus, in the Daisy, and in the *Leontodon Taraxacum*, in which latter a fusion of two or more flower-stems bearing at the top a composite flower, and made up of two, three, four, or more flowers combined together, and containing all the organs that would be present in the same flowers if separate, is very common.

11

Moquin's second objection is founded upon the fact that, in certain fasciated stems, the branches are not increased in number or altered in arrangement from what is usual; but however true this may be in particular cases, it is quite certain that in the majority of instances a large increase in the number of leaves and buds is a prominent characteristic of fasciated stems.

Another argument used by the distinguished French botanist to show that fasciated stems are not due to cohesion of two or more stems, is founded on the fact that a transverse section of a fasciated stem generally shows an elliptical outline with but a single central canal. On the other hand, if two branches become united and a transverse section be made, the form of the cut surface would be more or less like that of the figure 8[symbol: 8 turned 90°], although in old stems this may give place to an elliptical outline, but even then traces of two medullary canals may be found. This argument is very deceptive, for the appearance of the transverse section must depend, not only on the intimacy of their union, but also on the internal structure of the stems themselves. When two flowers cohere without much pressure they exhibit uniting circles somewhat resembling the figure of 8[symbol: 8 turned 90°], but when more completely combined they have an outline of a very elongated figure, and something similar is to be expected in herbaceous stems. Even the elongated pith of a transversely cut, woody, fasciated stem only marks the intimate union of several branches, and Prof. Hincks, whose views the writer entirely shares, has noticed[Pg 18] instances of the union of two, and of only two, stems where the internal appearance was the same as in other fasciations.

Moquin, moreover, raises the objection that it is unlikely that several branches should become united lengthwise in one plane only, and, further, that in the greater number of fasciations all the other branches which should be present are to be found—not one is wanting, not one has disappeared, as might have been anticipated had fusion taken place. In raising this objection, Moquin seems not sufficiently to have considered the circumstance that the buds in these cases are in one plane from the first, and are all about equal in point of age and size.

The last objection that Moquin raises to the opinion that fasciation is the result of a grafting process is, that in such a case, examples should be found wherein the branches are incompletely fused, and where on a transverse section traces of the medullary canals belonging to each branch should be visible. The arrangement of leaves or buds on the surface should also in such a case indicate a fusion of several spiral cycles or whorls. To this it may be replied that such cases are met with very frequently indeed. A figure is given by De Candolle[15] of a stem of *Spartium junceum* having several branches only imperfectly fasciated.

Fasciated stems, then, seem to be best explained, as is stated by Prof. Hincks, "on the principle of adhesion arising in cases where from superabundant nourishment, especially if accompanied by some check or injury, numerous buds have been produced in close proximity, and the supposition that these growths are produced by the dilatation of a single stem is founded on a false analogy between fasciated stems and certain other anomalous growths."

It will not, of course, be forgotten that this fasciated condition occurs so frequently in some plants as almost to constitute their natural state, *e.g. Sedum cristatum,*[Pg 19] *Celosia,* &c. This condition may be induced by the art of the gardener—"*Fit idem arte, si plures caules enascentes cogantur penetrare coarctatum spatium et parturiri tanquam ex angusto utero, sic sæpe in Ranunculo, Beta, Asparago, Hesperide Pinu, Celosiâ, Tragopogone, Scorzonerâ Cotula fœtida,*" Linnæus op. cit.

Plot, in his 'History of Oxfordshire,' considers fasciation to arise from the ascent of too much nourishment for one stalk and not enough for two, "which accident of plants," says Plot, the German virtuosi ('Misc. Curios. Med. Physic. Acad. Nat. Cur.,' Ann. i, Observ. 102,) "think only to happen after hard and late winters, by reason whereof, indeed, the sap, being restrained somewhat longer than ordinary, upon sudden thaws may probably be sent up more forcibly, and so produce these fasciated stalks, whereas the natural and graduated ascent would have produced them but single." Prof. Hincks' explanation is, however, more near to the truth, and his opinion is borne out by the frequency with which this change is met with in certain plants which are frequently forced on during their growth, as lettuce, asparagus, endive, &c., all of which are very subject to this change. In the 'Transactions of the Horticultural Society of London,' vol. iv, p. 321, Mr. Knight gives an account of the cultivation of the cockscomb, so as to ensure the production of the very large flower-stalks for which this plant is admired. The principal points in the culture were the application of a large quantity of stimulating manure and the maintenance of a high temperature. One of them so grown measured eighteen inches in width.

The list which is appended is intended to show those plants in which fasciation has been most frequently observed. It makes no pretension to be complete, but is sufficiently so for the purpose indicated: the * denotes the especial frequency of the change in question; the ! indicates that the writer has himself seen the plant, so marked, affected in this way. The remainder have been copied from various sources.

[Pg 20]

EXOGENS.

α. *Herbaceous.*

- Ranunculus tripartitus.
○   *bulbosus!
○   Philonotis.
- Delphinium elatum.
○   *sp.!
- Hesperis matronalis.
- *Cheiranthus Cheiri!
- *Matthiola incana!
- *Brassica oleracea! var. pl. inflor.
- Linum usitatissimum!
- Althæa rosea!
- Lavatera trimestris.
- Geranii sp.
- Tropæolum majus!
- Viola odorata inflor.!
- Reseda odorata!
- Fragaria vesca.
- Ervum lens.
- Trifolium resupinatum.
○   repens!
○   pratense!
- Saxifraga mutata.
○   irrigua.
- Bupleurum falcatum.
- Bunium flexuosum.
- *Sedum reflexum!
○   cristatum!
- Epilobium augustifolium!
- Momordica Elaterium!
- Gaura biennis.
- Cotula fœtida.
- Barkhausia taraxacifolia.

13

- Carlina vulgaris!
- Apargia autumnalis.
- *Leontodon Taraxacum inflor.!
- Centaurea Scabiosa.
- *Cichorium Intybus!
- Hieracium Pilosella.
  - aureum.
  - umbellatum.
- *Chrysanthemum Leucanthemum.
  - indicum!
- Anthemis nobilis.
  - arvensis.
- Cirsium lanceolatum.
- Conyza squarrosa!
- Inula dysenterica!
- Tragopogon porrifolium.
- Cnicus palustris.
- Carduus arvensis!
- Helianthus tuberosus!
  - annuus.
- Cineraria palustris.
- Helianthus sp.!
- Dahlia variabilis.
- Bellis perennis inflor.!
- Coreopsis sp.!
- Crepis virens.
- Lactuca sativa!
- Zinnia elegans.
- *Campanula medium!
  - rapunculoides.
  - thyrsoidea.
- Dipsacus pilosus.
  - fullonum.
  - silvestris.
- Knautia arvensis.
- Phyteuma orbiculare.
- Jasione montana.
- *Linaria purpurea!
- Antirrhinum majus!
- Veronica amethystea.
- Veronica maritima.
  - sp.

- Russellia juncea!
- Digitalis purpurea!
- Ajuga pyramidalis.
- Hyssopus officinalis.
- Dracocephalum moldavicum.
- Myosotis scorpioides.
- Echium pyrenaicum.
-         simplex.
- Stapeliæ sp.
- Lysimachia vulgaris!
- Androsace maxima.
- Primula veris inflor.!
-         denticulata inflor.!
- Polemonium cœruleum.
- Convolvulus sepium!
-         arvensis!
- Plantago media.
- *Euphorbia Characias.
-         exigua.
-         *Cyparissias.
- Suæda maritima.
- *Celosia sp.
- Beta vulgaris inflor.!
- Phytolacca sp.

β. *Woody.*

- Berberis vulgaris.
- Hibiscus syriacus!
- Acer pseudo-platanus!
- Dodonæa viscosa.
- Sterculia platanifolia.
- Euonymus japonicus!
- Vitis vinifera inflor.![Pg 21]
- Spartium Scoparium!
- Spartium junceum!
- Cytisus Laburnum.
-         nigricans.
- Chorozema ilicifolium.
- Amorpha sp.
- Phaseolus sp.
- Prunus sylvestris.
-         Laurocerasus!
- Rosa sp.!

15

- Spiræa sp.!
- Cotoneaster microphylla!
- Ailanthus glandulosus.
- *Fraxinus Ornus!
  - *excelsior!
- Melia Azedarach.
- Xanthoxylum sp.!
- Sambucus nigra.!
- Aucuba japonica.
- Erica sp. cult.
- Jasminum nudiflorum!
  - officinale!
- Olea europœa.
- Punica Granatum.
- Ilex aquifolium!
- Daphne indica.
- Daphne odora.
- Suæda fruticosa.
- Ulmus campestris.
- Alnus incana.
- Salix vitellina, &c.!
- Thuja orientalis.
- Pinus pinaster!
  - sylvestris!
- Abies excelsa!
- Taxus baccata.
- Larix europœa.

ENDOGENS.

- Lilium Martagon.
  - candidum!
- *Fritillaria imperialis!
- Asparagus officinalis!
- Hyacinthus orientalis!
- Tamus communis!
- Narcissi sp.!
- Gladiolus sp.
- Zea Mays.
- Filices.

See also—Moquin-Tandon, 'Elem. Ter. Veget.,' p. 146; C. O. Weber, 'Verhandl. Nat. Hist.,' Vereins, f. d. Preuss., Rheinl. und Westphal., 1860, p. 347, tab. vii; Hallier, 'Phytopathol.,' p. 128; Boehmer, 'De plantis Fasciatis,' Wittenb., 1752.

Cohesion of foliar organs.—This takes place in several ways, and in very various degrees; the simplest case is that characterised by the cohesion of the margins of the same

16

organ, as in the condition called perfoliate in descriptive works, and which is due either to a cohesion of the margins of the basal lobes of the leaf, or to the development of the leaf in a sheathing or tubular manner. As an abnormal occurrence, I have met with this perfoliation in a leaf of *Goodenia ovata*. The condition in question is often loosely confounded with connation, or the union of two leaves by their bases. In other cases the union takes place between the margins of two or more leaves.

Cohesion of margins of single organs.—The leaves of Hazels may often be found with their margins coherent at the[Pg 22] base, so as to become peltate, while in other cases, the disc of the leaf is so depressed that a true pitcher is formed. This happens also in the Lime *Tilia*, in which genus pitcher- or hood-like leaves (*folia cucullata*) may frequently be met with. There are trees with leaves of this character in the cemetery of a Cistercian Monastery at Sedlitz, on which it is said that certain monks were once hung: hence the legend has arisen, that the peculiar form of the leaf was given in order to perpetuate the memory of the martyred monks. ('Bayer. Monogr. *Tiliæ*,' Berlin, 1861.) It is also stated that this condition is not perpetuated by grafting.

FIG. 8.—Pitcher-shaped leaf of *Pelargonium*.

I have in my possession a leaf of *Antirrhinum majus*, and also a specimen of *Pelargonium*, wherein the blade of the leaf is funnel-like, and the petiole is cylindrical, not compressed, and grooved on the upper surface, as is usually the case. A comparison of the leaves of *Pelargonium peltatum* with those of *P. cucullatum* ('Cav.[Pg 23] Diss.,' tab., 106) will show how easy the passage is from a peltate to a tubular leaf. In these cases the tubular form may rather be due to dilatation than to cohesion. M. Kickx[16] mentions an instance of the kind in the leaves of a species of *Nicotiana*, and also figures the leaf of a rose in which two opposite leaflets presented themselves in the form of stalked cups. Schlechtendal[17] notices something of the same kind in the leaf of *Amorpha fruticosa*; Treviranus[18] in that of *Aristolochia Sipho*.

M. Puel[19] describes a leaf of *Polygonatum multiflorum*, the margins of which were so completely united together, as only to leave a circular aperture at the top, through which passed the ends of the leaves. The Rev. Mr. Hincks, at the meeting of the British Association at Newcastle (1838), showed a leaf of a Tulip, whose margins were so united that the whole leaf served as a hood, and was carried upwards by the growing flower like the calyptra of a Moss.

The margins of the stipules are also occasionally united, so as to form a little horn-shaped tube. I have met with instances of this kind in the common white clover, *Trifolium repens*, where on each side of the base of the petiole the stipules had the form just indicated. That the bracts also may assume this condition, may be inferred from the peculiar horn-like structures of *Marcgraavia*, which appear to originate from the union of the margins of the reflected leaf.

Tubular petals occur normally in some flowers, as *Helleborus*, *Epimedium*, *Viola*, &c., and as an exceptional occurrence I have seen them in *Ranunculus repens*, while in *Eranthis hyemalis* transitions may frequently be seen between the flat outer segments of the perianth and the tubular petals. To Dr. Sankey, of Sandywell Park, I am indebted for the flower of a Pelargonium,[Pg 24] in which one of the petals had the form of a cup supported on a long stalk. This cup-shaped organ was placed at the back of the flower, and had the dark colour proper to the petals in that situation. I have seen a petal of Clarkia similarly tubular, while some of the cultivated varieties of *Primula sinensis* exhibit tubular petals so perfect in shape as closely to resemble perfect corollas.

FIG. 9.—*Eranthis hyemalis*. Transition from flat sepal to tubular petal.

Like the petals, the stamens, and even the styles, assume a hollow tubular form. This change of form in the case of the stamens is, of course, usually attended by the petaloid expansion of the filament, or anther, and the more or less complete obliteration of the pollen sacs, as in Fuchsias, and in some double-flowered Antirrhinums.[20] So also in some semi-double varieties of *Narcissus poeticus*, and in *Aquilegia*. By the late Professor Charles Morren, this affection of the stamens and pistils was called *Solenaidie*,[21] but as a similar

17

condition exists in other organs, it hardly seems worth while to adopt a special term for the phenomenon, as it presents itself in one set of organs.

In many of these cases it is difficult to say whether the cup-like or tubular form is due to a dilatation or hollowing out of the organ affected, or to a fusion of its edges. The arrangement of the veins will in some[Pg 25] cases supply the clue, and in others the regularity of form will indicate the nature of the malformation, for in those instances where the cup is the result of expansion, its margin is more likely to be regular and even than in those where the hollow form is the result of fusion.

Cohesion of several organs by their margins:—leaves, &c.—The union of the margins of two or more different organs is of more common occurrence than the preceding, the leaves being frequently subjected to this change. Occasionally, the leaflets of a compound leaf have been observed united by their margins, as in the strawberry, the white trefoil, and others. Sometimes the union takes place by means of the stalks only. I have an instance of this in a Pelargonium, in *Tropæolum majus*, and *Strelitzia regina*; in other cases, the whole extent of the leaf becomes joined to its neighbour, the leaves thus becoming completely united by their edges, as in those of *Justicia, oxyphylla*.[22] M. Clos[23] has observed the same thing in the leaves of the lentil *Ervum lens*, conjoined with fasciation of the stem, and many other examples might be given. Some of the recorded cases are probably really due to fission of one leaf into two rather than to fusion. Although usually the lower portions of the leaf are united together, leaving the upper parts more or less detached, there are some instances in which the margins of the leaf at their upper portion have been noticed to be coherent, while their lower portions, with their stalks, were completely free.[24]

Cohesion of the leaves frequently accompanies the union of the branches and fasciation as might have been anticipated. Moquin cites the fenestrated leaves of *Dracontium pertusum*, as well as some cases of a similar kind that are occasionally met with, as instances[Pg 26] of the cohesion of the margins at the base and apex of the leaf, which thus appears perforated. This appearance, however, is probably due to some other cause. When the leaves are verticillate and numerous, and they become coherent by their margins, they form a foliaceous tube around the stem. When there are but two opposite leaves, and these become united by their margins, we have a state of things precisely resembling that to which the term connate is applied.

Fusion of the edges of the cotyledons also occasionally takes place, as in *Ebenus cretica*.[25] It has also been observed in *Tithonia*, and is of constant occurrence in the seed leaves of some *Mesembryanthema*. This condition must be carefully distinguished from the very similar appearance produced by quite a different cause, viz., the splitting of one cotyledon into two, which gives rise to the appearance as if two were partially united together.

Some of the ascidia or pitcher-like formations are due to the cohesion of the margins of two leaves, as in a specimen of *Crassula arborescens*, observed by C. Morren.

FIG. 10.—Two-leaved pitcher of *Crassula arborescens*, after C. Morren.

The stipules may also be fused together in different[Pg 27] ways; their edges sometimes cohere between the leaf and the stem, and thus form a solitary intra-axillary stipule. At other times they become united in such a manner as to produce a single notched stipule opposite to the leaf. Again, in other cases, they are so united on each side of the stem, that in place of four there seem only to exist two, common to the two leaves as in the Hop.

To the Rev. M. J. Berkeley I am indebted for specimens of a curious pitcher-like formation in the garden Pea. The structure in question consisted of a stalked foliaceous cup proceeding from the inflorescence. On examination of the ordinary inflorescence, there will be seen at the base of the upper of two flowers a small rudimentary bract, having a swollen circular or ring-like base, from which proceeds a small awl-shaped process, representing the midrib of an abortive leaf. In some of Mr. Berkeley's specimens, the stipules were developed as leafy appendages at the base of the leaf-stalk or midrib, the latter retaining its shortened form, while, in others, the two stipules had become connate into a cup, and all trace of the midrib was lost. The cup in question would thus seem to have been formed from the connation of two stipules which are ordinarily abortive.

Cohesion of the bracts by their edges, so as to form a tubular involucre, or by their surfaces, so as to form a cupule, is not of uncommon occurrence, under natural conditions, and may be met with in plants which ordinarily do not exhibit this appearance.

Cohesion of the sepals in a normally polypetalous calyx renders the latter gamosepalous, and is not of uncommon occurrence, to a partial extent, though rarely met with complete. I have observed a junction of the sepals to be one of the commonest malformations among Orchids, indeed such a state of things occurs normally in *Masdevallia Cypripedium*, &c. An illustration of this occurrence is given by Mr. J. T. Moggridge in *Ophrys insectifera*, in 'Seemann's Journal[Pg 28] of Botany,' 1866, p. 168, tab. 47. In Orchids, this cohesion of sepals is very often co-existent with other more important changes, such as absence of the labellum, dislocation of the parts of the flower, &c.

FIG. 11.—Gamopetalous flower of *Papaver bracteatum*.

Cohesion of the petals.—Linnæus mentions the occurrence of cohesion of the petals in *Saponaria.[26]* Moquin notices a Rose in which the petals were united into a long tube, their upper portions were free and bent downwards, forming a sort of irregular limb. An instance of the polypetalous regular perianth of *Clematis viticella* being changed into a monopetalous irregular one, like the corolla of Labiates, is recorded by Jaeger.[27] There is in cultivation a variety of *Papaver bracteatum*, in which the petals are united by their margins so as to form a large cup. Under[Pg 29] normal circumstances, the petals become fused together by their edges along their whole extent, at the base only, at the apex only, as in the Vine, or at the base and apex, leaving the central portions detached. Indications of the junction of the petals may generally be traced by the arrangement of the veins, or by the notches or lobes left by imperfect union. In Crocuses I have frequently met with cohesion of the segments of the perianth, by means of their surfaces, but the union was confined to the centre of the segment, leaving the rest of the surfaces free.

Cohesion of the stamens.—Under natural circumstances, cohesion of the stamens is said to take place either by the union of their filaments, so as to form one, two, or more parcels (Monadelphia, Diadelphia, Polyadelphia); at other times, by the cohesion of the anthers (Syngenesia), in which latter case the union is generally very slight. It must be remembered, however, that the so-called cohesion of the filaments is in many cases due rather to the formation of compound stamens, *i.e.* to the formation from one original staminal tubercle of numerous secondary ones, so that the process is rather one of over development than of fusion or of disjunction. These conditions may be met with as accidental occurrences in plants or in flowers, not usually showing this arrangement. Thus, for instance, Professor Andersson, of Stockholm, describes a monstrosity of *Salix calyculata*, in which the stamens were so united together as to form a tube open at the top like a follicle.[28] This is an exaggerated degree of that fusion which exists normally in *Salix monandra*, in Cucurbits and other plants.

Cohesion of the pistils is also of very frequent occurrence in plants, under ordinary circumstances, but is less commonly met with than might have been expected as a teratological phenomenon.

[Pg 30]

Further details relating to cohesion of the various parts of the flower are cited in Moquin-Tandon, 'El. Ter. Veg.,' p. 248; 'Weber. Verhandl. Nat. Hist. Vereins f. d. Preuss. Rheinl. und Westphal.,' 1860, p. 332, tabs. 6 et 7.

Formation of ascidia or pitchers.—In the preceding paragraphs, the formation of tubular or horn-like structures, from the union of the margins of one organ, or from the coalescence, or it may be from the want of separation of various organs, has been alluded to, so that it seems only necessary now, by way of summary, to mention the classification of ascidia proposed by Professor Charles Morren[29], who divides the structures in question into two heads, according as they are formed from one or more leaves. The following list is arranged according to the views of the Belgian savant, and comprises a few additional illustrations. Those to which the ! is affixed have been seen by the writer himself; the * indicates the more frequent occurrence of the phenomenon in some than in other plants. Those plants, such as *Nepenthes*, &c., which occur normally and constantly, are not here included. Possibly some of the cases would be more properly classed under dilatation or excavation.

ASCIDIA.

A. *Monophyllous.*

1. Sarracenia-like pitchers, formed by a single leaf, the edges of which are united for the greater portion of their length, but are disunited near the top, so as to leave an oblique aperture.

- *Brassica oleracea (several of the cultivated varieties)!
- *Tilia europæa!
- Pelargonium inquinans!
- Staphylea pinnata.
- Amorpha fruticosa.
- Pisum sativum!
- Lathyrus tuberosus.
- Vicia sp.
- Gleditschia sp.
- Ceratonia siliqua.
- Trifolium repens!
- Cassia marylandica.[Pg 31]
- Mimosa Lophantha.
- Rosa centifolia.
- gallica.
- Begonia sp.
- Bellis perennis!
- Nicotiana sp.
- Goodenia ovata!
- Antirrhinum majus!
- Vinca rosea.
- Polygonum orientale.
- Aristolochia sipho?
- Codiæum variegatum var.!
- Spinacia oleracea.
- Corylus avellana!
- Polygonatum multiflorum.
- Xanthosoma appendiculatum!

2. Calyptriform or hood-like pitchers, formed by the complete union of the margins, and falling off by a transverse fissure (as in the calyx of Escholtzia).

- Tulipa Gesneriana.

B. *Polyphyllous.*

1. Diphyllous, formed by the union of two leaves into a single cup, tube, or funnel, &c.

- Pisum sativum (stipules)!
- Crassula arborescens.
- Polygonatum multiflorum.

20

2. Triphyllous, formed by the union of three leaves.

- Paris quadrifolia var.

Besides the above varieties of ascidia formed from the union of one or more leaves, there are others which seem to be the result of a peculiar excrescence or hypertrophy of the leaf. Such are some of the curious pitcher-like structures met with occasionally in the leaves of cabbages, lettuces, Aristolochia, &c. See Hypertrophy, cup-like deformities, &c.

In addition to other publications previously mentioned, reference may be made to the following treatises on the subject of ascidia:—Bonnet, 'Rech. Us. Feuilles,' p. 216, tab. xxvi, f. 1, *Brassica*; De Candolle, 'Trans. Hort. Soc.,' t. v, pl. 1, *Brassica*; Id., 'Org. Veget.,' I, 316; 'Bull. Soc. Bot. Fr.,' I, p. 62, *Polygonatum*; 'Bull. Acad. Belg.,' 1851, p. 591, *Rosa*; Hoffmann, 'Tijdschrift v. Natuur. Geschied.,' vol. viii, p. 318, tab. 9, *Ceratonia*; C. Mulder, 'Tijdschrift, &c.,' vol. vi, p. 106, tab. 5, 6, *Trifolium, Mimosa,Staphylea*;' Molkenboer,' p. 115, t. 4, *Brassica*.

FOOTNOTES:

[10]See a curious instance of this kind in the branches of *Pinus*. 'Regel. Garten Flora,' vol. 8, tab. 268.

[11]'Bull. Soc. Bot. France,' 1860, p. 881.

[12]Ibid., 1861, p. 708.

[13]Ibid., 1860, p. 923.

[14]'Proc. Linn. Soc.,' April 5, 1853.

[15]'Organ. Végét.,' pl. iii, fig. 1.

[16]'Bull. Acad. Roy. Bruxelles,' t. xviii, p. i and p. 591.

[17]'Linnæa,' tom. 13, p. 383.

[18]'Verhandl. Nat. Hist. Vereins,' 1859, Bonn, tom. xvi, tab. 3.

[19]'Bull. Soc. Bot. Fr.,' vol. i, p. 62.

[20]'Report of Internat. Bot. Congress,' London, 1866, p. 131, tab. vii, figs. 10–13.

[21]'Bull. Acad. Roy. Belg.,' t. xviii, 2nd part, p. 179.

[22]D. C., 'Organ. Végét.,' pl. xvii, fig. 3, and pl. xlviii, fig. 2.

[23]'Mém. Acad. Toulouse,' 1862.

[24]Bonnet, 'Recherches Us. feuill.,' pl. xxi, fig. 2.

[25]De Candolle, 'Mém. Lég.,' pl. v, fig. 14.

[26]'Phil. Bot.,' § 125.

[27]'Nov. Act. Acad. Nat. Cur.,' 14, p. 642, t. xxxvii.

[28]'Journal of the Linn. Soc. Bot.,' vol. iv, p. 55.

[29]'Bull. Acad. Roy. Bruxelles,' 1838, t. v, p. 582. 'Bull. Acad. Roy. Belg.,' 1852, t. xix, part iii, p. 437.

[Pg 32]

CHAPTER II.
ADHESION.

Adhesion, so called, occurs either from actual union of originally distinct members of different whorls or from the non-occurrence of that separation which usually takes place between them. It is thus in some degree a graver deviation than cohesion, and is generally a consequence of, or at least is coexistent with, more serious changes; thus if two leaves of the same whorl are coherent the change is not very great, but if two leaves belonging to different whorls, or two leaves in the same spiral cycle are adherent, a deformation in the axis or a certain amount of dislocation must almost necessarily exist. Adhesion as a normal occurrence is usually the result of a lack of separation rather than of union of parts primitively separate. Instances of adhesion between different organs is seen under ordinary circumstances in the bract of the Lime tree, which adheres to the peduncle, also in *Neuropeltis*, while in *Erythrochiton hypophyllanthus* the cymose peduncles are adherent to the under surface of the leaf.

Adhesion between the axes of the same plant is sufficiently treated of under the head of Cohesion, from which it is in this instance impossible to make a distinction. Adhesion of the inflorescence is necessarily a frequent accompaniment of fasciation and cohesion of the branches.

Adhesion of foliar organs may occur either between the margins or between the surfaces of the affected parts; in the former case there is almost necessarily more or less displacement and change of direction, such as a twisting of the stem and a vertical rather than a horizontal attachment of the foliar organ to it; hence[Pg 33] it generally forms but a part of other and more important deviations.

Adhesion of leaves by their surfaces.—The union of leaves by their surfaces is not of very frequent occurrence, many of the instances cited being truly referable to other conditions. Bonnet describes the union of two lettuce leaves, and Turpin that of two leaves of *Agave americana*, in which latter the upper surface of one leaf was adherent to the lower surface of the leaf next above it, and I have myself met with similar instances in the wallflower and in lettuce and cabbage leaves; other instances have been mentioned in *Saxifraga, Gesnera, &c.*[30]

In these cases, owing to the non-development of the internodes, the nascent leaves are closely packed, and the conditions for adhesion are favorable, but in most of the so-called cases of adhesion of leaf to leaf by the surface, a preferable explanation is afforded either by an exuberant development (hypertrophy) or by chorisis (see sections on those subjects). Thus, when a leaf of this kind is apparently so united, that the lower surface of one is adherent to the corresponding surface of another, the phenomenon is probably due rather to extra development or to fission. There is an exception to this, however, in the case of two vertically-erect leaves on opposite sides of the stem; here the two upper or inner surfaces may become adherent, as in an orange, where two leaves were thus united, the terminal bud between them being suppressed or abortive.

Adhesion between the membranous bract of *Narcissus poeticus* and the upper surface of the leaf is described by Moquin.[31] The same author mentions having seen a remarkable example of adhesion in the involucels of *Caucalis leptophylla*, the bracts of which were soldered to the outer surface of the flowers. M. Bureau[32] mentions[Pg 34] an instance wherein the spathe of *Narcissus biflorus* was partially twisted in such a manner that the lower surface of its median nerve was adherent to the corresponding surface of one of the sepals, mid-rib to mid-rib, thus apparently confirming a law of G. de Hilaire, that when two parts of the same individual unite, they generally do so by the corresponding surfaces or edges, but the rule is probably not so general in its application as has been supposed.

Adhesion of foliar to axile organs.—The appendicular organs may likewise be found united to the axile ones. This union takes place in many ways; sometimes the leaves do not become detached from the stem for a considerable distance, as in the so-called decurrent leaves, at other times the leaves are prolonged at their base into lobes, which are directed along the stem, and are united with it. Turpin records a tendril of a vine which was fused with the stem for some distance, and bore leaves and other tendrils. Union of the leaf or bract with the flower-stalk is not uncommon. It occurs normally in the Lime and other plants.

Adhesion of the sepals to the petals is spoken of by Morren as calyphyomy, καλυξ φυομαι.[33] Moquin cites an instance in *Geranium nodosum*, in which one petal was united by its lower surface to one of the segments of the calyx. A similar circumstance has been observed in*Petunia violacea* by Morren. Duchartre describes an instance wherein one of the outer sepals of *Cattleya Forbesii* was adherent to the labellum.[34]

Adhesion of the stamens to the petals is of common occurrence under natural circumstances. Cassini has described a malformation of *Centaurea collina*, in which two of the five stamens were completely grafted with the corolla, the three others remaining perfectly free. Adhesion of the petals to the column is not of infrequent[Pg 35] occurrence among Orchids. I have observed cases of the adhesion of the segments of the perianth to the stamen in *Ophrys aranifera, Odontoglossum, sp.* &c. It is the ordinary condition in *Gongora* and some other genera. I have seen it also in *Lilium lancifolium*. Some forms of *Crocus*, occasionally met with, present a very singular appearance, owing to the adhesion of the stamens to the outer segments of the perianth, the former, moreover, being partially petaloid in aspect. M. de la Vaud[35] speaks of a similar union in *Tigridia pavonia*. Morren[36] describes a malformation of *Fuchsia* wherein the petals were so completely adherent to the stamens, that the former were dragged out of their ordinary position, so as to become opposite to the sepals; the fusion was here so complete that, no trace of it could be seen externally. It should be remarked that it was the outer series of stamens that were thus fused.[37]

FIG. 12.—*Crocus*. Adhesion of petaloid stamens to perianth.

Adhesion of stamens to pistils.—The stamens also may be united to the pistils, as in gynandrous plants. Moquin speaks of such a case in a *Scabious*; M. Clos in *Verbascum australe*.[38] I have seen cases of the same kind in the Wallflower, Cowslip (*Primula veris*), Tulip, Orange, in the garden Azalea and other plants.

Miscellaneous adhesions.—Sometimes organs, comparatively speaking, widely separated one from the other, become united together. Miquel has recorded the union of a stigma with the middle lobe of the lower[Pg 36] lip of the corolla of *Salvia pratensis*.[39] In the accompanying figure [fig. 13], taken from a double wallflower, there is shown an adhesion between a petal and an open carpel on the one side, and a stamen on the other.

Moquin speaks of some pears, which were united, at an early stage, with one or two small leaves borne by the peduncle and grafted to the fruit by the whole of their upper surface. As the pear increased in size the leaves became detached from it, leaving on the surface of the fruit an impression of the same form as the leaf, and differing in colour from the rest of the surface of the fruit. Traces of the principal nerves were seen on the pear.

FIG. 13.—*Cheiranthus cheiri*. Adhesion of petal to stamen and open carpel.

It is curious to notice how very rare it is for the calyx to adhere to the ovary in flowers where that organ is normally superior. The "*calyx inferus*" seems scarcely ever to become "*calyx superus*," while, on the other hand, the "*calyx normaliter superus*" frequently becomes inferior from detachment from, or from want of union with the surface of the ovary.

Adhesion of fruit to branch.—Of this Mr. Berkeley[40] cites an instance in a vegetable marrow (*Cucumis*), where a female flower had become confluent with the branch, at whose base it was placed, and also with two or more flowers at the upper part of the same branch, so as to make an oblique scar running down from the apex of the fruit to the branch.

Synanthy.—Adhesion of two or more flowers takes place in various ways; sometimes merely the stalks[Pg 37] are united together, so that we have a single peduncle, bearing at its extremity two flowers placed in approximation very slightly adherent one to the other. In this manner I have seen three flowers of the vegetable marrow on a common stalk, the flowers themselves being only united at the extreme base. Occasionally cases may be met with wherein the pedicels of a stalked flower become adherent to the side of a sessile flower. I have noticed this commonly in *Umbelliferæ*. Union of this kind occurs frequently in the common cornel (*Cornus*), wherein one of the lower flowers becomes adherent to one of the upper ones. In De Candolle's 'Organographie Végétale,' Plates 14 and 15, are figured cases of fusion of the flower stems of the Hyacinth and of a *Centaurea*. In other cases the union involves not only the stalk but the flowers themselves; thus fusion of the flowers is a common accompaniment of fasciation, as was the case in the *Campanula* figured in the cut (fig. 14).

FIG. 14.—Synanthic flowers of *Campanula medium*.

Synanthy may take place without much derangement of the structure of either flower, or the union may be attended with abortion or suppression of some of the[Pg 38] parts of one or both flowers. Occasionally this union is carried to such an extent that a bloom appears to be single, when it is, in reality, composed of two or more, the parts of which have become not only fused, but, as it were, thrust into and completely incorporated one with another, and in such a manner as to occupy the place of some parts of the flower which have been suppressed. It must not be overlooked that this adhesion of one flower to another is a very common occurrence under natural circumstances, as in *Lonicera*, in the common tomato, in *Pomax*, *Opercularia*, *Symphyomyrtus*, &c., while the large size of some of the cultivated sunflowers is in like manner due to the union of two or more flower-heads.

23

One of the simplest instances of synanthy is that mentioned by M. Duchartre,[41] in which two flowers of a hyacinth were united together simply by means of two segments of the perianth one from each flower. A similar occurrence has been cited by M. Gay in *Narcissus chrysanthus*. In like manner the blossoms of Fuchsias or Loniceras occasionally become adherent merely by their surface, without involving any other change in the conformation of the flowers. M. Maugin alludes to a case of this kind in *Aristolochia Clematitis*.[42]

But it is more usual for some of the organs to be suppressed, so that the number of existing parts is less than would be the case in two or more uncombined flowers. A few illustrations will exemplify this. In two flowers of *Matthiola incana*, that I observed to be joined together, there were eight sepals, eight petals, and ten perfect stamens, eight long and two short, instead of twelve. Closer examination showed that the point of union between the two flowers occurred just where, under ordinary circumstances, the two short stamens would be. In this instance but little suppression had occurred. In similar flowers of *Narcissus incomparabilis* I remarked a ten-parted perianth,[Pg 39] ten stamens within a single cup, two styles, and a five-celled ovary. Here, then, it would appear that two segments of the perianth, two stamens, and one carpel were suppressed. In a Polyanthus there were nine sepals, nine petals, nine stamens, and a double ovary.

FIG. 15.—Union of three flowers of *Calanthe vestita*.

FIG. 16.—Shows the abortion of the central spur in synanthic flowers of *Calanthe vestita*.

As an illustration of a more complicated nature reference may be made to three flowers of *Aconitum Napellus*, figured by A. de Chamisso, 'Linnæa,' vol. vii, 1832, p. 205, tab. vii, figs. 1, 2. In this specimen the two outer blossoms had each four sepals present, namely, the upper hooded one, one of the lateral sepals, and both of the inferior ones; the central flower had only the upper sepal and one other, probably one of the lower sepals; thus there were but ten sepals instead of fifteen. The nectary-like petals, the stamens, and pistils were all present in the lateral flowers, but were completely suppressed in the middle one. A less degree of suppression was exemplified in a triple flower of *Calanthe vestita* sent me by Dr. Moore, of Glasnevin, in which all the parts usually existing in[Pg 40] three separate flowers were to be found, with the exception of the spur belonging to the labellum of the middle flower (figs. 15, 16).

One of the most common malformations in the Foxglove (*Digitalis*) results from the fusion of several of the terminal flowers into one. In these cases the number of parts is very variable in different instances; the sepals are more or less blended together, and the corollas as well as the stamens are usually free and distinct, the latter often of equal length, so that the blossom, although truly complex, is, as to its external form, less irregular than under natural circumstances. The centre of these flowers is occupied by a two to five-celled pistil, between the carpels of which, not unfrequently, the stem of the plant projects, bearing on its sides bracts and rudimentary flowers. (See Prolification.) An instance of this nature is figured in the 'Gardeners' Chronicle,' 1850, p. 435, from which the cut (fig. 17) is borrowed.

FIG. 17.—Synanthy and other changes in a Foxglove.

One of the most singular recorded instances of changes connected with fusion of the flowers is that[Pg 41] cited by Reinsch,[43] where two female flowers of *Salix cinerea* were so united with a male one as to produce an hermaphrodite blossom.

It follows, from what has been said, that the number of parts that are met with in these fused flowers varies according to the number of blossoms and of the organs which have been suppressed. Comparatively rarely do we find all the organs present; but when two flowers are united together we find every possible variety between the number of parts naturally belonging to the two flowers and that belonging to a single one. Sometimes instances are met with wherein the calyx does not present the normal number of parts, while the other parts of the flower are in excess. I have seen in a *Calceolaria* a single calyx, with the ordinary number of sepals, enclosing two corollas, adherent simply by their upper lips, and

24

containing stamens and pistils in the usual way. In this instance, then, the sepals of one flower must have been suppressed, while no such suppression took place in the other parts of the flower.

Professor Charles Morren paid special attention to the various methods in which the flowers of Calceolarias may become fused, and to the complications that ensue from the suppression of some parts, the complete amalgamation of others, &c. Referring the reader to the Belgian savant's papers for the full details of the changes observed, it is only necessary to allude to a few of the most salient features.

FIG. 18.—Synanthic flowers of Calceolaria in which, with two upper lips, there was but a single lower one.

Sometimes the upper lips of two flowers are fused into one, the two lower remaining distinct. In other cases, the upper lip disappears altogether, while there are two lower lips placed opposite one another;, of the stamens, sometimes[Pg 42] the outermost, at other times the innermost disappear.[44]

Occasionally there appears to be, as it were, a transference of the parts of one flower to another. One of the simplest and most intelligible cases of this kind is recorded by Wigand in the 'Flora' for 1856, in a compound flower of *Polygonatum anceps*, in which within a twelve-parted perianth there were twelve stamens and two pistils, one four-celled, the other two-celled; hence it would appear as if a carpel belonging to one flower had become united to those constituting the pistil of the adjacent one. Among Orchids this fusion of some of the elements of different flowers, together with the suppression of others, is carried to such an extent as to render the real structure difficult to decipher. Sometimes flowers of *Ophrys aranifera*, at first sight seeming normal as to the number, and almost so as regards the arrangement of their parts, have yet, on examination, proved to be the result of a confluence of two flowers. Mr. Moggridge has observed similar phenomena in the same species at Mentone.

Sometimes the fusion affects flowers belonging to different branches of the same inflorescence, as in *Centranthus ruber*, described by Buchenau, 'Flora,' 1857, p. 293, and even a blossom of one generation of axes may be united with a flower belonging to another generation. Thus M. Michalet[45] speaks of a case wherein the terminal flower of *Betonica alopecuros* was affected with Peloria, and fused with an adjacent one belonging to a secondary axis of inflorescence, and not yet expanded. This latter flower had no calyx, but in its place were three bracts, surrounding the corolla; this again was united to the calyx of the terminal bloom in a most singular manner, the limb of the corolla and that of the calyx being so joined one to the other[Pg 43] as to form but a single tube. It is not uncommon, as has been before stated, to find two corollas enclosed within one calyx, but this is probably the only recorded instance of the fusion of the calyx and corolla of two different flowers belonging to two different axes.

From the preceding details, as well as from others which it is not necessary to give in this place, it would appear that synanthy is more liable to occur where the flowers are naturally crowded together[46] than where they are remote; so too, the upper or younger portions of the inflorescence are those most subject to this change. In like manner the derangements consequent on the coalescence of flowers are often more grave in the central organs, which are most exposed to pressure, and have the least opportunities of resisting the effects of that agency, than they are in the outer portions of the flowers where growth is less restricted.

Morren in his papers on synanthic *Calceolarias*, before referred to, considers that the direction in which fusion acts is centripetal, *e.g.* from the circumference towards the centre of the flower, thus reversing the natural order of things. He considers that there is a radical antagonism between the normal organizing forces and the teratological disorganizing forces, and explains in this way the frequent sterility of monsters from an imperfect formation of stamens, or pistils, or both.

The greater tendency in synanthic flowers of parts of one whorl to adhere to the corresponding organs in another flower has often been remarked, though the dislocation of parts may be so great as to prevent this from being carried out in all cases. It appears also

25

that synanthy is more frequently met with among flowers which have an inferior ovary than in those in which the relative position of the organ in question[Pg 44] is reversed. This remark applies particularly to individual cases; the proportion as regards the genera may not be so large. The explanation of this must of course depend on the circumstances of each particular case; and it would be wrong to attempt to lay down a general rule, when organogenists have not yet fully decided in what plants the inferior ovary is an axial structure, and in what others the appearance is due to the adhesion of the base of the calyx to the carpels.

The list which follows is not intended as a complete one, but it may serve to show what plants are more particularly subject to this anomaly; the * indicates unusual frequency of occurrence, the ! signifies that the writer has himself seen instances in the plants named. Many of the recorded cases of Synanthy are really cases of adhesion of the inflorescence rather than of the flowers.

- Ranunculus Lingua.
o   bulbosus!
- Aconitum Napellus.
- Delphinium sp.!
- Matthiola incana!
- Arabis sagittata.
- Silene sp.
- Reseda odorata!
- Vitis vinifera.
- Citrus aurantium.
- *Fuchsia var. hort.!
- Œnothera sp.
- Saxifraga sp.
- Podalyria myrtillifolia.
- Prunus Armeniaca.
o   spinosa.
- Pyrus Malus.
- Persica vulgaris.
- Cratægus monogyna.
- Robinia pseudacacia.
- Gleditschia triacanthos.
- Syringa persica.
- Cornus sanguinea.
- Viburnum sp.
- *Lonicera sp. plur!
- Centranthus ruber!
- Valantia cruciata.
- Centaurea moschata.
o   Jacea.
- Zinnia elegans.
- Zinnia revoluta.
- Helianthus sp.!

- Spilanthes oleracea.
- Dahlia.
- *Leontodon Taraxacum!
- Senecio Doria.
- Cichorium Intybus.
- Lactuca sativa.
- Anthemis retusa.
- *Campanula medium!
  - persicifolia.
- Azalea indica!
- Vinca minor.
- Atropa Belladonna.
- *Solanum Lycopersicum!
- *Petunia violacea!
- Galeopsis ochroleuca.
- Betonica alopecuros.
- *Digitalis purpurea!
- *Antirrhinum majus!
- *Linaria purpurea!
- *Pedicularis sylvatica!
- *Calceolaria var. hort.!
- Scrophularia nodosa.
- Salpiglossis straminea.
- Streptocarpus Rexii.
- *Gesnera var. hort.!
- Æschynanthus sp.!
- Thyrsacanthus rutilans!
- Anagallis collina.[Pg 45]
- *Primula veris!
  - Auricula.
- *Primula acaulis, var. umbellata!
  - elatior?
  - *sinensis!
- Aristolochia Clematitis.
- Blitum sp.
- Chenopodium sp.
- Rumex sp.
- Salix cinerea.
- *Hyacinthus orientalis!
- Lilium bulbiferum!
  - croceum, et sp. alix, pl.
- Tulipa, sp.

27

- Polygonatum anceps.
- Fritillaria imperalis!
- Agave americana.
- Iris versicolor.
  ○ sambucina.
- Crocus, sp.
- Colchicum autumnale.
- Narcissus incomparabilis!
  ○ Tazetta.
  ○ biflorus.
  ○ chrysanthus.
- *Ophrys aranifera!
- Calanthe vestita!
- Oncidium bicolor.
  ○ ornithorhyncum.
  ○ &c. &c.

In addition to the works before cited, additional information on this subject may be gained from the following:—Jaeger, 'Missbilld.,' p. 92. v. Schlechtend, 'Bot. Zeit.,' 1856, *Robinia*. Weber, 'Verhandl. Nat. Hist. Vereins. Preuss. Rheinl.,' 1849, p. 290, *Primula*. Hincks, 'Rep. Brit. Assoc. Newcastle,' 1838, *Salpiglossis*. Clos, 'Mém. Acad. Toulouse,' vol. vi, 1862, *Anagallis*. Wigand, 'Flora,' 1856, tab. 8, *Pedicularis*. Henfrey, 'Botan. Gazette,' i, p. 280, *Reseda*. P. Reinsch, 'Flora,' 1860, tab. 7,*Petasites*. Weber, Verhandl. Nat. Hist. Vereins. f.d. Preuss. Rheinl. u. Westphal.,' 1860, p. 332, tabs. 6 et 7, *Prunus, Persica, Campanula,Taraxacum, Saxifraga, Silene, Hyacinthus, &c*. Miquel, 'Linnæa,' xi, p. 423, *Colchicum*. Michel, 'Traité du Citronnier,' tab. 6, *Citrus*.

Syncarpy.—In the preceding section it has been shown that the carpels, like other parts of the flower, are subject to be united together. This union may either take place between the carpels of a single flower or between the pistils of different flowers. In the latter case the other floral whorls are generally more or less altered. Where, however, the ovary is, as it is called, inferior, it may happen that the pistils of different flowers may coalesce more or less without much alteration in the other parts of the flower, as happens normally in many *Caprifoliaceæ, Rubiaceæ*, &c. &c. In some of these cases it must be remembered that the real structure of the apparent fruit is not made out beyond dispute, the main points of controversy being as to what, if any, share the dilated fruit-stalk or axis takes in the formation of such organs. Again, it will be borne in mind that in some cases the so-called fruit is made up of a number of flowers all fused together, as in the Mulberry or the Pineapple, in which plants what[Pg 46] is, in ordinary language, called the fruit really consists of the whole mass of flowers constituting the inflorescence fused together. Union of the fruits may also in some cases take place between the carpels after the fall of the other floral whorls, particularly when the outer layers of the pericarp assume a succulent condition, so that under the general head of syncarpy really different conditions are almost necessarily grouped together, and, in seeking to investigate the causes of the phenomenon, the particular circumstances of each individual case must be taken into account. Syncarpy takes place in various degrees; sometimes only the stalks are joined; at other times the whole extent of the fruit, as in cherries, &c. This peculiarity did not escape the observant mind of Shakespeare—

"A double cherry seeming parted.
But yet a union in partition,
Two lovely berries moulded on one stem."
'Midsummer Night's Dream,' act iii, sc. 2.

A similar union has been observed in peaches, gooseberries, gourds, melons, and a great many other fruits. In the Barbarossa grape I have frequently seen a fusion of two, three, four or more berries quite at the end of the bunch, so that the clusters were terminated by a compound grape. Seringe has remarked sometimes two, sometimes three, fruits of *Ranunculus tripartitus* soldered together. He has also seen three melons similarly joined.[47] Turpin mentions having seen a complete union between the three smooth and leathery pericarps which are naturally separate and enclosed within the spiny cupule of the chestnut.[48] Poiteau and Turpin have figured and described in their treatise on fruit trees, under the name of Néfle de Correa, four or five medlars, joined together and surmounted by all the persistent leaflets of the calyces.[49]

[Pg 47]A very remarkable example of Syncarpy has been recorded by E. Kœnig in which nine strawberries were borne on one stem (*Fragaria botryformis*),[50] and a similar malformation has been observed in the Pineapple.

When two fruits are united together they may be of about equal size, while in other cases one of the two is much smaller than the other. This was the case in two cucumbers given to me by Mr. James Salter. These were united together along their whole length excepting at the very tips; the upper one of the two was much larger than the lower, and contained three cells, the lower fruit was one-celled by suppression. Both fruits were curved, the curvature being evidently due to the more rapid growth of the upper as compared with the lower one.

FIG. 19.—Adhesion of two apples.

FIG. 20.—Section of united apples.

In many of these cases, where the fruits are united by their bases, the summits become separated one from the other, so as to resemble the letter V. Such divergence[Pg 48] is of frequent occurrence where fruits are united by their stalks, because, as growth goes on, the tendency must necessarily be towards separation and divergence of the tips of the fruit.

In some cases of Syncarpy the fusion and interpenetration of the carpels is carried to such an extent that it is very difficult to trace on the outer surface the lines of union. The fruit in these cases resembles a single one of much larger size than usual. Moquin mentions a double apple in which the connection was so close that the fruit was not very different in form from what is customary, and a similar thing happens with the tomato. In the case of stone-fruits it sometimes happens, not only that the outer portions are adherent, but that the stones are so likewise.

M. Rœper has observed two apples grafted together, one of which had its stalk broken, and seemed evidently borne and nourished by the other apple;[51] and a similar occurrence happens not infrequently in the cucumber. Moquin has seen three united cherries having only a single stalk jointed to the central fruit, the lateral cherries having each a slight depression or cicatrix marking the situation of the suppressed stalks. Schlotterbec has figured three apples presenting precisely similar appearances.[52]

Fusion of two or more nuts (*Corylus*) is not uncommon; I have seen as many as five so united.[53] In these cases the fruits may be united together in a ring or in linear series.

In some *Leguminosæ*, contrary to the general rule in the order, more than one carpel is found; thus peas, French beans, and other similar plants, are occasionally met with having two or more pods within the same calyx, and in *Gleditschia triacanthos* and *Cæsalpinia digyna* this is so commonly the case as to be considered almost the normal state. (De Cand. 'Mem.[Pg 49] Leg.,' pl. 2, fig. 6; pl. 3, fig. 2.) At times these carpels become fused together, and it becomes difficult, when the traces of the flower have disappeared, to ascertain whether these carpels were formed in one flower, or whether they were the result of the fusion of several blossoms. I have seen an instance of this kind in a plum in which there were two carpels in the same flower, the one being partially fused to the other. The nature of such cases may usually be determined by an inspection of the peduncle which shows no traces of fusion. (See chapter on Multiplication.)

When, however, the fruits are sessile, and they become grafted together, the kind of syncarpy is difficult to distinguish. It, may, nevertheless, be said as a general rule that the union brought about by the approximation of two fruits, after the fall of the floral whorls, is

29

never so complete or so intimate as that determined by synanthy; and also that in those cases where there are supernumerary carpels in the flower, and those carpels become united together, they are rarely so completely fused that their individuality is lost.

An analogous phenomenon takes place not uncommonly in mosses, the spore capsules of which become united together in various ways and degrees. Schimper[54] cites the following species as subject to this anomaly:—*Buxbaumia indusiata, Leskea sericea, Hypnum lutescens,Anomodon alternatus, Clinacium dendroides, Bryum cæspititium,Brachythecium plumosum, Mnium serratum, Splachnum vasculosum.* It has also been observed in *Trichostomum rigidulum* and *Hypnum triquetrum.*

In addition to the authorities already mentioned, the reader may consult Moquin-Tandon, 'El. Ter. Veg.,' p. 270. Turpin. 'Mém. greffe. Ann. Sc. Nat.,' ser. i, t. xxiv, p. 334. De Candolle, 'Organ. Veget.,' t. i. Duhamel, 'Phys. des Arbres,' t. i, p. 304, tab. xiii, xiv. Weber. 'Verhandl. Nat. Hist. Vereina f. d. Preuss. Rheinl. u. Westphal.,' 1860, p. 332, tab. vi. et vii.

[Pg 50]

Synspermy, or Union of the Seeds.—Seeds may be united together in various degrees, either by their integuments,[55] or by their inner parts. Such union of the seeds, however, is of rare occurrence. It takes place normally, to a slight extent, in certain cultivated forms of cotton, wherein the seeds are aggregated together into a reniform mass, whence the term kidney cotton. Union of the parts of the embryo is treated under another head (see Synophty).

Adhesion between the axes of different plants.—Under this head may be classed the union that takes place between the stems, branches, or roots of different plants of the same species, and that which occurs between individuals of different species; the first is not very different in its nature from cohesion of the branches of the same plant (figs. 21, 22). It finds its parallel, under natural circumstances, among the lower cryptogams, in which it often happens that several individual plants, originally distinct, become inseparably blended together into one mass. In the gardening operations of inarching, and to some extent in budding, this adhesion of axis to axis occurs, the union taking place the more readily in proportion as the contact between the younger growing portions of the two axes respectively is close. The huge size of some trees has been, in some cases, attributed to the adnation of different stems. This is said to be the case with the famous plane trees of Bujukdere, near Constantinople, and in which nine trunks are more or less united together.[56]

FIG. 21.—Adhesion of two distinct stems of oak, or possibly cohesion of branches of the same tree. 'Gard. Chron.,' 1846, p. 252.

A similar anastomosis may take place in roots. Lindley cites a case wherein two carrots, of the white Belgian and the red Surrey varieties respectively, had grown so close to each other that each twisted half round the other, so that they ultimately became soldered together; the most singular thing with reference to this union was, that the red carrot[Pg 51] (fig. 23,*b*), with its small overgrown part above the junction, took the colour and large dimensions of the white Belgian (*d*), which, in like manner, with its larger head above the joining (*a*), took the colour and small dimensions of the red one at and below the union (*e d*). The respective qualities of the two roots[Pg 52] were thus transposed, while the upper portions or crowns were unaffected: the root of one, naturally weak, became distended and enlarged by the abundant matter poured into it by its new crown; and in like manner the root of the other, naturally vigorous, was starved by insufficient food derived from the new crown, and became diminutive and shrunken (see Synophty).

FIG. 22.—Adhesion of the branches of two elms. 'Gard. Chron.,' 1849, p. 421.

The explanation of the fact that the stumps of felled fir trees occasionally continue to grow, and to deposit fresh zones of wood over the stump, depends on similar facts. In *Abies pectinata*, says Goeppert,[57] the roots of different individuals frequently unite; hence if one be cut down, its stump may continue to live, being supplied with nourishment from the adjacent trees to which it is adherent by means of its roots.

[Pg 53]

FIG. 23.—**Adhesion of two roots of carrot. 'Gard. Chron.,' 1851, p. 67.**

A not uncommon malformation in mushrooms arises from the confluence of their stalks (fig. 24), and when the union takes place by means of the pilei, it sometimes happens, during growth, that the one fungus is detached from its attachment to the ground, and is borne up with the other, sometimes, even, being found in an inverted position on the top of its fellow.[58]

The garden operations of budding, grafting and inarching have already been alluded to as furnishing illustrations of adhesion, but it may be well to refer briefly to certain other interesting examples of adhesion[Pg 54] induced artificially; thus, the employment of the root as a stock, "root-grafting," is now largely practised with some plants, as affording a quicker means of propagation than by cuttings; and a still more curious illustration may be cited in the fact that it has also been found possible to graft a scion on the leaf in the orange.[59]

FIG. 24.—**Section through two adherent mushrooms, the upper one inverted.**

Mr. Darwin, in his work on the 'Variation of Animals and Plants,' vol. i, p. 395, alludes to the two following remarkable cases of fusion:—"The author of 'Des Jacinthes' (Amsterdam, 1768, p. 124) says that bulbs of blue and red hyacinths may be cut in two, and that they will grow together, and throw up a united stem (and this Mr. Darwin has himself seen), with flowers of the two colours on the opposite sides. But the remarkable point is, that flowers are sometimes produced with the two colours blended together." In the second case related by Mr. Trail, about sixty blue and white potatoes were cut in halves through the eyes or buds, and the halves were then joined, the other buds being destroyed. Union took place, and some of the united tubers produced white, others[Pg 55] blue, while some produced tubers partly white and partly blue.

Adhesion of the axes of plants belonging to different species is a more singular occurrence than the former, and is of some interest as connected with the operation of grafting. As a general rule horticulturists are of opinion, and their opinion is borne out by facts, that the operation of grafting, to be successful, must be practised on plants of close botanical affinity. On the other hand, it is equally true that some plants very closely allied cannot be propagated in this manner. Contact between the younger growing tissues is essential to successful grafting as practised by the gardener, and is probably quite as necessary in those cases where the process takes place naturally. Although there is little doubt but that some of the recorded instances of natural or artificial grafting of plants of distant botanical affinities are untrustworthy, yet the instances of adhesion between widely different plants are too numerous and too well attested to allow of doubt. Moreover, when parasitical plants are considered, such as the Orobanches, the Cuscutas, and specially the mistleto (*Viscum*), which may be found growing on plants of very varied botanical relationship, the occurrence of occasional adhesion between plants of distant affinity is not so much to be wondered at. Union between the haulms of wheat and rye, and other grasses, has been recorded[60]. Moquin-Tandon[61] relates a case wherein, by accident, a branch of a species of *Sophora* passed through the fork, made by two diverging branches of an elder (*Sambucus*), growing in the Jardin des Plantes of Toulouse. The branch of the *Sophora* contracted a firm adhesion to the elder, and what is remarkable is that, although the latter has much[Pg 56] softer wood than the former, yet the branch of the harder wooded tree was flattened, as if subjected to great pressure[62]. It is possible that some of the cases similar to those spoken of by Columella, Virgil[63], and other classical writers, may have originated in the accidental admission of seeds into the crevices of trees; in time the seeds grew, and as they did so, the young plants contracted an adhesion to the supporting tree. Some of the instances recorded by classical writers may be attributed to intentional or accidental fallacy, as in the so-called "greffe des charlatans" of more modern days.

Adhesion of the roots of different species has been effected artificially, as between the carrot and the beet root, while Dr. Maclean succeeded in engrafting, on a red beet, a scion of the white Silesian variety of the same species. In all these cases, even in the most successful grafts, the amount of adhesion is very slight; the union in no degree warrants the term fusion, it is little but simple contact of similar tissues, while new growing matter is formed all round the cut surfaces, so that the latter become gradually imbedded in the newly formed matter.

Synophty or adhesion of the embryo.—This often occurs partially in the embryo plants of the common mistleto (*Viscum*), but is not of common occurrence in other plants, even in such cases as the orange (*Citrus*), the*Cycadeæ, Coniferæ*, &c., where there is frequently more than one embryo in the seed. Alphonse De Candolle has described and figured an instance of the kind in *Euphorbia helioscopia*, wherein two embryo plants were completely grafted together throughout the whole length[Pg 57] of their axes, leaving merely the four cotyledons separate. A similar adnation has been observed by the same botanist in *Lepidium sativum* and *Sinapis ramosa*, as well as in other plants.[64] I have met with corresponding instances in*Antirrhinum majus* and in *Cratægus oxyacantha*, in the latter case complicated with the partial atrophy of one of the four cotyledons. It is necessary to distinguish between such cases and the fallacious appearances arising from a division of the cotyledons. M. Morren has figured and described the union of two roots of carrot (*Daucus*), which were also spirally twisted. He attributes this union to the blending of two radicles, and applies merely the term "rhizocollesy" to this union of the roots.[65] Mr. Thwaites cites a case wherein two embryos were contained in one seed in a *Fuchsia*, and had become adherent. What is still more remarkable, the two embryos were different, a circumstance attributable to their hybrid origin, the seed containing them being the result of the fertilisation of*Fuchsia coccinea* (quere *F. magellanica?*) by the pollen of *F. fulgens*.

FOOTNOTES:

[30]Wydler, 'Flora,' 1852, p. 737, tab. ix.

[31]'El. Ter. Veg.,' p. 254.

[32]'Bull. Soc. Bot. Fr.,' 1857, p. 451.

[33]'Bull. Acad. Belg.,' vol. xix, part ii, p. 335.

[34]'Bull. Soc. Bot. Fr.,' 1860, p. 25.

[35]'Bull. Soc. Bot. Fr.,' 1861, p. 147.

[36]'Bull. Acad. Belg.,' vol. xviii, part ii, p. 498.

[37]See also Prillieux, 'Bull. Soc. Bot. Fr.,' 1861, p. 195.

[38]'Mém. Acad. Toulouse,' 5th Series, vol. iii.

[39]Linnæa, vol. ii. p. 607.

[40]'Journal Roy. Hort. Soc.,' new ser., vol. i. 1866, p. 200.

[41]'Bull. Soc. Bot. Fr.,' 1861, p. 159.

[42]Ibid., 1859, p. 467.

[43]'Flora,' 1858, p. 65, tab. ii.

[44]C. Morren. 'Bull. Acad. Belg.,' vol. xv (Fuchsia, p. 89); vol. xviii, p. 591. (Lobelia, p. 142); vol. xix, p. 352; vol. xx, p. 4.

[45]'Bull. Soc. Bot. Fr.,' vol. vii, p. 625.

[46]Cramer, 'Bildungsabweichungen,' p. 56, tab. vii, fig. 10, figures a case wherein the two central flowers of the capitulum of *Centaurea Jacea*were united together.

[47]'Bull. Bot.' tab. iii, figs. 4–6.

[48]'Mém. greffe Ann. Science Nat.,' ser. i, t. xxiv, p. 334.

[49]"Mespilus portentosa." Poit. et Turp., 'Pomol. Franc.,' liv, xxxi, p. 202, pl. 202.

[50]Duchesne, 'Hist. Nat. Frais.,' p. 79.

[51]De Cand., 'Phys. Végét.,' tom. ii, p. 781.

[52]Sched. de monstr. plant. 'Act. Helv.,' tab. i, fig. 8.

[53]'Mém. greffe,' loc. cit., tab. xxiv, p. 334.

[54]'Bull. Soc. Bot. Franc.,' 8, pp. 73 and 351, tab. ii; and Röse. 'Bot. Zeit.,' x, p. 410.

[55]*Nymphæa lutea, Æsculus Hippocastanum*, &c. See Moquin, 'El. Ter. Veg.,' p. 277.

[56]C. Martins, 'Promenade Botanique,' p. 8.

[57]'Ann. Sc. Nat.,' t. xix, 1843, p. 141, tab. iv.

[58]'Ann. Nat. Hist.,' ser. 2, vol. ix, tab. xvi. 'Phytologist,' 1857. p. 352, &c.

[59]Quoted from the 'Revue Hortic.' in 'Gard. Chron.,' 1866, p. 386.

[60]Senebier, 'Phys Végét.,' t. iv, p. 426. The same author also cites Romer as having found two plants of *Ranunculus*, from the stem of which emerged a daisy. As it is not an

uncommon practice to stick a daisy on a buttercup, it is to be hoped no hoax was played off on M. Romer.

[61]'El. Ter. Veg.,' p. 289.

[62]An instance of this kind is cited in Dr. Robson's memoir of the late Charles Waterton, from which it appears that two trees, a spruce fir and an elm, were originally planted side by side, and had been annually twisted round each other, so that they had in places grown one into the other, with the result of stunting the growth of both trees, thus illustrating, according to the opinion of the eccentric naturalist above cited, the incongruous union of Church and State!

[63]See Daubeny, 'Lectures on Roman Husbandry,' p. 156.

[64]A. P. De Candolle, 'Organ Végét.,' t. ii, p. 72, tab. liv, fig. 1.

[65]'Bull. Acad. Belg.,' t. xx, part i, 1852, p. 43.

[Pg 58]

PART II.
INDEPENDENCE OR SEPARATION OF ORGANS.

Under this head are included all those instances wherein organs usually entire, or more or less united, are, or appear to be, split or disunited. It thus includes such cases as the division of an ordinarily entire leaf into a lobed or partite one, as well as those characterised by the separation of organs usually joined together. Union, as has been stated in a previous chapter, is the result either of persistent integrity or of a junction of originally separate organs, after their formation; so in like manner, the separation or disjunction of parts may arise from the absence of that process of union which is habitual in some cases, or from an actual *bonâ fide* separation of parts originally united together. In the former case, the isolation of parts arises from arrest of development, while in the latter it is due rather to luxuriant growth. A knowledge, as well of the ordinary as of the unusual course, of development in any particular flower is thus required in order to ascertain with accuracy the true nature of the separation of parts. The late Professor Morren[66] proposed the general term Monosy (μονωσις) for all these cases of abnormal isolation, subdividing the group into two, as follows—1, Adesmy (α-δεσμος), including those cases where the separation is congenital; and 2, Dialysis (διαλυω), comprising those instances where the isolation is truly a result of the separation of parts previously joined together. Adesmy, moreover,[Pg 59] was by the Belgian savant said to be homologous when it occurred between members of the same whorl, *e.g.* between the sepals of an ordinary monosepalous calyx, or heterologous when the separation took place between members of different whorls, as when the calyx is detached from the ovary, &c. The former case would thus be the converse of cohesion, the latter of adhesion.

To the adoption of these words there is this great objection, that we can but rarely, in the present state of our knowledge, tell in which group any particular illustration should be placed.

The terms adopted in the present work are, for the most part, not necessarily intended to convey any idea as to the organogenetic history of the parts affected. Where a single organ, that is usually entire, becomes divided the term Fission is used; in cases where parts of the same whorl become isolated, the word Dialysis is employed, and in the same sense in which it is generally used by descriptive botanists, and where the various whorls become detached one from the other, the occurrence is distinguished by the application of the term Solution.

FOOTNOTES:

[66]'Bull. Acad. Belg.,' t. xix, part iii, 1852, p. 315.

CHAPTER I.
FISSION.

When an organ becomes divided it receives at the hands of descriptive botanists the appellations cleft, partite, or sect, according to the depth of the division; hence in considering the teratological instances of this nature, the term fission has suggested itself as an appropriate one to be applied to the subdivision of an habitually entire or undivided organ. It thus corresponds pretty nearly in its application with the term Chorisis[Pg 60] or "dédoublement," or with the "disjonctions qui divisent les organes" of Moquin-Tandon.[67]It is usually, but not always, a concomitant with hypertrophy, and dependent on luxuriance of growth.

It must be understood therefore that the term, as generally applied, does not so much indicate the cleavage of a persistent organ, as it does the formation and development of two or more growing points instead of one, whence results a branching or forking (di-tri-chotomy) of the affected organ. In some instances it seems rather to be due to the relative deficiency of cellular, as contrasted with fibro-vascular tissue.

Fission of axile organs.—This condition is scarcely to be distinguished from multiplication of the axile organs (which see). A little attention, however, will generally show whether the unusual number of branches is a consequence of the development of a large number of distinct shoots, as happens, for instance, when a tree is pollarded, or of a division of one. M. Fournier[68] gives as an illustration the case of a specimen of *Ruscus aculeatus* in which there occurred a division of the foliaceous branches into two segments, reaching as far as the insertion of the flower, but no further. He also mentions lateral cleavage effected by a notching of the margin, the notch being anterior to the flowers and always directed towards their insertion. In the allied genus *Danaë*, Webb, 'Phyt. Canar.,' p. 320, describes the fascicles of flowers as in "crenulis brevibus ad marginem ramulorum dispositis." Sometimes, on the other hand, *Danaë*has a fascicle of flowers inserted on the middle of the upper surface, as in*Ruscus*. Wigand mentions an instance in *Digitalis lutea*, where the upper part of the stem was divided into six or seven racemes; possibly this was a case of fasciation, but such a division of the inflorescence is by no means uncommon in the spicate species of *Veronica*. I have[Pg 61] also seen it in*Plantago lanceolata*, *Reseda luteola*, *Campanula medium*, *Epacris impressa*, and a bifurcation of the axis of the spikelet within the outer glumes in *Lolium perenne*[69] and *Anthoxanthum odoratum*. In the Kew Museum is preserved a cone of *Abies excelsa*,[70] dividing into two divisions, each bearing bracts and scales. A similar thing frequently occurs in the male catkins of *Cedrus Libani* (fig. 25).

FIG. 25.—**Bifurcated male inflorescence,** *Cedrus Libani.*

This subdivision of axial organs is not unfrequently the result of some injury or mutilation, thus Duval Jouve alludes to the frequency with which branched stems are produced in the various species of *Equisetum*, as a consequence of injuries to the main stem, but this is rather to be considered as a multiplication of parts than as a subdivision of one.

FIG. 26.—**Bifurcated leaf of** *Lamium album***, &c.**

Fission of foliar organs.—Many leaves exhibit constantly the process of fission, such as the *Salisburia adiantifolia*, and which is due perhaps as much to the absence or relatively small proportion of cellular as compared with vascular tissue, as to absolute fission. In the same way we have laciniated leaves of the Persian lilac, *Syringa persica*, and Moquin mentions instances in a species of[Pg 62] *Mercurialis* in which the leaves were deeply slashed. In *Chenopodium Quinoa* the leaves were so numerous and the clefts so deep, that the species was hardly recognisable, while on a branch of *Rhus Cotinus* observed by De Candolle the lobes were so narrow and so fine as to give the plant the aspect of an *Umbellifer.* Wigand ('Flora,' 1856, p. 706) speaks of the leaves of *Dipsacus fullonum* with bi-partite leaves; Moquin mentions the occurrence of a leaf of an oleander bi-lobed at the summit, so as to give the appearance of a fusion of two leaves. Steinheil has recorded an instance in *Scabiosa atropurpurea* in which one of the stem leaves presented the following peculiarities. It was simple below, but divided above into two equal lobes, provided each with a median nerve.[71] Steinheil has also recorded a *Cerastium* in which one of the leaves was provided with two midribs; above this leaf was a group of ternate leaves. I have seen similar instances in the common Elm, *Ulmus campestris*, and also in the common nettle, *Urtica dioica*,[Pg 63] leaves of which latter thus resembled those of *Urtica biloba*, which are habitually bilobed at the summit. M. Clos[72] mentions an instance where the terminal leaf and first bract of *Orchis sambucina* were divided into two segments. The same author also mentions the leaves of *Anemiopsis californica*, which were divided in their upper halves each into two lobes—also leaves of a lentil springing from a fasciated stem and completely divided into two segments, but with only a single bud in the axil. The axillary branches in like manner showed traces of cleavage. Fig. 26 represents a case of this kind in *Lamium album*, conjoined with suppression of the flowers on one side of the stem. I have also in my herbarium a leaf of *Arum maculatum*, with a stalk single at the base, but dividing into two separate stalks, each bearing a hastate lamina, the form of which is so perfect that were it not from the venation of the sheath it would be considered that there was here a union of two leaves rather than a bifurcation of one. A garden Pelargonium presented the same appearance.

FIG. 27.—Bifurcated leaf of *Pelargonium*.

Fern fronds are particularly liable to this kind of subdivision, and they exhibit it in almost every degree, from a simple bifurcation of the frond to the formation of large tufts of small lobes all formed on the same plan by the repeated forking of the pinnules. These may be considered as cases of hypertrophy.

Moquin-Tandon, at a meeting of the Botanical Society[Pg 64] of France (April 3rd, 1858) exhibited a leaf of *Cerasus Lauro-Cerasus* divided in such a manner as to resemble a leaf of *Citrus* or of *Phyllarthron*. In this case, therefore, the disunion must have taken place laterally, and not from apex towards base, as is most common. The leaves of the common horse-radish,*Cochlearia Armoracia*, are very subject to this pinnated subdivision of the margin, and numerous other illustrations might be given.

FIG. 28.—Bifurcated frond, *Scolopendrium vulgare*.

A. Braun describes a singular case in a leaf of *Irina*[Pg 65] *glabra* wherein the blade of the leaf on one side was deeply and irregularly laciniated, the other side remaining entire. (Verhandl., d. 35, Naturforscherversammlung, tab. 3.) Laciniate varieties of plants are of frequent occurrence in gardens where they are often cultivated for their beauty or singularity; thus, there are laciniated alders, fern-leaved beeches and limes, oak-leaved laburnums, &c. A list of several of these is subjoined. A similar fission takes place constantly in the cotyledons of some plants, sometimes, as in *Coniferæ*, to such an extent as to give an appearance as if there were several cotyledons.[73]

It is not always easy to recognise, at a first glance, whether the division be the result of disunion or of an incomplete union of two leaves, but we may be guided by the number of leaves in the cycle or the whorl. The number is complete in cases of partial disjunction, while in cases of fusion it is incomplete. Again, in instances of disjunction, there is only one point of origin, but, when two leaves are grafted together, two such points may generally be detected at the base of the leaf, or a transverse section of the leaf-stalk will show indications of fusion. The number and position of the midribs will also serve as a guide, as in cases of fusion there are generally two or more midribs, according to the number of fused leaves; but as Moquin well remarks, this latter character cannot be always depended upon, for the median nerve may divide without any corresponding separation of the cellular portions of the leaf. The author just quoted cites examples of this kind in *Cardamine pratensis*, *Hedera Helix*, *Plantago major*, *Geranium nodosum*.

The following list of plants commonly producing leaves that are cleft or divided, to a greater extent than is usual in the species, is mainly taken from one given by Schlechtendal, 'Bot. Zeit.,' 1844, p. 441, with additions from other sources. The ! indicates that the author has himself met with the deviation in[Pg 66] question. Many are cultivated as garden varieties under the names here given.

- Trollius europæus dissectus.
- Chelidonium majus laciniatum!
- Glaucium luteum.
- Brassica oleracea!
- Tilia parvifolia laciniata.
  -
    - asplenifolia!

35

- Acer platanoides laciniatum.
  -
    - crispum.
- Æsculus Hippocastanum incisum!
  -
    - asplenifolium.
- Vitis vinifera apiifolia!
  -
    - laciniosa.
- Ilex Aquifolium!
- Rhus Toxicodendron quercifolium.
  - Cotinus.
- Ervum Lens.
- Cytisus Laburnum quercifolium!
  -
    - incisum.
- Rubus fraticosus laciniatus!
- Pyrcis communis.
- Cerasus Lauro-cerasus.
- Apium graveolens!
- Pimpinella magna.
  - Saxifraga.
- Cratægus Oxyacantha laciniata.
  -
    - quercifolia!
- Ribes nigrum.
- Sambucus nigra laciniata!
  - racemosa laciniata.
- Dipsacus fullonum.
- Scabiosa atropurpurea!
- Symphoricarpus racemosus.
- Helianthus sp.!
- Lonicera Periclymenum quercifolia!
- Syringa persica laciniata!
- Syringa vulgaris!
- Nerium Oleander!
- Lamium purpureum.
  - album!
- Salvia officinalis.
- Solanum Dulcamara!
- Fraxinus excelsior crispa.
- Veronica austriaca.
- Polemonium cæruleum.

- Juglans regia laciniata!
-
  - heterophylla.
  - filicifolia.
- Anemiopsis californica.
- Chenopodium Quinoa.
- Ulmus americana incisa.
- Fagus sylvatica heterophylla!
-
  - laciniata!
  - aspleniifolia!
  - incisa.
  - salicifolia!
- Mercurialis perennis.
- Urtica dioica.
- Quercus Cerris laciniata!
  - pubescens filicina.
- Betula populifolia laciniata.
  - alba dalecarlica.
- Alnus incana laciniata!
  - glutinosa laciniata!
    - quercifolia.
    - oxyacanthifolia.
- Corylus Avellana heterophylla!
-
  - laciniata!
  - urticifolia.
- Carpinus Betulus incisa!
-
  - quercifolia.
  - heterophylla.
- Castanea vesca heterophylla.
-
  - quercifolia.
  - incisa.
- Populus alba acerifolia.
-
  - palmata.
  - quercifolia.
  - balsamifera.
- Orchis sambucina.
- Arum maculatum.
- Filices sp. pl.

See also Schlechtendal, 'Bot. Zeit.,' tom. xiii, p. 823. A. Braun, loc. supra citat. For Ferns too numerous for insertion, see Moore, 'Nature-Printed Ferns,' 8vo ed., 2 vols. Clos, 'Mém. Acad. Toulouse,' 1862, p. 51.

Fission of the petals, &c.—The floral leaves are subject to a similar process of cleavage to that which has just[Pg 67] been mentioned as taking place in the leaves. This, indeed, occurs very often as a normal occurrence as in the petals of mignonette (*Reseda*), or those of *Alsine media* and many other plants. Here, however, we have only to allude to those instances in which the cleavage occurs in flowers whose sepals or petals are usually entire. Under this category Moquin mentions a petal of *Brassica oleracea* completely split into two. Linné in his 'Flora Lapponica' (pp. 145 and 164) mentions quadrifid petals of *Lychnis dioica*, and much divided petals of *Rubus arcticus*. Among other plants subject to this division of sepals or petals may be mentioned as having come within the writer's personal observation, *Ranunculus Lingua*, *R. acris*, *Papaver somniferum*, and others of this genus, *Saponaria sp.*, *Dianthus*, *Narcissus*, &c.

In some of the garden varieties of *Cyclamen* the corolla looks at first sight as if double, and the plan of the flower is oblong or elliptical, instead of circular. In these flowers each lobe of the corolla is divided almost to the base into two lobes, so that there appear to be ten lobes to the corolla instead of five, as usual. The stamens are normal in form and number in these flowers.

In the paroquet tulips of gardeners the segments of the perianth are deeply and irregularly gashed, the segments occasionally becoming rolled up and their margins coherent so as to form little tubular spurs. I have also noticed the segments of the perianth in *Crocus* and *Colchicum* deeply cleft, so much so sometimes, as to equal in this particular the stigmas. In the flowers of a species of *Oncidium*, communicated to me by Mr. Currey, the lip was divided into three segments perfectly distinct one from the other, but confluent with the column; the two side pieces had callosities at the upper edge close to the base, the central piece had a similar wartlike process in its centre. In these flowers the ovary, the stigma, and the anther were all in a rudimentary condition. Some verbenas raised by Mr.[Pg 68] Wills offer a curious illustration of this condition. It will be remembered that some of the lobes or petals of a verbena are normally divided at the base to a slight degree, but in the flowers in question this is carried to such an extent that the enlarged lobes are pushed into the centre of the flower and simulate, at a first glance, a distinct and separate organ, though in reality it is but an enlargement of what occurs normally.[74]

FIG. 29.—Flower of *Oncidium sp.* seen from the back. The lip is divided into three unequal segments.

Moquin mentions having seen the stamens of *Matthiola incana* and *Silene conica* completely divided, each section bearing half an anther, exactly as happens in *Polygalaceæ*. In tulips and lilies the same author mentions division of the anther only, the filament remaining entire, as happens naturally in many species of *Vaccinium*.

A division of the individual carpels occurs very frequently when those organs become more or less leafy, as in *Trifolium repens*, and other plants to be hereafter mentioned.

The instances given in this chapter have all been cases wherein the division or the accessory growth has taken place in one plane only and that plane[Pg 69] the same as that of the affected organ, but there are other examples, probably equally due to fissiparous division, where the new growth is either parallel to, or even at angle with the primary organ. Of such nature are some of those instances wherein two leaves appear to be placed back to back. These partake of the nature of excrescences or of exaggerated developments, and hence will be more fully treated of under the head of hypertrophy. It must be remembered that in some of these cases the fission may be a resumption of characters proper to the species under natural conditions, but lost by cultivation or otherwise. Thus, Mr. Buckman accounts for "finger-and-toe" in root-crops on the principle of reversion to the wild form.

FOOTNOTES:

[67]Loc. cit., p. 295.

[68]'Bull. Soc. Bot. France,' 1857, p. 758.

[69]Masters, 'Jourl. Linn. Soc.,' vol. vii, p. 121.

[70]Cramer, 'Bildungsabweichungen,' p. 4, tab. vi, fig. 4, figures a case of the same kind in *Pinus Cembra.*

[71]'Ann. des Science Nat.,' 2nd series, t. iv, p. 147, tab. v, figs. 3 and 4.

[72]'Mém. Acad. Scien. Toulouse,' 5th series, vol. iii.

[73]Duchartre, 'Ann. Sc. Nat.,' 3rd series, 1848, vol. x, p. 207.

[74]Masters, 'Rep. Bot. Congress,' London, 1866, p. 136, tab. 7, f. 15, 16.

CHAPTER II.
DIALYSIS.

This term is here made use of in the same sense as in descriptive botany, to indicate the isolation of parts of the same whorl; it is thus the opposite of cohesion. Morren, as has been previously stated, employed the word in a different sense, while Moquin-Tandon[75] included cases of this description under the category of "Disjonctions qui isolent les organes."

Dialysis, as here understood, may be the result of an arrest of development, in consequence of which parts that under ordinary circumstances would become fused, do not do so; or, on the other hand, it may be the result of an actual separation between parts primitively undivided. As it is not possible in every case to distinguish between the effects of these two diverse causes, no attempt is here made to do so.

[Pg 70]

Dialysis of the margins of individual foliar organs.—In cases where the leaf or leaf-like organ is ordinarily tubular or horn-like in form, owing to the cohesion of its edges, it may happen either from lack of union or from actual separation of the previously united edges, that the tubular shape is replaced by the ordinary flattened expansion. Thus, in *Eranthis hyemalis*, wherein the petals (nectaries) are tubular and the sepals flat, I have met with numerous instances of transition from the one form to the other, as shown in fig. 9, p. 24.

It is, however, in the carpels that this separation occurs most frequently. When these organs appear under the guise of leaves, as they often do, their margins are disunited, so that the carpel becomes flat or open. This happens in the strawberry (*Fragaria*), the columbine (*Aquilegia*), in *Trifolium repens, Ranunculus Ficaria,* &c.[76]

Dialysis of the parts of the same whorl:—calyx.—The separation of an ordinarily coherent series into its constituent parts is necessarily of more common occurrence than the foregoing. As here understood, it is the precise converse of cohesion, and it may be represented diagrammatically by a dotted line above the letters denoting the sepals, petals, &c. When this change happens in the calyx we have the gamosepalous condition replaced by the polysepalous one, as thus represented:

.... S S S S S instead of _____ S S S S S

as in a calyx of five coherent sepals.

Detachment of this kind occurs not unfrequently, as in *Primula vulgaris,Trifolium repens,* &c. In *Rosaceæ* and *Pomaceæ* this separation of the calyx is of the more moment, as it has reference to the structure of the[Pg 71]inferior ovary, as will be more fully mentioned hereafter. Here, however, a case recorded by M. J. E. Planchon may be alluded to[77] wherein a quince fruit (*Cydonia*) was surmounted by five leaves, the surface of the pome being marked by as many prominences, which apparently corresponded to the five stalks of the calycine leaves. In this specimen, then, the inferior position of the ovary appeared to be not so much due to an expansion of the fruit stalk, as to the fusion of the hypertrophied stalks of the sepals. Some of the malformations among Cucurbits point to a similar structure. It is probable that in many of these cases the so-called inferior ovary is partly axial partly foliar, *i.e.,* sepaline, and partly carpellary in its nature.

Dialysis of the sepals in calyces that are usually gamosepalous has been most frequently observed in *Rosaceæ, Pomaceæ, Umbelliferæ,* less commonly in *Leguminosæ,* also in the following genera:—*Primula,Symphytum, Gentiana, Campanula,* &c.

FIG. 30.—Dialysis of the sepals and petals in *Correa.*

Dialysis of the corolla is likewise of frequent occurrence, either partially or to such an extent as to render the corolla truly polypetalous. Among*Labiatæ* the upper lip of the

39

corolla may be often met with partially[Pg 72] cleft, as it is constantly in *Phlomis biloba*, or more markedly among the *Lobeliaceæ*.

In the *Compositæ*, a similar separation of the petals is not infrequent, thus showing frequent transitional stages between the labiatifloral and tubulifloral divisions respectively. The ligulate corollas also may often be found in Chrysanthemums, Dahlias, &c., more or less deeply divided into their component parts.

A more complete separation occurs not unfrequently in *Campanula*, *Rhododendron*, *Phlox*, *&c*. Figs. 30 and 31 illustrate dialysis of the corolla; the first in *Correa*, the second in *Campanula*.

FIG. 31.—Dialysis of the corolla in *Campanula sp.*, after De Candolle.

In the last-named genus, *C. rotundifolia* has been found with polypetalous flowers in a wild state in the mountains of Canton Neufchatel, Switzerland, and gave rise to the creation of a new genus. This form is now introduced into gardens.

It must be remembered that in some genera, where this separation of the petals has been met with, there are species in which a similar isolation occurs normally, as in *Rhododendron*. *R. linearilobum*, a Japanese species, offers a good illustration of this.

The following list contains the names of the genera[Pg 73] in which this separation of the petals of an ordinarily gamopetalous flower takes place most frequently.

- Correa.
- Campanula! sp. pl.
- Polemonium.
- Phlox!
- Cobœa!
- Rhododendron!
- Erica!
- Rhodora.
- Azalea!
- Compositæ! sp. pl.
- Lonicera!
- Convolvulus!
- Pharbitis.
- Antirrhinum!
- Verbascum!
- Mimulus.
- Digitalis!
- Orobanche.
- Solanum.
- Nicotiana.
- Gentiana!
- Anagallis.
- Primula!
- Lamium!
- Convallaria!
- Lilium!
- Colchicum!

40

- &c. &c.

This list does not include those very numerous cases in which this change is associated with more or less complete frondescence or leafy condition of the petals.

Dialysis of the stamens.—A similar isolation of the stamens occurs occasionally; for instance, when Mallows (*Malvaceæ*) become double, one of the first stages of the process is often the disjunction of the stamens, and a similar dissociation occurs in *Leguminosæ* and *Compositæ*, as in *Tragopogon*, as related by Kirschleger, in *Hypochæris* by Wigand, and in *Coreopsis* by Schlechtendal.

Dialysis of the carpels.—In the case of the carpels this disunion is more frequent than in the stamens. M. Seringe[78] figures carpels of *Diplotaxis tenuifolia* more or less completely separated one from the other; indeed, this separation is very common amongst *Cruciferæ* and *Umbelliferæ*.

Generally speaking, the disunion is complicated with frondescence—but not always so. I have, in my herbarium, specimens of *Convallaria majalis*, *Commelyna sp.*, and of *Lilium auratum*, in all of which the three carpels are completely disjoined, and present three[Pg 74] styles, three stigmas, &c., without any other change. Engelmann[79] speaks of three classes of this malformation. 1st, that in which the carpels separate one from the other without opening, as in the lily just alluded to; 2nd, that in which the ovary remains closed, but loses its internal partitions, as in a case mentioned by Moquin in *Stachys sylvatica*, in which, owing to imperfect disjunction, the two bi-lobed carpels were changed into a nearly one-celled capsule;[80] and 3rd, those cases in which the carpels are open and foliaceous.

FIG. 32.—Anomalous form of orange.

Disjunction is more frequent in dry fruits than in fleshy ones. In the latter instance it happens at an early stage of existence, and the pericarp becomes more or less leafy, losing its faculty of becoming fleshy, as in *Prunus Cerasus* and *Amygdalus persica*; nevertheless, fleshy fruits sometimes become disunited. I have seen a case similar to that mentioned by M. Alphonse de Candolle in *Solanum esculentum*, in which the pericarp became ruptured, and the placentas protruded. A like occurrence has also been observed in a species of *Melastoma*.[81] This is analogous to what happens in *Caulophyllum* and *Slateria*. Disjunction of the carpels[Pg 75] is not rare in oranges. Sometimes this takes place regularly, at other times irregularly; occasionally in such a manner as to give the appearance of a hand and fingers to the fruit. Of one of these, Ferrari,[82] in the curious volume below cited, speaks thus: "Arbor profusissima, quia dat utraque manu; imo quia vere manus dat in poma conversis; utque magis munifica sit poma ipsa convertit in manus."

M. Duchartre[83] mentions a semi-double flower of orange with eight to ten distinct carpels in a whorl, and occasionally several whorls one above another. De Candolle[84] considers the rind of the orange as a production from the receptacle, and this view is confirmed by the specimens of Duchartre, in which the carpels were quite naked or had a common envelope truncated, and open above to allow of the passage of the styles and stigmas.

FIG. 33.—Orange. Showing disjunction of carpels, after Maout.

FIG. 34.—Section of orange shown in fig. 33 after Maout.

It frequently happens in conjunction with this separation of the carpels one from the other, that a lack of union manifests itself between the margins of the individual carpels themselves. Very numerous cases of this kind have been recorded, and the double tulips of gardens may be referred to as showing this condition[Pg 76] very frequently. In connection with this detachment of the carpels, a change in the mode of placentation is often to be observed, or two or more kinds may be seen in the same pistil, as in double-flowered saponarias, many Crucifers, &c., as alluded to under the head of displacements of the placenta.

FOOTNOTES:

[75] *Loc. cit.*, p. 298.

[76]Masters in Seemann's 'Journal of Botany,' 1867, p. 158.

[77]Bull. Soc. Bot. France,' t. xiii, 1866, p. 234.

[78]'Bull. Bot.,' pl. i, figs. 8–12.

[79]'De Anthol.,' p. 37.

[80]Moquin, loc. cit., p. 305.

[81]'Neue Denkschr. der Allg. Schweiz. Gesell.,' band v, pl. ii. p. 5.

[82]'Hesperides,' auctore Ferrario. Rome, 1646, fig. 415, pp. 213 and 215. See also Michel, 'Traité du Citronnier.'

[83]'Ann. des Science Nat.,' 3rd series, 1844, vol. i, p. 294.

[84]'Org. Véget.,' vol. ii., p. 41.

CHAPTER III.
SOLUTION.

The isolation or separation of different whorls that are ordinarily adherent together is by no means of rare occurrence. Were it not that the isolation is often congenital, the word detachment would be an expressive one to apply to these cases, but as the change in question occurs quite as often from a want of union, an arrest or stasis of development, as from a *bonâ fide* separation, the word solution seems to be, on the whole, the best. It corresponds in application to the word *liber* (*calyx liber*, &c.), in general use by descriptive botanists. As here employed, the term nearly corresponds with the "adesmie hetérologue" of Morren. Moquin Tandon does not make any special subdivision for the class of cases here grouped together, but places them all under "Disjonctions qui isolent les organes." It seems, however, desirable to have a separate word to express the converse condition of adhesion, and for this purpose the term solution, as above stated, is here employed. Diagrammatically, the condition may be expressed by placing a dotted line at the side of the letters thus:

: S S S S S :   : C C C C C :

would indicate the disjunction of the sepals from the[Pg 77] carpels (c), in contradistinction to adhesion, which may be represented by the unbroken line thus:

| S S S S S | | C C C C C |

Solution of the calyx from the ovary.—Of all the instances of adhesion which take place under ordinary circumstances, that between the calyx and the ovary is perhaps the most common. The *calyx adhærens* or *superus* is a structural characteristic to which all botanists attach considerable importance; so that when exceptional cases occur in which the calyx becomes detached from the ovary, becomes, that is, *inferus* or *liber*, a proportionate degree of interest attaches to the irregularity. It is not within the scope of the present work to inquire whether this detachment be real or merely apparent, arising from a want of union between parts ordinarily united together. This point must be left to the organogenists to decide in each particular case. So also the question as to what share, if any, the expanded and dilated flower-stalk may take in what are usually called inferior ovaries, can be here only incidentally touched upon.

Among *Rosaceæ*, the change in question is very common, especially in conjunction with an elongation of the axis of the flower (apostasis) and with prolification, though it is by no means always co-existent with these malformations. When this alteration in the apparent relative position of calyx and carpels occurs in roses (*Rosa*) the appearances are generally such as to indicate that the "hip" of the rose is a dilatation of the peduncle, continuous above with the coherent bases of the sepals; this inference seems also to be borne out by what happens in the *Pomaceæ*. In some cases in this sub-order, the calyx becomes detached from the carpels, so that the latter organs become more or less "superior," and distinct one from the other. This happens constantly in the double-flowered[Pg 78] thorn, *Cratægus Oxyacantha*, in some blossoms of which the hollowed end of the peduncle still invests the base of the carpels, leaving the upper portions detached. In apples flowers are occasionally met with of greater size than usual and on longer stalks, so that the whole looks more like a rose than an apple blossom. In these cases it will usually be found that the calyx consists of distinct sepals, without a trace of the ordinary swelling beneath the flower. The petals are often more numerous than usual; the stamens variously changed, and the carpels sometimes absent; at other times, as in the instance figured in the adjacent woodcuts, figs. 36, 37,

42

consisting of separate, superior ovaries, sometimes destitute of ovules, or, at other times, having two of these bodies.[85]

FIG. 35.—Proliferous Rose. Showing an absence of the usual dilatation of the flower-stalk, and other changes.

This condition accords precisely with the account[Pg 79] of the development of the flowers in *Pomaceæ* as given by Payer, Caspary, and others, so that the flowers above described would owe their deficiency of the swollen receptacle to an arrest of development. M. Germain de Saint Pierre, among other malformations of the rose, presented to the Botanical Society of France in 1854[86] two specimens which are of special interest as relating to this contested point. In the one, the swollen portion beneath the flower was surmounted by five perfect leaves, as, indeed, is not infrequent in such malformations; here, then, the calyx could have had little or no share in the production of the swelling in question. In the other, the swollen portion was actually above the insertion of the sepals here represented by five perfect leaves.

FIG. 36.—Section through Apple blossom, showing detachment of calyx from ovaries, absence of dilated flower-stalk, &c.

FIG. 37.—Calyx detached from carpels in Apple.

On the other hand, M. Planchon's specimen of the Quince before alluded to, not to mention other instances, tends to show that the bases of the sepals do sometimes enter into the composition of the pome. And, indeed, in many of these cases it would be impossible to say where the axial or receptacular portion ended, and the foliar portion began. As both from[Pg 80]normal organogeny as well as from unusual conformation contradictory inferences may be drawn, it would obviously be unsafe to attempt the explanation of the so-called calyx-tube in general from any particular instances; so far as *Rosaceæ* are concerned, there is so much variation in the relative position of calyx and carpels under ordinary circumstances, that it is no matter for surprise that similar diversities should exist in teratological cases. A similar remark will apply to *Saxifragaceæ*,*Cucurbitaceæ*, *Myrtaceæ*, *Bruniaceæ*, *Rubiaceæ*, and other families of like conformation.

FIG. 38.—Flower of *Œnanthe crocata*, in which the five sepals were completely detached from the ovaries, here three in number and destitute of stylopods.

In *Umbelliferæ*, a detachment of the calyx from the ovaries frequently occurs, sometimes without any other change; at other times attended by more serious alterations. So far as can be judged from exceptional occurrences of this kind, it would appear that in this order the axis or flower-stalk does not, in any material degree, enter into the composition of the fruit.

In the Rubiaceous genus *Bikkhia*, as mentioned by Duchartre, the ovary is completely inferior, but when the fruit arrives at maturity four small leaves are detached from its surface which had previously adhered to it, and which it seems reasonable to consider as the sepals.

In *Campanulaceæ* a similar separation of calyx from the ovary may be occasionally met with. On the other hand, the occasional formation of a leaf on the inferior ovary of those plants would indicate the axial nature of the fruit. In *Campanumæa* and *Cyclodon* the calyx is inferior, while the corolla is superior. In the last-named genus this peculiarity "is carried to the highest degree, the sepals being, in *C. parviflorum*, placed on the peduncle of the flower far removed from the base of the corolla and ovary, whilst in*C. truncatum* and in[Pg 81] *Campanumæa* they adhere to the base of the tube of the corolla."[87] In this order, then, as in *Saxifragaceæ*, *Bruniaceæ*, &c., no hasty conclusion should be drawn as to the nature of the fruit. In *Brunia microphylla* the ovary is superior, enclosed within but not adnate to the cup-like calyx, to which latter, however, the petals and stamens are attached.

In *Onagraceæ* (*Jussieua*), as also in *Cactaceæ* (*Opuntia*), buds have been observed on the surface and edges of the inferior ovary. Indeed, in the former genus, they have been produced artificially, but as buds may be formed on foliar as well as on axial organs, the fact cannot be made great use of in support either of the foliar or axial nature of the inferior ovary. In *Epilobium*, I have met with four perfect leaves at the summit of the ovary, in the place usually occupied by the sepals. This would also favour the notion that the axis entered into the constitution of the fruit in this genus.

Mr. B. Clarke, in his 'New Arrangement of Phanerogamous Plants,' p. 4, cites a case wherein the perianth was completely detached from the surface of the ovary in *Cannabis sativa*.

It must be borne in mind that some of the recorded instances of change in the relative position of the calyx and pistil ought more properly to be referred to a substitution of carpels for stamens, as in *Begonia*, *Fuchsia*, &c. Among *Cucurbitaceæ*, examples have been recorded, both of the detachment of the calyx from the ovary,[88] and of the partial conversion of some of the anthers of the male flower to carpels.

The very singular mode of germination of *Sechium edule* in which the fruit, instead of rotting, becomes thickened into a kind of rhizome or tuber, is a fact that should not be overlooked in investigating the true nature of the fruit in this order.

[Pg 82]

The following are the genera in which the change has been most frequently observed:

- *Rosa!
- *Pyrus!
- *Cratægus!
- *Daucus!
- Pastinaca.
- Torilis.
- Apium.
- Œnanthe!
- Heracleum,
- Athamanta.
- Selinum.
- Carum.
- Imperatoria.
- Rudbeckia!
- *Campanula!
- Lonicera!
- Cucumis!
- Cannabis.

Solution of the stamens from the petals.—A separation of the stamens from the petals in flowers, wherein those organs are usually adherent one to the other does not often occur unattended by other changes. It has been observed in *Cobæa scandens* (Turpin), in *Antirrhinum majus*, and in many double flowers.

Partial detachment of the stamens from the styles occurs frequently in semi-double flowers of *Orchis*.[89]

FOOTNOTES:

[85]'Gard. Chron.,' 1865, p. 554; 1867, p. 599.

[86]'Bull. Soc. Bot. Fr.' 1854, p. 303.

[87]Hook et Thoms, 'Præcurs. ad Flor. Ind.,' Journ. Linn. Soc., vol. ii, 1858, p. 6.

[88]Lindley, 'Veget. Kingd.,' p. 315.

[89]Masters, 'Journal of Linnean Society,' 1866, vol. viii, p. 207. On the subject of this chapter the reader should also consult Moquin-Tandon, 1. c., p. 298. Engelmann, 'De Antholysi,' p. 37, tab. v. C. Morren, 'Bull. Acad. Belg.,' xix, part 3, p. 318. Cramer,

'Bildungsabweichungen,' p. 64. Fleischer, 'Missbild. Cultur. Pflanzen.' As to the nature of inferior ovaries, see also Payer, 'Bull. Soc. Bot. Fr.' i, 1854, p. 283. Germain de Saint Pierre, *ibid.*, p. 302. Caspary, 'Bull. Soc. Bot. Fr.,' t. vi, 1859, p. 235. Schleiden, 'Principles of Botany,' English translation, p. 368. Duchartre, 'Elements de Botanique,' p. 574. Le Maout et Decaisne, 'Traité général de Botanique,' p. 57. Bentham, 'Journ. Linn. Soc.,' vol. x, p. 104 (Structure of *Myrtaceæ*), and other treatises on Organography.

[Pg 83]

PART III.
ALTERATIONS OF POSITION.

Necessarily connected with changes in the arrangement of organs are similar alterations in their position; so closely, indeed, that but for convenience sake, it would be unnecessary to treat them separately. There are, however, some anomalous developments affecting the relative position of organs that could hardly be treated of under any of the preceding paragraphs. There are, also, certain rare instances where an organ is not so much displaced as misplaced; that is to say, it is developed on or from a portion of the plant, which under usual circumstances does not produce such an organ. In the former instance, the altered position is due to or coexistent with other changes, but in the latter case the new growth may spring from organs otherwise in nowise different from ordinary. The word Displacement is here used to signify the unusual position of an organ; while Heterotaxy may serve to include those cases where a new growth makes its appearance in an unwonted situation, as, for instance, a leaf-bud on a root, &c. Prolification is also included under this heading, the unusual position of the buds in these cases being of graver import than the mere increase in number. Alterations in the position of the sexual organs are spoken of under the head of Heterogamy.

[Pg 84]

CHAPTER I.
DISPLACEMENT.

Real or apparent displacement of organs from their usual position is an almost necessary consequence of, or is, at least, coexistent with a large number of teratological phenomena. It is obvious that abnormal unions or disunions, suppressions, hypertrophies, &c., are very liable to bring about or to be accompanied with changes in the position, either of the parts directly affected or of adjoining organs.

In this place, then, it is merely necessary to allude to some of the more important displacements, and to refer for further details to the sections relating to those irregularities of growth on which the displacement depends.

Displacement of bulbs.—I owe to the kindness of Mr. James Salter a tulip bulb which had been dug up after flowering, and from the base of which were suspended several small bulbs; and I have since seen another specimen showing the same unusual arrangement. The explanation of these formations seems to be that they correspond to the bulbils ordinarily found in the axils of the scales of the parent organ, and which, in some way or another, have been displaced and thrust into the ground. Professor de Vriese figures something of the same kind in *Ixia carminosa*.[90]

Of somewhat different nature to those above described was an anomaly described by M. Gay at a meeting of the Botanical Society of France, April 8th, 1859. The plant affected was *Leucoium æstivum*, and the changes observed were apparently attributable to a simple separation of two leaves that are usually contiguous. "Suppose," says M. Gay in describing this[Pg 85] malformation, "the first leaf of the terminal bud separated by a long internode from the other leaves, which remain closely packed; and further, suppose an evident thickening of the upper portion of the lengthened internode, and there will be not only a single bulb, bearing with the leaves of the present year all the remnants of the leaves of the two preceding years, but two bulbs placed one above another, on the same axis, separated by the length of the internode."

FIG. 39.—Unusual position of bulbs of tulip; the parent-bulb cut open.

The formation of bulbs in the axils of the leaves, as happens occasionally in tulips, is further alluded to under the head of hypertrophy.

Displacements affecting the inflorescence.—These are, for the most part, dependent on hypertrophy, elongation, atrophy, spiral torsion, &c., but there are a few instances of a different nature, which may here be alluded to as not being coincident with any of the phenomena just mentioned. Sometimes these deviations from the ordinary position have the more interest as affecting[Pg 86] characters used to distinguish genera; thus one of the distinctions between rye-grass (*Lolium*) and wheat (*Triticum*) resides in the relative position of the spikelets and the main stem; in *Triticum* the spikelets are placed with their backs against the rachis, in *Lolium* with one edge against it; but in a specimen of rye-grass that has come under my own observation, the arrangement was that of *Triticum*.

M. Kirschleger relates having found a specimen of *Leucanthemum pratense*, in which the ligulate female flowers were growing singly in the axils of the upper leaves of the stem.[91] The ordinary capitulum would here seem to have been replaced by a spike or a raceme. A less degree of this change wherein a few flowers may be found, as it were, detached from the ordinary capitulum may often be observed in *Compositæ*,*Dipsacaceæ*, &c. I have also met with specimens of *Lamium album* in which some of the fascicles or clusters of flowers of being placed at the same level on opposite sides of the stem were placed alternately one above another.

Caspary[92] mentions a flower of *Aldrovanda vesiculosa*, which was elevated on a stalk that was adherent to the stem for a certain distance, and then separated from it. This flower, with the leaf to which it was axillary, evidently belonged to the whorl beneath, where there was a corresponding deficiency. Another flower of the same plant bore on its pedicel a small leaf, which was doubtless the bract raised above its ordinary position.

M. Fournier mentions an instance in *Pelargonium grandiflorum*, where, owing to the lengthening of the axis, the pedicels, instead of being umbellate, had become racemose; and I owe to the kindness of Dr. Sankey a somewhat similar specimen, but in a less perfect condition. Here there was but a single flower, and that rudimentary, placed at the extremity of the[Pg 87] axis. There were several bracts beneath this flower disposed spirally in the 1/3 arrangement, all being empty, excepting the terminal one. In like manner, a head of flowers becomes sometimes converted into an umbel.

Displacement of leaves.—A cohesion of parts will sometimes give rise to an apparent displacement, but the true nature of the malformation can, in general, be readily made out.

Steinheil[93] found a specimen of *Salvia Verbenaca*, the leaves of which presented very curious examples of displacement arising from cohesion. Two of these leaves placed at the base of a branch were completely fused in their lower thirds, and divided into two distinct lobes at the upper part; each of these lobes seemed to be as large as the limb of an ordinary leaf. Above these was another very broad one, apparently entire, but evidently produced by a complete cohesion of two. This completely fused leaf alternated in position with the imperfectly fused one below it; the alternation is explained by supposing that the opposite leaves of each pair were directed one towards the other, and became fused, and that thus resulted the displacement. The dislocation of the organs took place in one direction for one pair of leaves, and in another direction for the other pair, hence the alternation. Thus, leaves normally opposite and decussate may, by fusion, become alternate. A similar instance occurred to the writer in*Lysimachia vulgaris*, wherein the changes arising from fusion and suppression of parts, &c., were very considerable; as far as the leaves were concerned they presented the following arrangement in succession from below upwards:—first verticillate, then opposite, then spirally alternate, lastly opposite.[94] The term "diremption" has sometimes been applied to cases where leaves are thus apparently dragged out of position.

[Pg 88]In *Tradescantia virginica* I have met with opposite connate leaves; the altered position, however, being due to the union of two stems.

FIG. 40.—**Large-coloured leaf occupying the position of the inflorescence in***Gesnera***, after Morren.**

FIG. 41.—**Ordinary arrangement of leaves in fascicles of three in** *Pinus pinea* **and unusual arrangement of leaves of same plant in spires.**

Twisting of the stem is a frequent cause of the displacement of leaves (see spiral torsion), as also hypertrophy,[Pg 89] whether that excess of development take place laterally or lengthwise (see elongation). Atrophy or suppression will also frequently bring about an alteration in the position of leaves; sometimes in such a manner that the place of the suppressed organ is occupied by another one. One of the most curious instances of displacement of leaves arising from suppression is that mentioned by Morren,[95] where, in *Gesnera Geroltiana*, a large leaf apparently occupied[Pg 90] the extremity of the axis, a position which, under ordinary circumstances, no leaf could assume. The explanation given by the Belgian professor is, that the axis in this case, instead of throwing off a pair of leaves, one on each side, had from some cause or another produced only one; this one not only being much larger than ordinary, but brightly coloured, thus assuming some of the characteristics as well as the position of the inflorescence.

Alterations in the usual arrangement of leaves, however, are not always dependent on or coexistent with other teratological changes, but may simply depend on a natural elongation of the internodes, or on fission or multiplication; for instance, in some conifers, such as the Larch, (*Abies Larix*) or *Pinus pinea*, there may be found at different stages in the growth of the branches leaves in crowded fascicles or tufts; while, when growth is more rapid, the leaves may be disposed in a spiral or alternate manner.

In the yew (*Taxus*) the leaves at the ends of the shoots not unfrequently lose their usual distichous arrangement and become arranged in a close spiral manner, the elongation of the shoot being arrested. This appears to be the result of the injury effected by some insect.

FIG. 42.—**Altered arrangement of leaves of yew, *Taxus baccata*.**
[Pg 91]

So, too, the alteration from verticillate to spiral, or *vice versâ*, may take place without any other notable change.[96] This may frequently be seen in Rhododendrons.

Displacement of the parts of the flower.—This subject is partly touched on in the chapters on solution, adhesion, and in those on hypertrophy, elongation, prolification, &c., so that in this place it is only requisite to offer a few general remarks, and to refer to other sections for further details. Morren, in referring to displacement of the floral organs, mentions an instance in a *Fuchsia*, wherein the four petals in place of being alternate with the sepals were placed in front of them, owing to the adhesion that had taken place between the petals and the stamens. He speaks of this transposition as metaphery.[97] The same author also gives an account of the displacement of several of the organs of the flower in *Cypripedium insigne*, the displacement being consequent, apparently, on a spiral torsion proceeding from right to left, and involving the complete or partial suppression of several of the organs of the flower. The dislocation of organs in a spiral direction led Morren to apply the term "speiranthie" to similar deviations from the usual construction. Changes of this kind among *Orchidaceæ* are by no means uncommon; the following may be cited by way of illustration. In a specimen of *Oncidium cucullatum* furnished me by Mr. Anderson, well known for his success as a cultivator of these plants, there was, associated with a cohesion of one sepal with another, and probably dependent on the same cause, a displacement of the sepals and petals—so that all were dragged out of place. This dislocation may be better appreciated by the accompanying formula than even[Pg 92] by the woodcut. Let the usual arrangement be thus represented:

S   P ST P   L   S   S

S standing for sepal, P for petal, L for lip, ST for stamen; then the dislocated form may be represented thus:

S   P   P   T   S   S_S   L

FIG. 43.—**Flower of *Oncidium cucullatum*, showing union of two lower sepals, displacement of column and lip, &c.**

In a specimen of *Cypripedium* also furnished by Mr. Anderson the appearance was as represented in the accompanying figure and diagrams, figs. 44, 45. Referring to the plan of the natural arrangement at fig. 46, it will be seen that an explanation of the peculiar

47

appearance of the flower may be arrived at by supposing a disunion and lateral displacement of the upper segment of the outer perianth together with the[Pg 93] complete absence of the lower one. In the second or inner whorl of the perianth the lip is merely a little oblique on one side, but the lateral petals are distorted, displaced, and adherent one to the other and to the column, while the posterior shield-like rudimentary anther is completely wanting.

FIG. 44.—Malformed flower of *Cypripedium*.

FIG. 45.—Diagram of malformed *Cypripedium*. *o*, outer segments; *i*, inner segments of perianth; *e*, lip; *s*, stigma; *a*, anther.

FIG. 46—- Diagram showing ordinary arrangement in *Cypripedium*. *o*, outer, *i*, inner segments of perianth; *e*, lip, *a*, anther, *a'*, abortive stamen; *s*, stigma.

FIG. 47.—Plan of flower of *Lycaste Skinneri* showing displacement of organs.

In a specimen of *Lycaste Skinneri* similar changes were observed, as shown in the plan, fig. 47. Here the posterior sepal was deficient, the two lateral ones were present, one of them with a long tubular spur, *o o*; of the two lateral petals, *i i*, one was twisted out of place, so as partially to occupy the place of the deficient sepal; the lip was represented by two three-lobed segments, *l*, one above and within the other. The[Pg 94] column and ovary of this flower were in their normal condition.

Cohesion of two or more segments of the perianth is frequently associated with displacements of this nature: thus, in a flower of *Dendrobium nobile*, a diagram of which is given at fig. 48, the uppermost sepal was coherent with one of the lateral ones, and at the same time diminished in size, and, as it were, dragged out of position. All the other organs of the flower are also more or less displaced, forming a minor degree of the change already alluded to, and which Morren termed speiranthy. The changes will be better appreciated by comparing them with fig. 49, a diagram showing the natural arrangement of parts in this species.

FIG. 48.—Plan of malformed flower of *Dendrobium nobile*.

FIG. 49.—Plan of natural arrangement in *Dendrobium nobile*. The x x represent processes of the column, perhaps rudiments of stamens.

Sometimes the displacement seems consequent on hypertrophy of one of the parts of the flower, the disproportionate size of one organ pushing the others out of place. This was the case in a violet, fig. 50, in which one of the sepals *s* was greatly thickened, and the petals and stamens were displaced in consequence.

FIG. 50.—Plan of flower of violet showing displacement of petals, &c. At *b* was a rudiment of a stamen.

It is curious to observe in many of these cases that the transposed organ not only[Pg 95] occupies the place of a suppressed or abortive organ, but frequently assumes its colour, and, to some extent, its function. This has been alluded to in the case of the leaf of *Gesnera* (see p. 88) and in Orchids this replacement seems to be very common; thus, in addition to the cases before mentioned, in a flower of an Odontoglossum, for which I am indebted to Professor Oliver, the two lateral sepals were united together and occupied the position of the labellum, which was absent. A similar occurrence happens occasionally in *Lycaste Skinneri*, thus recalling the structure of *Masdevallia*, where the labellum is normally very small. The arrangement in Lycaste may thus be symbolised:

S   P   st   P   +   S S   ---

[Transcriber's note: The underscores represent a horizontal curly brace in the original.]

the + indicating the position of the absent labellum.

Cases of this kind are the more interesting from their relation to the fertilization of these flowers by insects; it seems as though, when the labellum, which performs so

48

important an office in attracting and guiding insects, is deficient, its place is supplied by other means.

Displacement of the parts of the flower from elongation of the receptacle is a not infrequent teratological occurrence, resulting sometimes in the conversion of the verticillate into the spiral arrangement. Instances of this are cited under Elongation, Prolification, &c. In this place it is merely necessary to refer to a curious circumstance that is met with in some double flowers, owing to this separation of some parts of the flower and the cohesion or adhesion of others. Thus, in some double flowers of *Primula sinensis* and in the Pea (*Pisum sativum*), I have seen a gradual passage of sepals to petals, so that the calyx and corolla formed one continuous sheet, winding spirally around the[Pg 96] central axis of the flower, after the fashion of a spiral tube.[98]

Displacement of the carpels arises from one or other of the causes above alluded to, and when suppression takes place in this whorl it generally happens that the place of the suppressed organ is occupied by one of the remaining ones, which thus becomes partially dislocated.

Displacement of the placentas and ovules is a necessary result of many of the changes to which the carpels are subject. The disjunction or dialysis of the carpels, for instance, frequently renders axile placentation marginal. Moreover, it frequently happens, when the carpels become foliaceous and their margins are disconnected, that the ovules, in place of being placed on the suture, or rather on the margins of the altered carpel, are placed on the surface of the expanded carpel. Thus, in some double flowers of *Ranunculus Ficaria* that came under the writer's notice the carpels were open, *i.e.* disunited at the margins, and each bore two imperfect ovules upon its inner surface a little way above the base, and midway between the edges of the carpel and the midrib, the ovules being partly enclosed within a little depression or pouch, similar to the pit on the petals. On closer examination the ovules were found to spring from the two lateral divisions of the midrib, the vascular cords of which were prolonged under the form of barred or spiral fusiform tubes into the outer coating of the ovule. In this instance, then, the ovules did not originate from the margins of the leaf, nor from a prolonged axis, but they seemed to spring, in the guise of little buds, from the inner surface of the carpellary leaf.[99]

The occurrence, also, of different forms of placentation[Pg 97] in different flowers on the same plant is no unusual thing in malformed flowers; thus, in double flowers of *Saponaria officinalis* I have met with sutural, parietal, and free central placentation in the same plant.[100]

Professor Babington describes in the 'Gardeners' Chronicle,' 1844, p. 557, a curious flower of *Cerastium*, in which, in addition to other changes, the five carpellary leaves "were partially turned in without touching the placenta, which bears a cluster of ovules, and is perfectly clear of all connection with those partitions" (fig. 51). See also Lindley, 'Veg. Kingdom,' p. 497.

FIG. 51.—1. Monstrous flower of a *Cerastium*; sepals and petals leafy. 2. Stamens and pistils separate. 3. Ovary cut open to show the imperfect dissepiments and the attachment of the ovules. 4. A deformed ovule.

M. Baillon[101] records flowers of *Bunias*, some with ovules on the margins of the carpels, others with a central branch bearing the ovules; hence he concludes[Pg 98] very justly that no fair inference can be drawn from these facts as to the normal placentation of Cruciferæ.

The same excellent observer has recorded the occurrence of free central placentation in malformed flowers of *Trifolium repens.*[102]

In malformed flowers of *Digitalis* the change from axile to parietal placentation may often be seen. Mr. Berkeley describes an instance of this nature where the placentas were strictly parietal, and therefore receded from the distinctive characters of the order, and approximated to those of *Gesneraceæ*.

The same author alludes to certain changes in the same flower where two open carpels "were soldered together laterally, as was clear by the rudiments of two styles, the placenta being produced only at the two united edges, the outer margins remaining in the normal condition. This may possibly tend to the explanation of some cases of anomalous placentation, for the only indication of the true nature of the placentation is afforded by the two rudimentary styles, in the absence of which the spongy receptacle of the seeds must have been supposed to spring from the medial nerve."

In other cases the placentas were parietal above, but axile at the base of the capsule, a striking instance of the facility with which axile placentation becomes parietal, the change being here effected by the prolongation of the axis, and the formation on it of a second whorl of carpellary leaves.

In double flowers of *Primulaceæ* similar alterations in the placentation may often be observed. I have seen in *Primula sinensis* sutural, parietal, axile, and free central placentation all on the same plant; nay, even in the same capsule the ovules may be attached in various ways, and transitions from one form of placentation to another are not infrequent. The late Professor E. Forbes describes[103] an instance of true foliar[Pg 99] and true axile placentation in the same flower in *Vinca minor.*

These and many similar changes, which it is not necessary further to allude to, are not so much to be wondered at when it is borne in mind how slight an alteration suffices to produce a change in the mode of placentation, and how frequent is the production of adventitious buds or of foliar outgrowths, as may be seen in the sections relating to those subjects and to Substitutions.

It will be remembered, also, how, in certain natural orders, under ordinary circumstances, considerable diversity in placentation exists, according as the margins of the carpels are merely valvate or are infolded so as to reach the centre. Often this diversity is due merely to the changes that take place during growth; thus, the placentation of *Caryophylleæ, Cucurbitaceæ,Papaveraceæ,* and many other orders, varies according to the age of the carpel, and if any stasis or arrest of development occurs the placentation becomes altered accordingly.

It is not necessary, in this place, to enter into the question whether the placenta is, in all cases whatsoever, a dependence of the axis, as Payer, Schleiden, and others, have maintained, or whether it be foliar in some cases, axial in others. This question must be decided by the organogenists; teratologically, however, there can be no doubt that ovules may be formed from both foliar and axial organs, and, moreover, that, owing to the variability above referred to, both in what are called natural and in what are deemed abnormal conditions, it can rarely happen that any safe inferences as to the normal or typical placentation of any family of plants can be drawn from exceptional or monstrous formations.

On the subject of placentation the following authors may be consulted:

R. Brown, 'Ann. Nat. Hist.,' 1843, vol. xi, 35. Brongniart, 'Ann. Sc. Nat.,' 1834, sér. 2. i, p. 308. Alph. De Candolle, 'Neue Denkschrift der[Pg 100] Allg. Schweizer Gesellsch.,' Band v. 1841, p. 9. Duchartre, 'Ann. Sc. Nat.,' 3rd ser., 1844, vol. ii, p. 290. Ibid., 'Elem. Bot.,' p. 574; 'Rev. Bot.,' 1846–7, p. 213. Babington, 'Gard. Chron.,' 1844, p. 557. Lindley, 'Elements,' p. 89; 'Veg. King.,' pp. 313, 497, &c. Berkeley, 'Gard. Chron.,' 1850, p. 612. Unger, 'Nov. Act. Acad. Nat. Cur.,' 1850; and in Henfrey's, 'Bot. Gazette,' 1851, p. 70. Schleiden, 'Principles,' English edit., p. 385. Payer, 'Elem. Bot.,' pp. 196, 211, 224. Baillon, 'Adansonia.' iii, p. 310. tab. iv. Cramer, 'Bildungsabweichungen,' p. 20, &c. Clos, 'Ann. Sc. Nat.,' 5th ser., iii, 313, as well as any of the general treatises on botany. Reference may also be made to the chapters on Prolification and Substitutions (in the case of the carpels and ovules), and to the authorities therein cited.

FOOTNOTES:

[90]'Tijdschr. voor. nat. Gesch.,' viii, 1841. tab. ii, p. 178.

[91]Communication to the Internat. Bot. Congress, Paris, 1867.

[92]'Bot. Zeit.,' 1859, p. 117, tab. v.

[93]'Ann. Sc. Nat.,' ser. 2, vol. iv, 1835, p. 143. tab. v.

[94]See Kirschleger, 'Flora.' 1844. p. 566 (*Scabiosa*).

[95]'Bull. Acad. Belg.,' t. xvii. part ii, p. 387.

[96]'Clos. Mem. Acad. Toulouse,' 5th ser., t. vi. pp. 51, 70.

[97]'Bull. Acad. Roy. Belg.,' xviii. part ii, p. 505, and vol. xvii, part i, p. 196, and vol. xix. part i. p. 260.

[98]See also Schlechtendal, 'Bot. Zeit.,' iv, p. 804. *Primula veris, partibus perigonii spiræ in modum confluentibus.*

[99]Seemann's 'Journal of Botany,' vol. v, 1867, p. 158.

[100]'Journ. Linn. Soc.,' i, 1857, p. 161. *c. xylog.*

[101]'Adansonia,' ii, 306.

[102]'Adansonia,' iv, p. 70, t. i.

[103]Henfrey's 'Bot. Gazette,' i, 265.

CHAPTER II.
PROLIFICATION.

Moquin-Tandon and other writers have classed the production of buds in unwonted situations under the head of multiplication, but, as the altered arrangement is of graver import than the mere increase in number, it seems preferable to place these cases under this heading rather than under that of alterations of number.

The adventitious bud may be a leaf-bud or a flower-bud; it may occupy the centre of a flower, thus terminating the axis, or it may be axillary to some or other of its component parts, or, again, it may be extra-floral. In this last case the prolification is of the inflorescence, and is hardly distinguishable from multiplication or subdivision of the common flower-stalk. In accordance with these differences we have median, axillary, and extra-floral prolification, each admitting of subdivision into a leafy or a floral variety, according to the nature of the adventitious bud. Under the head of each variety certain special peculiarities are noticed, but it may here be advisable to add a few general remarks on the subject.

Axillary prolification is a much less frequent malformation[Pg 101] than the median form. If only the number of orders and genera be reckoned, the truth of this statement will be scarcely recognised; but if individual cases could be estimated, the difference in frequency between the two would be very much more obvious. This may, perhaps, be explained by the fact that the branch has a greater tendency to grow in length than it has to develop buds from the axils of the leaves. The flower is admitted to be homologous with the branch, and it is also known that, up to a certain time, the branch-bud or leaf-bud and the flower-bud do not essentially differ.[104] At a later stage the difference between the two is manifested, not only in the altered form of the lateral organs in the flower-bud, but in the tendency to an arrest of growth, thus limiting the length of the central axial portion. Now, in prolified flowers the functions and, to a considerable extent, the appearance of a leaf-bud or of a branch are assumed, and with them the tendency to grow in length is developed. Median prolification, therefore, is in this sense, a further step in retrograde metamorphosis than is the axillary form. To grow in length, and to produce axillary buds, are alike attributes of the branch; but the former is much more frequently called into play than the latter; for the same reason, median prolification is more common than the axillary form. This is borne out by the frequency with which apostasis, or the separation of the floral whorls one from another, to a greater degree than usual, is met with in prolified flowers.

In both forms the adventitious growth is much more frequently a flower-bud or an inflorescence than a leaf-bud or a branch. This may be due to the position of the flowers on a portion of the stem of the plant especially devoted to the formation of flower-buds, to the more or less complete exclusion of leaf-buds, *i.e.* on the inflorescence. This conjecture is borne out by the comparative rarity with which prolification has been observed in flowers that are solitary in the axils of the[Pg 102] ordinary leaves of the plant. If the lists of genera appended hereto be perused, it will be seen that nearly all the cases occur in genera where the inflorescence is distinctly separated from the other branches of the stem. In direct proportion, then, to the degree in which one region of the axis or certain branches of a plant are devoted to the formation of flower-buds to the exclusion of leaf-buds, is the frequency with which those flowers become affected with floral prolification.

Flowers produced upon indefinite inflorescences are liable to be affected with either form of prolification more frequently than those borne upon definite inflorescences. Prolification in both varieties is also more frequently met with in branched inflorescences than in those in which the flowers are sessile; but the degree of branching seems less material, inasmuch as this malformation is more commonly recorded as occurring in racemes than in the more branched panicles, &c. From the similar arrest of growth in length, in the case of the flower, to that which occurs in the stem in the case of definite inflorescence, it might have been expected that axillary prolification would be more frequent in plants having a cymose arrangement of their flowers than in those whose inflorescence is indefinite; such, however, is not the case. The reason for this may be sought for in the lengthening of the floral axis, so common in prolified flowers—a condition the reverse of that which happens in the case of definite inflorescence.

Median prolification occurs frequently in double flowers; the axillary variety, on the other hand, is most common in flowers whose lateral organs have assumed more or less of the condition of leaves. The other coincident changes are alluded to elsewhere or do not present useful points of comparison, and may therefore be passed over.

Prolification of the inflorescence.—This consists in the formation of leaf-buds or of an undue number of flower-buds[Pg 103] on the inflorescence. It must be distinguished from virescence, or the mere green colour of the floral organs, and from chloranthy, in which all or the greater portion of the parts of the flower are replaced by leaves. Prolification is, in fact, a formation of supernumerary buds, leafy or floral, as the case may be, these buds being sessile or stalked, the ordinary buds being not necessarily changed. Prolification of the inflorescence, like the other varieties, admits of subdivision, not only according to the foliar or floral nature of the bud, but according to its position, terminal or median and lateral.

Terminal prolification of the inflorescence, whether leafy or floral, is hardly to be looked upon in the light of a malformation[105] seeing that a similar condition is so commonly met with normally, as in *Epacris,Metrosideros, Bromelia, Eucomis,* &c., wherein the leafy axis projects beyond the inflorescence proper; or as in *Primula imperialis,* in which plant, as also in luxuriant forms of *P. sinensis,* tier after tier of flowers are placed in succession above the primary umbel. Nevertheless, when we meet with such conditions in plants which, under ordinary circumstances, do not manifest them, we must consider them as coming under the domain of teratology.

Median foliar prolification of the inflorescence is frequently met with in*Coniferæ,* and has of late attracted unwonted attention from the researches of Caspary, Baillon, and others, on the morphology of these plants. The scales and bracts of the cone in these abnormal specimens frequently afford transitional forms of the greatest value in enabling morphologists to comprehend the real nature of the floral structure. It would be irrelevant here to enter into this subject; suffice it merely to say that an examination of very numerous specimens of this kind, in the common larch and in*Cryptomeria Japonica,* has enabled me to verify nearly the whole of Caspary's observations. A similar prolongation of the axis occurred in some of the male catkins of *Castanea*[Pg 104] *vesca,* each of which had a tuft of small leaves at their extremity. In the common marigold and in *Lotus corniculatus* I have also seen instances of this kind. Kirschleger[106]describes a tuft of leaves as occurring on the apex of the flowering spike after the maturation of the fruit in *Plantago,* and a similar growth frequently takes place in the common wallflower, in *Antirrhinum majus,* &c. In cases where a renewal of growth in the axis of inflorescence has taken place after the ripening of the fruit, the French botanists use the term recrudescence, but the growth in question by no means always occurs after the ripening of the fruit, but frequently before. Professor Braun cites the case of a specimen of *Plantago lanceolata,* in which the spike was surmounted by a tuft of leaves and roots, as well as a still more singular instance in *Eryngium viviparum,* in which not only did particular branches terminate in rosettes of leaves provided with roots, but similar growths proceeded from the heads of flowers themselves. Baron de Mélicoq[107]gives a case in *Primula variabilis,* in which at the top of the flower-stalk, in the centre of six flowers, was placed a complete plant in miniature, having three leaves, from the axil of one of which proceeded a rudimentary flower. Mr. W. B. Jeffries also forwarded me a polyanthus (fig. 52) in which the peduncle was surmounted by a small plant, forming a crown above the ordinary flower-stalk, just as the crown of the pineapple surmounts that fruit. A similar instance was exhibited at the Scientific Committee of the Horticultural Society on July 11th, 1868, by Mr. Wilson Saunders; the species in this case was *P. cortusoides.* To Mr. R. Dean I am indebted for a similar proliferous cyclamen, which seems similar to one mentioned by

Schlechtendal.[108] This author alludes to an analogous circumstance in the inflorescence of *Cytisus nigricans*, where, however, the change was not[Pg 105] so great as in the preceding cases. The instances just cited all occur in plants having an indefinite form of inflorescence; but the production of a tuft of leaves or of a leafy shoot above or beyond the inflorescence is not confined to plants with this habit of growth, for Jacquin figures and describes an instance of this nature in the cymose flower-stems of a Sempervivum. "*Hi racemi*," says he, "*ultra flores producuntur in ramos, foliosos duo bifidos qui tandem trium unciarum longitudinem adepti fuerunt.*"[109]

FIG. 52.—Inflorescence of *Polyanthus*, bearing a tuft of leaves at the top of the scape intermixed with the flowers.

Median floral prolification of the inflorescence, wherein a new inflorescence projects beyond the primary one, is not uncommon in plants having their flowers arranged in close heads or umbels, as in the common[Pg 106]wild celery and other *Umbelliferæ*.[110] I have also met with it in *Trifolium repens*, in the umbellate variety of the common primrose, and in the scarlet geranium. Engelmann cites it in *Triticum repens*, Roëper in *Euphorbia palustris*.[111]

Lateral foliar prolification of the inflorescence is of more common occurrence than the preceding. I have met with it, amongst other plants, frequently in *Brassica oleracea, Pelargonium zonale*, SCABIOSA, BELLIS, and many other composites, also in *Leguminosæ*, e.g. *Lupinus, Trifolium,Coronilla*, &c. Prof. Oliver forwarded me a specimen of *Euphorbia geniculata* in which, in addition to other changes, there was a series of stalked buds bearing tufts of green scales, but without any trace of stamens or pistil; these adventitious buds occurred within the ordinary involucre of the plant, between it and the stamens. The pistil was unaffected in some cases, while in some others it was entirely wanting, the gynophore being surmounted by a cup-like involucre, divided into three acutely pointed lobes, each with a midrib; these encircled a series of stalked involucels, as before, and among which were scattered a few stamens, some perfect, others partially frondescent.

In a specimen of *Scrophularia nodosa* examined by me one of the lateral buds on each of the cymes was represented, not by a flower, but by a tuft of leaves, the other buds being unchanged. As the inflorescence was much contracted in size, the appearance of the whole plant was greatly changed.

Many of the instances of so-called viviparous plants, *e.g., Polygonum viviparum*, may be cited under this head.[112] Many species of *Allium,Lilium, Saxifraga, Begonia, Achimenes*, normally produce leaf-buds or bulbs in the inflorescence; so, too, leafy shoots are sometimes[Pg 107] found in*Alisma natans, Juncus uliginosus, Chlorophytum Sternbergianum*, &c. As an accidental occurrence, a similar thing has been noticed in *Lychnis coronaria, Phaius grandifolius, Oncidium cebolleta, Epidendrum elongatum*,[113] &c. &c.

Here, too, may be mentioned those cases wherein a leaf-bud is found upon the surface of the so-called inferior ovary; generally a leaf only is found, but a leaf-bud may also originate in this situation, and in either case the inference is that the ovary is, in part at least, made of the dilated and hollowed axis. Leaves may occasionally be found in this way on the so-called calyx-tube or on the inferior ovaries of roses, pears, apples,*Pereskia, Cratægus tanacetifolia*, &c.

The fruits of *Opuntia Salmania* and of *O. fragilis* ('Bull. Soc. Bot. France,' vol. i, p. 306; vol. v, p. 115) have been observed to form small fruit-like branches around their summits. This circumstance is more fully treated of in the succeeding chapter relating to Heterotaxy.

Lateral floral prolification of the inflorescence.—This, which is termed by Engelmann Ecblastesis foliorum sub floralium,[114] is much the most common of all these deviations, and it is met with in every degree, from the presence of a single supernumerary flower in the axil of a bract to the existence of a small cluster or panicle of such flowers.

FIG. 53.—Lateral prolification in inflorescence of *Pelargonium*.

It is common in the *Anemone coronaria* and *hortensis*, also in the common scarlet *Pelargonium* (fig. 53). It has been frequently recorded in *Poterium sanguisorba*, and in *Sanguisorba officinalis*, and is especially common in*Umbelliferæ, Dipsaceæ*, and *Compositæ*; a

53

familiar illustration in the latter order is afforded by the hen-and-chicken daisy. In some species of Compositæ, indeed,[Pg 108] it is a normal and constant occurrence, while in other cases, such as *Filago germanica*, usually described as proliferous, there is not, strictly speaking, any prolification, for the branching of the stalk takes place below the inflorescence, and the branches originate from the axils of ordinary leaves, not from the floral leaves or bracts. *Convolvulus Sepium* is very commonly subject to the production of flower-buds from the axils of the floral leaves. The several species of Plantain (*Plantago*) seem very liable to this and similar changes. Schlechtendal[115] gives a summary of the various kinds of malformation affecting the inflorescence in *Plantago*, and divides them into five groups, as follows:—1st, bracteate, wherein the inferior bracts are quite leaf-like, as is frequently seen in *Plantago major*. 2nd, roseate; bracts leafy in tufts or rosettes, without flowers, as in the so-called rose plantain, common in old-fashioned gardens in this country. 3rd, polystachyate; spike-branched, bearing other spikes in the axils of the bracts, as in *P. lanceolata*, *P. maritima*, &c. 4th, proliferous, where the flower-stalk bears a rosette, a spike, or a[Pg 109] head with other rosettes. 5th, paniculate, in which the inflorescence has become a much-branched pyramidal panicle, covered with little bracts, and with very rudimentary flowers.[116] The first two groups belong rather to frondescence of the bracts; but with regard to the whole of them it will easily be surmised that intermediate forms occur, linking one group to the other, and defying exact allocation in either. Thus, in the borders of richly cultivated fields in the neighbourhood of London I have frequently gathered specimens of *Plantago major* with a branched spike provided with large leafy bracts, the branches of the spike being but little less in diameter than the ordinary single spike. These specimens would therefore seem to be intermediate between Schlechtendal's bracteate and polystachyate divisions.

Wigand[117] also describes an anomalous specimen of *Plantago major* similar to those just mentioned, but having small lateral spikes in place of large ones. The instance quoted from Professor Braun would fall under the roseate section, as would also that of Kirschleger, though we are expressly told that the tuft of leaves in this last case was not developed until after the ripening of the seed-vessel. One of the characters of the roseate group, according to Schlechtendal, is the absence of flowers, but most persons who have had the opportunity of[Pg 110] watching the growth of the rose plantain must have observed the occasional production of flowers, sometimes stalked, in the axils of the leafy bracts, and at the same time have noticed that the internodes become elongated, so that an approach is made to the ordinary spike-like form of the inflorescence. The proliferous group would include such specimens as that of *P. lanceolata*[Pg 111] mentioned by Dr. Johnston,[118] wherein were several spikes, some sessile, others stalked and pendent, the whole intermixed with leaves and disposed in a rose-like manner. I have myself gathered specimens of this nature, occurring in the same plant, at Shanklin, Isle of Wight (fig. 56).

FIG. 54.—*Plantago major*, with panicled inflorescence.

FIG. 55.—Inflorescence of *Plantago major*, with bracts partly replaced by leaves and spike branched.

FIG. 56.—Inflorescence of *Plantago lanceolata*, bearing a tuft of leaves and flowers at the end of the flower-scape.

It is rather singular that each species of *Plantago* seems to have its own perverse mode of growth; for instance, the bracteate, polystachyate and paniculate forms are almost exclusively confined to *P. major*, the roseate form to *P. media*, the proliferous form to *P. lanceolata*.

The instances wherein flower-buds originate from the surface of an inferior ovary, as in those cases where the top of the stem is dilated so as to form part of the fruit, would be properly classed under the head of prolification[Pg 112]of the inflorescence. As, however, there is still some difference of opinion as to the correct morphological interpretation to be put on some of these cases, it has been thought better to include them under the head of heterotaxy than of prolification.

FIG. 57.—Branched inflorescence of Reseda luteola.

Some of the cases of prolification of the inflorescence resulting in a branching of an ordinarily simple inflorescence, as in *Reseda luteola* (fig. 57), might equally well be placed with fission or multiplication of the axile organs. Branched spikes of this character are not so common among Orchids as might be expected.[Pg 113] Professor Reichenbach enumerates a few instances in the Report of the International Botanical Congress of London, 1866, p. 121, and the same author gives an illustration in his 'Orchidographia Europœa,' tab. 150.

In Grasses, as indeed in other plants with a spicate inflorescence, this change occurs not unfrequently. The common Ray Grass (*Lolium*) is especially subject to the change in question, and among cultivated cereals, maize and wheat occasionally show this tendency to subdivision. One variety of the latter grain is cultivated in hot countries under the name of Egyptian wheat—*Triticum vulgare*, var. *compositum*.

Prolification of the inflorescence has been most frequently observed in the following genera:

	Leafy.	Floral.
Ranunculaceæ	Ranunculus.	Ranunculus!
	Anemone.	Anemone.
Cruciferæ.	*Brassica!	
Caryophyllaceæ.	Lychnis!	
	Dianthus!	
Geraniaceæ.	*Pelargonium!	*Pelargonium!
Leguminosæ.	*Trifolium!	Trifolium!
	Lotus!	Lotus!
	Coronilla!	
	Cytisus.	Cytisus.
Rosaceæ.		Poterium.
	*Pyrus!	*Pyrus!
	*Cratægus!	Cratægus!
	*Rosa.	Rosa!
		Sanguisorba.
Philadelphaceæ.		Philadelphus.
Crassulaceæ.	Sempervivum.	
	Echeveria.	
	Crassula.	
Ficoideæ.		?Tetragonia.
Cactaceæ.	Opuntia.	Opuntia.

	Pereskia.	
Saxifragaceæ.	Saxifraga!	
Umbelliferæ.	Seseli.	
		*Apium!
		Cnidium.
		Chærophyllum
	Eryngium.	Eryngium.
		Silaus.
	Heracleum!	Heracleum!
	Hydrocotyle.	Hydrocotyle.
	Daucus.	[Pg 114]
		Carum.
		Selinum.
		Angelica!
		Conium.
		Astrantia.
	Œnanthe.	Œnanthe.
Begoniaceæ.	Begonia!	
Valerianaceæ.	Valeriana.	
Dipsacaceæ.	*Scabiosa!	*Scabiosa!
	Knautia!	Knautia!
Compositæ.		*Bellis!
		Centaurea.
	Calendula.	Calendula.
		Anthemis.
		Coreopsis.
		Apargia.
		Lampsana.
		Carlina.

		Arnoseris.
	Tragopogon!	Tragopogon!
		Rudbeckia!
		Senecio!
		Carlina.
	Bidens!	Pyrethrum.
		Filago.
		Hedypnois.
		Cirsium.
		Lactuca.
Campanulaceæ.	Prismatocarpus	
Lobeliaceæ.		Jasione.
Ericaceæ.	Azalea!	
Convolvulaceæ.	Convolvulus!	Convolvulus!
		Calystegia!
Scrophulariaceæ.	Scrophularia!	
	Antirrhinum!	
Gesneraceæ.	Achimenes!	
Primulaceæ.	Primula!	Primula!
	Cyclamen!	Cyclamen!
Plumbaginaceæ.		Armeria.
Plantaginaceæ.	*Plantago!	*Plantago!
Polygonaceæ.	Polygonum!	
Euphorbiaceæ.	Euphorbia!	
Urticaceæ.		Ficus.
Amentaceæ.		Corylus!
	Castanea!	Castanea.
Coniferæ.	*Larix!	
	*Cryptomeria!	

57

	Taxodium!	Pinus.
Orchidaceæ.	Phaius!	Ophrys!
	Epidendrum!	
	Oncidium!	
Liliaceæ.	*Allium!	
	*Ornithogalum!	[Pg 115]
	*Lilium!	
Amaryllidaceæ.	Fourcroya	
Alismaceæ.	Alisma!	
Palmaceæ.	Cocos.	
Juncaceæ.	*Juncus!	
Restiaceæ.	Restio!	Restio!
	Elegia!	Elegia!
	Willdenovia!	Willdenovia!
Cyperaceæ.		Carex.
Graminaceæ.		Dactylis.
		*Lolium!
		Festuca.
		*Zea!
		*Triticum!
		*Hordeum!
		Secale.
		Phleum.

In addition to the papers already cited the following works may be consulted with reference to prolification of the inflorescence:

Moquin-Tandon. 'El. Ter. Veg.,' p. 376. Engelmann, 'De Antholysi,' §§ 85–87. Fleischer, 'Missbild. Versch. Cultur. Pflanz.' For figures of Hen and Chicken Daisy (*Bellis prolifera*). see Lobel, 'Ic.,' 477. Sweert, 'Florileg.,' pl. 98, f. 5. 'Hort. Eystett. Plant. Vern.,' fol. iv, f. i. &c. For similar malformations in marigold (*Calendula*), see Lobel, 'Ic.,' 553. 'Act. Acad. Nat. Cur.,' vol. x, p. 208. Jaeger, 'Missbilld.,' 192–195. 'Hort. Eystett.,' pl. æstiv. fol. iii, f. i. Klinsmann, 'Linnæa,' t. x, p. 607.

For monstrous plantains, in addition to previous citations, see Camerarius, 'Epist.,' p. 261, *P. rosea.* Matthioli, 'Krauterb,' 245. Lobel, 'Stirp. Advers. Nov.,' p. 128, *P. major paniculata.* J. Bauhin, 'Hist. Plant.,' i, p. 503 *b.* Ibid., p. 503, *a, c, P. major rosea, bracteata paniculata, prolifera,* &c. 'Hort. Eystett.,' pl. æstiv., t. vii, f. 2, *P. rosea* et *P. bracteata.* Lobel, 'Stirp.

Hist.,' p. 162. Dodonæus, 'Pempt.,' 1–4, cap. xxiii, P. major spica multiplex, *i.e.* paniculata. Gerard, 'Herbal.' Clusius, 'Plant. Rar. Hist.,' lib. v, p. 109–10, *Plantago augustifolia Gareti prolifera.* Marchand, 'Adansonia,' iv, p. 156.

Coniferæ.—Richard, 'Mem. Conif.,' tab. xiii, f. 9. A. Braun, 'Das Individ.,' 1853, p. 65. De Cand., 'Organogr.,' tab. xxxvi. Wigand, 'Bot. Untersuch.,' 154. Schlechtendal, 'Bot. Zeit.,' 1859, p. 239. Caspary, 'De Abiet. flor. fem. struct. morphol.' Parlatore, 'Ann. Sc. Nat.,' 1862, vol. xvi, p. 215. Cramer, 'Bildungsabweich.,' p. 4, &c., &c.

Gramineæ.—Bauhin, 'Pinax.,' 21. Morison, 'Hist. Plant.,' t. i. Winckler, 'Ephem. Nat. Cur.,' dec. i, ann. 7, 8, p. 151. Irmisch, 'Flora,' 1858, p. 40, &c.

See also under Chloranthy, Viviparous plants, &c.

Prolification of the flower.—In the preceding sections the formation of adventitious buds of a leafy or floral nature on the inflorescence has been considered. A similar production of buds may take place in the flower itself,[Pg 116] either from its centre or from the axil of some of its constituent parts. Prolification of the flower is therefore median or axillary, and the adventitious bud itself may be of a leafy or a floral nature.

Median leafy prolification.—In this malformation the centre of the flower is occupied by a bud or a branch; the growing point or termination of the axis which ordinarily ceases to grow after the formation of the carpels, takes on new growth. This is well shown in the accompanying illustration (fig. 58), representing the thalamus of a strawberry prolonged beyond the fruits into a small leaf-bearing branch.

FIG. 58.—Receptacle of strawberry prolonged into a leafy branch. From the 'American Agriculturist.'

FIG. 59.—Flower of *Verbascum* with five disunited sepals, five similar green petals, and a prolonged branch in the centre of the flower.

In other cases the carpels are entirely absent and their place is supplied by a leafy shoot as in a species of *Verbascum*, which came under my own observation. In this case the petals were virescent, and the stamens and pistils were entirely absent, hence in truth, the so-called[Pg 117] flower more nearly resembled a branch. In a flower of a May Duke cherry, for which I am indebted to Mr. Salter, there was a gradual change from the floral to the foliar condition; thus there were five distinct lanceolate sepals, the arrangement of whose veins betokened that they were leaf-sheaths rather than perfect leaves, ten petals partly foliaceous and sheath-like as to their venation, one of them funnel-shaped, but whether from dilatation or cohesion of the margins could not be determined. The stamens were eight or ten in number, their connectives prolonged into foliaceous or petaloid appendages, so that the filament represented the stalk of the leaf. The pistil was entirely absent and its place was supplied by a branch with numerous perfectly formed stipulate leaves.

Some flowers of *Anagallis arvensis* described by Dr. Marchand[119] are so interesting and show so well the gradual stages by which this malformation is arrived at, that it is desirable to cite the summary of Dr. Marchand's researches as given in the 'Gardeners' Chronicle' by Mr. Berkeley, taking that instance first in which the parts of the flower departed least from the normal condition, and then the others in their proper order. In all the parts there was a greater or less tendency to assume a green tint; in some they were entirely green, in others the brighter colours were confined to the more recently developed parts.

"1. In the first case then, the sepals and petals were in their normal position, though rather more dilated than usual; the anthers were fertile, the principal change existing in the ovary, the upper part of which was wanting, so that the ovules were exposed seated on the central placenta.

2. In the next step the calyx, more developed than usual, was separated from the corolla by a long peduncle, and the ovary, which was ovate, contained instead of a placenta a sort of plumule or young shoot.

[Pg 118]

3. In this case the corolla and calyx were distant from each other; there was no trace of stamens, but the axis was continued from the centre of the corolla, and ended in a leaf-bud.

4. The calyx and corolla nearly as before, but instead of stamens a whorl of little leaves was developed, in the centre of which the axis was continued, bearing at its tip two whorls of leaflets, alternately three and three.

5. In this case two out of the five stamens were normal, the other three changed into leaves, showing clearly the origin of the leaflets, in the last case, which took the place of the stamens.

6. The ovary varied in different flowers. In some the placenta was crowned with ovules; in others the ovules were replaced by a single whorl of leaflets; in others there was every shade of change from ordinary ovules to perfect leaflets; while in others, again, every ovule was converted into a leaf with a long petiole.

7. In these flowers shoots were developed in the axils of the sepals, or on the face of the petals between the point of their insertion and that of the stamens, and, what is most curious, in the interior of the ovaries round the foot of the placenta.

8. Here, again, a very singular condition presented itself: the calyx and corolla separated from each other, the stamens partly developed, the axis continued beyond the corolla, branched and bearing normal leaves so as exactly to resemble an ordinary stem, while in consequence of the calyx and corolla being bent down to the ground, adventitious roots were developed from the axis on the under side above each of them. In another case, where the calyx and corolla were approximated, the ovary was open above, and sent out six shoots from within, perfectly developed, clearly representing the central placenta and five axile buds, and each giving out a number of adventitious roots at its base."

In other genera of the same order (*Primulaceæ*) an[Pg 119] extension of the placenta into a leafy branch has been observed, as in *Lysimachia*, where in one case the prolonged placenta was removed and struck as a cutting.[120]

In *Ericaceæ* too, the axile placenta has been seen ovuliferous at the base and prolonged above into a leafy branch.[121]

Median floral prolification.—This is of more frequent occurrence than the preceding. The prolonged axis is more frequently terminated by a flower-bud than by a leaf-bud, though it must be remarked, that the lengthened and protruded stem frequently bears leaves upon its sides, even if it terminate in a flower, and thus the new growth partakes of a mixed leafy and floral nature. Instances of this kind have long been familiar to observers, and have always excited attention from the singularity of their appearance. In one of the old stained-glass windows, apparently of Dutch manufacture, in the Bodleian Picture Gallery at Oxford, is a representation of a *Ranunculus* affected with median floral prolification.[122] In pinks the affection is not unfrequently met with. Fig. 60 shows an instance of the kind copied from Schotterbec.

A singular instance of prolification in the central flower of one of the verticillasters of *Phlomis fruticosa* fell under my own notice; it was a case wherein the calyx was torn on one side, and one of its lobes had become petaloid. Between the calyx and the corolla were three or four spathulate, hairy, bract-like organs; the corolla and stamens were unchanged; but in place of the usual four-lobed ovary there was a single carpel with a basilar style, terminated by a forked stigma. Occupying the place of the other lobes of the pistil was an oblong woolly flower-bud, consisting of calyx, corolla, and stamens, but with no trace of pistil. I[Pg 120] have been unable to find recorded any instance of malformation among Labiates or Borages at all similar to this. It differed from most other examples of prolification in that the axis was not prolonged, the adventitious bud occupying precisely the position of the three lobes of the ovary that were absent. The sole remaining carpel had a style and a stigma as perfect in appearance as though the pistil had been complete.

FIG. 60.—Flower of *Dianthus* affected with median floral prolification.

In a flower of *Conostephium* (*Epacridaceæ*) forwarded to me by Mr. Bentham, there was a similar adventitious bud placed by the side of the pistil, but as the latter contained the usual number of cells it is probable that the supernumerary bud in this case originated rather from the side than the end of the axis.

Certain families of plants present this deviation from their ordinary structure with greater frequency than others: the following orders seem to be the most frequently affected by it: *Ranunculaceæ, Caryophyllaceæ,*[Pg 121]*Rosaceæ,* while it is commonly met with in *Scrophulariaceæ, Primulaceæ*and *Umbelliferæ*. Of genera which seem peculiarly liable to it may be mentioned the following: *Anemone, Ranunculus, Cheiranthus, Dianthus,Dictamnus, Daucus, Rosa, Geum, Pyrus, Trifo lium, Antirrhinum,Digitalis, Primula.*

A reference to the subjoined list of genera affected by this malformation, and the knowledge of its comparatively greater frequency in some than in others of them, will show that it is more often met with in plants having an indefinite form of inflorescence than in those having a definite one. The change may affect some only, or the whole of the flowers constituting an inflorescence; and though it is by no means a constant occurrence, it very frequently happens that the central or terminal flower in a definite inflorescence is alone affected, the others remaining in their ordinary condition, as in pinks (*Dianthus*); and in the indefinite forms of inflorescence, it is equally common that the uppermost flower or flowers are the most liable to be thus affected.

In those plants which present this deviation from the ordinary condition with the greatest frequency, it often happens that the axis is normally more or less prolonged, either between the various whorls of the flower, as in the case of the gynophore, &c., or into the cavity of the carpels, as in the instances of free central placentation. To bear out this assertion, the following instances taken from those genera having definite inflorescence, and which are very commonly affected with prolification, may be cited; thus, in *Anemone* and *Ranunculus* the thalamus is prolonged to bear the numerous carpels; in *Dianthus* there is a marked internode separating the carpels from the other parts of the flower; in *Primulaceæ* central prolification is very common, and this is one of the orders where the placenta seems from the researches of Duchartre and others, to be truly a production of the axis within the carpels;[123] in *Thesium* also, another genus with[Pg 122] free central placenta, this malformation has been found.

So also among plants with indefinite inflorescence, prolification seems very frequently to affect those wherein the axis is normally prolonged; thus it is common in *Dictamnus*, which plant has an internode supporting the pistil; it is frequent among *Umbelliferæ*, where the carpophore may be truly considered an axile production; it is common among *Rosaceæ* and*Ranunculaceæ*, in many of which the axis or thalamus is well-marked, and it is by no means infrequent in the flowers of the Orange, where the floral internodes are also slightly elongated; on the other hand, there is no case on record in *Magnoliaceæ*, and some other orders where the floral part of the axis is at some point or other elongated; still, on the whole, there can be but little doubt that there is a real relation between prolification and the normal extension of the floral internodes.

Under these circumstances, those instances wherein the parts of the flower become separated one from the other by the elongation of the internodes (apostatis), constitute a lesser degree of the same change, which operates most completely in the formation of a new bud at the extremity of the prolonged axis. Some specimens of *Geum rivale* (a plant very liable to become prolified) in my possession show this very clearly. In the wild plant the thalamus is elevated on a short stalk; in the abnormal ones the thalamus is simply upon a longer stalk than usual, or in a more advanced stage of the deviation the lengthened thalamus takes the form of a branch provided with leaves and terminated by a flower; it is noticeable, also, in these specimens, that the sepals of the lower flower have assumed entirely the dimensions and appearance of leaves.

Median prolification has occasionally been recorded in flowers that have, in their ordinary condition, but one carpel, as in *Leguminosæ* and in*Santalaceæ*. In *Leguminosæ*, as also in *Amygdalus*, it would seem as if[Pg 123] the adventitious bud were strictly a lateral and axillary production, and moreover that the carpel itself is not strictly terminal but lateral in position, though apparently terminal from the abortion of other carpels. In the only recorded instance that I am aware of, of this malformation affecting the genus *Thesium*, the pistil was altogether absent, and occupying its place was the new bud or branch.[124]

FIG. 61.—*Daucus Carota*, showing leafly carpels, prolification, &c.

[Pg 124]
As the carpels are not unfrequently absent in cases of median prolification, it has been thought that the pistil in such cases was metamorphosed into a stem bearing leaves or flowers. Setting aside the physiological difficulties in the way of accepting such an opinion, an examination of any number of cases is sufficient to refute it; for, as Moquin well remarks, the carpels may frequently be found either in an unaltered condition or more or less modified.

If the pistil be normally syncarpous, its constituent carpels, if present at all in the prolified flower, become disjoined one from the other to allow of the passage between them of the prolonged axis; thus in some malformed flowers of *Daucus Carota* gathered in Switzerland (fig. 61), not only was the calyx partially detached from the pistil, but the carpels themselves were leaf-like, disjoined, and unprovided with ovules; between them rose a central prolongation of the axis, which almost immediately divided into two branches, each terminated by a small umbel of perfect flowers, surrounded by minute bracts.[125]

[Pg 125]
Not only are the carpels thus frequently separated one from the other by the prolonged axis, but they undergo commonly a still further change in becoming more or less completely foliaceous, as in the *Daucus* just mentioned, where the carpels were prolonged into two lance-shaped leaves, whose margins in some cases were slightly incurved at the apex, forcibly calling to mind the long "beaks" that some Umbelliferous genera have terminating their fruits—for instance, *Scandix*. Dr. Norman, in the fourth series of the 'Annales des Sciences,' vol. ix, has described a prolification of the flower of *Anchusa ochroleuca*, in which the pistil consisted of two leaves, situated antero-posteriorly on a long internode, with a small terminal flower-bud between them; and numerous similar instances might be cited.

In this place may also be noticed those instances wherein the placenta elongates so much that the pericarp becomes ruptured to allow of the protrusion of the placenta, although this prolongation is not attended by the formation of new buds. Cases of this kind occurring in *Melastoma* and *Solanum* have been put on record by M. Alph. de Candolle.[126] This is a change analogous with that which occurs in some species of *Leontice* or *Caulophyllum*, as commented on by Robert Brown. See 'Miscellaneous Botanical Works' of this author, Ray Society, vol. i, p. 349.

If the pistil be apocarpous, and the carpels arranged spirally on an elevated thalamus, it then frequently happens that the carpels, especially the upper ones,[Pg 126] become carried up with the prolonged axis, more widely separated one from the other than below, and particularly liable to undergo various petalloid or foliaceous changes as in proliferous *Roses, Potentilla*, &c.

FIG. 62.—Median floral prolification, &c., in flower of *Delphinium*.

Fig. 62, copied from Cramer, shows an instance of this kind in *Delphinium elatum*, where not only is the thalamus prolonged, and the carpels separated, but from the axils of some of the latter which have[Pg 127] assumed from the disunion of their margins somewhat of the appearance of leaves, other flowering branches proceed—axillary prolification. If, on the other hand, the carpels be few in number, and placed in a verticillate manner, the axis then generally passes upwards without any change in the form or position of the carpels being apparent, as in a proliferous columbine, figured in the 'Linnean Transactions,' vol. xxiii, tab. 34, fig. 5.

When a flower with the ovary naturally inferior or adherent to the calyx becomes prolified, a change in the relative position of the calyx and ovary almost necessarily takes place, the latter becoming superior or detached from the calyx; this has been already alluded to in *Umbelliferæ*. In a species of *Campanula* examined by me, the calyx was free, the corolla double, the stamens with petaloid filaments, and in the place of the pistil there was a bud consisting of several series of green bracts, arranged in threes, and enclosing quite in the centre three carpellary leaves detached from one another and the other parts of the flower, and open along their margins, where the ovules were placed. In other similar instances in the same species of *Campanula*, the styles were present, forming below an imperfect tube which surrounded the adventitious bud; in another, contrary to what occurs usually in such cases, the ovary was present in its usual position, but surmounted by a bud of leafy scales, enclosed within the base of a tube formed by the union of the styles. A similar relative change in the position of the calyx and the ovary takes place when the *Compositæ* are affected with central prolification, or even in that lesser degree of change which merely consists in the separation and disunion of the parts of the flower, but which in these flowers appear to be, as it were, the first stage towards prolification. I owe to the kindness of Professor Oliver a sketch of a species of *Rudbeckia?* showing this detachment of the calyx from the ovary. In a monstrous *Fuchsia* that I have had the opportunity of recently examining, the calyx was[Pg 128] similarly detached from the ovary simultaneously with the extension of the axis. Here the petals were increased in number and variously modified, the stamens also; while in the centre and at the top of the flower, conjoined at the base with some imperfect stamens, was a carpel open along its ovuliferous margins. Such instances as these seem to be the first stages of a change which, carried out more perfectly, would result in the formation of a new bud on the extremity of the prolonged axis.

In *Orchidaceæ*, among which family I have now met with several instances of prolification, the ovary seems usually to be absent. Fig. 63 shows a prolified flower of *Orchis pyramidalis* in which the perianth was nearly regular, the central portions of the flower absent, and their place supplied by a new miniature raceme. This specimen was forwarded to me by Dr. Moore, of Glasnevin.

FIG. 63.—Median prolification in *Orchis pyramidalis*, the outer segments of the perianth regular and reflexed.

As might be expected, it very rarely happens that median prolification occurs without some other deviation in one or more parts of the flower being simultaneously manifested. Some of these changes have been already mentioned, but others are commonly met with, as, for instance, the multiplication or doubling, as it is termed, of the petals; others, though less frequent, are of more[Pg 129] interest. Fusion of two or more flowers in association with prolification is especially common in cultivated specimens of *Digitalis purpurea*; the uppermost flowers of the raceme become fused together so as to form one large, regular, erect, cup-shaped corolla, to the tube of which the stamens are attached, in greater number than ordinary, and all of equal length; the bracts and sepals are confusedly arranged on the exterior of the flower; while in the centre, in the place usually occupied by the pistil, there rises a conical prolongation of the axis, bearing at its outer or lower portion a number of open carpels, provided, it may be, with styles and ovules; these enclose an inner series of scale-like bracts, from whose axils proceed more or less perfect florets; so that in the most highly developed stage a perfect raceme of flowers may be seen to spring from the centre of a cup-shaped regular flower, whose lobes show its compound character. All intermediate stages of this malformation may be found from cases where there is a simple fusion of two flowers with a second verticil of carpels within the outer, up to such cases as those which have been just mentioned. It is worthy of special remark, that in all these cases the flowers at the uppermost part of the raceme are alone affected, and that, in addition to the prolification, there is fusion of two or more flowers, and regularity in the form of the compound corolla and stamens.

The calyx of a prolified flower is either unchanged, or it is modified in harmony with the changes in the central part of the flower. If the ovary be normally superior or free from the calyx, then the latter is comparatively rarely altered; for instance, in proliferous pinks (*Dianthus*) the calyx is seldom affected, except, indeed, in those instances where the floral axis is prolonged, and produces from its side a successive series of sepals, as in what is called the wheat-ear carnation; but though these instances may be, as I believe, an imperfect degree of prolification, they do not affect the general truth of the above opinion, that the calyx, if it be free[Pg 130] from the ovary, is but rarely changed in a prolified flower; but that this is not

63

a universal rule is shown by proliferous flowers of *Geum rivale*, where the sepals are usually large and leaf-like, as they likewise are frequently in proliferous roses and pears.

FIG. 64.—Proliferous rose. Hip absent, sepals leafy, stamens wanting, axis prolonged bearing supplementary flower, &c. (Bell Salter).

Proliferous roses have a special interest, inasmuch as they show very conclusively that the so-called calyx-tube of these plants is merely a concave and inverted thalamus, which, in prolified specimens, becomes elongated[Pg 131] (fig. 64) after the fashion of *Geum rivale*, &c.[127] Occasionally from the middle of the outer surface of the urn-shaped thalamus proceeds a perfect leaf, which could hardly be produced from the united sepals or calyx-tube; a similar occurrence in a pear is figured in Keith's 'Physiological Botany,' plate ix, fig. 12.

The change which the calyx undergoes when flowers with an habitually adherent ovary become prolified, and wherein the calyx is disjoined from the ovary, has been before mentioned, but it may also be stated that, under such circumstances, the constituent sepals are frequently separated one from the other, and not rarely assume more or less of the appearance of leaves, as in proliferous flowers of *Umbelliferæ*, *Campanulaceæ*,*Compositæ*, &c.

As to the corolla, it was long since noticed that prolification was especially liable to occur in double flowers; indeed, Dr. Hill, who published a treatise on this subject, setting forth the method of artificially producing prolified flowers, deemed the doubling to be an almost necessary precursor of prolification;[128] but, though frequently so, it is not invariably the case that the flower so affected is double—*e.g. Geum*. If double, the doubling may arise from actual multiplication of the petals, or from the substitution of petals for stamens and pistils, according to the particular plant affected. Occasionally in prolified flowers the parts of the corolla, like those of the calyx, become foliaceous, and in the case of proliferous pears fleshy and succulent. There is in cultivation a kind of *Cheiranthus*? in which there is a constant repetition of the calyx and corolla, conjoined with an entire absence of the stamens and pistils; a short internode separates each flower from the one above it, and thus frequently[Pg 132] ten or a dozen of these imperfect flowers may be seen on the end of a flower-stalk, giving an appearance as if they were strung like beads, at regular intervals, on a common stalk. I have seen a similar instance in a less degree in a species of *Helianthemum*.

The stamens are subject to various changes in prolified flowers; they assume, for instance, a leaf-like or petal-like condition, or take on them more or less of a carpellary form, or they may be entirely absent; but none of these changes seem to be at all necessarily connected with the proliferous state of the flower. Of more interest is the alteration in the position of these organs which sometimes necessarily accrues from the elongation of the axis and the disjunction of the calyx; thus, in proliferous roses the stamens become strictly hypogynous, instead of remaining perigynous. In *Umbelliferæ* the epigynous condition is changed for the perigynous, &c.

The condition of the pistillary organs in prolified flowers has already been alluded to. Hitherto those instances have been considered in which either the carpels were absent, or the new bud proceeded from between the carpels. There is also an interesting class of cases where the prolification is strictly intra-carpellary; the axis is so slightly prolonged that it does not protrude beyond the carpels, does not separate them in any way, but is wholly enclosed within their cavity. Doubtless, in many cases, this is merely a less perfect development of that change in which the axis protrudes beyond the carpels. This intra-carpellary prolification occurs most frequently in plants having a free central placenta, though it is not confined to them, as it is recorded among *Boragineæ*. A remarkable instance of this is described by Mr. H. C. Watson in the first volume of Henfrey's 'Botanical Gazette,' p. 88. In this specimen a raceme of small flowers was included within the enlarged pericarp of a species of *Anchusa*. But the most curious instances of[Pg 133] this form of prolification are, no doubt, those which are met with among *Primulaceæ* and other orders with free central placentation.

Duchartre, in his memoir on the organogeny of plants with a free central placenta, in the 'Ann. des Sc. Nat.,' 3 sér., 1844, p. 290, among other similar instances, mentions two flowers of *Cortusa Matthioli*, wherein the placenta was ovuliferous at the base; but the upper portion, instead of simply elongating itself into a sterile cone, had produced a little flower with its parts slightly different from those of the normal flowers. M. Alph. de Candolle has likewise described somewhat similar deviations, and one in particular in *Primula Auricula*, where the elongated placenta gave off long and dilated funiculi bearing ovules, while other funiculi were destitute of these bodies, but were much dilated and foliaceous in appearance.[129]In some flowers of *Rhododendron* I have observed a similar condition of the ovules, which, moreover, in the primary flowers, were attached to the walls of the carpels—parietal placentation.

In speaking of these as cases of intra-carpellary prolification, it is, of course, impossible to overlook the fact that they differ in degree only from those cases where the lengthened axis projects beyond the cavity of the carpels; nevertheless they seem to demand special notice, because in these particular plants the placenta or its prolongation appears never to protrude beyond the carpels, or at least very rarely. There are, however, numerous instances of such an extension of the placenta and of prolification occurring among *Primulaceæ* in conjunction with the more or less complete arrest of growth of the carpels.[130] An instance of this kind has come under my own notice in a monstrosity of the chinese primrose, in which the carpels were reduced to a hardly discernible rim[Pg 134] surrounding an umbel of five rays, each terminated by a small normally constituted flower-bud.

The ovules of a prolified flower are either unaffected, or they occur in a rudimentary form, or, lastly, they may be present in the guise of small leaves.

Under the term prolification of the fruit two or three distinct kinds of malformation appear to have been included. The term seems usually to be applied to those cases where from the centre of one fruit a branch bearing leaves, flowers, or another fruit, is seen to project, as happens occasionally in pears. Now, in many instances, not only the fruit, is repeated, but also the outer portions of the flower, which wither and fall away as the adventitious fruit ripens; so that at length the phenomenon of one fruit projecting from another is produced. It is obvious that this form of prolification in no wise differs from ordinary central prolification. Sometimes some of the whorls of the adventitious flower are suppressed; thus, M. Duchartre describes some orange blossoms as presenting alternating series of stamens and pistils one above another, while the calyces and corollas belonging to each series of stamens and pistils were entirely suppressed.[131] In other cases, doubtless, the carpellary whorl is alone repeated, the other whorls of the adventitious flower being completely absent.

Another condition, apparently sometimes mistaken for prolification of the fruit, is that in which the carpellary whorl becomes multiplied; so that there is a second or even a third series within the outer whorl of carpels. If the axis be at all prolonged, then these whorls are separated one from the other, and produce in this way an appearance of prolification. This happens frequently in oranges, as in the variety called Mellarose.[132]

[Pg 135]

Moquin has given an explanation of the St. Valery Apples, wherein the petals are sepaloid, the stamens absent, and where there is a double row of carpels, by supposing these peculiarities to be due to "a prolification combined with penetration and fusion of two or more flowers," but it is surely more reasonable to conceive a second row of carpels placed above the first by the prolongation of the central part of the axis. Supposing this view to be correct, the inner calyx-like whorl might be considered either as a repetition of the calycine whorl, or it might be inferred that the corolla was present in the guise of a second calyx.

Moquin-Tandon suggests another explanation—namely, that though the stamens are absent in these curious flowers, at least in their ordinary shape, they are represented by the lower row of carpels, which become, in process of development, fused with the upper or true carpels. If this were so, surely some intermediate conditions between stamen and carpel would occasionally be present; but such does not appear to be the case.[133]

In some of the instances of so-called proliferous pears the carpels would seem to be entirely absent, and the dilated portion of the axis to be alone repeated. Thus, the axis dilates to form the lower fruit without any true carpels being produced, but at its summit a whorl of leaves (sepals) is formed; above these another swelling of the axis takes place also without the formation of carpels, and this, it may be, is terminated in its turn by a branch producing leaves. In these cases there is no true prolification, but simply an extension of the axis. That the outer portion (so-called calyx-tube) of these fruits is really an axile product there can now be little doubt; and, as if to show their axile nature, they occasionally produce leaves from their sides, as[Pg 136] before mentioned. Moquin, in the tenth volume of the 'Bulletin of the Botanical Society of France,' p. 73, says that when the case is one of prolification the lower fruit is larger and is formed of a fleshy mass; moreover, the line of demarcation between the fruits is more distinct, and there are traces of the seed-bearing cavity in the interior, and of calycine lobes at the top. On the other hand, if the case be one of hypertrophy merely, the lowermost fruit is the smallest, and there is no trace of seed-bearing cavity nor of sepals. See also under Hypertrophy.

Some other malformations usually referred to prolification of the fruit seem due to branching of the inflorescence, as in *Plantago*, wheat, maize; or to a simple extension of the axis beyond its ordinary limit, as in some cones of firs, &c. It is obvious that the true fruits in these cases are in no wise affected.

From these considerations it would appear better to abandon the use of the expression prolification of the fruit, as unnecessary where it is really applicable, and as delusive in the numerous other cases where it is employed.

Median prolification of one or other kind has been met with in the following genera:

	Leafy.	*Floral.*
Ranunculaceæ.		Clematis.
	Anemone!	*Anemone!
	Ranunculus!	*Ranunculus!
		Delphinium.
		Caltha.
		Aquilegia!
Cruciferæ.		Bunias.
		*Cheiranthus!
		Erucago.
		*Matthiola!
		Sisymbrium!
		Brassica!
		Nasturtium.
		Hesperis.
		Sinapis!
		Diplotaxis.
		Lunaria.
		Erysimum.[Pg 137]

66

		Alyssum.
		Peltaria.
		Cardamine!
		Cleome.
Cistaceæ.		Helianthemum!
Caryophylleæ.	Dianthus!	*Dianthus!
		Silene!
		Lychnis!
Violaceæ.		Viola!
Tiliaceæ.	Triumfetta!	
Geraniaceæ.		Geranium!
Sapindaceæ.	Pavia!	Pavia!
Malvaceæ.		Paritium.
		Hibiscus!
Malpighiaceæ.		Byrsonima!
Rutaceæ.	Genera not specified.	*Dictamnus!
Resedaceæ.		Reseda.
		Caylussa!
Aurantiaceæ		*Citrus!
Vitaceæ.	Vitis.	Vitis.
Umbelliferæ		Heracleum.
		Angelica.
		Thysselinum.
		*Athamanta.
		*Daucus!
		*Torilis.
Rosaceæ.	*Rosa!	*Rosa!

		*Geum!	*Geum!
		Agrimonia.	Amygdalus.
			Prunus!
		Spiræa!	Spiræa!
			Rubus.
		*Pyrus!	*Pyrus!
	?Leguminosæ		Trifolium!
			Medicago!
			Melilotus.
			Pisum!
	Cucurbitaceæ.		Cucumis.
	Passifloraceæ.		Passiflora.
	Philadelphaceæ.		Philadelphus.
	Onagraceæ.	Epilobium!	
	Epacridaceæ.		Epacris!
	Ericaceæ.		*Erica.
			Rhododendron!
	Convolvulaceæ.	Convolvulus.	
	Gentianaceæ.	Gentiana.	Gentiana.
	Apocynaceæ.		Vinca.
	Jasminaceæ.		Jasminum!
	Scrophulariaceæ.	Verbascum!	Antirrhinum!
			*Digitalis!
			*Linaria!

Amaryllidac		Narcissus!
eæ.		
		Leucojum.
Orchidaceæ.		Orchis!
		Habenaria.
Cyperaceæ.		Carex.
Gramineæ.		Phleum.

Axillary prolification is the term applied to those cases wherein one or more adventitious buds spring from the axils of one or more of the parts of the flower. Engelmann makes use of the word ecblastesis to denote the same condition. Both terms are open to the objection that they do not clearly enable us to distinguish prolification occurring within the flower from a similar state originating outside the flower, within the bracts of the inflorescence. This latter condition, called by Moquin-Tandon lateral prolification (see Prolification of the Inflorescence), is as truly axillary as that to which the name is restricted. In consequence of certain peculiarities in the structure of some flowers, to be hereafter alluded to, it is not in all cases easy to decide whether the new growth springs from the[Pg 139] interior of the flower, or from the inflorescence beneath the flower.

The accessory bud presents itself as a leaf-bud, a branch, a flower-bud, or a miniature inflorescence; it may be sessile, but is far more frequently stalked, and in more than half the number of cases it is a flower-bud or an inflorescence. There may be one or more of these buds; if two only, then they are usually placed directly opposite one to the other, on the opposite sides of the flower.

It will be seen, from the appended list, that the orders and genera in which this description of adventitious growth occurs most frequently are the following:—*Cruciferæ*, especially the genus *Brassica*; *Caryophyllaceæ*, e.g. *Dianthus*; *Resedaceæ*, *Leguminosæ*, e.g. *Melilotus*, *Trifolium*, &c.;*Rosaceæ*, e.g. *Rosa*, *Potentilla*, &c.; *Umbelliferæ*, and *Campanulaceæ*. For the most part, these are groups also peculiarly liable to central prolification.

All the parts of the flower may be thus affected; but, as might have been anticipated from the foliaceous nature of the sepals, the new bud usually arises from within the axil of one of those organs. Next in frequency to the calyx, the pistil is subjected to this change— the carpels in such a case being disunited and leaf-like. The petals rank next, and lastly the stamens; these latter, indeed, are usually, but not invariably, absent, the new growth occupying their position. Hence it may well be that when such is the case, there is no real axillary prolification, but rather the substitution of a bud for a stamen. Generally, however, the position of the accessory bud is such that it may properly be referred to the axil of an undeveloped or rudimentary stamen.

The largest number of instances of this malformation, not merely generically, but also individually, occurs in plants the members of whose floral whorls are not united one to the other; thus, it is far more common in polypetalous plants than in gamopetalous[Pg 140] ones. In the prolified flowers belonging to the latter group, the sepals, if not actually uncombined, are only united for a short distance. The same relationship, but in a much less degree, exists in the case of median prolification, as that aberration is likewise most commonly met with in polypetalous flowers. Another feature of interest is the rarity with which axillary prolification is found in irregular gamopetalous blooms. It may be that the irregular and comparatively excessive growth in some parts of these flowers, as compared with others, may operate in checking any luxuriant tendency in other directions.

As in the case of median prolification, plants having an indefinite inflorescence are more liable to be affected with ecblastesis than those having a definite one. The degree of branching of the inflorescence may be noticed, as this deformity is far more common in plants whose peduncles are branched than in those which have either a solitary flower or an

70

unbranched flower-stalk. More than two thirds of the entire number of genera cited as the subjects of this malformation have a branched inflorescence of some form or other; and about two thirds of the cases occur in genera having some form of indefinite inflorescence. If individual instances could be accurately computed, the proportion would be even higher.

Fully three fourths of the entire number of genera recorded as occasionally the subjects of this irregularity possess in their usual state some peculiarity of the thalamus; for instance, in about a third of the whole number of genera the thalamus is more or less prolonged between some or other of the floral whorl, e.g. *Caryophyllaceæ, Potentilla, Anemone, Dictamnus,Umbelliferæ*, &c. About one fourth of the genera have numerous stamens or numerous carpels, or both, springing naturally from the thalamus. In others (about one sixth) the thalamus is enlarged into a disc, or else presents one or more[Pg 141] glandular swellings, *e.g. Reseda, Nymphæa,Cruciferæ*. In the last-named family, as has been already remarked, prolification is very common. It would be interesting to ascertain precisely what part of an inflorescence is most liable to this affection; but as information on this point is but rarely given in the records of these cases, I can only give the results of my own observations, which go to show that, in a many-flowered inflorescence, those flowers at the outside, or at the lower portion, seem to be more frequently the subjects of this change than those situated elsewhere. This may probably be accounted for by the fact that the malformation is met with most generally in plants with an indefinite form of inflorescence, and therefore the lowermost or outermost flowers are most fully nourished; the upper flowers being in a less advanced condition, the change is more likely to be overlooked in them; or it may be that from the unusual luxuriance in the lower flowers, the upper ones may be either present in their ordinary condition, or may be (as indeed frequently happens) stunted in the size and proportion of their several parts.

Axillary foliar prolification of the flower.—The formation of an adventitious leaf-bud in the axil of any of the parts of the flower is not of such common occurrence as the development of a flower-bud in similar situations, nor is it so frequent as median foliar prolification. I have seen leafy shoots proceeding from the axils of the sepals in the flowers of*Brassica*, and a similar occurrence has been noticed in *Caltha palustris,Herreria parviflora*, and other plants. Dr. Marchand's flowers of*Anagallis*, previously referred to at p. 117, showed good illustrations of this occurrence, as also some specimens described by Kirschleger in *A. phœnicea*.[134] Steinheil has figured and described[135] a flower of*Scabiosa*[Pg 142] in which there was an adventitious formation of leafy shoots in the axil of the outer calyx. In some flowers, such as *Convolvulus,Anemone*, &c., the exact nature of the sub-floral leaves is uncertain, *i.e.* it is open to doubt whether the organs in question are bracts or leaves pertaining to the inflorescence, or whether they are really parts of the flower. When leafy shoots are formed in the axils of such organs, the adventitious growth may be referred to extra-floral prolification, prolification of the inflorescence that is, or to axillary prolification, according to the view taken of the real nature of the sub-floral leaves. So far as the mere occurrence of prolification is concerned, it is not very material which view be adopted. The same remark applies to cases where leaf-buds occur on the outer surface of inferior ovaries, as in *Rosaceæ,Pomaceæ, Philadelphus,* or *Tetragonia expansa*, as elsewhere mentioned.

It would seem more consistent with the general arrangements of parts, that the adventitious buds should be formed more frequently outside than within the flower proper.

Knight[136] figures and describes the occurrence of small tubers or fleshy leaf-buds in the axils of the sepals of a potato, a curious illustration of the real morphological nature of the tuber.

Axillary floral prolification of the flower.—As already stated, this is of more common occurrence than the formation of a leaf-bud in a similar situation. Any of the parts of the flower may thus subtend a flower-bud, though probably the new buds more frequently originate in the axils of the sepals than in the other whorls. In *Cruciferæ* the change in question is, relatively speaking, very common. In cauliflowers and broccoli I have frequently met with stalked flowers proceeding from the axils of the sepals, so also in some fuchsias I have seen a ring of stalked flower-buds alternating[Pg 143] with the petals, which, together with the stamens and pistil, remained unaffected. The number of parts in the supernumerary structures is generally less than the normal flowers.

In Mr. Herbert Spencer's 'Principles of Biology,' part iv, p. 37, are figured and described some monstrous inflorescences in *Angelica* and other*Umbelliferæ*, from which, amongst other things, the author draws the conclusion that there is no absolute distinction between leaf and branch. Without staying for the moment to discuss this matter, it may here be said that the Umbellifers in question apparently owe their peculiarities rather to axillary prolification within the flower, or to prolification of the inflorescence, than to an actual transformation of a flower or any portion of a flower into an umbellule.[137]

In the 'Gardeners' Chronicle,' 1855, p. 551, an instance is figured of the production of a supernumerary flower proceeding from the axil of a stamen in a species of *Nymphæa* (fig. 65). The ovary in this case was wanting, but in its place was a tuft of small leaves. It is curious that among Dr. Kirk's drawings of east tropical African plants now at Kew, there should be one representing a precisely similar state of things. The species in both instances was *Nymphæa Lotus*, or a cultivated variety of it.

M. Wesmael[138] describes a very singular case of what appears to have been referable to axillary prolification in the flowers of *Carex acuta*. The rachillus is described as prolonged through the utricle by the side of the stigmas, bearing on its side a bract, then a secondary utricle, from the axil of which sprung a short stem surmounted by an ovary. Wigand, 'Flora,' 1856, mentions a similar change in *Carex glauca*. In this instance the base of the female inflorescence bore lateral spikes, which projected from the utricles; some of these adventitious spikes were female, others[Pg 144] female below and male above, others, again, wholly male.

FIG. 65.—Flower of *Nymphæa Lotus*, var., showing axillary floral prolification. The section also shows the tuft of leaves that occupied the place of the ovary.

Various changes in the form and arrangement of the several floral whorls accompany axillary prolification; some of these affect the particular organ or organs implicated, and these only, while in other cases some other parts of the flower likewise undergo modification. The changes most commonly met with are such as may be classed under Goethe's theory of retrograde metamorphosis; for instance, if a supplementary bud be developed in the axil of a sepal, that sepal is likely to be more than ordinarily leaf-like in appearance. The dislocation of the affected sepal from its fellows is a very frequent occurrence; in cases of this[Pg 145] kind the detached sepal is placed below the others, thus approximating, in position as well as in function, to the bracts. In some of the instances of proliferous pears, on which I shall have occasion to comment, the sepals are described as sharing in the succulent character of the fruit.

The petals, under such circumstances, often exist in the guise of sepals or of small leaves; and instances are recorded wherein the place of the calyx and corolla was supplied by a succession of overlapping green scales, from the axils of which the new buds arose. M. Germain de Saint Pierre records such a case in *Trifolium repens*, wherein the calyx and corolla were replaced by overlapping scales, in the axils of each one of which arose a flower; above there was a row of stamens, and in the centre a pistil in the guise of a trifoliate leaf.[139] Such instances seem to afford an extreme degree of a more common change, viz., the diminished size and contracted appearance of the sepals and petals when affected with axillary prolification. They have also a close relationship to such developments as we see in the wheat-ear carnation, in certain species of the genus *Mæsa*and others, wherein the calyx is repeated over and again, to the partial or complete suppression of the other parts of the flower. All these cases may be in part explained by the operation of the principle of compensation.

So far as the <u>androecium</u> is concerned, the stamens either remain unaltered, or they are present in a more or less petal-like condition; but it far more frequently happens that the stamens are entirely suppressed, the adventitious bud supplying their place; thus was it in the *Dianthus*represented in the adjoining woodcut, fig. 66, where the stamens were entirely absent, and their places supplied by flower-bearing branches. This*Dianthus* has the more interest from its similarity to the one described by Goethe, Metam. der Pflanzen,[Pg 146] cap. 16, sect. 105; but in that instance median prolification also existed. For my specimens I am indebted to Mr. T. Moore.

FIG. 66.—**Flower of *Dianthus* sp., calyx removed; petals turned down so as to show the stalked flower-buds springing from their axils.**

The pistil, too, is necessarily subject to very grave alterations when affected with this malformation. It is separated into its constituent carpels; and these assume a leaf-like aspect, and are in the great majority of instances destitute of ovules. Indeed, virescence or chloranthy is very intimately connected with this aberration, as might have been anticipated, for if the parts of the flower assume more or less of the condition of stem-leaves or bracts, it is quite natural to expect that they will partake likewise of the attributes of leaves, even at the expense of their own peculiar functions.

It occasionally happens that an adventitious bud arises from the axil of a monocarpellary pistil. This takes place sometimes in *Leguminosæ*, and seems to have been more frequently met with in *Trifolium repens* than in other plants. The species named is, as is well known, particularly subject to a reversion of the outer whorls of the flower to leaves, and even to a leaf-like condition of the pistil. There are on record instances wherein a leaf-bud has been placed in the axil of a[Pg 147] more or less leaf-like carpel; while at other times a second imperfect carpel has been met with in the axil of the first.[140] I have myself seen numerous imperfectly developed cases of this kind.

It may be asked whether such cases are not more properly referable to central prolification—whether the axis is not in such flowers terminated by two, rather than by one carpel? It is, however, generally admitted by morphologists that the solitary carpel of *Leguminosæ* is not terminal, but is the sole existing member of a whorl of carpels, all the other members of which are suppressed as a general rule, though exceptional instances of the presence of two and even of five carpels have been described.[141]

Again, the adventitious bud or carpel is placed, not laterally to the primary one, or opposite to it, on the same level, but slightly higher up—in fact, in the axil of the primary carpellary leaf. Griffith figures and describes[142] an instance of the kind in a species of *Melilotus*. The stalk of the ovary is mentioned as having a sheathing base, bearing in its axil a prolongation of the axis of inflorescence, in the form of a short spike with hairy bracts and imperfect flowers, the latter having a well-formed calyx and rudimentary petals and stamens. Griffith infers, from this specimen, that the legume is not to be considered as a terminal leaf.
[Pg 148]

List of Genera in which Axillary Prolification has been observed.

Order	Genus.	Leaf-bud or Branch	Flower-bud or Inflorescence	From what organ.
Ranunculaceæ	Clematis		Flower-bud	Sepals.
	Caltha		Ditto	Ditto.
	Aconitum			Ditto.
	Delphinium		Ditto	Sepals, carpels, &c.
	Anemone!		Ditto	Involucre?
Nymphæaceæ	Nymphæa!			Fruit?
	Nymph		Flower	Petal.

73

Cruciferæ	*Brassical!	Leaf-bud	Flower-bud	Sepals and petals.
	Brassica!		Ditto	Stamens.
	Brassica!	Ditto	Ditto	Pistil.
	Cardamine!		Ditto	Sepals.
	Matthiola!		Ditto	Sepals and petals.
	Cheiranthus!		Ditto	Sepals.
	Erysimum	Ditto		Sepals and pistils.
	Lepidium!		Ditto	Petals and stamens.
	Arabis		Ditto	Sepals.
	Diplotaxis		Flower, inflorescence	Pistil, calyx and corolla.
	Capsella			
Capparidaceæ	Cleome		Flower-bud	Sepals.
Resedaceæ	*Reseda		Ditto	Ditto.
Caryophyllaceæ	Arenaria	Branch		Ditto.
	Agrostemma	Leaf-bud		Ditto.
	*Lychnis	Ditto		
	Stellaria	Ditto		
	Silene	Ditto[Pg 149]		
	*Gypsophila	Ditto	Ditto	Sepals and stamens.

		*Dianthus!	Ditto		Ditto	Sepals.
		Dianthus!	Ditto	nce	Inflorescence	Petals and stamens.
		Cucubalus				Sepals
		Saponaria!				Sepals and petals.
æ	Malvace	Alcea		bud	Flower-	Stamen.
ceæ	Aurantia	Citrus!			Ditto	Ditto.
	Rutaceæ	Dictamnus!	Ditto			Pistil leafy.
aceæ	Tropæol	Tropæolum!	Ditto			Petals.
eæ	Celastrac	Celastrus	Ditto			Sepals.
osæ	Legumin	*Melilotus!		nce	Inflorescence	Sepals and petals.
		o Medicago		bud	Flower-	Sepals.
		a Coronilla			Ditto	Ditto.
		m! Trifolium	Ditto	Second carpel axillary to first		Pistil.
		s! Melilotus			Ditto	Ditto
		m! Trifolium		bud	Flower-	Sepals and petals.
	Rosaceæ	Pyrus!			Fruit?	Fruit?
		Cerasus!		bud	Flower-	Petals and stamens.
		a! Potentilla			Ditto	Leafy carpels.
		s! Cratægus			Ditto	Petals.

Order	Genus			Remarks
	*Rosa!	Ditto	Ditto	Sepals, petals, stamens and pistil.
Myrtaceæ	Lecythis	Ditto		Fruit?
Tetragoniaceæ	Tetragonia?		Ditto	Ditto.
Cactaceæ!	Opuntia	Fruit-like branch		Tufts of spines.
	Pereskia	Ditto		Sepals?
	Echinocactus	Ditto		Ditto.
Philadelphaceæ	Philadelphus		Ditto	Sepals.
Umbelliferæ	*Athamanta		Ditto	Calyx.
	*Daucus!		Ditto	Calyx and pistil.
	Bupleurum		Ditto	Ditto ditto.
	Torilis		Ditto	Ditto ditto.[Pg 150]
	Apium		Flower-bud	Calyx and pistil.
	Pastinaca		Ditto	Ditto ditto.
	Heracleum!		Ditto	Ditto ditto.
	Angelica!		Umbel	Ditto ditto.
Campanulaceæ	*Campanula!	Branch		Sepals.
	Prismatocarpus	Ditto	Fruit	Sepals, &c.
Gentianaceæ	Gentiana!		Flower-bud	Sepals.
Convolvulaceæ	*Convolvulus!		Ditto	Outer calyx.

Family	Genus			Result
Solanaceæ	Solanum!		Ditto	Sepals.
	Solanum	Tubers		Sepals and petals.
Scrophulariaceæ	*Digitalis!		Ditto	Petals, &c.
	Veronica		Raceme	Calyx.
Primulaceæ	Anagallis!	Branch	Ditto	Petals.
	Primula	Ditto		Petals and carpels.
Polygonaceæ	Rumex		Ditto	Sepals.
Santalaceæ	Thesium	Leaf-bud		In place of stamens and pistils, both absent.
Euphorbiaceæ?	Euphorbia?	Ditto	?	Outer bracts?
Orchidaceæ	Orchis!		Flower-bud	Perianth.
Amaryllidaceæ	Leucoium		Ditto	Ditto.
Iridaceæ	Iris		Ditto	Pistil.
Liliaceæ	Herreria	Ditto		Sepals.
	Hyacinthus		Flower and raceme	Perianth.
	Convallaria		Flower-bud	Ditto.
	Allium		Ditto	Ditto.
Cyperaceæ	Carex		Inflorescence	Utricle.

[Pg 151]

FIG. 67.—Proliferous Rose. Calyx leafy; petals normal, some reflexed; stamens and pistil absent; in their places a branch with leaves and flowers.

FIG. 68.—Rose exhibiting median, axillary, lateral, floral, and leafy prolification in same flower.

77

Complicated prolification.—From what has been before stated it may be seen that prolification of two or more kinds may coexist in the same flower. Mixed leafy and floral prolification is not unfrequent in proliferous roses, where a shoot is, as it were, prolonged through the centre of the original flower and terminated by a[Pg 152] second flower, or even by a cluster, as is well shown in the accompanying figure (fig. 67). Median and axillary prolification, also, not unfrequently coexist in the same flower; thus, in a proliferous rose forwarded to me by Mr. W. Thomson (fig. 68), the following changes were observed:—the swollen portion below the calyx, the "hip," was entirely absent; the sepals were leaf-like in aspect, the petals unaffected; above the petals the axis was prolonged for a short distance and then bore a circlet of miniature, sessile roses, destitute, indeed, of calyx, but provided with numerous petals, stamens, and pistils. Above these lateral flowers, the prolonged axis bore a number of scales in many rows. The scales were in their turn surmounted[Pg 153] by a whorl of five perfect leaves, beyond which, again, the axis was prolonged into a leafy shoot terminated by a flower bud, the whole constituting a remarkably complicated admixture of elements belonging to the flower, the bud, the inflorescence, and the leafshoot.[143]

Proliferous flowers of Orchids also occasionally present great complexity in the arrangement of their parts. An instance of this kind was described by myself from specimens furnished by Dr. Moore, of Glasnevin, in the 'Journal of the Linnean Society,' vol. ix, p. 349, tabs. x, xi, and from which the following summary is extracted:

FIG. 69.—Proliferous Orchis. Diagram showing the arrangement of the several organs in the seven outer circles of the flower. Each whorl is numbered, and the position of the axillary buds shown by the small circles.

The primary flowers were composed of five distinct whorls, and of at least two others less perfectly developed. These primary flowers did not give rise to[Pg 154] median formations, but they produced secondary buds in the axils of the segments of the perianth. These latter buds were themselves the subject of tertiary prolification of both kinds, median and axillary. The tertiary median growths, like the primary flower, did not develop median buds, but only lateral ones—quaternary axillary prolification.

The accompanying diagrams are intended to show the plan of arrangement in these flowers. Fig. 69 shows the disposition of parts in the primary flower and the situation of the axillary buds. Fig. 70 shows the primary flower without any central prolongation, but giving off axillary buds, two of which are shown in the diagram, 2, 2; these are, each of them, the subject of both median, 3, 3, and axillary prolification, 4', 4'.

FIG. 70.—Diagram to explain the construction of the double-flowered*Orchis*.
1. The primary flower, with no median bud, the position of which, had it been present, is shown by the dotted line.
2. Two axillary buds proceeding from 1, and themselves giving origin to
3, 3. Median buds, and 3', 3', axillary buds.
4' 4'. Axillary buds, proceeding from 3. No median bud is produced from 3; its situation, had it been present, is indicated by the dotted line.

In *Narcissus major* a similar combination of both forms of prolification exists, as described by Morren.[144]

On the general subject of Prolification in flowers, in[Pg 155] addition to the authorities already cited, the reader may refer to the following among many others:

Linnæus, 'Prolepsis,' §§ vi et vii. Goethe, 'Versuch. Metamorph.,' cap. xv and xvi §§ 103–106. Moquin-Tandon,' El. Ter. Veg.,' p. 362, &c. Engelmann, 'De Antholys.,' §§ 52–62, &c. Cramer, 'Bildungsabweichungen,' &c. *Orchidaceæ*, *Umbelliferæ*, *Compositæ*,*Leguminosæ*, *Primulaceæ*, *Ranunculaceæ*. Fleischer, 'Missbild. Cultur Gewachs.' Schlechtendal, 'Linnæa,' xv, p. 408, *Rosa*. 'Bot. Zeit.' vol. xx, 1862, p. 382, *Cyclamen*. 'Bot. Zeit.,' vol. xx, p. 301, *Asphodelus*, et*Lilium*. Seringe, 'Bull. Bot.,' i, t. xi, f. 7, 8, *Arabis*, *Diplotaxis*. Clos, 'Mem. Acad. Toulouse,' 5th sér., 1862, *Papaver*. Wigand, 'Flora,' 1856, p. 716, *Hypochæris*; et 'Bot. Untersuch.,' p. 19. Buchenau,' Flora,' 1857, p. 295, *Reseda*. Roeper, 'Bot. Zeit.,' 1852, p. 427, *Orchis*. Presl., 'Linnæa,' vi, p. 599, tab. ix, figs. 5– 8, *Sisymbrium*, Vrolik., 'Flora,' 1846, p. 97, t. i et ii, id. 1844, t. i, *Digitalis*. See also

Schlechtendal, 'Bot. Zeit.,' vol. ix, 1851, p. 579. Klinsmann, 'Linnæa,' x, p. 604, t. v, *Hesperis.* Fuckel, 'Flora,' 1848, p. 609. *Melilotus.* De Candolle, 'Organogr.,' i, 396, t. 33. Turpin, 'Atlas de Goethe,' p. 65, t. 5, figs. 12, 13. Fenzl. 'Sitzungsbericht d. k. Akad. d. Wissensch. Wien.,' heft, iii, tabs. 3, 4, *Rosa.* Kirschleger, 'Flora,' 1845, 613, *Dianthus, Rosa.* 'Institut.,' 1841, No. 413, p. 421,*Tragopogon.* Baron de Melicoq., 'Ann. Sc. Nat.,' 3rd ser., vol. v. 1846, p. 61, *Antirrhinum.* Reichenbach, 'Icon. Fl. Germ.,' tab. 100, *Reseda*—"monstrosa anticipatio Euphorbiacearum et Capparidearum." Duhamel, 'Phys. Arbres.,' liv. iii, cap. 3, p. 303, pl. xii, f. 306, *Rosa.* Caspary, 'Bull. Soc. Bot. Fr.,' vol. vi, 1859, p. 235, Rev. Bibl., *Pyrus.* Eichler, 'Flora,' 1865, tab. ix, *Cleome.* Lindley, 'Elements of Botany,' p. 63, &c., *Rosa,Epacris, Anagallis, Pyrus.* Irmish, 'Flora,' 1858, p. 38, *Pyrus;* and 'Bot. Zeit.,' xix, 1861, p. 342, *Hyacinthus.* Duchartre, 'Bull. Soc. Bot. France,' 1861, p. 451, *Rosa.* Weber, 'Verhandl. Nat. Hist. Verein. Rhein. Preuss., &c.' 1858 et 1860. Landrin, 'Mem. Soc. Sc. Nat. Seine et Oise,' 1866?[145] Masters, 'Trans. Linn. Soc.,' vol. xxiii, p. 359, tab. 34 and p. 481, tab. 54.

Prolification of the embryo.—This term was applied by Moquin-Tandon to a peculiar condition of the almond (*Amygdalus*), in which, though it is not of unfrequent occurrence. In these cases one almond encloses within its cotyledons a second embryo, and this, again, in some instances, a third, the little plants being thus packed like so many boxes one within the other. The supplementary embryos are, in the ripe state at least, quite separate and detached one from another. These cases differ from the ordinary instances wherein there is an increased number of embryos in one seed in their[Pg 156] position. In the latter case, as often happens in the seeds of the orange, the new products are placed by the side one of another.[146]

For other cases of prolification or the adventitious formation of buds on leaves, roots, &c., see under Heterotaxy.

FOOTNOTES:

[104]Linn., 'Prolepsis,' § vii; Goethe, 'Metamorph.,' §§ 96, 103, 106.

[105]"Diaphysis inflorescentiarum." Engelmann, 'De Anthol.,' § 85.

[106]'Flora,' 1844, p. 565.

[107]'Ann. Sc. Nat.,' ser. 3, vol. v, 1846, p. 64.

[108]'Bot Zeit.,' vol. xx, p. 382.

[109]'Miscel. Austriac. Bot.,' vol. i, Vindob, 1778, p. 133.

[110]"*Umbellati dum prolificantur, augent umbellulam, ut ex umbellula simplici altera exeat.*" 'Linn. Phil. Bot.,' § 124.

[111]'En. Euphorb.,' p. 36.

[112]Meisner. 'Mon. Gen. *Polygoni* Prodrom.,' p. 20, tab. v, considers the bulbils of this plant to be modifications of the pedicels of the flower.

[113]See A. Braun. 'Ann. Scienc. Nat.,' 4th series, 1860, vol. xiv, p. 13.

[114]"*Prolificatio e latere ex calyci communi proles plurimos pedunculatos emittens, fit in compositis aggregatis proprie dictis.*" 'Linn. Phil. Bot.,' § 124.

[115]'Bot. Zeit.,' 1857, p. 873. See also 'Verhandl. Nat. Hist. Vereins. Preuss. Rheinl. u. Westphal.,' 1854, t. ix.

[116]"Pannicula spicatim sparsa onusta innumera fœtura herbaceorum flosculorum racematim cohærentium," 'Lobel. Stirp. Hist.,' p. 163. This is the "Besome Plantain, or Plantain with spoky tufts," of Ray, 'Synopsis,' p. 314. Gerard's 'Herbal,' Ed. Johnson, p. 420. Parkinson, 'Theat. Bot.,' p. 494. Baxter, 'Loudon. Mag. Nat. Hist.,' vol. ix. p. 204, and vol. iii, p. 482. fig. 118.

[117]'Flora.' 1856. p. 706.

[118]'Flora of Berwick-on-Tweed,' vol. i. p. 38.

[119]'Adansonia,' vol. iv. 1864, p. 150, tab. vii. 'Gard. Chron.,' November 19th, 1864.

[120]'Ann. Sc. Nat.,' ser. 3, tom. ii, p. 290; and 'Adansonia,' iii, tab. iv; see also Bureau, in 'Bull. Soc. Bot. France,' x, p. 191.

[121]Baillon, 'Adansonia,' i, 286.

[122]See also figure in 'Hort. Eystett. Ic. Plant. Vern.,' fol. 15, fig. 1.*Ranunculus asiaticus.*

[123]Duchartre, 'Ann. des sc. nat.,' 3me série, vol. ii, 1844, p. 293.

[124]Reissek, 'Linnæa,' vol. xvii, 1843, p. 641, tab. xix.

[125]The tube of the calyx in these specimens was traversed by ten ribs, apparently corresponding to the primary ridges of the normal fruit; these ribs were destitute of spines, and the bristly secondary ridges were entirely absent. Those portions of the carpels which were detached from the calyx had each three ribs, a central and two lateral ones, which appeared to be continuous with the ribs of the calyx below,—although in the case of the calyx there were ten, in the case of the carpels six ribs, three to each. This diversity in number is thus explained:—A circle of vascular tissue ran round the interior of the calyx-tube, at its junction with the limb, and at the point of insertion of the petals and stamens. The vascular circle seemed to be formed from the confluence of the ten ribs from below. Of the five ribs in each half of the calyx, the three central ones were joined together just at the point of confluence with the vascular circle, above which they formed but a single rib—that traversing the centre of the carpellary leaf; the two lateral ribs of each half of the calyx seemed to be continuous, above the vascular rim, with the lateral ribs of the carpel; these lateral ribs were connected on either side with the central one by short branches of communication. The disposition of the ten ribs may be thus represented:—

1 1 1   1 1 1   3 2 3 2 3   3 2 3 2 3   1 1 1 1 1   1 1 1 1 1

The lower line of figures represents the calycine ribs, the middle row shows how each of these ribs is divided at the vascular rim, and the uppermost row shows their distribution above the rim. From this it will be seen that six of the calycine ribs divide into three branches, one prolonged upwards as a lateral or median rib into the carpellary leaf, the other running horizontally to join with similar branches sent out from the neighbouring rib; the four intermediate calycine ribs divide into two branches only, which join the side branches of the first mentioned, but have no direct upward prolongation into the carpel. The ten ridges are placed opposite to the sepals and petals.

[126]'Neue Denkschriften der allgemeine Schweizerischen Gesellschaft,' band 5. 1841. tab. 2.

[127]Bell Salter, 'Gard. Chron.,' March 13th, 1847, and 'Ann. Nat. Hist.,' 1847, vol. xix, p. 471. &c.

[128]'The Origin and Production of Proliferous Flowers, with the Culture at large for raising Double Flowers from Single, and Proliferous from the Double.' By J. Hill, M.D. London, 1759.

[129]A. de Candolle, 'Neue Denkschriften,' op. cit., p. 9; also Unger as cited in 'Botanical Gazette,' May, 1351. p. 70.

[130]Duchartre, op. cit.

[131]'Ann. Sc. Nat.,' 1844, vol. i, p. 297.

[132]Maout, 'Leçons Elémentaires de Botanique,' vol. ii. p. 488; Ferrari. 'Hesperides.' pls. 271, 315, 405.

[133]Moquin-Tandon, loc. cit., p. 386, &c.; see also Trécul, in the 'Bull. Soc. Bot. France,' tom. i, p, 307.

[134]'Bull. Soc. Bot. Fr.,' 1863, vol. x, p. 461.

[135]'Ann. Sc. Nat.,' 1835, p. 65. See also Le Maout, 'Leçons Element.,' vol. ii, p. 426.

[136]'Proc. Hort. Soc.,' vol. i, p. 39, fig. 2.

[137]See also 'Nat. Hist. Review,' 1865, p. 377.

[138]'Acad. Roy. Belg.,' April 11th. 1863.

[139]'Bull. Soc. Bot. Fr.,' tom. iii, 1856, p. 479.

[140]'Linnæa,' vol. xv, p. 266, *c. ic.* Caspary, 'Schriften d. Physik.-Oek. Gesell. zu Königsberg,' bd. ii, p. 5, tab. iii, fig. 39, &c.

[141]Lindley, 'Veg. King.,' p. 545; also Clarke on the Position of Carpels, Linn. Soc.,' December, 1850. 'Proc. Linn. Soc.,' ii, p. 105.

[142]'Notulæ,' vol. i, Dicot. p. 127. 'Atlas,' pl. xliii.

[143]Moquin-Tandon gives the following references to cases of proliferous roses, but some I have not been able to verify. 'Journ. des Sav.,' 22 Mai 1679. Hottinger, 'Ephem. Nat. Cur.,' dec. 3 ann. 9 et 10, p. 249. Marchant, 'Mem. Acad. Scienc. Paris.' 1707, p. 488. Preussius, 'Ephem. Nat. Cur.,' cent. 7 et 8. App. p. 83. Schuster, 'Act. Acad. Nat. Cur.,' vol. vi, p. 185. Spadoni, 'Mem. Soc. Ital.,' t. v, p. 488. See also at the end of this section for numerous other references.

[144]'Bull. Acad. Belg.,' t. xx, part ii, p. 271. See also Bellynck, 'Bull. Soc. Bot. Belg.,' t. vi, ex. 'Bull. Soc. Bot. France,' t. xiv, 1867, Rev. Bibl., p. 241. *Orchis ustulata.*

[145]I have not been able to meet with this, but it is said to contain a paper on prolification, with numerous bibliographical references.

[146]'El. Ter. Veg.,' p. 364, Adnot.

CHAPTER III.
HETEROTAXY.

Under this category are here included a variety of deviations from the ordinary arrangement and position of parts which cannot conveniently be classed under the preceding or under other headings. The term heterotaxy is intended to apply to the production of organs in situations where, under usual circumstances, they would not be formed. It thus does not include cases of substitution, where one part is replaced by another, or more or less metamorphosed, nor cases of multiplication, nor of prolification which are characterised not only by the production of members in unwonted situations, but also in unwonted numbers. From the very nature of the anomalies, and specially from the scanty knowledge we possess concerning their mode of development, it is not possible to allocate them in all cases correctly, and moreover many of them might as well be placed in one group as in another.

Formation of adventitious roots.—This is of exceedingly common occurrence in a vast number of plants, so much so that in most cases it cannot be considered as in any way abnormal; there are, however, a few instances where the formation of these organs may be[Pg 157] considered to come within the scope of teratology, or, at least, where their production is the result of injury or of some unfavorable condition to which the plant is exposed.

Thus the production of adventitious roots on the stem of the vine is considered to be due to untoward circumstances impairing the proper action of the ordinary subterranean roots. So, too, the formation of roots on the upper portions of stems that are more or less decayed below, as in old willows, is to be considered as an attempt to obtain fresh supplies through a more vigorous and healthy channel.

A similar occurrence often arises as a consequence of some injury. Virgil had this circumstance in view when he wrote

"*Quin et, caudicibus sectis, mirabile dictu,Truditur e sicco radix oleagina ligno.*"—'Georg.' Bk. ii.

I have seen many specimens of adventitious roots produced on the olive in the way just mentioned.

In the 'Gardeners' Chronicle,' January 8th, 1853, p. 21, is described a curious formation of roots in the fissure between two divisions of a laburnum stem. In the same journal, January 1st, 1853, p. 4, Mr. Booth mentions the case of a Cornish elm, the trunk of which was divided at the top into two main divisions, and from the force of the wind or from some other cause the stem was split down for several feet below the fork. Around the edges of the fracture, layers of new bark were formed, from which numerous roots issued, some measuring an inch in diameter and descending into the cleft portion of the tree: similar instances must be familiar to all observers.

It may happen that these roots sent down into the cavity of a decaying trunk may, after a time, become completely concealed within it, by the gradual formation and extension of new wood over the orifice of the cavity formed by the death and decay of the old wood. Such is presumed to be the explanation of a specimen of[Pg 158] this kind in the possession of the writer, and taken from a cavity in an apparently solid block of rosewood; externally there were no marks to indicate the existence of a central space, but when the block was sawn up for the use of the cabinet-maker, this root-like structure was found in the centre and attached to one end of the cavity.

The production of roots which ultimately serve as props to support the branches, or as buttresses to compensate for the increasing weight of branches and foliage, is also a familiar occurrence. The huge gnaurs and burrs met with occasionally on some trees often produce great quantities, not only of adventitious buds, but of roots also.

FIG. 71.—Production of adventitious roots from leaf stalk of celery.

The leaves, equally with the stems, have the power of emitting roots under certain conditions, as when the leaves are in close contact with moist soil or as the result of injury. This happens in some plants more readily than in others—*Bryophyllum calycinum* is a well-known instance. Mr. Berkeley has described the formation of roots from the fractured leaves of celery,[147][Pg 159] and also in a cabbage where a snail "having gnawed a hole into the middle of a leaf at its junction with the stem, a fascicle of roots was formed, bursting through the tissue lining the cavity, and covered with abundant delicate hairs after the fashion of ordinary radicles."

FIG. 72.—Germinating plant of mango, showing production of roots from one of the cotyledons (from the Kew Museum).

The production of adventitious roots is not limited to the ordinary leaves of the plant, but may be manifested on the cotyledons; thus Irmisch describes cases of this kind in the cotyledons of *Bunium creticum* and *Carum Bulbocastanum*.[148] I have figured and described an analogous case in the cotyledons of the Mango (fig. 72).[149]

To this formation of adventitious roots the gardener owes the power he has of propagating plants by cuttings, *i.e.*, small portions of the stem with a bud or buds attached, or in some cases from portions of the[Pg 160] leaves, of the roots themselves, or even of the fruit, as in the case of the cactus (Baillon). Care also has to be exercised in grafting certain fruit trees not to allow the grafted portion to be too close to the ground, else the scion throws out roots into the soil, and the object of the cultivator is defeated.

FIGS. 73 and 74 show formation of roots from leaves induced by the art of the gardener.

Layering is another garden operation dependent on the formation of these organs, and advantage is also sometimes taken of this tendency of some plants to produce roots when injured to reduce the dimensions of a plant when getting too large for the house in which it is growing. By gradually inducing the production of new roots from the central or upper portions of the stem, it becomes possible, after a time, to sever the connection between the original roots and the upper portion of the trunk, and thus secure a shortened plant.

On the subject of adventitious roots, &c., reference may be made to Trécul, 'Ann. Sc. Nat.,' 1846, t. v, p. 340, et vi, p. 303. Duchartre, 'Elements de Botanique,' p. 219. Lindley, 'Theory and Practice of Horticulture.' Thomson's 'Gardener's Assistant,' pp. 374, *et seq.*; and any of the ordinary botanical text-books.

Formation of adventitious buds on roots.—One of the characteristics by which roots are distinguished from stems in a general way consists in the absence of buds; but, as is well known, they may be formed on the roots under certain circumstances, and in certain plants, e.g.,[Pg 161] *Pyrus Japonica, Anemone Japonica*, &c. What are termed suckers, owe their origin to buds formed in this situation.

If roots be exposed or injured, they will frequently emit buds. The well-known experiment of Duhamel, in which a willow was placed with the branches in the soil and the roots in the air, and emitted new buds from the latter and new roots from the former, depended on this production of adventitious organs of either kind.

Gardeners often avail themselves of the power that the roots have of producing buds to propagate plants by cuttings of the roots, but in many of these cases the organ "parted" or cut is really an underground stem and not a true root.

M. Claas Mulder has figured and described a case in the turnip-radish of the unusual formation of a leafy shoot from the root, apparently after injury.[150] From the figure it appears as if the lower portion of the root had been split almost to the extremity, while the upper portion seems to have a central cavity passing through it. From the angle, formed by the split segments below, proceeds a tuft of leaves, some of which appear to have traversed the central cavity and to have emerged from the summit, mingling with the other leaves in that situation. The production of a flower-bud has even been noticed on the root of a species of *Impatiens*.

Formation of shoots beneath the cotyledons.—The tigellar or axial portion of the embryo plant, as contrasted with the radicle proper, is very variously developed in different cases; sometimes it is a mere "collar" bearing the cotyledons, while at other times it is of considerable size. Generally it does not give origin to shoots or leaves other than the seed-leaves, but occasionally shoots may be seen projecting from it below the level of the cotyledons. This happens frequently in seedling plants of *Anagallis arvensis, Euphorbia*[Pg 162] *peplus*, and other species, *Linaria vulgaris*, some *Umbelliferæ*, &c.[151]

Adventitious formation of leaves.—The term phyllomania has been vaguely applied both to the production of an unwonted number of leaves and to their development in unusual situations. Under the present heading the latter class of cases are alone included. The extraordinary tendency in some Begonias to develop leaves or leafy excrescences from their surfaces is elsewhere alluded to, and is, in reality, a species of hypertrophy or over-luxuriant growth.

In some flowers where the inferior ovary is supposed to be, in part at least, formed by a dilatation of the top of the flower-stalk, leaves have been met with proceeding from the surface of the ovary or fruit, as in *Cratægus tanacetifolia*, roses, pears, gooseberries, &c. In a specimen of *Nymphæa alba* I have met with scale-like leaves projecting from the surface of the fruit (or torus?), and which did not appear to be metamorphosed stamens or styles (fig. 76).

FIG. 75.—Leaf proceeding from hip of the Rose.

FIG. 76.—Leaves proceeding from the ovary of *Nymphæa*.
[Pg 163]
For other illustrations of increased leaf-formation, see Multiplication of foliar organs.

FIG. 77.—*Leontodon*. Scape with two leaves; the bracts of the involucre are also leafy.

Production of leaves on a usually leafless inflorescence.—The development of the bracts of an inflorescence to such an extent that they resemble ordinary leaves is elsewhere alluded to as of common occurrence. It happens far less frequently that leaves are developed on an inflorescence usually destitute of them, without any metamorphosis or substitution, and without any formation[Pg 164] of adventitious buds, such as happens in prolification. Such a partial change from a floriferous to a foliiferous branch may be seen in a specimen of *Sambucus nigra* in the Smithian herbarium in the Linnean Society, where the ultimate branches of the cyme bear small leaves. My attention was directed to this specimen by the Rev. W. Newbould.

Jacquin figures an analogous case in *Sempervivum sediforme*,[152] in which the branches of the inflorescence were prolonged into leafy shoots.

Sometimes from the side of a flower-stalk or scape, which usually does not bear leaves, those organs are produced. The common dandelion, *Taraxacum*, sometimes offers an illustration of this, and also the daisy (*Bellis*).[153] In a specimen of fasciated cowslip given me by Mr. Edgeworth there was a similar formation of leaves on the flattened stalk.

Production of leaves or scales in place of flower-buds.—The position of the leaf and of the flower-buds respectively is, in most plants, well defined, but occasionally it happens that the former is formed where, under ordinary circumstances, the latter organ should be. This may happen without the formation of any transitional organs between the two, and without actual increase in the number of the buds. Where there is evidently a passage from leaf-bud to flower-bud, or *vice versâ*, the case would be one of metamorphy. If the number of buds be augmented, or they be mixed with the flower-buds, then it would be referable to leafy prolification of the inflorescence. There remains a class of cases wherein there is a complete substitution of one structure for the other, it may be without the slightest indication of transition between the two, and without any admixture of leaf-buds among flower-buds,[Pg 165] or any absolute increase in the number of organs, as in Prolification. Such a case is represented in fig. 78, which shows a portion of the stem of a species

83

of *Valeriana*, bearing at the summit, not an inflorescence, but a tuft of leaves without the slightest indication of flowers.

Drs. Hooker and Thomson relate that in Northern India the flowers of *Anemone rivularis* are very generally absent, and their place supplied by tufts or umbels of leaves.[154] In the collection of the late Mr. N. B. Ward was a specimen of lupin in which the flowers were all absent, and their place supplied by tufts of leaves.

FIG. 78.—Tuft of leaves replacing the inflorescence in a species of *Valeriana*.

A similar appearance has been noticed in *Compositæ*, and I owe to the kindness of Professor Oliver the communication of a specimen of a species of *Bidens* from[Pg 166] Peru, in which the capitula, instead of consisting of florets, as usual, contained tufts of linear ciliolated bracts within the involucre, without a trace of flowers. In the eleventh volume of the 'Linnæa,' 1837, p. 301, Von Cesati figures and describes an analogous case in *Carduus crispus*. The same author[1] records a similar instance in the umbel of *Seseli coloratum*, where the place of the flowers was occupied by stalked tufts of leaves. In the 'Gardeners' Chronicle,' October 6th, 1860, p. 894, is mentioned an instance where the blossoms of the pea were entirely absent, and their place supplied by accumulations of small, ovate, green scales, thus presenting an appearance similar to that brought about by the inordinate multiplication of the sepals in the "wheat-ear carnation," and in the Sweet William, and not unlike the condition met with in *Bryophyllum proliferum*. In *Digitalis purpurea* a similar anomaly is sometimes met with.

In the apple I have observed leafy shoots bearing terminal tufts of leaves where the flower should have been, so that what, under ordinary circumstances would be a corymb of flowers, is here represented by a series of tufts of leaves. In the cultivated azaleas also, leafy shoots occupying the position of the flower may occasionally be met with.

In *Bouchea hyderabadensis* I have seen the inflorescence more than usually branched and covered with little tufts of bracts, without a trace of true flower. A similar condition seems not infrequent in *Gentiana Amarella*, as I have not only met with the plant myself in this condition, but have been favoured with specimens by Mr. Pamplin, Mr. Darwin, and others. In *Phyteuma spicatum* an analogous appearance has been recorded.

Among Griffith's collections from Affghanistan is a species of willow (*Salix*) in which the inflorescence replaced by a much branched panicle, bearing a quantity of minute bracts, in the axils of which nestle numerous small buds. In another specimen the inflorescence[Pg 167] preserves its usual catkin-like shape, but the flowers are replaced by little tufts of leaves. M. Germain de Saint Pierre mentions a case wherein the flowers of *Alisma parnassifolia* were completely replaced by leaf-buds.[155]

FIG. 79.—Spikelets of *Willedenovia*, composed entirely of scales to the exclusion of flowers.

FIG. 80.—Rose Willow, *Salix*, sp.

Here, also, may be mentioned the curious aggregations of scales which occur in some grasses, in *Restiaceæ*, *Juncaceæ*, and other orders, in which the inflorescence[Pg 168] is made up of collections of scales or bracts with no trace of floral structure. Fig. 79 shows this in a species of *Willdenovia*, and a very good example is figured in a bamboo, *Pseudostachyum polymorphum*, by General Munro.[156]

"Rose willows" (fig. 80) owe their peculiar appearance to a similar cause, the scales of the catkin being here replaced by closely crowded leaves. These aggregations of scales or leaves are not confined to the inflorescence, but may be found in other parts of the plant, and may be frequently met with in the willow, birch, oak, &c., generally as the result of insect puncture. On the other hand, the production of leaves or leaf-buds in place of flowers is, as is well known, generally the consequence of an excess of nutrition, and of the continuance rather than of the arrest of vegetative development.[157] It has even been asserted that a flower-bud may be transformed into a leaf-bud by removing the pistil at a very early stage of development, but this statement requires further confirmation.[158]

Viviparous plants.—The spikelets of certain grasses are frequently found with some of their constituent parts completely replaced by leaves, like those of the stem, while the true flowers are usually entirely absent. A shoot, in fact, is formed in place of a series of flowers. In these cases it generally happens that the outermost glumes are changed, sometimes, however, even the outer and inner paleæ are wholly unchanged, while there is no trace of squamulæ or of stamens and pistils within them, but in their place is a small shoot with miniature leaves arranged in the ordinary manner.

[Pg 169]

The grasses most commonly affected in this manner are *Dactylis glomerata!, Poa bulbosa!, Poa annua!, P. trivialis!, pratensis!, alpina!,angustifolia*, and *laxa, Cynosurus cristatus, Festuca nemoralis, F. ovina!,Glyceria fluitans!, Gl. aquatica, Aira alpina!, cæspitosa!, Phleum phalaroides, Lolium perenne!, Alopecurus pratensis!, Agrostis alba,Holcus mollis!*

FIG. 81.—Portion of panicle of *Aira vivipara* and separate floret.

From an examination of the structure of viviparous grasses Von Mohl was led to the conclusion that the lower palea is to be considered as a bract, and not a perianthial leaf, because the base of the palea surrounds the stem or axis of the spikelet entirely, and both its margins cohere towards its lower extremity.[159]

A similar condition occurs not infrequently in *Polygonum viviparum*, and in *Juncaceæ, Cyperaceæ*, &c.

[Pg 170]

In the genus *Allium* an analogous formation of little buds or bulbils takes place in lieu of flowers; this is specially the case with *A. vineale*, the flowers of which are rarely seen.

Other illustrations of a similar character, where the adventitious leaf-buds are mixed in amongst the flower-buds, are cited under the head of Prolification of the Inflorescence.

Formation of buds on leaves.—The formation of little bulbs upon the surfaces or edges of leaves, forming what are called viviparous leaves, has long been familiar to botanists amongst Alliums. Professor Alexander Braun,[160] who has paid much attention to this subject, divides cases of this kind according to the position of the buds; thus, for instance, they are sometimes formed upon the upper portion of the leaf or petiole, as in many ferns, in *Nymphæa guineensis*, some *Arads*, &c. The same condition has been met with as a teratological occurrence in the leaves of *Cardamine pratensis, Hyacinthus Pouzolzii, Drosera intermedia*,[161] *Arabis pumila,Chelidonium majus, Chirita sinensis*,[162] *Episcia bicolor*,[163] *Zamia*, &c.[164] Many species of *Begonia* possess the power of emitting buds from the petioles and veins of the leaf; the little ramenta or scales which so plentifully beset the surface of some of these plants likewise, in some instances, pass gradually into leaves. *B. phyllomaniaca*, Mart., is the species best known as manifesting this tendency, but others have it also.[165]

Buds are also very often formed upon the margins of the leaf, the best known instance of which occurs in[Pg 171] *Bryophyllum calycinum,* Weinmann[166] figures an instance of this kind in *Alchemilla minima*, or they may occur upon the lower surface of the leaf, as in *Ornithogalum scilloides* and *longe-bracteatum*. M. Duchartre[167] mentions a case in the tomato in which the leaves gave origin to small leaf-bearing branches, which, of course, must have originated from buds, just in the same way as in the *Drosera* before mentioned.

FIG. 82.—Formation of shoot on leaf of *Episcia bicolor*.

Gardeners occasionally avail themselves of this formation of buds from leaves to propagate plants, *e.g. Hoya, Gesnera, Gloxinia*, &c.

Formation of buds in the pith.—This is said to be a[Pg 172] normal condition in the curious *Stangeria paradoxa*,[168] and Mr. Berkeley records an instance of this in sea-kale[169] (fig. 83) where the crown had been injured, and buds were seen sprouting from its centre.

FIG. 83.—Adventitious buds in sea kale.

FIG. 84.—Hyacinth bulb cut across to induce the formation of new bulbs.

FIG. 85.—**Showing the formation of new bulbs on the cut edges of an old hyacinth bulb.**

It will be remarked that the adventitious production[Pg 173] of buds, like that of roots, is very often consequent on decay or injury. The Dutch bulb-growers have availed themselves of this latter circumstance in the propagation of hyacinths. Mr. Fortune, who published some articles on this subject in the 'Gardener's Chronicle,'[170] describes two special modes as adopted by these skilful horticulturists—the one to make two or three deep cuts at the base of the bulb, destroying the nascent flower-stalk when, after a time, small bulbs are formed along the edges of the cut surfaces (figs. 84, 85). The other method is effected by scooping out the interior of the base of the bulb, thus leaving exposed the cut ends of the sheathing leaves arranged concentrically; along these lines the new bulbs are, after some time, formed in great numbers (fig. 86).

FIG. 86.—**Showing the production of small bulbs on the inner surface of the scooped-out bulb of hyacinth.**

For the formation of supernumerary leaves on the surface of the normal one, see Multiplication and Hypertrophy.

Production of gemmæ in place of spores.—An instance of[Pg 174] this is recorded by Dr. Montagne[171] in the case of a moss, *Encamptodon perichætialis*, in which, in the interior of the capsule, in lieu of spores numerous minute gemmæ of the same nature as those in the cup of *Marchantia* were seen.

Formation of flowers on leaves.—It is very doubtful whether a flower-bud has ever been found actually on a leaf. Mere adhesion of the pedicels of the leaf, such as happens in *Ruscus*, in *Helwingia*, *Erythrochiton hypophyllanthus*, and a few other plants, is, of course, not really to be considered in the light of an actual growth from the leaf, and it is very doubtful in the present state of our knowledge whether the case of the Nepaul barley should find a place here, but for convenience sake it is placed in this section, as it is uncertain at present where it properly belongs.

FIG. 87.—**Three-lobed end of outer palea of Nepaul barley bearing supplementary florets.**

FIG. 88.—**Three spikelets of Nepaul barley.**

FIG. 89.—**Lip of outer palea of Nepaul barley.**

FIG. 90.—**Supplementary rachillus or outer palea of Nepaul barley bearing florets.**

FIG. 91.—**Diagram showing arrangement of supplementary rachillus and florets.**

FIG. 92.—**Supplementary floret of Nepaul barley; palea removed.**

This curious plant has been described and figured[Pg 175] by Irmisch in the 13th volume of the 'Linnæa,' p. 124, t. iv; also by Professor Henslow, 'Hooker's Journal of Botany,' 1849, vol. i, p. 33, tabs. 2, 3. The lower palea of this plant forms an inverted flower-bud upon its midrib. In some fresh specimens which I have lately examined I find the structure to be as follows:—On each notch of the rachis there are three spikelets (fig. 88), each one-flowered, and each provided with two linear glumes; the outer palea in all cases is three-lobed at the summit, the central lobe being oblong and hollow, forming a kind of hood (figs. 87–89), and covered with hairs, which are directed downwards towards the centre of the plant. The two lateral lobes are more[Pg 176] pointed than the central one; like it they are provided with hairs, but the hairs, in this case, are turned away from the centre of the plant. The cavity of the side lobes is generally empty, but that of the central lobe is occupied by a very slender stalk, which is apparently the termination of the midrib, but which is bent inwards at an acute angle, so as to occupy the hollow space (figs. 90–91). On this slender axis are developed two florets, more or less imperfect in their structure. Only one of the florets that I have seen contained a perfect ovary. The tips of the lateral lobes of the paleæ in the primary flower are sometimes extended into a long awn. A similar awn may also be occasionally found on the tips of the paleæ of the rudimentary florets. The occurrence of an adventitious axial structure with rudimentary flowers has been adduced in support of the opinion that the lower paleæ is, at least so far as its midrib is concerned, an axial rather than a foliar structure, but in the present uncertain state of our knowledge as to the morphology of grasses it is hazardous to risk any explanation founded on so exceptional a case as that of the Nepaul barley.[172]

Production of flower-buds in place of leaf-buds.—Under natural circumstances this does not appear to be of so common occurrence as the change above alluded to, but by the art of the gardener the change is often effected. In rhododendrons and in peach trees and roses I have met with this change occurring without human agency. The means adopted by the gardener are such as check the luxuriance of the leaf-shoots,[173] and this is effected in various ways, as by continuous "pinching" or removal of the leaf-buds, by pruning, ringing the bark, confining the roots, limiting the[Pg 177]supply of nutriment, and other means all based on the same principle. Some of the Cape bulbs (*Cyrtanthus*) are known not to produce their flowers till their leaves have received, in some manner, a check. Fires which often destroy the herbage thus have the effect of throwing the plant into bloom. A very remarkable instance is recorded of the production of flower-buds after an injury to the leaf-buds in the 'Bulletin of the Botanical Society of France,' vol. ix, p. 146. It appears that during the war of the French against the Arabs in Algiers, the latter planted several hundreds of Agaves with a view to obstruct the passage of the French cavalry. The soldiers hacked these plants with their sabres, and cut out the central tuft of leaves, or the heart, as gardeners call it. The following season almost every one of these Agaves sent up their large handsome flower-spikes. It is well known that, under ordinary circumstances, these plants do not flower except at long intervals of time.

Presence of flowers on spines.—That the spine, as a contracted branch, should occasionally produce flowers is not to be wondered at, though the occurrence is by no means common. M. Baillon showed at a meeting of the Botanical Society of France ('Bulletin,' vol. v, 1858, p. 316) a branched spine of *Gleditschia* bearing a flower at the end of each of the sub divisions. This was, therefore, strictly analogous with those cases in which the peduncle is normally spiney.

Formation of flower-bud on the petals.—An instance of this, it is believed, the only one on record, is cited in the 'Gardeners' Chronicle' for 1865, p. 760, by the Rev. M. J. Berkeley, who describes the formation of a flower-bud on the surface of a petal of *Clarkia elegans*. Reasoning from analogy there seems no reason why buds should not be formed on the petals as well as on the leaves.

[Pg 178]

Formation of buds on fruits.—This is a point of some moment with reference to the share which the axis takes in the production of "inferior" fruits. A very frequent malformation in pears is one wherein a second pear proceeds from the centre of the first, and even a third from the centre of the second.[174] Pears are occasionally also observed arising either from the axils of the sepals of the primary pear or from the axil of leaves originating on the outer surface of the fruits—using the term fruit in its popular sense. These cases afford strong confirmation of the view that the outer portion of the so-called fruit in these plants is rather to be considered as an expansion and hollowing-out of the flower-stalk, than as formed from the calyx-tube. It is noteworthy that the true carpels and seeds are frequently entirely absent in these cases.[175] Further reference to these fruits will be made under the head of Hypertrophy.

M. Trécul has described and figured an instance in a species of *Prismatocarpus*, in which a second flower proceeded from the axil of a bract attached to the side of the fruit of the first flower.[176] A similar growth was observed in the fruit of *Philadelphus speciosus* by M. A. Gris, who observed that the so-called calyx-tube was provided with two small bracts, from the axil of one of which proceeded a small flower-bud.[177]

FIG. 93.—**Small buds projecting from the edges of the fruit in** *Opuntia.*

The fruits of *Opuntia Salmiana*, *O. fragilis*,[178] *O. monacantha*, and of some species of *Echinocactus*, have been observed to form small fruit-like branches around their summits. M. Napoléon Doumet describes the fruit as ripening as usual, but as being destitute of seeds in the interior; after a little while the fruit begins to wither,[Pg 179] and then a circle of small buds, like those of the stem, may be seen at the top of the fruit, each bud springing from the axil of a little tuft of wool and spines found on the fruit. These little buds elongate into long shoots, produce flowers the following year, which flowers exhibit the same peculiarity. Gasparini and Tenore are said to have recorded the same fact as long since as 1832. The specimen from which the figure (fig. 93) was taken produced its fruits in the Royal Gardens at Kew, and is now preserved in the museum of that establishment. The adventitious growth in these cases appears to arise from the tufts of spines, which, it has been suggested, are the homologues of the sepals. There can, however, be little doubt that the outer and lower portion of the fruit of *Opuntia* and its allies is a dilatation of the flower-stalk. This is borne out by the fruits of *Pereskia*, which bear leaves on their surface arranged spirally; indeed, the fruits of *Pereskia Bleo* are mentioned as producing buds from their[Pg 180] summits, in the same way as the *Opuntia* just cited. *P. Bleo* is said, by M. Delavaud,[179] to present this anomaly as a constant occurrence. On the summit of the primary fruit, arising apparently from the axils of the sepals, or of small leafy bracts in that situation, are a series of fruit-like branches, which, in their turn, are surmounted by others, even to the fourth generation.

The fruits of *Tetragonia expansa* frequently have attached to their side a secondary flower or fruit in such a position as to lead to the inference that it springs from the upper portion of the peduncle which is dilated to invest the true carpels. In other instances it is due to an adhesion of the pedicel to the side of the fruit. In either case the production of an adventitious bud might be considered as an illustration of prolification of the inflorescence, though not as was supposed by Moquin and others of axillary prolification.[180]

Buds have also been produced artificially on the surface of some of the fruits in the construction of which the axis is supposed to share; thus, the unripe fruits of some species of *Lecythis* were stated by Von Martius, at a meeting of the German Naturalists at Carlsruhe, to produce buds when placed in the earth. The fruit of these plants is probably of the same nature as that of the *Pomaceæ*, and Baillon[181] succeeded in producing buds on the surface of the inferior ovary of *Jussiæa.*

Some of the cases just mentioned have been considered to be instances of prolification of the fruit, but the fruit has little to do with the appearances in question.

Formation of adventitious flowers and fruits within the ovary.—This generally arises either from substitution of a[Pg 181] flower-bud for an ovule or from prolification; there are certain cases, however, where the new growth seems not to be either due to metamorphosis or to prolification strictly.

The cut, fig. 94, represents a case where, in the dilated upper portion of the ovary of *Sinapis arvensis*, two flower-buds were found projecting from a raised central line, corresponding, as it would seem, to the midrib, and not to the margins of the carpel. Similar cases have occurred in *Nasturtium amphibium*, *Brassica Rapa*, and *Passiflora quadrangularis.*

FIG. 94.—**Distended pod of** *Sinapis arvensis* **bearing in the interior stalked flower buds.**

In Bromfield's 'Flora Vectensis,' p. 35, the following account is given of an abnormal development in *Cardamine pratensis*: "On the lower part of the corymb were several seed vessels on pedicels changed from their usual linear to an ovate elliptical figure, so as to resemble a silicula. These, on being opened, were found to contain petals of the usual colour, which in the pods above had burst from their confinement and appeared as semi-double flowers; the valves of the pod answering to the true calyx. * * * From their verticillate arrangement it is evident that these petaloid expansions were not transformed seeds, but simply a development of the common axis within the ovary into an abortive whorl of floral organs, besides which there were evident rudiments both of stamens and germens[Pg 182]in the centre of the bundle." Baillon[182] also records a case of the same nature in *Sinapis arvensis.*

88

FIG. 94*.—Portion of the interior of the silicle in *Cheiranthus Cheiri*, showing adventitious pod in the place of an ovule.

FIG. 95.—Adventitious pod from fig. 94, enlarged.

Here, too, may also be mentioned the presence of an adventitious siliqua within the ordinary one attached along the same line as the ovules, and partially divided by a replum into two cavities. In this case there was nothing to indicate the presence of floral envelopes (figs. 94, 95). A similar occurrence has been brought under my notice in some grapes which were observed to be cracking before they were perfectly ripe, and in which adventitious fruits were found within the parent grape, occupying the position of seeds (figs. 96, 97).

Similar anomalous growths are noticed under the heads of Substitution and Prolification.

Formation of stamens within the cavity of the ovary.—The only instance of this that has come under the author's observation occurred in some flowers of *Bæckea diosmæfolia*,[Pg 183] Rudge, for an examination of which he is indebted to Mr. Bentham.

FIG. 96.—Section of Barbarossa grape showing adventitious grape in the position of a seed.

FIG. 97.—Grape with supplementary fruit in the interior

In the normal flower there is a turbinate hollow calyx, whose limb is divided into five serrated lobes; alternating with these latter, and springing from the throat of the calyx, are the petals. Originating from the same annular disk as the petals are the stamens, seven or eight in number. The ovary is partially adherent, is surmounted by a style, and has two or three loculi with an axile placenta, to which several small curved ovules are attached. The malformed flowers did not present anything peculiar in their outer parts, nor did the ovary, partially immersed within the expanded top of the flower-stalk and the calyx-tube, which is continuous with that organ, show externally any indication of the change within. On cutting it across, however, in any direction, numerous perfect stamens (filaments and anthers) were seen projecting from the walls of the cavity (fig. 98). In most of the flowers the ovary was one-celled; but in a few there was the usual axile placenta; yet even in these latter cases the stamens originated from the walls of the cavity, and not from the placenta. The stamens presented different degrees of development; in some cases they were fully formed, the anther-lobes open, and the pollen exposed; while in other instances the[Pg 184]filaments were involute or circinate, just as the ordinary stamens are in the unexpanded flower-bud. In some cases imperfect stamens were found, mere barren filaments, with or without rudimentary anthers at the top. In no instance was there a perfect ovule, or, indeed, any trace of ovules. The stamens appeared to be arranged irregularly on the walls of the ovarian cavity; and while they were certainly more numerous at the lower portion (that now generally considered to be formed by the cup-like end of the pedicel), they were not wanting in the upper half of the ovary (or that which is probably formed from the carpellary leaves).

FIG. 98.—1. Vertical section of flower of *Bæckea diosmæfolia*, showing stamens within the ovary; magnified ten times. 2. Transverse section of ovary. 3. Stamen. 4. Imperfect stamen.

This case differs from most that have been recorded, and in which there has been a more or less complete substitution of anther for carpel, or where the tissues of the carpel have produced pollen, and so taken upon themselves the appearance and functions of anthers. Instances of this latter kind are not uncommon; but in the *Bæckea* there were perfect stamens proceeding[Pg 185] from perfect and completely closed ovaries. Moquin-Tandon[183] cites from Agardh an instance which seems more closely to resemble the state of things in the *Bæckea*, and which occurred in a double hyacinth, wherein both anthers and ovules were borne on the same placenta. Probably, though the fact is not stated, the ovary of the hyacinth was open; and we are told that the flower was double—that it was, in fact, modified and changed in more organs than one; while in the *Bæckea* nothing at all unusual was observed till the ovary was cut open. The style was present even in those flowers where there was no axile placenta; hence in these cases it could not be, as Lindley stated it to be in the closely allied *Babingtonia*, a prolongation of the placenta.[184]

Formation of pollen within the ovules.—This has now been recorded in two instances by Mr. S. J. A. Salter in *Passiflora cærulea* and in *P. palmata*,[185] and by the author in *Rosa arvensis*.[186]

FIG. 99.—**Pollen within the ovule of *Passiflora*** (after Salter).

In the case of the passion-flower there were various malformations in the ovaries, which were all more or[Pg 186] less split open at the distal end, indicating a tendency towards dialysis. The pollen-bearing ovules were borne on the edges of these ovaries, and presented various intermediate conditions between anthers and ovules, commencing at the distal extremity of the carpel with a bi-lobed anther, and passing in series to the base of the ovary, an antheroid body of ovule-like form, a modified ovule containing pollen, an ovule departing from a perfectly natural condition only in the development of a few grains of pollen in its nucleus, and, finally, a perfect, normal ovule.

In the flowers of the Rose the stamens exhibited almost every conceivable gradation between their ordinary form and that of the carpels, while some of the ovules contained pollen in greater or less abundance. Speaking generally, the most common state of things in these flowers was the occurrence on the throat of the calyx, in the position ordinarily occupied by the stamens, and sometimes mingled with those organs, of twisted, ribbon-like filaments, which bore about the centre one or more pendulous, anatropous ovules on their margins. Immediately above the latter organs were the anther-lobes, more or less perfectly developed, and surmounting these a long style, terminating in a fringed, funnel-shaped stigma. Sometimes the ovules were perfect, at other times the nucleus protruded through the foramen, while in a third set the nucleus was included within the tegument, the ovules having in all respects their natural external conformation, containing, however, not only pollen-grains, but also a layer of those peculiar spheroidal cells, including a fibrous deposit, which are among the normal constituents of the anther. In one case, where the coat of the ovule was imperfect, and allowed the nucleus to protrude, the pollen was evidently contained within the central mass of the structure. In this instance the fibrous cells were not detected, these being only found in cases where the investment of the ovule was perfect; and hence it seems likely that the fibrous cells were part of the coat[Pg 187] of the ovule, while the pollen was formed within the nucleus. In no case was any trace of embryo sac to be seen.

The main interest, as Mr. Salter remarks, in these cases is physiological; so far as structure alone is concerned, there does not appear any reason why pollen-grains should not be developed in any portion of the plant; the mother cells in which the pollen is formed not differing, to all outward appearance, from any other cells, unless it be in size.

The fundamental unity of construction in all the organs of plants could hardly be better illustrated than by these cases; while, in spite of their exceptional nature, they must be of great interest physiologically, as showing the wide limits of possible variation which thus may even involve the sex, "for an ovule to develop pollen within its interior," says Mr. Salter, "is equivalent to an ovum in an animal being converted into a capsule of spermatozoa. It is a conversion of germ into sperm, the most complete violation of individuality and unity of sex. * * * * The occurrence of an antheroid ovule and a normal ovule on the same carpellary leaf realises the simplest and the most absolute form of hermaphroditism."

It must, however, be remarked that the term substitution would be preferable to conversion. There is, at present, no evidence to show that the germinal vesicles were present in these cases; on the other hand, it seems most probable that they were not, so that the presence of the pollen-cells must be considered as simply adventitious. It can hardly be that they were, in the first instance, germinal vesicles, which, in course of time, became so modified as to assume the appearance of pollen-grains. Between the nucleus of the ovule and the tubercle of cellular tissue constituting the primordial anther, there is little or no difference, so that it may be said that, for a time, there is no distinction of sex in the nascent flower, but as development goes on, the difference becomes perceptible.[Pg 188] It cannot at present be stated what precise circumstances induce the one mass to form mother-cells and

90

pollen-grains, and the other to develop an embryo sac and germinal vesicles. Position and external circumstances may have some indirect effect, and it may, perhaps, be significant that in all the instances of polliniferous ovules, the ovular structures have been exposed on an open carpel or otherwise, in place of being confined within the cavity of a closed ovary, as under ordinary circumstances. Even among Conifers the ovuligerous scales are so closely packed that there is little or no exposure of the ovules. But, apart from all speculative notions as to the relation between the structure and functions of the anther and of the ovule respectively, and of the possibility or the reverse of parthenogenesis, it will clearly be necessary in any future alleged occurrence of the latter phenomenon to ascertain whether any or all of the apparent ovules are, or are not, anthers in disguise.

Homomorphic flowers of "Compositæ."—In a large section of the *Compositæ* there is, as is well known, a distinction between the florets of the "disc" and those of the "ray," the latter being ligulate, the former tubular.

In what are erroneously called double flowers in this order, *e.g.* in the Chrysanthemum, Dahlia, &c. &c., the florets are all ligulate. This change is sometimes classed with peloria, but there is no abnormal regularity in these cases. On the other hand, were the ligulate florets to be all replaced by tubular ones, the term peloria would be more strictly applicable. It will be remembered that in the sub-order *Ligulifloræ*, the florets are naturally all ligulate, so that the change above mentioned is not in itself a very grave one.

Heterotaxy affecting the inflorescence.—Under the head of Prolification, Heterogamy, &c., various deviations from the normal inflorescence are alluded to. In this place, therefore, it is only necessary to mention certain rare[Pg 189] deviations from the customary arrangement of the inflorescence, such as the change from a definite centrifugal form of inflorescence to an indefinite centripetal one. This occurs occasionally in roses, where the shoot, instead of terminating in a flower-bud, lengthens and bears the flower-bud on its sides as in a raceme.

In the hyacinth, the inflorescence of which is properly indefinite, the terminal flower may frequently be found to expand first, though in order of development it may have been the last formed.

It occasionally happens that certain plants will, contrary to their usual custom, bloom twice in the same season; this usually arises from the premature development of buds which, under ordinary circumstances, would not unfold till the following spring. In these instances of what the French term "fleuraison anticipée," the position of inflorescence is not changed, but there are other cases where the position of the inflorescence is altered, as in the laburnum, where, in some seasons, racemes may be seen springing from short lateral "spurs" along the sides of the branches, as well as from the extremities of long shoots.

Of a similar nature are those cases wherein stems or branches usually sterile become fertile; this happens in *Equisetaceæ*,[187] in *Restiaceæ*, and other orders. In the equisetums, the condition in question has been specially noticed to occur after prolonged drought.

Equisetaceæ are likewise subject to an anomaly called by Duval Jouve interruption of the spike, and wherein the scales bearing the spore cases are separated by whorls of branches instead of forming one compact unbroken spike as usual.

This alternation of the organs of vegetation and reproduction may also be seen occasionally in *Typha*, and other plants.

Kirschleger describes a case in which the male catkins of *Salix cinerea* were placed at the ends of the[Pg 190] branches instead of being lateral productions; moreover the usual articulation was not formed, so that the catkin was persistent instead of deciduous.[188]

Supra-soriferous ferns.—In the great majority of ferns the sori or clusters of spore cases are placed on the under surface of the fronds; nevertheless, a few cases are on record where the fructification is produced on the upper as well as on the lower surface, and sometimes abundantly so. This occasionally happens from the elongation of the normally placed sorus, which thus extends to the margin, and returns on the upper side, when the sori chance to be placed opposite to the marginal crenatures. But it is also frequently the case that the sori are produced on the upper side, distinctly within the margin, and where there are no corresponding sori beneath. Those varieties which have the margin crenated or lobed seem most liable to assume this abnormal supra-soriferous condition. Among the ferns in

91

which this condition has been observed are the following: *Scolopendrium vulgare, Polypodium anomalum,* Hook., *Asplenium Trichomanes,Cionidium Moorei.*[189]

FOOTNOTES:

[147]'Gard. Chron.' 1852, p. 51.

[148]'Flora.' 1858, pp. 32–42.

[149]'Journ. Linn. Soc.,' vol. vi; "Botany," 1862, p. 24.

[150]'Tijdschrift voor Natuur. Geschied,' 1836, vol. iii, tab. vii, p. 171.

[151]Rœper, 'Enum. Euphorb.,' p. 19. Bernhardi, 'Linnæa,' vii, p. 561, tab. xiv, f. 1. Wydler, "Subcotyled. sprossbildung," 'Flora,' 1850, p. 337. Hooker, 'Trans. Linn. Soc.,' vol. xxiv, p. 20 (*Welwitschia*).

[152]'Misc. Austriac. ad Bot.,' vol. i, p. 133, t. 5.

[153]See also Carrière, 'Revue Horticole,' 1866, p. 442; and as to pears, Radlkofer in 'Bericht über die Thätigkert der Baierischen Gartenbau Gesellschaft,' 1862, p. 74, t. i.

[154]'Flora Indica,' p. 23.

[155]'Bull. Soc. Bot. Fr.,' 1856, p. 53.

[156]'Trans. Linn. Soc.' xxvi, p. 142, tab. iv, B.

[157]"Si arbusculam, quæ in ollâ antea posita, quotannis floruit et fructus protulit, deinde deponamus in uberiori terra calidi caldarii, proferet illa per plures annos multos ac frondosos ramos, sine ullo fructu. Id quod argumento est, folia inde crescere, unde prius enati sunt flores; quemadmodum vicissim, quod in folia nunc succrescit, id, naturâ ita moderante, in flores mutatur, si eadem arbor iterum in ollâ seritur."—Linnæus, 'Prolepsis,' § iii.

[158]'Rev. Hortic.' May, 1868, 'Gardeners' Chronicle,' 1868, pp. 572, 737.

[159]Cited in 'Annals Nat. Hist.,' 1845, vol. xv, p. 177.

[160]'Ann. Scienc. Nat.,' vol. xiv, 1860, p. 13.

[161]Naudin, 'Ann. Sc. Nat.,' 2nd ser., 1840, vol. xiv, p. 14, fig. 6, pl. i (*Drosera*). St. Hilaire, 'Comptes Rendus,' ix, p. 437.

[162]Hance, 'Hook. Journ. Botany,' 1849, vol. i, p. 141, pl. v.

[163]Booth, 'Gard. Chron.,' Jan. 1st, 1853, p. 4.

[164]Lindley, 'Theory of Horticulture,' ed. 2, p. 273.

[165]'Hook. Journ. of Botany,' 1852, iv, p. 206. See also the curious *Begonia gemmipara,* 'Hook. fil. Illust. Himal. Plant.,' t. xiv.

[166]'Phytanth.,' n. 36, *d.*

[167]'Ann. Scienc. Nat.,' 3rd series. 1853. vol. xix, p. 251, tab. 14.

[168]Carrière, 'Revue Horticole.' 1868, p. 184.

[169]'Gard. Chron.,' 1858, p. 556.

[170]1863, p. 556, &c.

[171]'Ann. Nat. Hist.,' 1845, vol. xvi, p. 355.

[172]See also Lindley, 'Veg. Kingd.,' p. 109 et 116*a*, where the views of Raspail, R. Brown, Mohl, Henslow, and others, are discussed.

[173]It has been observed that if a plant is supplied with copious nourishment the flowering-period is delayed; but that moderate or even scanty nourishment accelerates it. Goethe, 'Metam.,' § 30. See also Wolff, 'Theoria Generationis,' 1759; Linn. 'Prolepsis,' §§ 3 and 10.

[174]Moquin-Tandon, p. 384; also Lindl., 'Elements of Botany,' p. 65, fig. 130; "Theory of Horticulture," p. 86. 'Gard. Chron.,' 1851, p. 723; Irmish, 'Flora,' 1858, p. 38, &c.

[175]Caspary, 'Bull. Soc. Bot. Fr.,' vol. vi, 1859, p. 235; also Payer, ibid., vol. i, 1854. p. 283.

[176]Trécul, 'Ann. Sc. Nat.,' 2nd ser., vol. xx, p. 339.

[177]'Bull. Soc. Bot. Fr.,' vol. vii, 1858, p. 331.

[178]'Bull. Soc. Bot. Fr.,' vol. i. p. 306, vol. v, p. 115. 'Illustr. Hortic.,' xii, 1865, Misc. 79. 'Rev. Horticole,' 1860 p. 204, et 1867 p. 43.

[179]'Bull. Soc. Bot. Fr.,' 1858, p. 685.

[180]The structure of this flower is discussed at some length in a paper by the author on axillary prolification. 'Trans. Linn. Soc.,' vol. xxiii, p. 486, t. liv. fig. 3. See also 'Clos. Bull.

Soc. Bot. Fr.,' vol. v, 1855, p. 672. Seringe et Heyland, 'Bull. Bot.,' i, p. 8. 'Pallas Enum. Plant. Hort. Demidoff,' append, c, ic.

[181]'Adansonia,' i, 181.

[182]'Adansonia.' vol. iii, p. 351, tab. xii.

[183]'Elém. Térat. Végét.,' p, 218.

[184]Masters, 'Journ. Linn. Soc.,' vol. ix, 1866, p. 334.

[185]'Trans. Linn. Soc.,' vol. xxiv, p. 143. tab. xxiv.

[186]'Brit. Assoc. Report,' Dundee, 1867; and Seemann's 'Journal of Botany,' 1867, p. 319, tab. lxxii, figs. B 1–9.

[187]Duval Jouve, 'Hist. Equiset. France.' 1864, p. 154.

[188]'Flora,' t. xxiv, 1841, p. 340.

[189]Moore, 'Nature-Printed British Ferns,' 8vo edition, vol. ii. p. 135. tab. lxxxv, B, &c.

CHAPTER IV.
HETEROGAMY.

This term is here intended to apply to all those cases in which the arrangement of the sexual organs is different from what it is habitually. It is evident that in many instances there is no malformation, no monstrosity, but rather a restoration of organs habitually[Pg 191] suppressed, a tendency towards structural completeness rather than the reverse. It must be also understood that the following remarks apply to structural points only, and are not intended to include the question of function. The occurrence of heteromorphic unions renders it necessary to keep in mind that plants hermaphrodite as to structure are by no means necessarily so as to function.

The simplest case of this alteration in the relative position of the sexes is that which occurs in monœcious plants, where the male and female flowers have a definite position, but which in exceptional instances is altered.

Change in the relative position of male and female flowers may thus occur in any monœcious plant. Cultivated maize, *Zea Mays*, frequently exhibits alterations of this kind; under ordinary circumstances, the male inflorescence is a compound spike, occupying the extremity of the stem, while the female flowers are borne in simple spikes at a lower level, but specimens may now and then be found where the sexes are mixed in the same inflorescence; the upper branching panicle usually containing male flowers only, under these circumstances, bears female flowers also.[190] In like manner, but less frequently, the female inflorescence occasionally produces male flowers as well.

Among the species of *Carex* it is a common thing for the terminal spike to consist of male flowers at the top, and female flowers at the base; the converse of this, where the female flowers are at the summit of the spike, is much more uncommon. An illustration of this occurrence is given in the figure (fig. 100). Among the *Coniferæ* numerous instances have been recorded of the presence of male and female flowers on the same spike, thus Mr. now Professor Alexander Dickson exhibited at the Botanical Society of Edinburgh[Pg 192] in July, 1860, some malformed cones of *Abies excelsa*, in which the inferior part of the axis was covered with stamens, whilst the terminal portion produced bracts and scales like an ordinary female cone. The stamens of the lower division were serially continuous with the bracts above. Some of the lower scales of the female portion were in the axils of the uppermost stamens, which last were somewhat modified, the anther cells being diminished, whilst the scale-like crest had become more elongated and pointed, in fact, more or less resembling the ordinary bracts.[191] Mohl, Schleiden, and A. Braun have observed similar cones in *Pinus alba*, and Cramer figures and describes androgynous cones in *Larix microcarpa*. C. A. Meyer ('Bull. Phys. Math.,' t. x, 1850) also describes some catkins of *Alnus fruticosa* which bore male flowers at the top, and female flowers at the base.

FIG. 100.—Spike of *Carex acuta*, with female flowers at the summit.

On the subject of this section the reader may consult A. Braun,. 'Das Individ.,' 1853, p. 65. Caspary, 'De Abietin. flor. fem. struct. morphol.' Schleiden. 'Principles,' English edition, p. 299. Mohl, 'Verm. Schrift.,' p. 45. Meyen in 'Wiegm. Archiv.,' 1838, p. 155.

Cramer, 'Bildungsabweich,' p. 4, tab. v, figs. 13–17. Parlatore, 'Ann. Sc. Nat.,' ser. iv, vol. xvi, p. 215, tab. 13A. See also under the head of Prolification, Substitutions, &c.

[Pg 193]

Change from the monœcious to the diœcious condition.—This is of less frequent occurrence than might have been anticipated. In the 'Gardeners' Chronicle,' 1847, pp. 541 and 558, several instances are noted of walnut trees bearing female flowers to the exclusion of males. The mulberry tree has also been noticed to produce female blossoms only, while in other plants male flowers only are developed.

It seems probable that the age of the plant may have something to do with this production of flowers of one sex to the exclusion of the other.

Change from the diœcious to the monœcious condition.—Androgynism.—This is of far more common occurrence than the preceding.

FIG. 101.—Monœcious inflorescence of Hop.

In the hop (*Humulus Lupulus*), when monœcious, the female catkins are usually borne on the ends of the branches as shown in the cut (fig. 101), and a similar[Pg 194] thing has been noticed in *Urtica dioica* by Clos, 'Bull. Soc. Bot. France,' vol. 9, p. 7.

Baillon ('Etudes du groupe des Euphorbiacées,' p. 205) mentions the following species of that order as having been seen by him with monœcious inflorescence: *Schismatopera distichophylla, Mozinna peltata, Hermesia castaneifolia.* Oliver mentions ('Hook. Icon. Plant.,' t. 1044) that in *Leitneria floridana* the upper scales of the male catkin occasionally subtend an ovary.

It would seem that external conditions have some effect in determining the formation of one sex, as in some species of *Carex*, while in the case of *Salix repens*, Hampe[192] says that when grown partially or for a time under water, those twigs which are thrust up above the surface bear female flowers, while those twigs that blossom after the water is dried up, produce male flowers only.

Carrière[193] says that a plant of *Stauntonia latifolia* which for some years produced stamens only, now produces flowers of both sexes; it was diœcious, but is now monœcious. The same author alludes to a similar occurrence in *Juniperus Virginiana.* The hops is also said to vary in sexual characteristics from time to time.[194] In addition to the genera, already named, in which this production of flowers of both sexes has been observed may be mentioned *Taxus! Gunnera! Urtica! Mercurialis! Restio! Cannabis! Salix! Humulus!* as well as others in which the change is less frequent.

Among cryptogams a similar change occurs. As an illustration may be cited *Leucobryum giganteum*, as quoted from Müller in Henfrey's 'Botanical Gazette,' i, p. 100.

As to androgynous willows, in addition to the references given under the head of Substitution of stamens for pistils, see Schlechtendal, 'Flora[Pg 195]Berol.,' ii. p. 259. Tausch, 'Bot. Zeit.,' 1833, i. p. 229. Koch, 'Synops. Flor. Germ.,' 740. Host, 'Flor. Aust,.' ii, p. 641 (*S. mirabilis*). See also Hegelmaier, 'Württemberg Naturwissenshaft Jahreshefte,' 1866, p. 30. Other references to less accessible works are given in 'Linnæa,' xiv, p. 372.

Change from hermaphroditism to unisexuality.—Many flowers ordinarily hermaphrodite as to structure, become unisexual by the abortion or suppression of their stamens, or of their carpels, as the case may be. This phenomenon is lessened in interest since the demonstration of the fact by Darwin and others, that many plants, structurally hermaphrodite, require for the full and perfect performance of their functions the cooperation of the stamens and pistils, belonging to different individuals of the same species.

Some of the *Ranunculaceæ* constantly exhibit a tendency towards the diœcious condition, and the rarity with which perfect seeds of *Ranunculus Ficaria* are formed is to be attributed, in great measure, to the deficiency of pollen in the anthers of these flowers. *Ranunculus auricomus* also is frequently sterile. Specimens of *Ranunculus bulbosus* may be met with in which every flower is furnished with carpels, most of which have evidently been fertilised, although there are no perfect stamens in the flowers.

Knight and other vegetable physiologists have been of opinion that a high temperature favours the production of stamens, while a lower degree of heat is considered more favorable to the production of pistils, and in this way the occurrence of "blind" strawberries has been accounted for. Mr. R. Thompson, writing on this subject, speaks of a plantation of Hautbois strawberries which in one season were wholly sterile, and accounts for the circumstance as follows: the plants were taken from the bearing beds the year previous, and were planted in a rich well-manured border, in which they started rapidly into too great luxuriance, the growth being to leaves rather than to fruit. The following season these same plants bore[Pg 196] a most abundant crop, hence these plants were accidentally prevented from perfecting their female organs.[195]

Mr. Darwin[196] cites from various sources the following details relating to strawberries which it may be useful to insert in this place, as throwing some light upon the production of unisexual flowers. "Several English varieties, which in this country are free from any such tendency, when cultivated in rich soils under the climate of North America commonly produce plants with separate sexes. Thus, a whole acre of Keen's seedlings in the United States has been observed to be almost sterile in the absence of male flowers; but the more general rule is, that the male plants over-run the females.... The most successful cultivators in Ohio plant, for every seven rows of pistillate flowers, one row of hermaphrodites, which afford pollen for both kinds; but the hermaphrodites, owing to their expenditure in the production of pollen, bear less fruit than the female plants."

Stratiotes aloides has been said to produce its carpels with greater abundance towards the northern limits of its geographical distribution, and its stamens, on the other hand, are stated to be more frequently developed in more southern districts.

Honckenya peploides affords another illustration of the sexual arrangements in the flower being altered as it would seem by climatal conditions. Thus, in the United States, according to Professor Asa Gray, the flowers are frequently hermaphrodite, while in this country they are usually sub-diœcious.[197]

Treviranus[198] says that the flowers of *Hippuris* and *Callitriche* are apt to be hermaphrodite in summer, but female only at a later period.

For further remarks on this subject, see sections relating to suppression of stamens and pistils.

[Pg 197]

Change from unisexuality to hermaphroditism.—This occurrence depends on one of two causes, either organs are developed (stamens or pistils as the case may be), which are habitually absent in the particular flower; or some of the stamens may be more or less completely converted into or replaced by pistils, or *vice versâ*.

The first condition is the opposite of suppression; it is, as it were, a restoration of symmetry, and might be included under the head of regular peloria, inasmuch as certain organs which habitually undergo suppression at a certain stage in their development, by exception, go on growing, and produce a perfect, instead of an imperfect flower. In teratological records it is not always stated clearly to which of the two above-named causes the unusual hermaphroditism belongs, though it is generally easy to ascertain this point. Very many, perhaps all, diclinous flowers may, under certain conditions, become perfect, at least structurally. I have myself seen hermaphrodite flowers in *Cucurbita*,[199] *Mercurialis*, *Cannabis*, *Zea Mays*, and *Aucuba japonica*, as well as in many *Restiaceæ*, notably *Cannamois virgata* and *Lepyrodia hermaphrodita*. *Spinacia oleracea*,*Rhodiola rosea*, *Cachrys taurica*, and *Empetrum nigrum* are also occasionally hermaphrodite.

Gubler[200] alludes to a similar occurrence in *Pistacia Lentiscus*, wherein, however, he adds that there was a deficiency of pollen in the flowers.

Schnizlein[201] observed hermaphrodite flowers in the beech, *Fagus sylvatica*, the ovaries being smaller than usual, and the stamens epigynous.

Baillon[202] enumerates the following *Euphorbiaceæ* as having exceptionally produced hermaphrodite flowers,[Pg 198] *Crozophora tinctoria*,*Suregada* sp., *Phyllanthus longifolius*, *Breynia* sp., *Philyra brasiliensis*,*Ricinus communis*, *Conceveiba macrophylla*, *Cluytia semperflorens*, *Wall*, non *Roxb. Mercurialis annua* and *Cleistanthus polystachyus*.

In some of these cases the hermaphroditism is due to the development of anthers on the usually barren staminodes, though, in other cases, the stamens would seem to be separate, independent formations, as they do not occupy the same relative position that the ordinary stamens would do if developed.[203]

95

FIG. 102.—Flower of *Fuchsia* in which the calyx was leafy, the petals normal (reflexed in the figure), the stamens partially converted into ovaries, the ordinary inferior ovary being absent. See Substitution.

Robert Brown[204] observed stamens within the utricle of *Carex acuta*, and Gay is stated by Moquin ('El. Ter.[Pg 199] Veg.,' p. 343) to have observed a similar occurrence in *Carex glauca*.

Paasch[205] observed a similar occurrence in *C. cæspitosa*, and Schauer, in *C. paludosa*,[206] though in the latter instance the case seems to have been one of transformation or substitution rather than one of hermaphroditism.

The second cause of this pseudo-hermaphroditism is due either to the more or less perfect mutation of male and female organs, or it may be to the complete absence of one and its replacement by another, as when out of many stamens, one or more are deficient, and their places occupied by carpels. This happens very frequently in willows and poplars, and has been seen in the beech.[207]

FIG. 103.—Hermaphrodite flower of *Carica Papaya*.

In *Begonia frigida*[208] the anomaly is increased by the position of the ovaries above, the perianth, a position due, not to any solution or detachment of the latter from the former, but simply to the presence of ovaries where, under ordinary circumstances, stamens only are[Pg 200] formed, as happened also in a garden variety of a *Fuchsia*, wherein, however, the change was less perfect than in the *Begonia*, and in which, as the flower is naturally hermaphrodite, the alteration is of the less importance.

FIG. 104.—Ovuliferous anthers—*Cucurbita*.

In hermaphrodite flowers of *Carica Papaya* (fig. 103) there is a single row of five stamens instead of two rows of five each as in the normal male flowers, the position of the second or inner row of stamens being occupied by five carpels, which, however, are not adherent to the corolla as the stamens are, thus, supposing the[Pg 201] arrangement of parts in the normal male flowers to be as follows:

```
--------------------------    S  S  S  S    --------------------------    |  p  p
p  p  p    |    | st st st st st    |    | st st st st st    |
```

That of the hermaphrodite blossoms would be, in brief, as follows:

```
| 5  S  |------------  | 5    p  |    | 5  st  |    | 5    c  |
```

One of the most curious cases of this kind recorded is one mentioned by Mr. Berkeley,[209] wherein a large white-seeded gourd presented a majority of flowers in which the pollen was replaced by ovules. It would seem probable from the appearances presented by the figure that these ovules were, some of them, polliniferous, like those of the *Passiflora*, &c., described at p. 185, but nothing is stated on the subject.

See also section on Regular Peloria, Substitution, Pistillody of the stamens, &c.

FOOTNOTES:

[190]See also Clos., 'Mem. Acad. Toulouse,' sixth ser., t. iii, pp. 294–305. Scott, 'Trans. Bot. Soc. Edinburgh,' t. viii, p. 60. Wigand, 'Flora,' 1856, p. 707.

[191]Professor Dickson concludes from the examination of these structures that the male cone, consisting of simple stamens developed on one common axis, must be regarded as a simple male flower, while the axillary scales of the female cone are by him compared with the flattened shoots of *Ruscus*.

[192]'Linnæa,' xiv, 367.

[193]Rev. Hortic.,' January, 1867.

[194]See Royle, 'Man. Materia Medica,' ed. 1, p. 567.

[195]Thomson, 'Gardener's Assistant,' p. 577.

[196]'Variation of Animals and Plants,' i, 353.

[197]Babington, 'Ann. Nat. Hist.,' vol. ix, 1852, p. 156.

[198]'Phys. der Gewächse,' ii, p. 323.

[199]See also Schlechtendal, 'Linnæa,' viii, p. 623, and Lindley, 'Veg. Kingd.,' p. 315.

[200]'Bull. Soc. Bot. France,' vol. ix, p. 81.

[201]Cited in Henfrey, 'Bot. Gazette.' 3, p. 11.

[202]Baillon. 'Etudes du Groupe des Euphorbiacées,' p. 205, tab. xv, fig. 19, tab. xix, fig. 31.

[203]See also Guillemin, 'Mém. Soc. Nat. Hist. Paris,' I, p. 16; hermaphrodite flowers in *Euphorbia esula*.

[204]'Prod. Flor. N. Holl.,' p. 242.

[205]'Bot. Zeit.,' 1837, p. 335.

[206]'Pflanz, Terat.,' von Moquin-Tandon, p. 208.

[207]Schnizlein, loc. cit.

[208]'Bot. Mag.,' tab. 5160, fig. 4. See also 'Gard. Chron.,' 1860, pp. 146, 170; 1861, p. 1092.

[209]'Gard. Chron.,' 1851, p. 499.

CHAPTER V.
ALTERATIONS IN THE DIRECTION OF ORGANS.

The deviations from the ordinary direction of organs partake for the most part more of the nature of variations than of absolute malposition or displacement. It must also be borne in mind how frequently the direction of the leaves, or of the flower, varies according to the[Pg 202] stage of development which it has arrived at, to unequal or disproportionate growth of some parts, or to the presence of some impediment either accidental or resulting from the natural growth of the plant. These and other causes tend to alter the direction of parts very materially.

Change in the direction of axile organs, roots, stems, &c.—The roots frequently exhibit good illustrations of the effect of the causes above mentioned in altering the natural direction. The roots are put out of their course by meeting with any obstacle in their way. Almost the only exception to the rule in accordance with which roots descend under natural circumstances, is that furnished by *Trapa natans*, the roots of which in germination are directed upwards towards the surface of the water. So in *Sechium edule*, the seed of which germinates while still in the fruit, the roots are necessarily, owing to the inverted position of the embryo, directed upwards in the first instance.

A downward direction of the stem or branches occurs in many weak-stemmed plants growing upon rocks or walls, or in trees with very long slender branches as in *Salix Babylonica*, and the condition may often be produced artificially as in the weeping ash.

The opposite change occurs in what are termed fastigiate varieties, where the branches, in place of assuming more or less of a horizontal direction, become erect and nearly parallel with the main stem as in the Lombardy poplar, which is supposed to be merely a form of the black Italian poplar.

M. de Selys-Longchamps has described a similar occurrence in another species of Poplar (*P. virginiana* Desf.), and amongst a number of seedling plants fastigiate varieties may frequently be found, which may be perpetuated by cuttings or grafts, or sometimes even by seed; hence the origin of fastigiate varieties of elms, oaks, thorns, chestnuts, and other plants which may be met with in the nurseries.

[Pg 203]

Sometimes when the top of the main stem is destroyed by disease or accident, one of the heretofore lateral shoots takes its place, and continues the development of the tree in the original direction. It is often an object with the gardener to restore the symmetry of an injured tree so that its beauty may ultimately not be impaired.[210]

Climate appears sometimes to have some influence[Pg 204] on the direction of branches, thus Dr. Falconer, as quoted by Darwin,[211] relates that in the hotter parts of India "the English Ribston-pippin apple, a Himalayan oak, a Prunus and a Pyrus all assume a fastigiate or pyramidal habit, and this fact is the more interesting as a Chinese tropical species of *Pyrus* naturally has this habit of growth. Nevertheless many of the fastigiate varieties seen in gardens have originated in this country by variation of seeds or buds."

M. Carrière has also recorded a curious circumstance with reference to the fastigiate variety of the false acacia *Robinia pseudacacia*; he states that if a cutting or a graft be taken from the upper portion of the tree, the fastigiate habit will be reproduced, and the branches will be furrowed and covered with short prickles; but if the plant be multiplied by detaching portions of the root-stock, then instead of getting a pyramidal tree with erect branches, a spreading bushy shrub is produced, with more or less horizontal, cylindrical branches, destitute of prickles.[212]

Eversion of the axis.—In the case of the fig, the peculiar inflorescence is usually explained on the supposition that the termination of the axis becomes concave, during growth, bearing the true flowers in the hollow thus formed. The cavity in this case would probably be due not to any real process of excavation, but to a disproportionate growth of the outer as contrasted with the central parts of the fig. Some species of *Sempervivum* have a similar mode of growth, so that ultimately a kind of tube is formed, lined by the leaves, the central and innermost being the youngest. The hip of the Rose may be explained in a similar manner by the greater proportionate growth of the outer as contrasted with the central portions of the apex of the flower-stalk. In cases of median prolification, already referred to, the process is reversed, the central portions[Pg 205] then elongate into a shoot and no cavity is formed. A fig observed by Zuccarini (figs. 105, 106) appears to have been formed in a similar manner, the flower-bearing summit of the stalk not being contracted as usual, the flowers projected beyond the orifice of the fig. If this view be correct the case would be one rather of lengthening of the axis than of absolute eversion since it was never inverted.

FIG. 105.—Fig showing prolonged inflorescence and projecting flowers.

FIG. 106.—Section of the same.

Altered direction of leaves.—The leaves partake more or less of the altered direction of the axis, as in fastigiate elms, but this is not universally the case, for though the stem is bent downwards the leaves may be placed in the opposite direction; thus in some specimens of *Galium Aparine* growing on the side of a cliff from which there had been a fall of chalk, the stems, owing apparently to the landslip, were pendent, but the leaves were abruptly bent upwards.

One of the most singular instances of an inverted[Pg 206] direction of the leaves is that presented by a turnip (fig. 107) presented to the Museum of King's College, London, by the late Professor Edward Forbes. The turnip is hollow in the interior and the majority of the leaves springing from its apex instead of ascending into the light and air become bent downwards so as to occupy the cavity, and in such a manner as to bring to mind the position of an inverted embryo in a seed.

FIG. 107.—Hollow turnip, showing some of the leaves inverted and occupying the cavity.

Altered direction of the flower and its parts.—The changes which take place in the relative position either of the flower as a whole or of its several parts during growth are well known, as also are the relations which some of these movements bear to the process of fertilisation, so that but little space need here be given to the subject beyond what is necessary to point out the frequent changes of direction which necessarily accompany[Pg 207] various deviations from the ordinary form and arrangement of parts.

In cases where an habitually irregular flower becomes regular, the change in form is frequently associated with an alteration in direction both of the flower as a whole and, to a greater or less extent, of its individual members, for instance of *Gloxinia*, the normal flowers of which are irregular and pendent, there is now in common cultivation a peloriate race in which the flowers are regular in form and erect in position.

FIG. 108.—Flower of normal *Gloxinia*.

FIG. 109.—Flower of *Gloxinia*, erect and regular (regular *Peloria*).

Fig. 108 shows the usual irregular form of *Gloxinia*, with which may be contrasted figs. 109, 110 and 111.

[Pg 208]

Fig. 109 shows the regular erect form; fig. 110 the calyx of the same flower; while in fig. 111 are shown the stamens and style of the two plants respectively. In the upper figure the style of the peloriate variety is shown as nearly straight, and the stamens undergo a corresponding change. No doubt the relative fertility and capacity for impregnation of the two varieties is affected in proportion to the change of form. The Gloxinia affords an instance of regular congenital peloria in which the regularity of form and the erect direction are due to an arrest, not of growth, but of development, in consequence of which the changes that ordinarily ensue during the progress of the flower from its juvenile to its fully formed condition do not take place.

FIG. 110.—Calyx of erect *Gloxinia*.

FIG. 111.—Stamens of erect regular, and of pendent irregular-flowered *Gloxinia*.

A similar alteration accompanies this form of peloria in other flowers (see Peloria). A change in direction may result also from other circumstances than those just alluded to. Abortion or suppression of organs will induce such an alteration; thus in a flower of *Pelargonium* now before me three of the five carpels, from some cause or other, are abortive and much smaller than usual, and the style and the beak-like[Pg 209] torus are bent downwards towards the stunted carpels instead of being, as they usually are, straight.

Amongst orchids, where the pedicel of the flower or the ovary is normally twisted, so that the labellum occupies the anterior or inferior part of the flower, it frequently happens, in cases of peloria and other changes, that the primitive position is retained, the twist does not take place, and so with other resupinate flowers. In Azaleas a curious deflexion of the parts of the flower may occasionally be met with. Fig. 112 shows an instance of this in which the corolla, the stamens and the style were abruptly bent downwards: as young flowers of this singular variety have not been examined it is difficult to form an opinion as to the cause of this variation. In one plant the change occurred in connection with the suppression of all the flowers but one in the cluster, or rather the place of the flowers was occupied by an equal number of leafy shoots.

FIG. 112.—Flower of *Azalea*, showing the corolla reflected.

Moquin[213] mentions a flower of *Rosa alpina* in which two of the petals were erect, while the remaining ones were much larger and expanded horizontally. The same author quotes from M. Desmoulins the case of a species of *Orobanche*, in which a disjunction of the petals constituting the upper lip took place, thus liberating[Pg 210] the style and allowing it to assume a vertical direction.

FIG. 113.—Flower of *Cuphea miniata* enlarged, showing protrusion and hypertrophy of an erect placenta, after Morren.

FIG. 114.—Placenta from the flower shown at fig. 113; the ovary is membranous and torn, the placenta, erect and ovuliferous, after Morren.

M. Carrière[214] has described an instance wherein two apples were joined together, a larger and a smaller one; the former was directed away from the centre of the tree as usual, while the smaller one was pointed in exactly the opposite direction. The larger fruit had the[Pg 211] customary parchment-like carpels, the smaller was destitute of them.

Sometimes the direction assumed by one flower as an abnormal occurrence is the same as that which is proper to an allied species or genus under natural circumstances; thus flowers of the vine (*Vitis*) have been met with in which the petals were spreading like a star (*fleurs avalidouires*), as in the genus *Cissus*.[215]

Morren describes a curious condition in some flowers of *Cuphea miniata*, in which the placenta protruded through an orifice in the ovary, and losing the horizontal direction became erect (figs. 113, 114). A similar occurrence happened in *Lobelia erinus*. To this condition the Belgian savant gave the name of gymnaxony.[216]

FOOTNOTES:

[210]The following details as to the method pursued by Mr. McNab, of the Edinburgh Botanic Garden, may not be uninteresting in this place. They are from the pen of Mr. Anderson, and originally appeared in the 'Gardeners' Chronicle.'

"The mode of inducing leaders to proceed from laterals is a matter of comparatively little concern among the generality of deciduous trees, for they are often provided with subsidiary branches around the leader, at an angle of elevation scarcely less perpendicular, but the laterals of all Conifers stand, as nearly as possible, at right angles. Imagine the consternation of most people when the leader of, say, *Picea nobilis, P. Nordmanniana*, or *P. Lowii* is destroyed."

In a specimen of the latter plant the leader had been mischievously destroyed, to remedy which Mr. McNab adopted means which Mr. Anderson goes on to describe. "Looking from the leader downward to the first tier of laterals, there appeared to have been a number of adventitious leaf-buds created, owing to the coronal bud being destroyed. These were allowed to plump up unmolested until the return of spring, when every one was scarified or rubbed off but the one nearest the extremity. To assist its development and restrain the action of the numerous laterals, every one was cut back in autumn, and this restraint upon the sap acted so favorably upon the incipient leader as to give it the strength and stamina of the original leader, so that nothing detrimental was evident twelve months after the accident had happened, and only a practical eye could detect that there had been any mishap at all. This beautifully simple process saved the baby tree.

"Another example of retrieving lost leaders may be quoted as illustrative of many in similar circumstances. *Picea Webbiana* had its leader completely destroyed down to the first tier of laterals. There was no such provision left for inducing leaf-buds as was the case with *P. Lowii* above referred to. Resort must, therefore, be had to one of the best favoured laterals, but how is it to be coaxed from the horizontal position of a lateral to the perpendicular position of a leader? The uninitiated in these matters, and, in fact, practical gardeners generally, would at once reply, by supporting to a stake with the all-powerful Cuba or bast-matting. But no. A far simpler method than that, namely, by fore-shortening all the laterals of the upper tier but the one selected for a leader. Nature becomes the handmaid of art here; for without the slightest prop the lateral gradually raises itself erect, and takes the place of the lost leader. All that the operator requires to attend to is the amputation of the laterals until this adventitious fellow has gained a supremacy. Singular provision in nature this, which, thanks to the undivided attention of a careful observer, has been fully appreciated and utilized."

[211]'Variation of Animals and Plants,' ii, p. 277.

[212]Quoted in 'Gard. Chron.,' 1867, p. 654.

[213]Loc. cit., p. 315.

[214]'Rev. Hortic.,' 1868, p. 110.

[215]Planchon and Marès, 'Ann. Sc. Nat.,' 5 ser., tom. vi, 1866, p. 228, tab. xii.

[216]'Bull. Acad. Belg.,' xviii, part ii, p. 293.

[Pg 212]

[Pg 213]

BOOK II.
DEVIATIONS FROM THE ORDINARY FORM OF ORGANS.

In a morphological point of view the form of the various parts or organs of plants and the changes to which they are subjected during their development are only second in importance to the diversities of arrangement and, indeed, in some cases, do not in any degree hold a second place.

Taken together, the arrangement, form, and number of the several parts of the flower, make up what has been termed the symmetry of the flower.[217] Referring to the assumed standard of comparison, see p. 4, it will be seen that in the typically regular flower all the various organs are supposed to be regular in their dimensions and form. At one time it was even supposed that all flowers, no matter how irregular they[Pg 214] subsequently became, began by being strictly symmetrical or regular, and that subsequent alterations were produced by inequality of growth or development. The researches of organogenists have, however, dispelled this idea of unvarying primordial regularity, by showing that in many cases flowers are irregular from the very first, that some begin by being irregular, and subsequently become regular, and even in some cases resume their original condition during the course of their development.[218] Under these circumstances an artificial standard of comparison becomes almost an absolute necessity for the time being.

Changes of form very generally, but not always, are accompanied with a change in regularity: thus a flower habitually bi-lateral may assume the characters of radiating symmetry and *vice versâ*. Increase or decrease of size very frequently also are co-existent with an alteration in the usual form.

In the case of the arrangement of organs it is often difficult or impossible, in the present state of our knowledge, to determine whether a given arrangement is congenital or acquired subsequently to the first development, whether for instance an isolation of parts be due to primordial separation or to a subsequent disunion of originally combined organs, see p. 58. With reference to the changes in the form of organs, however, it is in general more easy to ascertain the proximate cause of the appearance, and thus teratological changes of form may be grouped according as they are due to, 1, arrest of development; 2, undue or excessive development; 3, perverted development; and 4, irregular development; hence the use of the following[Pg 215] terms—Stasimorphy, Pleiomorphy, Metamorphy, and Heteromorphy—to include teratological changes really or apparently due to one or other of the causes above mentioned. The classification here adopted is of course to a considerable extent an arbitrary one and subject to correction or modification, as the knowledge of the development of the flowers in the various genera of plants advances.

FOOTNOTES:

[217]The word symmetry has been used in very different senses by different botanists, sometimes as synonymous with "regularity," at other times to express the assumed typical form of a flower. Payer understands it to be that arrangement of parts which permits of the whole flower being divided vertically into two symmetrical halves (bi-lateral symmetry). Others, again, have applied the term symmetry to the number of the parts of the flower, reserving the terms "regularity" or "irregularity" for the form. It is here used in a general sense to express the plan of the flower, and thus includes the arrangement, form, and number of its component elements.

[218]See Baillon, 'Adansonia,' v, 176.

[Pg 216]

PART I.

STASIMORPHY.[219]

Deviations from the ordinary form of organs arising from stasis or arrest of development are included under this heading.

There are many cases in which the forms proper to a juvenile condition of the plant are retained for a much longer period than ordinary, or even throughout the life of the individual growth goes on, but "development" is checked. Such conditions may even be propagated by seed or bud. It is a very general thing for botanists to consider these cases as reversions to a simpler, primitive type, and this may be so; but on the other hand, they may be degenerations from a complex type, or they may have no direct relation to any antecedent condition. Stasimorphic changes affecting principally the relative size of organs—such, for instance, as the non-development of internodes, or the atrophy or suppression of parts will be found mentioned in the sections relating to those subjects. In the present part those alterations which affect the form of organs principally are treated of.

FOOTNOTES:

[219]Στασις-μορφωσις.

[Pg 217]

CHAPTER I.

PERSISTENCE OF JUVENILE FORMS.

The retention in adult life of a form characteristic of an early stage of development, and therefore usually transient, may be manifested in any of the organs of the plant. As these cases are for the most part treated under separate headings, it is here only necessary to allude to a few, which it is difficult to allocate satisfactorily, while the reader may be referred for other instances of like nature to the sections on Peloria, Atrophy, Suppression, Dimorphy, Substitutions, &c.

FIG. 115.—*Juniperus sinensis*. **Two forms of leaves on branches of the same shrub.**

Stasimorphy in the leaves of conifers.—In many conifers the leaves produced in the young state of the plant are different, both in arrangement and form, from those subsequently developed (see pp. 89, 90). But it[Pg 218]occasionally happens that the plant continues to form throughout its existence leaves such as are usually produced only in a young state; thus M. Gubler ('Bull. Soc. Bot., Fr.,' vol. viii, 1861, p. 527) describes a plant of *Pinus pinea* in which the primordial, usually transitory, foliage was permanent, leaves of the ordinary shape not being developed at all. It more often happens that some only of the leaves retain their young form while others assume other shapes, see fig. 115. This happens frequently in the larch and constantly in the Chinese juniper when it has arrived at a considerable age. In *Cupressus funebris* two forms of leaves may often be found on the same plant, the one representing the juvenile state, the other the more developed condition. What is very singular, is that a cutting taken from the branch with leaves of the young form grows up into a shrub bearing leaves of no other shape, so that an ordinary observer unacquainted with the history of the plant would imagine that he had to deal with two distinct species. This fact is the more interesting when compared with the alternation of generations which takes place among the lower animals.

The regular development of all the parts of the flower in a plant habitually producing irregular flowers is referred to under the head of Peloria, but it still remains to consider those examples in which some only of the parts of the flower are affected in this manner.[220] Most of these cases are elsewhere referred to in this volume under the particular form of malformation assumed; but the following case may here be noticed as not coming under any of the previous heads. It is an instance recorded by Professor Babington ('Phytologist,' August, 1853), and in which the pod of*Medicago maculata*, which is usually rolled up like a snail shell and provided with spines, was sickle-shaped and unarmed.

FOOTNOTES:

[220]See a paper of Professor C. Morren's on "Floral Stesomy" in 'Bull. Acad. Belg.,' t. xix, part ii, p. 519.

[Pg 219]

CHAPTER II.

REGULAR PELORIA.

FIG. 116.—**Regular Peloria,** *Delphinium.*

FIG. 117.—**Sepal, petal, &c., of regular-flowered** *Delphinium.*

FIG. 118—**Regular peloria,** *Viola.*

FIG. 119—**Double Violet, flower regular, petals multiplied, stamens and pistils petaloid.**

When an habitually irregular flower becomes regular, it does so in one of two ways; either by the non-development of the irregular portions, or by the formation of irregular parts in increased number, so that the symmetry of the flower is rendered perfect, as in the original peloria of Linnæus, and which may be called irregular peloria, while the former case may be called regular peloria. This latter appearance is therefore congenital, and due to an arrest of development.[221] As the true nature of these cases has not been in all cases recognised (even Moquin places them under the head of deformities—they being less entitled to rank in that class than are the usual flowers), it may be well to cite a few instances taken from various families. In *Delphinium peregrinum* I have met with perfectly regular flowers having five sepals and five oblong stalked petals, and a similar occurrence has been noted[Pg 220] in other species of this genus. Baillon,[222] in referring to these flowers, points out the

102

resemblance that they bear to the double varieties of *Nigella*. In the stellate columbines (*Aquilegia*) of gardens the tubular petals are replaced by flat ones often in increased numbers. In violets both forms of peloria occur, that in which there is an unusual number of spurs, and that in which there are no spurs (var. anectaria). In the more perfect forms of regular peloria occurring in the last-named genus the following changes may be noticed: 1, an alteration in the direction of the flower so that it remains in an erect position, and is not bent downwards as usual; 2, equality of proportion in the sepals and petals; 3, absence of spurs, as also of[Pg 221] hairs on the lateral petals; 4, equal stamens whose anthers are sometimes entirely destitute of the prolonged crest which forms so prominent a feature under ordinary circumstances; 5, erect, not curved styles, and the stigmas not prolonged into a beak, but having a more or less capitate form; ovary with three or five cells, ovules normal.

These are cases where the change in question is most strongly marked, the bi-lateral is completely replaced by the radiating symmetry. The absence of the usual nectary, and of hairs on the side petals, the alterations in the form of the style, etc., all show how much the process of fertilisation must be altered from that which occurs under ordinary circumstances. In some of the double violets now cultivated in gardens, a similar regularity of proportion in the parts of the flower may be seen combined with the substitution of petals for stamens and pistils, and with the development of an increased number of petal-like organs.[223] Between these cases and the ordinary spurred forms as well as those with an increased number of spurs, many intermediate forms may be met with. That such regularity should occur in this family is not to be wondered at seeing that there is a whole subdivision of the order (*Alsodeiæ*) in which regular flowers are the rule.

In cultivated Pelargoniums the central flower of the umbel or "truss" frequently retains its regularity of proportion, so as closely to approximate to the normal condition in the allied genus *Geranium*; this resemblance is rendered greater by the fact that, under such circumstances, the patches of darker colour characteristic of the ordinary flower are completely wanting; the flower is as uniform in colour as in shape. Even the nectary which is adherent to the upper surface of the pedicel in the normal flower disappears—sometimes completely, at other tunes partially. The direction of the stamens and style, and even that of the whole flower, becomes[Pg 222]altered from the inclined to the vertical position. In addition to these changes, which are those most commonly met with, the number of the parts of the flower is sometimes augmented, and a tendency to pass from the verticillate to the spiral arrangement manifested. Schlechtendal mentions some flowers of *Tropæolum majus* in which the flowers were perfectly regular and devoid of spurs[224], while in the double varieties, now commonly grown in greenhouses, the condition of parts is precisely the same as in the double violet before alluded to. Among the *Papilionaceæ* the Laburnum and others have been noticed to produce occasionally a perfectly regular flower in the centre, or at the extremity of the inflorescence, though the peloria in this flower is usually irregular. In the Gentianaceous genus *Halenia*, *H. heterantha* is remarkable for the absence of spurs. Amongst *Gesneraceæ*, *Bignoniaceæ*, *Scrophulariaceæ*, and other families of like structure, regular peloria is not uncommon. Fig. 120 represents a case of this kind in *Eccremocarpus scaber*, conjoined, as is frequently the case, with dialysis or separation of the petals.[225] Many of the cultivated Gloxinias also show[Pg 223] erect, regular, five stamened flowers, but these are probably cases of irregular peloria.

FIG. 120.—Regular peloria, *Eccremocarpus scaber*.

A solitary flower of *Pedicularis sylvatica* was found by the Marquis of Stafford near Dunrobin Castle in Sutherlandshire, in which the usual ringent form of the corolla was replaced by the form called salver-shaped. There were six stamens, four long and two short. Sir W. Hooker and Mr. Borrer are stated to have found a similar flower in the same locality in 1809.[226]

The passage of ligulate to tubular corollas among *Compositæ* is not of such common occurrence as is the converse change. I owe to Mr. Berkeley the communication of a capitulum of a species of *Bidens*, in which there was a transition from the form of ligulate corollas to those that were deeply divided into three, four, or five oblong lobes. These then were instances of regular peloria.

103

FIG. 121.—Flower of *Cattleya marginata*. Lip replaced by a flat petal.

In *Orchidaceæ* a similar change is not by any means infrequent; in a few, indeed, a regular flower is the normal[Pg 224] character, as in *Dendrobium normale*, *Oncidium heteranthum*, *Thelymitra*, etc. Fig. 121, reduced from a cut in the 'Gardeners' Chronicle,' 1854, p. 804, represents an instance of this kind in *Cattleya marginata*.

From the same journal the following account of a case of peloria in *Phalænopsis Schilleriana* is also cited as a good illustration of this peculiar change. The terminal flower differed entirely from all the others; instead of the peculiar labellum there were three petals all exactly alike, and three sepals also exactly alike; the petals resembled those of the other flowers of the spike, and the upper sepal also; but the two lower sepals had no spots, and were not reflexed as in the ordinary way: thus, these six parts of the flower were all in one plane, and being close together at their edges, made almost a full round flower; the column and pollen-glands were unaffected. Professor Reichenbach also exhibited at the Amsterdam Botanical Congress, of 1865, a flower of *Selenipedium caudatum* with a flat lip.

M. Gris[227] has placed on record some interesting cases of peloria of this kind in *Zingiber zerumbet*; in the more complete forms the andrœcium or staminal series was composed of six distinct pieces, the three inner of which were fertile, while in the ordinary flower the andrœcium is composed of two pieces, "a lip" and a fertile stamen. "Is it not a matter of regret," says M. Gris, "to be obliged to call the latter the normal flower?"

Under this head may likewise be mentioned those cases in which the normal, or at least the typical symmetry of the flower is restored by the formation of parts usually suppressed; thus Moquin cites an abnormal flower of *Atriplex*[228] *hortensis* described by M. Fenzl as having a true calyx within the two bracts that usually alone encircle the stamens. Adanson, also cited by Moquin, found a specimen of *Bocconia* with a[Pg 225]corolla. *Arum maculatum* has likewise been met with provided with a genuine perianth as in *Acorus* and other Orontiads. The unusual development of the sexual organs in diclinous flowers has been alluded to under the head of heterogamy, and other cases where the symmetry of the flower is rendered regular, by the development of parts ordinarily suppressed, will be found in the chapters relating to deviations from the usual number of organs.

This change, or rather this persistence of a form that is usually transient, is generally accompanied by some other alterations. Change of direction, as has been already mentioned, is one of the most common of these; separation of the petals (*Antirrhinum*, *Verbascum*, &c.), and even their appearance in leaf-like guise, are not infrequent (*Delphinium*, *Antirrhinum*, *Verbascum*, &c.) At other times multiplication or increased number of the whorls of petals takes place, often, but not always, at the expense of the sexual organs of the flower. Perhaps even more frequent is the increased number of parts in the same whorl in cases of regular peloria; thus, in the Pelargoniums before alluded to, the parts of the flower are frequently regulated by the number six instead of five.

This form of peloria is most generally met with in flowers that are placed at the end or in the centre of the inflorescence, or in such flowers as occur singly at the end of the flower-stalk, as in *Tropæolum*, *Viola*, &c. It would hence seem as if the freedom from pressure or restriction on one side allowed the flower to develop equally in all directions, and thus to produce regularity of form.

It is obvious, from what has been before said, that the process of fertilisation is in many cases interfered with and altered by the change in the conformation or the flower.

From overlooking the occasional existence of this form of peloria, new genera have sometimes been formed on insufficient grounds. The genus *Aceranthus*,[Pg 226] for instance, consists of species of *Epimedium* in which the customary spurs are not formed.[229]

The occurrence both of regular and irregular peloria on the same plant has frequently been observed in *Linaria*. It has also been remarked that the seedlings raised from these forms are not always constant; thus, the late Mr. Crocker, formerly foreman in the Royal Gardens, Kew, informed me that he fertilised some flowers of a drooping Gloxinia with their own pollen, and that when the seedlings blossomed a large number of them produced the erect regular flowers.

From what has been already said it will be seen that regular peloria is closely allied to what Morren called epanody, or a return to the normal condition. The reversion of a monstrous form to the normal one, as, for instance, when the fern-leaved beech reverts to the normal type, was called by the same author epistrophy.[230]

The following are the genera in which regular peloria has been most often observed. It must, however, be remarked that in some of the flowers recorded as peloric there is no indication as to which form of peloria the case should be referred to. For other illustrations refer to chapters on Heterogamy, Number, Irregular Peloria, &c.

- *Delphinium peregrinum!
- *Nigella damascena!
- *Aquilegia vulgaris!
- *Viola odorata!
- hirta.
- Epimedium, sp.
- *Pelargonium zonale!
- *inquinans!
- Tropæolum majus!
- *Wistaria sinensis.
- Lupinus.
- *Cytisus Laburnum!
- Trifolium repens!
- *Compositæ, gen. pl.!
- Lonicera Periclymenum!
- Streptocarpus Rexii.
- *Digitalis purpurea.
- *Scrophularia aquatica.
- *Pentstemon.
- *Linaria vulgaris!
- *Antirrhinum majus!
- Verbascum nigrum!
- Columnea Schiedeana.
- Halenia heterantha.
- Galeobdolon luteum.
- Prunella vulgaris!
- Salvia, sp.!
- Teucrium campanulatum.
- Betonica alopecuros.
- Eccremocarpus scaber.[Pg 227]
- Pedicularis sylvatica.
- Zingiber Zerumbet.
- Phalænopsis amabilis!
- Phalænopsis Schilleriana.
- Habenaria.

105

- *Orchis morio.
o   mascula.
- *Dendrobium, sp.
- Atriplex, sp.
- Cattleya Mossiæ!
o   marginata.
- Calanthe vestita!
- Oncidium, sp.!
- Selenipedium caudatum.
- Arum maculatum.

In addition to the references already given, further information on this subject may be gained from consulting the following publications. See also Irregular Peloria.

Giraud, 'Bot. Soc. Edinb.,' Dec. 12, 1839, *Antirrhinum*. Dareste, 'Ann. Sc. Nat.,' ser. 2, 1842, xviii, p. 220, *Delphinium*. C. Morren, 'Fuchsia,' p. 90,*Calceolaria*, 'Bull. Acad. Belg.,' xx, part ii, p. 57; and E. Morren, 'Bull. Acad. Belg.,' 2nd ser., xix. p. 224, *Gloxinia*. Richard, 'Mém. Soc. d'hist. nat.,' ii, p. 212, tab. 3. Lindley, 'Journ. Linn. Soc.,' iii, p. 9, *Dendrobium*. Michalet, 'Bull. Soc, Bot. France,' vii, p. 625, *Betonica*. Gubler, 'Bull. Soc. Bot. Fr.,' ix, 81, 'Des anomalies aberrantes et regularisantes.' Reichenbach fil. 'De pollinis orchid. genesi ac structura,' 1852, *Oncidium*. Clos, 'Mém. Acad. Toulouse,' vi, 1862, *Salvia*. Caspary, 'Verhandl. Phys. Œkon. Gesell. Königsberg,' 1860, i, 59, *Columnea*. Bureau, 'Bull. Soc. Bot. Fr.,' 1861, vol. viii, p. 710, *Streptocarpus*. Darwin, 'Variation of Animals and Plants,' ii, pp. 59 and 396. Godron, 'Ex. Bull. Bot. Soc. Fr.,' xiv, p. 165, 'Rev. Bibl.,' *Wistaria*. Marchand, 'Adansonia,' iv, p. 172,*Lonicera*. Baillon, 'Adansonia,' v, p. 177, 'Sur la regularité transitoire de quelques fleurs irreg.,' shows that during the development of some flowers which begin and end by being irregular, there is an intermediate state when all the parts are regular. Helye, 'Revue Horticole,' Sept., 1868, p. 327. In this last paper, published as this sheet is going through the press, the author states that he has raised from seed three generations of plants of*Antirrhinum* with regular spur-less flowers. The original wild plant was only partially peloric, but all the flowers produced on its descendants were regular.

FOOTNOTES:

[221]"On the existence of two forms of Peloria," by M. T. Masters. 'Nat. Hist. Review,' April, 1863.

[222]Baillon, 'Adansonia,' iv. p. 149.

[223]Similar cases are figured in 'Hort. Eystettens. Ic. Pl. Vern.' fol. 4, f. 1, 2. *Viola martia* multiplici flore.

[224]'Linnæa,' 1837, p. 128.

[225]M. Bureau, 'Bull. Soc. Bot. Fr.,' ix, p. 91, describes two genera of*Bignoniaceæ* in which the flowers are *normally* regular and six parted.

[226]See 'Trans. Linn. Soc.,' vol. x. p. 227.

[227]'Ann. Sc. Nat.,' ser. 4, 1859. tom. xi, p. 264, tab. 3.

[228]'El. Ter. Veg.,' p. 342.

[229]Marchand, 'Adansonia,' vol. iv, p. 127.

[230]'Bull. Acad. Belg.,' xvii. p. 17. "Fuchsia," p. 169.

[Pg 228]

PART II.
PLEIOMORPHY.[231]

Most irregular flowers owe their irregularity to an unequal development of some of their organs as compared with that of others. When such flowers become exceptionally regular they do so either because development does not keep pace with growth, and a regular flower is thus the result of an arrest of the former process (regular peloria), or because the comparatively excessive development, which usually occurs in a few parts is, in exceptional cases manifested by all, hence the flower becomes regular from the increase in number of its irregular elements. These latter cases, then, are due to an excess of development, hence the application of the term pleiomorphy. It must be understood that mere increase in the number of the organs of a flower is not included under this head, but under that of deviations from the ordinary number of parts.

FOOTNOTES:

[231]Πλειος-μορφωσις.

CHAPTER I.
IRREGULAR PELORIA.

The term peloria was originally given by Linné to a malformation of *Linaria vulgaris*, with five spurs and five stamens, which was first found in 1742 near Upsal. This was considered so marvellous a circumstance that the term peloria, from the Greek πελωρ, a[Pg 229] prodigy, was applied to it.[232]After a time other irregular flowers were found in like condition, and so the term peloria became applied to all cases wherein, on a plant habitually producing irregular flowers, regular ones were formed. The fact that this regularity might arise from two totally different causes was overlooked, or at least not fully recognised, even by Moquin-Tandon himself. Where a flower retains throughout life the same relative size in its parts that it had when those parts first originated the result is, of course, a regular flower, as happens in violets and other plants. This kind of peloria may for distinction sake be called regular or congenital peloria (see chapter on that subject); but where a flower becomes regular by the increase in number of its irregular portions, as in the *Linaria* already alluded to, where not only one petal is spurred, but all five of them are furnished with such appendages, and which are the result of an irregular development of those organs, the peloria is evidently not congenital, but occurs at a more or less advanced stage of development. To this latter form of peloria it is proposed to give the distinctive epithet of irregular.

Peloria is either complete or incomplete; it is complete when the flower appears perfectly symmetrical, it is incomplete when only a portion of the flower is thus rendered regular. It is very common, for instance, to find violets or Linarias with two or three spurs, and these intermediate stages are very interesting, as they[Pg 230] serve to show in what way the irregularity is brought about. In *Antirrhinum*, *Linaria*, &c., intermediate forms show very clearly that it is to the repetition of the form usually assumed by the petals of the lower lip that the condition is due. This is also obvious in peloric flowers of the *Calceolaria*. The perfect peloria of this flower is in general erect, with five regular sepals, a regular corolla contracted at the base and at the apex, but distended in the centre so as to resemble a lady's sleeve, tight at the shoulder and wrist, and puffed in the centre!

FIG. 122.—Peloric flower of *Calceolaria*.

Morren[233] describes a form intermediate between the ordinary slipper-shaped corolla and the perfect peloria just described, and which he calls sigmoid peloria. This flower is intermediate in direction between the erect peloria and the ordinary reflected flower. The tube is curved like a swan's neck and is dilated in front into two hollow bosses, such as we see in the lower lip of an ordinary flower; beyond these it is contracted and is prolonged into a slender beak terminating in two hollow teeth, between which is the[Pg 231] narrow orifice of the corolla. The colour at the base of the tube inside is as in the perfect peloria; while round the summit of the tube, in both cases, the intensity of colour is greatest on the outside. Now, in a normal flower the deepest colour is within just opposite the orifice of the corolla; this deep colour is also seen outside of the central and most elevated portions of the lower lip. In the peloria the deep colour at the base of the tube represents that which is near the orifice under ordinary circumstances, while the outer patch of colour at the apex corresponds to that formed on the upper surface of the lower lip. On the other hand, in peloric flowers of *Cytisus Laburnum*, *Clitoria Ternatea*, *Trifolium repens*, and other Papilionaceæ, it is the "standard," the form of which is repeated. In the case of peloric aconites[234] the lateral and sometimes the inferior coloured sepals assume the hooded form usually peculiar to the upper sepal only, the number of the petals or nectaries being correspondingly increased. Balsams become peloric by the augmentation in the number of spurs.[235] So when orchids are affected with irregular peloria it is the form of the labellum that is repeated, the accessory lips being sometimes the representatives of stamens, which are usually suppressed in these flowers,[236] but at other times the appearance is due simply to the fact that all three petals assume the form usually confined to the lip, the staminal column being unaffected, except that its direction and relative position with reference to the other parts of the flower is different from ordinary. This was the case in some flowers of *Phalænopsis equestris* sent to me by Mr. Wentworth Buller. Fig. 123 represents a flower of *Aristolochia caudata* with two lips, for which I am indebted to Mr. W. H. Baxter.

From these cases it is evident that the flowers in[Pg 232] question become regular by the repetition of the irregular parts.

FIG. 123.—Two-lipped flower of *Aristolochia caudata*.

It is probable that peloria may occur in any habitually irregular flower, and that, if more attention were directed to the subject, illustrations might be obtained from a larger number of natural families than can be done at present. It is, however, necessary to exercise discrimination, and not to attribute to peloria all the cases that at first sight appear to be so referable. Thus, Professor Dickson exhibited at the Botanical Society of Edinburgh, December 13th, 1860, four abnormal flowers of the common Indian cress (*Tropæolum majus*), each presenting a supernumerary spur. On these he remarked that "in *Tropæolum* the posterior[Pg 233] part of the receptacle between the insertion of the petals and that of the stamens is dilated so as to form the spur which is so characteristic in the genus. The position of the spur in a line with the posterior sepal has led many botanists to consider it as a process of that sepal, but the fact of its being situated within the insertion of the petals is conclusive as to its receptacular origin. In the flowers exhibited the supernumerary spur (as if to show its want of connection with any sepal) was placed exactly between a lateral sepal and one of the anterior sepals, sometimes on the one side of the flower and sometimes on the other. These additional spurs were precisely similar to the normal ones, except that they were a little shorter. This abnormality, although at first sight seeming to indicate a pelorian tendency, is no approximation to regularity, from the fact of the extra spur being differently placed, with regard to the sepals, from the normal one."

Peloria of this kind, when perfect, is very often associated with other alterations. Change of direction is one of the most common of these; the usually drooping flower becomes erect, the stamens and style also are changed in direction, while, not unfrequently, either the one or the other (most often the stamens) are entirely suppressed. With this suppression an increase in the size of the flower very generally coincides. The number of parts is also frequently increased; thus, in *Antirrhinum majus* the corolla, when subjected to peloria, is very generally six-parted, and has six stamens. Fusion of one or more flowers is also a common accompaniment of peloria, as in *Digitalis purpurea*, in which plant prolification often adds increased complexity to the flower.

It has been stated by Moquin and others that the uppermost flower of an inflorescence is the most subject to peloria; the uppermost flower of *Teucrium campanulatum*, for instance, is very generally regular. In *Calceolaria* it is the central terminal flower which is usually peloriated; on the other hand, in *Linaria* and *Antirrhinum*[Pg 234] the lower flowers, or those on the secondary branches, are quite as often affected as the primary ones. Cassini considered that the spur of *Linaria* was developed from the lower petal rather than from the upper ones, because there is more room on the side of the flower farthest from the stem than on the opposite side. With reference to this point, M. Godron remarks that in habitually irregular flowers the apex of the peduncle is oblique, and hence the flowers are bent downwards or spread horizontally, but if the receptacle be quite flat and level then the flower is regular. The oblique position causes some of the organs to press on others, and hence induces abortion and suppression of some parts and increased growth in others that are not subjected to pressure. In a terminal peloriated flower of aconite, described by this naturalist, the flower was removed so far from the nearest bracts that all its parts had the chance of growing regularly. In ordinary cases M. Godron considers that the compression of the lateral bracts is the cause of the irregularity of the andrœcium and of the receptacle.[237]

It has also been somewhat too generally stated that peloria occurs principally on luxuriant vigorous plants. It seems quite as often to happen in plants characterised by their deficiencies in this respect. On this point M. de Melicoq[238] says, referring to *Linaria vulgaris* affected with peloria, that on the weakest plants the peloriated flower was at the top of the stem; while in stronger plants, with more numerous flowers and larger foliage, the peloriated flowers were principally to be found in the centre and at the base of the inflorescence, and their pedicels were much longer than usual.

Linné, as has been already stated, considered these flowers to be sterile, and only capable of multiplication by division of the root, but Willdenow obtained[Pg 235] seeds from the *Linaria* which reproduced the anomaly when sown in rich soil. Baron Melicoq obtained similar results.[239] Mr. Darwin[240] raised sixteen seedling plants of a peloric *Antirrhinum*, artificially fertilised by its own pollen, all of which were as perfectly peloric as the parent plant. On the other hand, the same observer alludes to the tendency that these peloric plants have to revert to the usual form, as shown by the fact that when the peloric flowers were crossed with pollen from flowers of the ordinary shape, and *vice versâ*, not one of the seedlings, in either case, bore peloric flowers. Hence, says Mr. Darwin, there is in these flowers "a strong latent tendency to become peloric, and there is also a still greater tendency in all peloric plants to reacquire their normal irregular structure." So that there are two opposed latent tendencies in the same plant. A similar remark has been made with reference to malformations in general by other observers.

It would be very interesting if some competent naturalist would collect information as to whether any variations in degree of fertility exist in the three forms of flowers in *Linaria*, viz. the ordinary one-spurred form, which is intermediate between the spur-less and the five-spurred form. It must be remembered, however, that in the latter cases the stamens are often deficient. In the *Compositæ*, where there are regular flowers in the disc and irregular ones in the ray, sexual differences, as is well known, accompany the diversities in form.

To Mr. Darwin the author is indebted for the communication of some flowers of *Corydalis tuberosa* (figs. 124, 125), provided with two spurs of nearly equal size. To these flowers allusion is made in the work already quoted[241] in the following terms:—"*Corydalis tuberosa* properly has one of its two nectaries colourless, destitute of nectar, only half the size of the other, and[Pg 236] therefore to a certain extent in a rudimentary state; the pistil is curved towards the perfect nectary, and the hood formed of the inner petals slips off the pistil and stamens in one direction alone, so that when a bee sucks the perfect nectary the stigma and stamens are exposed and rubbed against the insect's body. In several closely allied genera, as in *Dielytra*, there are two perfect nectaries; the pistil is straight, and the hood slips off on either side, according as the bee sucks either nectary." In the flowers of *Corydalis*, which were provided with two perfect nectaries containing nectar, Mr. Darwin considers that there has been a redevelopment of a partially aborted organ, accompanied by a change in the direction of the pistil, which becomes straight, while the hood formed by the petals slips off in either direction, "so that these flowers have acquired the perfect structure, so well adapted for insect agency, of *Dielytra* and its allies."

FIG. 124.—Two-spurred flowers of *Corydalis*.

FIG. 125.—Section through two-spurred flowers of *Corydalis*, Magnified.

Peloria, then, is especially interesting physiologically as well as morphologically; it is also of value in a systematic point of view, as showing how closely the[Pg 237] deviations from the ordinary form of one plant represent the ordinary condition of another; thus, the peloric Calceolarias resemble the flowers of *Fabiana*, and De Candolle,[242] comparing the peloric flowers of *Scrophulariaceæ* with those of *Solanaceæ*, concluded that the former natural order was only an habitual alteration from the type of the latter. Peloric flowers of *Papilionaceæ* in this way are indistinguishable from those of *Rosaceæ*. In like manner we may trace an analogy between the normal one-spurred *Delphinium* and the five-spurred columbine (*Aquilegia*), an analogy strengthened by such a case as that of the five-spurred flower of *Delphinium elatum* described by Godron.[243] The *Corydalis*, before referred to, is another illustration of the same fact, the structure being the same as in *Dielytra*, &c.

The ordinary irregular flowers may possibly be degenerated descendants of a more completely organized ancestor, and some of the cases of peloria may therefore be instances of reversion; some ancient *Linaria* may, perhaps, have had all its petals spur-shaped, and the cases of irregular peloria now found may be reversions to that original form. When both regular and irregular forms of peloria occur on the same plant, as they frequently do in *Linaria*, the one may be perhaps considered as a reversion to a very early condition, the other to a later state, when all the petals were irregularly formed. But before we can assert the truth of this surmise we must have better evidence as to what the original condition really was than we have at present.

The proximate cause of irregular peloria has been considered to be excess of nourishment, but evidence as to this point is very conflicting. Willdenow states that "radices peloriæ, solo sterili plantatæ, degenerant in Linariam," ('Sp. Plant.,' iii, p. 254); but this opinion is counterbalanced by that of others, while the frequent[Pg 238] existence of both forms on the same plant, at the same time, seems to negative the supposition of any direct effect from external circumstances.

The following are the plants in which irregular peloria has been most often observed:

- Aconitum Napellus.
- Delphinium elatum!
- Corydalis tuberosa.
- *Viola odorata!
o   hirta.
- Impatiens Balsamina.
- Clitoria Ternatea.
- Cytisus Laburnum!
- Trifolium repens!
- Lupinus polyphyllus!
- *Gloxinia, var. cult.!
- *Linaria vulgaris!
o   spuria.
o   Elatine.
o   triphylla.
o   æruginea.
o   triornithophora.
o   pilosa.
o   chalepensis.
o   cymbalaria!
o   purpurea!
o   decumbens.
o   Pelisseriana.
o   origanifolia.
- Digitalis orientalis.
o   *purpurea!
- Calceolaria crenatiflora.
o   rugosa.
o   *var. cult.!
- Chelone barbata.
- *Antirrhinum majus!
- Rhinanthus crista galli.
- Pedicularis sylvatica.

- Pedicularis euphrasioides.
- Scrophularia aquatica!
- Sesamum indicum.
- Lamium.
- Mentha.
- Sideritis.
- Nepeta diffusa.
- Galeopsis Ladanum.
○   Tetrahit.
- Galeobdolon luteum.
- Teucrium campanulatum!
- Plectranthus fruticosus.
- Cleonia lusitanica.
- Dracocephalum austriacum.
- Phlomis fruticosa!
- Vitex incisa.
- Aristolochia, sp.!
- Ophrys aranifera!
- Orchis simia.
○   pyramidalis!
○   latifolia!
○   morio!
○   papilionacea.
○   mascula.
○   latiflora.
○   conopsea.
- Habenaria bifolia.
- Corallorhiza innata.
- Aceras anthropophora.
- Cattleya Moasiæ!
- Phalænopsis equestris!
- Pogonia ophioglossoides!

The literature of peloria is very extensive. The following are the principal papers, not already mentioned, which relate to the subject, arranged under the genera, placing those first which are most subject to this anomaly (see also Regular Peloria).

Linaria.—Adanson, 'Fam. Plant.,' t. i, p. 110. Jussien, 'Gen. Plant.,' p. 120. Poiret, 'Encycl. Method, Suppl.,' t. iii, Jaeger, 'Missbilld. der Gewachs.,' pp. 94, 97, and 313. Cassini, 'Op. Phytol.,' t. ii, p. 331. Ratzebourg, 'Animadv. ad pelor. spectand.,' 1825. Turpin. 'Ic. Veget.,'[Pg 239]tab. xx, f. 16. Curtis, 'Flor. Londin.,' i, 118. Hopkirk, 'Flora Anom.,' pl. vii, figs. 1, 2, 3. Haller, 'Act. Helvet.,' 2, p. 25, t. iv. De Candolle, 'Flore Franc.,' t. iii, p. 583. Sowerby, 'Engl. Bot.,' iv, 260, ed. Syme, tab. 963. Chavannes, 'Mon. Antirrhin.' Delavaud, 'Bull. Soc. Bot. France,' 1858, p. 689; id., 1860, p. 175. Heufler, 'Linnæa,' xvii, tab. ii. Weber, 'Verhandl. des Nat. Hist. Vereins. f. d. Rh. Preuss.,' 1850, tab. i, figs. 1–8. 'Verh. Nat. Hist. Ver. Rh. Preus.,' 1849, vol. vi, p. 290, tab. xiii.—*Antirrhinum*, Clos, 'Mém. Acad. Toulous.,' vi, 1862. Chavannes, 'Mon. Antirrh.,' p. 62. Fresenius, 'Mus. Senkenb.,' ii, t. iv, fig. 10. 'Bot. Soc. Edinb.,' 1851, July 10.—*Calceolaria*, Chamisso, 'Linnæa,' t. vii, p. 206. Guillemin, 'Archiv.

Bot.,' t. ii, p. 1 et 136. Schlechtendal, 'Linnæa,' xii, p. 686. Ernst Meyer, 'Linnæa,' xvi, 26, tab. iii. Morren, 'Bull. Acad. Belg.,' t. xv, n. 7, et t. xviii, p. 583. 'Gard. Chron.,' 1850, p. 389; ibid., 1866, p. 612.—*Viola*, Leers, 'Flor. Herborn.,' p. 145. De Candolle, 'Organ. Veget.,' t. i, p. 519, pl. xlv. Forbes, 'Proc. Linn. Soc.,' June 6, 1848, p. 382. Hildebrand, 'Bot. Zeit.,' 1862, vol. xx, tab. viii.—*Orchidaceæ*, His, 'Jourl. Phys.,' 65, p. 241. Wydler, 'Arch. Bot.,' t. ii, p. 310, tab. xvi. R. Brown, 'Obs. organ. Orchid.,' p. 698. A. Richard, 'Mém. soc. d'hist. nat.,' t. i, p. 212. Greville, 'Flora Edinens.,' p. 87 (*Corallorhiza*). Curtis, 'Flora Londinensis,' t. lxxxii. Morren, C., 'Bull. Acad. Roy. Belg.,' t. xix, part ii, p. 171. Clos, 'Mém. Acad. Sc. Toulous.,' 5 ser., vol. iii. Caspary, 'Schrift. K. Gesellsch. Königsberg,' 1860, i, 59. Masters, 'Jourl. Linn. Soc.,' vol. viii, p. 208 (*Ophrys, Pogonia*). Duchartre, 'Bull. Soc. Bot. Fr.,' vol. vii, 1860, p. 26,*Cattleya.* Cramer, 'Bildungsabweich.'—*Limosella*, Baillon, 'Adansonia,' i, p. 305. (Flower normally irregular, becoming regular "à force d'irregularité.")—*Chelone*, Chamisso, 'Linnæa,' vii, p. 206,—*Clitoria*, Bonavia, 'Gard. Chron.,' 1868, p. 1013. In this latter communication, published as this sheet is passing through the press, the author gives an interesting account of the transitional stages between the ordinary papilionaceous condition and the regular form which is like that of a Rosaceous plant. The peloric form is stated to be transmitted by seed.

For other references see Moq.-Tandon, 'El. Terat. Veget.,' p. 186. Hallier, 'Phytopathol.,' p. 151.

FOOTNOTES:

[232]'Amœn. Acad.,' i, p. 55, t. iii (1744):—The following note refers to Linné's notion that these forms were due to hybridization. It is extracted from Gmelin's edition of the 'Systema Naturæ,' 1791, p. 931. "*Linariæ* proles hybrida, ejusdemque qualitatis et constans, radicibus infinite sese multiplicans charactere fructificationis diversissima, corolla regulari, quinque-corniculata, pentandra, ut genus proprium absolute constitueret et distinctissimum, nisi fructus frequentissime abortiret. Naturæ prodigium. Ita quidem a Linné. Verisimilar autem videtur ea opinio, quæ peloriam pro peculiari degeneratione monstrosa floris habet, in quam inclinare hoc genus (Linaria) præ aliis, similis a forma deflexio in aliis speciebus, e.g. *spurio Elatine,cymbalaria*, observata, ... Merk., 'Goett. gel. Anz.,' 1774, n. 121. Linck, 'Annal. Naturg.,' i, p. 32."

[233]'Bull. Acad. Belg.,' xviii, part i, p. 591. Lobelia, p. 137.

[234]See also Seringe, 'Esquisse d'une Monogr. du genre *Aconitum*,' p. 124.

[235]Schlotterbec, 'Act. Helvet.,' t. ii, pl. i, Roeper. Balsam, p. 10, note.

[236]Masters. "Peloria, &c., *Ophrys aranifera*," 'Journ. Linn. Soc.,' viii, p. 207.

[237]Godron, "Mém. sur les Fumarieès à fl. irreg.," 'Ann. Sc. Nat.,' sér. 5, vol. ii, tab. xvii, p. 280.

[238]'Bull. Soc. Bot. France,' vol. v, 1858, p. 701.

[239]'Bull. Soc. Bot. France,' vol. vi, 1859, p. 717.

[240]'Variation of Anim. and Plants,' ii, p. 70.

[241]Loc. cit., p. 59.

[242]'Théor. Elém.,' ed. 2, p. 266.

[243]Cited in 'Bull. Soc. Bot. France,' vol. xiii (Rev. Bibl.), p. 81.

[Pg 240]

PART III.

METAMORPHY.

Much of the objection with which Goethe's famous essay on the 'Metamorphosis of Plants' was met on its publication may be traced to a misapprehension of the sense in which Goethe employed the word. As used by him, it had nearly the same signification as now applied to the word development by organogenists. It does not necessarily imply that there has been a change in any particular organ, but rather that there has been, to some extent, a change in the plan of construction, in accordance with which a deviation from the customary form results. The particular organ was never anything else than what it is; it has not been metamorphosed in the ordinary sense of the word; for instance, in a double flower, where the stamens are, as it is said, changed or metamorphosed into petals, no absolute change really has taken place—the petal was never a stamen, although it occupies the position of the latter, and may be considered a substitute for it.

The term metamorphosis, then, really implies an alteration in the organizing force, taking effect at a very early period of the life of the flower, at or before the period when the primitive aggregation of cells, of which it is at that time composed, becomes separated or "differentiated" into the several parts of the flower. In other words, the "development" of the flower pursues a different course from what is usual. In the preceding sections the effects of arrest and of excess in this process have been partly treated of; other deviations arising from similar causes will be mentioned[Pg 241]elsewhere, but, under the present heading, are specially included cases not of merely diminished or increased, but of perverted development; the natural process is here not necessarily checked or enhanced, but it is changed. Hence, in the present work, the term metamorphy is employed to distinguish cases where the ordinary course of development has been perverted or changed. As it is applied solely for teratological purposes, the ordinary acceptation of the term, as nearly synonymous with "development," is not interfered with.

In order to avoid other possible misapprehensions, the terms retrograde and progressive metamorphosis employed by Goethe are not herein used, their place being, to a great extent, supplied by the more intelligible expressions arrest or excess of development.[244]

FOOTNOTES:

[244]See Goethe, 'Versuch. der Metam. der Pflanzen,' 1790. English translation by Emily M. Cox, in Seemann's 'Journal of Botany,' vol. i, 1863, p. 327. For a brief sketch of the origin and progress of the theory of vegetable morphology, prior to the publications of Wolff, Linné, and Goethe, as well as for an attempt to show what share each of these authors had in the establishment of the doctrine, the reader is referred to an article in the 'Brit. and For. Medico-Chirurgical Review,' January, 1862, entitled "Vegetable Morphology: its History and Present Condition," by Maxwell T. Masters.

CHAPTER I.
PHYLLODY.

This condition, wherein true leaves are substituted for some other organs,[245] must be distinguished from Virescence, q. v., in which the parts affected have simply the green colour of leaves, without their form or structure. The appearance of perfect leaves, in[Pg 242] place of other organs, is frequently looked on as due to retrograde metamorphosis, or to an arrest of development. But this is not strictly correct; for instance, suppose a petal, which is very generally merely the sheath of a leaf, with the addition of colouring matter, to be replaced by a perfect leaf, one in which all three constituent parts, sheath, stalk, and blade, are present, it surely can hardly be said that there has been any retrogression or arrest of development in the formation of a complete organ in place of an incomplete organ. The term retrograde here is used in a purely theoretical sense, and cannot be held to imply any actual degradation. Morphologically, as has been stated, the case is one of advance rather than the reverse, and hence the assignment of instances of this nature to a perversion of development, rather than to a diminution or to an exaltation of that process, seems most consistent with truth. The affected organs have really undergone no actual change, simply the direction of the organising force has been altered at a very early state, so that the usual differentiation of parts has not taken place.

FIG. 126.—'Rose plantain,' *Plantago media var.,* **spike contracted; bracts leafy.**
Phyllody of the bracts.—As bracts are very generally imperfect organs, so their replacement by perfect leaves[Pg 243] is not attributable to arrest of development or retrograde metamorphosis, but the reverse. The bracts of some species of *Plantago*[246] are very subject to this change. Thus, in the rose plantain of gardens, *P. media* (fig. 126), the bracts are leafy and the axis depressed or not elongated, so that it is surmounted by a rosette of small leafy organs. A similar condition of the bracts, unattended with arrest of growth in the axis, is common in *P. major* (fig. 127) and in *P. lanceolata* (see p. 108). It also occurs in the bracts of *Corydalis solida,Amorpha fruticosa, Ajuga reptans, Parthenium inodorum, Centaurea Jacea,* in the involucral bracts of the dandelion, the[Pg 244] daisy, and many other composites. In the 'Gardeners Chronicle,' 1852, p. 579, is figured a dahlia in which the bracts of the involucre

and the scales of the receptacle had all assumed the form, texture, and venation of leaves.[247]

FIG. 127.—Leaf-like bracts in *Plantago major*.

FIG. 128.—Dahlia. Scales of receptacle leafy.

In *Umbelliferæ* the substitution of leaves for involucral bracts is not infrequent. It has been observed among other plants in *Angelica Razoulzii*,*Carum carui*, *Daucus Carota*, &c. The scales of the hop (*Humulus Lupulus*) not infrequently manifest this change, as do also the bracts of many amentaceous plants, *e.g.* in the male catkins of the walnut, the female catkins of the alder,[248] of some willows,[249] &c. The bracts of some *Euphorbiaceæ*, as *E. pusilla*, *E. Lathyris*, *E. Cyparissias*, have been observed to undergo a similar alteration.[250]

[Pg 245]Amongst monocotyledons an analogous change occurs not unfrequently, as in some commelynaceous plants, *e.g.* *Tradescantia*, in *Musa*, &c.

The spathe of *Arum maculatum* is sometimes represented by a stalked leaf similar to that which occurs, under ordinary circumstances, in *Spathiphyllum*, but in which genus the spadix is more or less adherent to the leaf-like spathe.[251] In *Schœnus cephalotes* a similar exaggerated development of the bracts is figured by Rottboell.[252]

Phyllody in inflorescence of Conifers.—This demands passing notice by reason of the interest attaching to the morphological construction of these plants. The elongation of the axis which occurs in the female cones has been already alluded to under the head of prolification of the inflorescence. This change is frequently associated with a more or less foliaceous condition of the bracts, which, indeed, may be seen to be serially continuous, both above and below, with the ordinary leaves. The scales, too, become notched and bipartite, and show, between the lobes, the rudiment of a bud, which in a further stage becomes developed into a shoot bearing leaves. Such a change has been described by Parlatore in *Abies Brunoniana*, and examples may frequently be met with in the larch (*Larix europæa*), and specially in *Cryptomeria japonica*.[253] The scales of the male catkins of conifers likewise occasionally assume the appearance of leaves; this may be seen in monstrous catkins of *Araucaria*, as also in *Podocarpeæ* and *Cupressineæ* (Eichler).

Phyllody of the calyx.—Sepals under ordinary circumstances are so like leaves, that it is not wonderful that[Pg 246] they are often replaced by those organs.[254] A singular instance of this has been mentioned as occurring in *Cakile maritima*, wherein the sepals were found by M. Fournier to be pinnatifid like the ordinary leaves of the plant.[255] The sepals of *Ranunculaceæ* and *Rosaceæ*, for example, *Rosa*, *Geum*, are particularly liable to this change.

FIG. 129.—Flower of rose, sepals replaced by five perfect leaves; axis prolonged through the flower in the form of a leafy branch.

In a species of *Geranium* recently examined the sepals presented themselves in the form of three-lobed leaflets; so in fuchsias and in *Epilobium hirsutum* the sepals occasionally are not distinguishable from ordinary leaves (fig. 130). In roses, the change in question is a very frequent accompaniment of prolification (fig. 129). In the peach also this replacement of the sepals is[Pg 247] sometimes carried to such an extent, that five perfect, bistipulate leaves occur in the place of the calyx, but when this is the case it usually happens that the pistil is abortive.

FIG. 130.—Fuchsia, with one of the sepals leaf-like.

De Candolle[256] figures a curious instance wherein the pappus of *Podospermum laciniatum* was replaced by five linear, foliaceous lobes. A similar change has been noticed in other composites, as in *Tragopogon pratense*. Engelmann mentions as subject to this hypertrophy of the pappus, as it may be termed, *Scorzonera octangularis* and *Senecio vulgaris*. Wigand has observed a similar transformation in a species of *Centranthus* (*Valerianaceæ*).

In some cases the phyllody of the sepals has a special interest, as bearing on the question whether what is termed calyx-tube is or is not a portion of the calyx, and whether the sepals are modifications of the blade or of the sheath of the leaf. Thus in the primrose the phyllodic sepals seem to show clearly that the sepals are in that plant of a laminar nature (fig. 131). The so-called calyx-tube of roses is elsewhere alluded to. The leaf-like organs sometimes seen at the apex of a cucumber would seem to support the view that there was really a calyx-tube in *Cucurbitaceæ* adherent to the carpels. It is also shown in the cut,[Pg 248] fig. 132, borrowed from the 'Gardeners' Chronicle,' 1859, p. 654.

FIG. 131.—Primrose. Calyx of foliaceous segments.

FIG. 132.—Leafy calyx of melon.

[Pg 249]

Under ordinary circumstances, the sepals may be considered as the representatives of the sheath of the leaf (cataphyllary) or of the blade (euphyllary), the arrangement of the veins being different in the two cases; thus, in the vagina or sheath, there are generally several large veins of about equal size, either convergent towards the apex, or divergent; on the other hand, in the blade, there is usually but one central vein, the midrib, larger than the rest, and the smaller veins come off at a less acute angle, and are more reticulated.[257]

Now, when phyllomorphy occurs in sepals which ordinarily are vaginal, it is obvious that the case is one, not merely of increased relative growth, but also of the appearance or development of an organ habitually suppressed; on the other hand, when phyllomorphy occurs in sepals which usually are laminar in form and nervation, the case is one of unusual growth or hypertrophy, and not of the development of an organ habitually suppressed, so that the amount of change is greater in the former than in the latter instance.

Under normal circumstances it will be found that laminar venation is most common in gamosepalous and vaginal venation in polysepalous calyces. And the same holds good in cases where the calyx is abnormally leafy. The complete leaf development shows itself more frequently among the monosepalous[Pg 250] plants than in the polysepalous ones, as shown even in the subjoined list of species. This statement would be more fully verified were it possible to state the frequency with which the condition occurred in *individual plants*, when it would be found that phyllody of the calyx occurs much more often in individual gamosepalous plants than in polysepalous ones.

Phyllody of the calyx has been most often observed in the following plants:

- Ranunculus acris!
- Delphinium Ajacis.
- Caltha palustris.
- Anemone Pulsatilla.
  - sylvestris!
  - nemorosa!
  - hortensis!
  - coronaria!
- *Papaver orientale.
- Escholtzia crocea.
- Cakile maritima.
- Diplotaxis tenuifolia.
- Thlaspi arvense.
- Cheiranthus Cheiri.
  - incanus.
- Sinapis arvensis.
- Brassica oleracea!
- Peltaria alliacea.
- *Sisymbrium officinale.

115

- Caryophyllaceæ,[258] sp. pl.
- Geranium, sp.!
- *Fuchsia, var. hort.!
- Epilobium hirsutum!
- Cucurbita Pepo!
- *Rosa, var. hort.!
- Potentilla nepalensis.
- Fragaria sp.
- Geum rivale.
- Amygdalus communis.
- Persica vulgaris.
- Cerasus!
- Pyrus Malus.
- Daucus Carota.
- Athamanta Cervaria.
- *Trifolium repens!
- Centranthus macrosiphon.
- Tragopogon pratense.
o   orientale.
- Scorzonera octangularis.
- Hypochæris radicata.
- *Senecio vulgaris!
- Podospermum laciniatum.
- Cirsium arvense.
- Carduus heterophyllus
o   tataricus.
- Campanula, sp.
- Convolvulus sepium.
- *Primula officinalis, var. cult!
o   acaulis.
o   elatior.
- Gentiana campestris.
- *Petunia violacea!
- Lycium europæum.
- Laurus Sassafras.
- Tulipa Gesneriana.
- Convallaria maialis.
- Colchicum autumnale! (virescent?)

Consult also Turpin, 'Atlas de Goethe,' t. iv, f. 12, *Lycium*. Engelmann, 'De Anthol.,' § 35, p. 31. This author figures phyllodic sepals in *Senecio vulgaris*, tab. v, figs. 24–26; *Campanula*, tab. iii, f. 15, 16; *Athamanta cervaria*, tab. v, f. 14. Lindley, 'Elements of Botany,' 1847, pp. 64, 73, &c. 'Gard. Chron.,' 1858, p. 685; 1859, p. 654, *Cucurbita*. Petunnikoff, 'Bull. Soc. Imp.

Moscow,' 1862, *Cirsium*. Braun, 'Rejuvenescence,' Ray Society's Transl. See succeeding paragraphs.

[Pg 251]

Phyllody of the corolla.—The petals also are frequently replaced by leaves, though in many of the recorded instances the change has been one of colour only; these latter are strictly cases of virescence. M. Seringe[259]speaks of a flower of *Peltaria alliacea* in which the calyx was petal-like, while the corolla was leafy as if there had been transposition of the two organs, a very rare, if not unparalleled, instance. In a flower of *Campanula Medium*, provided, as is often the case, with a double corolla, the outer corolla was slit down on one side, the edges of the cleft being leafy.

FIG. 133.—Sepals and petals to leaves. *Geranium*.

The frondescent petals are very often completely disjoined, as in *Verbascum nigrum*, and *Lonicera Periclymenum*, in which, moreover, median prolification generally coexists. In the case of *Tropæolum majus*, the ordinary leaves of which are peltate and orbicular, the petals when frondescent have not the peltate arrangement, but are spathulate, and provided with very long, narrow stalks, so that, in some cases, they are, more properly speaking, enlarged virescent petals than true leaves; in other instances, however, the arrangement of the veins is more like that of the true leaves than that of the petals.

As might be expected, frondescence of the petals is frequently accompanied by other changes of a similar nature in other parts of the flower, and sometimes by the abortion of the sexual organs. Thus, in *Actæa spicata*, as observed by Fresenius, the petals were replaced by true petiolate, palminerved, lobed leaves,[Pg 252] the stamens and pistils being abortive. In *Ranunculus* the leaves that appear in the place of the petals have no scale at their base, and in *Tropæolum* the calyx (or receptacle) is free from the usual spur.

The absolute frequency of this occurrence seems to be greatest in those flowers which are normally polypetalous. The petals of these flowers, as a general rule, are more like the leaf-sheaths than the leaf-blades as to their venation, hence it would seem that the phyllomorphic condition in these petals is a manifestation of a greater degree of organizing force than that which occurs in those cases where the petals are normally present in the form of contracted blades or laminæ. (See the remarks in the preceding section.)

Frondescence of the petals has been observed most frequently in the following cases; some, perhaps, were cases merely of virescence, q. v.; see also under Chloranthy, Prolification.

- Ranunculus repens!
- Delphinium Ajacis.
- o   crassicaule.
- Aquilegia vulgaris.
- Actæa spicata.
- *Brassica oleracea!
- Diplotaxis muralis.
- Hesperis matronalis.
- Thlaspi bursa pastoris.
- Sisymbrium tenuifolium.
- Turritis glabra.
- Raphanus sativus.
- Peltaria alliacea.
- Alyssum incanum.
- Erysimum Barbarea.
- o   officinale!

- ○   cheiranthoides.
- Cheiranthus Cheiri.
- *Dictamnus Fraxinella!
- Lychnis sylvestris.
- ○   dioica!
- Alsine media.
- Cerastium vulgatum!
- ○   triviale.
- Reseda lutea.
- ○   Phyteuma.
- Malva sylvestris.
- *Tropæolum majus!
- Geranium, sp.!
- Triumfetta, sp.!
- Epilobium hirsutum!
- Œnothera striata.
- Rubus, sp.
- *Rosa, var. cult.!
- *Trifolium repens!
- Spiræa oblongifolia.
- Amygdalus communis.
- *Rosa!
- Cerasus vulgaris!
- Persica vulgaris!
- Potentilla nepalensis.
- Geum rivale.
- Daucus Carota!
- Heracleum Sphondylium.
- Torilis Anthriscus.
- Echinophora maritima.
- Campanula rapunculoides.
- ○   glomerata.
- Phyteuma spicatum.
- Calendula officinalis.
- Cirsium tricephalodes.
- Senecio vulgaris.
- Scabiosa columbaria.
- ○   agrestis.
- Lonicera xylosteum.
- ○   Periclymenum.[Pg 253]
- Gentiana Amarella.
- Gilia glomeriflora.

- *Symphytum officinale.
- Petunia violacea!
- Verbascum, sp.
- Antirrhinum majus!
- Stachys sylvatica.
- *Anagallis phœnicea?
- Primula sinensis!
- Polemonium cœruleum.

See Moquin-Tandon, 'El. Terat. Veg.,' p. 203. Engelmann, 'De Anthol.,' § 38 *et seq.*; tab. ii, figs. 8–14, *Gilia*; tab. v, 23–26, *Senecio*; tab. v, f. 1–13,*Torilis*; tab. iv, f. 3, *Erysimum.* 'Bull. Soc. Bot. Fr.,' vol. ii, 1855, p. 479,*Primula sinensis.* Giraud, 'Edinb. Phil. Magazine,' 1839, *Antirrhinum.* Jaeger, 'Act. Acad. Cæs. Nat. Cur.,' vol. xiii, 2, p. 1, tab. xli, *Tropæolum.* Bischoff, 'Lehrbuch,' 11, 2, p. 27, *note, Tropæolum.* Fresenius, 'Mus. Senkenb.,' ii, 35, tab. 4, fig. 5, *Actæa.* See also succeeding paragraphs and sections in Chloranthy, Virescence, &c.

Phyllody of the stamens happens less frequently than the corresponding condition in the neighbouring organs. The structure of the anther is so much removed from that of the leaf, that the change of the stamen from its ordinary condition to that of a leaf must be regarded as indicating a greater degree of perverted development than that which occurs in those cases where less highly differentiated organs, such as the sepals, petals, and pistils, are thus altered.[260]

In all cases it is desirable to ascertain, if possible, what parts of the stamen are thus transformed. In some Petunias the filaments are unchanged, but in place of the anther is a small lamina, representing precisely the blade of an ordinary leaf. Sometimes the connective only is replaced by a leaf. One of the most interesting cases of this kind that has fallen under the writer's observation was in *Euphorbia geniculata*, in which, in addition to other changes mentioned under prolification of the inflorescence, some of the stamens were partly frondescent,[Pg 254] half the anther being perfect, the other half leaf-like. Another filament bore just above the usual joint three leaflets, two lateral ones, somewhat conduplicate, and a third central one, half anther, half leaflet.

FIG. 134.—Flower of a *Petunia*, opened to show the stamens partially replaced by stalked leaves.

In the case of frondescent flowers of *Tropæolum majus* the stamens are usually absent or atrophied, but in other instances the filament is present as usual, representing the stalk of the leaf, and surmounted by a small lamina, but this latter, in place of being nearly flat, is pinched up in the centre from back to front, and surmounted by a two-lobed anther, so that the general appearance of the whole structure is that of a central anther, supported at the base on each side by two concave leaf-lobes, or it might be compared with a three-lobed leaf, the terminal lobe represented by the anther.

In *Jatropha Pohliana*, Müll. (*Adenorophium luxurians*, Pohl.), a singular condition has been observed by M. Müller (Argov.). In this flower the anther, in place[Pg 255] of being represented by the flat blade of a single leaf, had the appearance as if two such blades were present and coherent one with the other by their midribs, along their upper or inner surfaces, which were directed towards the centre of the flower (fig. 136), thus resembling the cases of adhesion of leaves by their surfaces already referred to (p. 33). In other cases, in the same plant, the anther appeared as if formed by two collateral leaves, the faces looking towards the circumference of the flower, and their margins so folded together as to represent an open anther lobe (fig. 135). These cases are apparently due, not to the formation and adhesion of two leaves, but rather to the exuberant development of one leaf into two blades.[261] The bearings of these and other similar malformations on the morphology of the anther are alluded to under the head of petalody of the anther.

FIG. 135.—Phylloid anther of *Jatropha*, after Müller (Arg.).

FIG. 136.—**Leaf-like anther of** *Jatropha Pohliana*, **after Müller.**

Phyllody of the stamens has been most often observed in the following plants: [Pg 256]

- Anemone nemorosa.
- coronaria.
- Delphinium crassicaule.
- Nymphæa dentata.
- Tropæolum majus!
- Dictamnus albus.
- *Trifolium repens!
- Torilis anthriscus.
- Heracleum Sphondylium.
- Daucus Carota
- Epilobium hirsutum!
- *Rosa, var. cult.!
- Lonicera Periclymenum.
- Anagallis arvensis.
- Primula sinensis!
- Petunia, var. cult.
- Jatropha Pohliana.
- Euphorbia goniculata.

In addition to the foregoing there are very numerous instances of similar substitution in chloranthic flowers. In the above list only those cases are given wherein the leafy change is confined to the stamens, or, at least, to a few only of the other parts of the flower.

Phyllody of the pistils.[262]—This is of more common occurrence than is the corresponding change in the case of the stamens. It is of interest, as it sometimes serves to illustrate the morphological nature of the pistil. Of this the double-flowering cherry is a well-known illustration, the pistil being here represented by two small foliar laminæ, whose midribs are prolonged with a short style, terminated by an imperfect stigma. It is usually the basal portion of the pistil, the ovary, which is thus specially affected, the margins being also often disunited so as to expose the ovules. These latter organs may be absent or they may themselves be the subjects of foliaceous development. Moquin[263] relates having found in the neighbourhood of Montpellier a flower of a tulip the ovary of which was represented by true leaves, which bore on their margins the ovules, and thus presented a striking analogy with the carpels of those Sterculias, like *S. platanifolia*, which are foliaceous in texture and open very early in the course of their development. A similar occurrence[Pg 257] has also been frequently noticed in the Columbine and also in *Cruciferæ* and *Umbelliferæ*. M. Germain de St. Pierre mentions an instance wherein the carpels of *Salix Babylonica* were converted into two leaves, provided with stipules. All the flowers of the catkins[Pg 258] were similarly changed, so that it became permanent, and resembled a branch.

FIG. 137.—**Rose, in which the axial portion of the flower was elongated and the carpels were more or less replaced by leaves.**

Substitutions of this kind form the green "eyes" or centres of certain varieties of *Ranunculus* and *Anemone*.

In proliferous roses, or in cases where the central axis of the flower is prolonged, it frequently happens that the pistils are more or less replaced by leaves. Fig. 137, from a specimen of Dr. Bell Salter's, given in the 'Gardeners' Chronicle,' shows the passage, from below upwards, of the ordinary carpels to perfect leaves; the so-called calyx-tube being completely deficient and the ovaries entirely superior. Like most similar specimens, this one bears out the notion that what is called the calyx-tube in roses is really an expansion and dilatation of the top of the flower-stalk.

FIG. 138.—Cucumber with leaf attached.

[Pg 259]

Fig. 138, for which I am indebted to Mr. S. J. Salter, represents a very singular conformation in the cucumber, described by that gentleman in 'Henfrey's Botanical Gazette,' i, p. 208, and considered by him to be due to the foliaceous condition of one of the three carpels of which the fruit is composed. The portion near the peduncle was binary, while the distal extremity of the fruit was ternary. The main difficulties attending the acceptance of this explanation reside in the peculiar reversed position of the leaf, and in the fact that the fruit of the *Cucurbitaceæ* is probably of axial nature, the dilated and succulent end of the peduncle adhering to and usually concealing the carpels; in some cases, however, these latter project beyond the axial portion, leaving no doubt as to the true nature of the structure in these particular instances.

Admitting the axial nature of the fruit, it might be supposed that in Mr. Salter's cucumber an adventitious leaf had been given off from the axis, but even on that supposition the reversed position offers a difficulty, and there still remains to be explained the fact that the proximal part of the fruit was binary in its constitution, the distal end ternary.

M. Norman[264] mentions a case wherein the carpels of *Anchusa ochroleuca* were replaced by two leaves; from this he draws the inference that the pistil of borages and labiates is really composed of two leaves, placed fore and aft, the margins of the leaves being congenitally fused. This tallies well with the account given of the development of these plants by Payer, Germain de St. Pierre, and others.

In an Indian species of *Triumfetta*, not only were the petals virescent, but the ovary also was much enlarged, and in some flowers it was divided half way down into five lanceolate leaves (fig. 139), the sepals and stamens being in their normal condition.

[Pg 260]

In the preceding instances the foliaceous condition has pervaded the entire pistil, or at any rate the basal portion or ovary, and it may be noticed that the ovary is thus shown to consist in some cases of the sheath of the leaf, as in *Aquilegia*; in other cases of the blade, as in *Cerasus, Daucus*, &c.

FIG. 139.—Flower of *Triumfetta*, sp., carpels represented by five leaves.

There are cases, however, in which a part only of the pistillary structure thus becomes foliaceous. Linnæus, 'Prolepsis,' § 9, mentions some flowers of *Carduus heterophyllus* and *C. tataricus* in which the style had grown into two green leaflets, and in which the calyx and corolla were also leaf-like. A very singular instance is recorded by Baillon,[265] wherein the pistil of *Trifolium repens* consisted of three carpels, either separate, or combined so as to form a one-celled ovary with three parietal, pluri-ovulate placentæ; the ovary in these flowers was formed of the basal vaginiform part of the leaf; the three styles were formed by the petioles, while the stigmas were represented by trifoliolate leaves. The back of the leaf in these cases is usually directed away from the centre of the[Pg 261] flower. When this change occurs it is commonly attended by an increased number of parts, as in the trefoil just mentioned, or in the double cherry, where usually two foliaceous carpels may be met with, and sometimes more.

The change is also of interest when it affects such orders as the *Umbelliferæ*, which have their ovaries inferior under ordinary circumstances; but when these organs assume a leafy condition they become superior also, *i.e.* they are detached from the calyx.

As regards the position of the ovules in these foliaceous pistils, they may be placed, as in *Aquilegia, Delphinium*, &c., on the edges of the carpel or on the surface, as in some flowers of *Ranunculus repens* and R. *Ficaria*. A similar position of the ovules is recorded in the case of the vine (*Vitis*), where the pistil consisted of leaves bearing the ovules on their inner surface.[266] The supposed causes of this and other similar malformations are alluded to under the head of chloranthy, but it may be here remarked that semi-double flowers, fertilised by the pollen of similar flowers, are said to produce flowers with a centre of small green leaves, this central tuft resulting from the expansion and frondescence of the pistils.

As this condition rarely occurs without corresponding changes in other parts of the flower, further remarks on this subject will be found in the chapter relating to Chloranthy.

Phyllody of the pistil has been most frequently recorded in the following plants:

- Pæonia officinalis.
- Ranunculus repens!
- *Aquilegia vulgaris!
- Delphinium elatum.
  - crassicaule.
  - Ajacis.
  - amænum.
- Nymphæa dentata.
- Sinapis arvensis!
- Diplotaxis tenuifolia.
- *Brassica oleracea!
- *Sisymbrium officinale!
- Dianthus. sp
- Reseda Phyteuma.[Pg 262]
- Triumfetta, sp.!
- Lychnis dioica.
- Cerastium, sp.!
- *Dictamnus Fraxinella!
- Cerasus avium.
  - vulgaris!
- *Rosa, var. cult.!
- *Daucus Carota!
- Heracleum, sp.
- Epilobium hirsutum!
- Lathyrus latifolius.
- *Trifolium repens!
  - hybridum.
- Melilotus, sp.
- Medicago, sp.
- Lonicera Periclymenum.
- Carduus heterophyllus.
  - tataricus.
- Scrophularia aquatica.
- Symphytum officinale.
- Anchusa ochroleuca.
  - paniculata.
- *Primula sinensis!

- Salix babylonica.
- Hyacinthus, sp.
- Tulipa, sp.

Some of the above are probably cases of mere virescence rather than of phyllody. For further illustrations, references to authorities, &c., see under Chloranthy, Virescence, Prolification, &c.

Phyllody of the ovules.—Pending the settlement of the existing differences of opinion with reference to the morphological nature of the ovule and its component parts, much interest attaches to the malformations to which they are occasionally subject. Considered purely in a teratological point of view, it seems clear that the ovular coats are usually, if not always, of foliar nature, while the central nucleus is an axial organ; but if this be so there still remains the question whether the leafy coats of the ovule are processes of the carpel itself, or distinct independent formations, like the scales of a leaf-bud; as to this latter point, the evidence is at present very conflicting. Prof. Al. Braun, who has devoted much attention to the subject, describes and figures ovules of *Nigella* and *Adonis*, wherein the outer coat of the ovule was converted into a leafy, lobed mass, like the ordinary leaves, and these he considers to be a portion, not of the carpel, but of the ovular bud; he, however, hesitates to pronounce an opinion on the nature of the pedicel of the ovule. In *Primulaceæ*, wherein ovular changes are very common, the leafy coat of the ovule would seem, from the nature of the placenta, to be independent of the carpel. Morren, who studied the changes in the[Pg 263] ovules of *Primula sinensis*, applied the term lepyrophylly (λεπυρον, a scale) to the foliaceous condition of the testa in this plant. Unger[267] describes a series of malformations in *Primula sinensis*, consisting chiefly of reversions of the part of the flower to leaves. The carpels were entirely absent in this case, and the place of the free central placenta was occupied by a circle of leaves, sometimes bearing imperfect ovules on their edges. An instance of a similar kind has been described by A. de Candolle.[268]

In these flowers the placenta seemed to be composed of several funiculi soldered together, and bearing imperfect ovules. In other cases no traces of ovules are visible, but the funiculi are in a foliaceous condition. Moquin also alludes to a case of the same nature in *Cortusa Mathioli*, in which the funiculi bore little rounded leaves. Brongniart has described some malformations of *Primula sinensis* in which the ovules were transformed wholly or partially into small leaves with three to five lobes.[269] Dr. Marchand[270] mentions similar changes in *Anagallis arvensis* and *Lonicera Periclymenum*.

Cramer[271] figures ovules of *Primula sinensis* in the form of stalked leaves, often becoming infolded at the margins, and giving origin to a small nucleus on their inner surface.

M. Tassi[272] records an instance in *Symphytum officinale* wherein the ovules were replaced by two small linear leaves arising entirely from the axis, and not from the carpels.

In most of the foregoing illustrations the foliar portion of the ovule must have been independent of the carpel; this independence is less manifest, though probably as[Pg 264] real in the cases now to be mentioned. In *Sinapis* and in *Brassica oleracea* foliaceous ovules may occasionally be seen, attached to the placenta by long stalks. No trace of the nucleus is visible in these specimens.

FIG. 140.—*Sinapis*, replum and ovules; the dotted line shows the position of the carpels.

Griffith, in alluding to a similar case in *Sinapis*,[273] describes the ovules as foliaceous, and having their backs turned away from the axis, the raphe being next to the axis and representing the midrib the funicle corresponding to the petiole. The outer tegument of the ovule, according to Griffith, is a leaf united along its margins, but always more or less open at its apex. No inversion can, therefore, really take place in anatropous ovules, but the blade of the leaf is bent back on the funicle, with which its margins also cohere.

Caspary, in an elaborate paper on phyllomorphy occurring in *Trifolium repens*, figures foliaceous ovules springing from the edge of an open, leafy carpel. The nucleus of the ovule,

123

in these cases, appears to originate as a little bud from the surface of the leafy ovule (figs. 141, 142).

[Pg 265]

FIG. 141.—Leafy ovules, &c., *Trifolium repens*.

In a species of *Triumfetta* (see p. 260), of which I examined dried specimens, the ovary was open and partly foliaceous; it bore on its infolded margins ten erect leaflets, representing so many ovules; each leaflet was conduplicate, the back being turned towards the placenta.

FIG. 142.—Leafy ovules of *Trifolium repens*, showing formation of nucleus, &c. After Caspary.

On the other hand, there are cases in which the leafy coat of the ovule, in place of being a distinct organ, seems to originate from the margin of the carpellary leaf itself—to be, as it were, a lobule or small process of the carpel, and not an absolutely new growth. Thus, Planchon[274], from an examination of some monstrous flowers of *Drosera intermedia*, was led to the inference that the ovules are analogous to hairs on the margins of the leaves. This acute botanist was enabled to trace all the gradations between the simple[Pg 266] cup formed by the confluence of four glanduliferous hairs and the concave leaf and the perfect ovule.

Brongniart[275] records ovules of *Delphinium elatum* existing in the form of marginal lobes of the carpellary leaf itself; so that each ovule corresponds to a lobe or large tooth of this leaf, the funiculus, as well as the raphe, being formed by the median nerve of the lateral lobe. M. Clos[276] mentions a similar instance in *Aquilegia Skinneri*; and another is figured in Lindley's 'Elements of Botany,' p. 88, f. 180.

FIG. 143.—Portion of an open foliaceous carpel of *Delphinium*, with ovules on the lobules.

Cramer[277], from an examination of several ovular malformations, as well as from the investigation of the mode of evolution of the ovules, is led to a similar conclusion with reference to the production of ovules[Pg 267] from the modified lobes of the carpellary leaf. Figs. 143–145, copied from Cramer, show how the nucleus of the ovule is formed as a new growth from the surface of the lobes of the leaf in *Delphinium elatum*.

FIG. 144.—Section through marginal lobe of carpel (*Delphinium*), showing the nucleus (*n*).

FIG. 145.—Section through marginal lobe of carpel, showing nucleus and tegument (*Delphinium*).

FIG. 146.—1. Placenta of *Dianthus*, bearing ovules and carpels. 2. One of the ovaries separated.

FIG. 147.—Ovules of *Dianthus* passing into carpels.

One of the most singular instances of ovular malformation in record is that cited by the Rev. M. J. Berkeley, in the 'Gardener's Chronicle,' September 28th, 1850, p. 612. The plant was a carnation, and its placenta bore, not only ovules, but also carpels (fig. 146), the latter originating in a perverted development[Pg 268] of the former, so that many intermediate stages could be traced between the ordinary ovule and the ovary (fig. 147, 1, *a*, 2, *b*). Some of these carpels, thus derived from the ovules, themselves bore secondary ovules on a marginal placenta, as shown in the sections at *c*, *d*,*e*. Could such a change occur in the animal kingdom, there would be the unfertilised ovum[Pg 269] converted into an ovary, and this again bearing Graafian vesicles! In Mr. Berkeley's carnation the change was not so great, seeing that the nucleus of the ovule was not developed, and sufficient evidence has been above given as to the foliar nature of the primine, while for a leaf to be folded up so as to form a carpel is an ordinary occurrence.

124

It is worthy of remark that in these foliaceous ovules there is never more than one coat, the secondine and other integuments do not make their appearance in these cases, and that very generally the change in question accompanies a similar foliaceous condition in the carpel, the margins of which are more or less disunited.

Prof. A. Braun remarks that up to this date no such change has been observed in the ovules of Monocotyledons.

Changes in the nucleus of the ovule.—The preceding remarks have had reference especially to the ovular coats, but it is desirable also to allude to certain points connected with the nucleus. Very frequently, when the coat of the ovule is phylloid, as before described, the nucleus is altogether wanting, though sometimes it is present as a small cellular papilla; very rarely is it to be found in its perfect state. Occasionally the nucleus is present in the guise of a small elongated branch. Wigand cites ovular buds in every stage of progress into a branch, sometimes even bearing indications of anthers. Wydler has observed a similar occurrence in ovules of *Alliaria officinalis*, and Schimper has described and figured specimens of *Nigella damascena* in which the outer coats of the ovule were but little changed, while the nucleus was replaced by a leafy shoot. On one of the leaves of this latter was found an imperfect ovule—an ovule on an ovule!

Fig. 148 shows a floret of a species of *Gaillardia*, in which the ovule was replaced by a leafy shoot which had made its way through a chink in the ovary. In[Pg 270] this specimen, however, there was no evidence to show whether the shoot in question was a perverted development of the nucleus, or whether it was wholly independent of the ovule.

FIG. 148.—Floret of *Gaillardia*, showing leafy shoot occupying the place of the ovule.

From this occasional elongation of the nucleus, as well as from the foliar nature of the ovular coats, Prof. Alex. Braun arrives at the conclusion that the ovule is to be looked on as a bud, the ovular coatings, so often variable in number, representing the scales of the bud, the nucleus corresponding to the end of the axis or growing point. Griffith had previously expressed the same opinion from his observations on malformed ovules of *Sinapis* and *Lonicera*, while Caspary's conclusions from the foliaceous ovules of *Trifolum repens* are somewhat similar. The latter observer considers that the funiculus, with the integuments, is the equivalent of a leaflet, the petiolule or midrib of which answers to the funiculus, and its hollow expansion to the integument. The nucleus itself is considered to be a new formation analogous to a shoot.

[Pg 271]

M. van Tieghem's conclusion[278] from the examination, of flowers of *Tropæolum majus*, in which the ovules were replaced by perfect peltate leaves, is that the ovules are foliar productions springing, not directly from a prolonged floral axis, as in *Primulaceæ*, but from branches of the axis arising from the axils of the carpellary leaves.

Phyllody of the ovules has been met with most often in the following species:

- *Aquilegia vulgaris!
o   Skinneri.
- Delphinium crassicaule.
o   elatum.
o   dictyocarpum.
o   Ajacis.
- Nigella damascena.
- Adonis autumnalis.
- Cheiranthus Cheiri!
- Nasturtium, sp.
- Sisymbrium officinale!
- Brassica napus!

125

- ○   *olcracea!
- *Alliaria officinalis!
- Sinapis arvensis!
- Turritis, sp.
- Thlaspi arvense.
- Erucastrum Pollichii.
- Stellaria media.
- *Reseda lutea.
- Drosera intermedia.
- Agrostemma Githago.
- Stellaria media.
- Triumfetta, sp.!
- Tropæolum majus!
- Dictamnus albus.
- ○   Fraxinella!
- Caram carui
- Pastinaca sativa.
- Torilis anthriscus.
- Thysselinum palustre.
- Epilobium palustre.
- Rosa, sp.
- Fragaria alpina.
- *Trifolium repens!
- Medicago maculata.
- Desmodium canadense.
- Melilotus macrorhiza.
- Lonicera, sp.
- Gaillardia!
- Crepis, sp.
- Phyteuma odorata.
- Symphytum Zeyheri.
- ○   *officinale.
- Stachys sylvatica.
- Anagallia arvensis.
- ○   phœnicea.
- Lysimachia ephemerum.
- *Primula sinensis!
- ○   Auricula.
- ○   prænitens.
- Gilia glomeruliflora.
- Rumex arifolius.
- ○   scutatus.

126

- Salix capræa.

The following list of publications relating to ovular malformations is copied from A. Braun, 'Ueber Polyembryonie und Keimung von Cælobogyne' (Appendix),[279] to which are also added some others not alluded to by[Pg 272] that author and not specially referred to in the preceding pages:

Jaeger, 'Missbilld. d. Gewächse,' p. 78, 79, f. 47. Rœper, 'Enum. Euphorb.,' 1824. p. 45, *Delphinium.*—Schimper, 'Flora,' 1829, pp. 437–8, et 'Mag. fur Pharmacie de Geiger,' 1829–30, pl. iv-vi, text wanting,*Primula, Reseda, Cheiranthus.*—Engelmann, 'De Antholysi,' 1832.—Valentin, 'Act. Acad. Nat. Cur.,' 1839, p. 225, *Lysimachia.*—Unger, 'Act. Acad. Nat. Cur.,' xxii, 11, 1850, p. 543, t. 5 B, *Primula.*—'Flora (B. Z.)', 1842, p. 369, t. ii, *Trifolium.*—Brongniart, 'Ann. Sc. Nat.,' 1834, ii, p. 308; also 'Archives Mus. d'Hist. Nat.,' 1844, t. iv, p. 43, pl. iv, v,*Primula.*—Reissek, 'Linnæa,' xvii, 1843, *Alliaria.*—Wydler, 'Denkshrift. d. Regensb. Bot. Gesell.,' 1855, iv, s. 77, t. vii, *Alliaria.*—Wigand. 'Grundlegung der Pflanzen Teratol.,' 1850, p. 39, *Turritis.*—Wigand, 'Bot. Untersuchungen,' 1853, p. 23, *Rosa, Turritis, Crepis.*—Germain de St. Pierre, 'L'Institut,' 1853, n. 1051, p. 351.—Rossmann, "Entwicklung der Eiknospen aus dem Fruchtblatte," &c., 'Flora,' 1855, pp. 647 and 705.—Dareste, 'Ann. Sc. Nat.,' 1842, p. 220, *Delphinium.*—Fresenius, 'Mus. Senkenb.,' ii, p. 39, t. iv, f. 9, *Primula.*—Schultz, 'Flora o. d. Bot. Zeit.,' 1834, xvii, p. 121, *Nasturtium.*—Seringe and Heyland, 'Bull. Bot.,' 1–7,*Diplotaxis.*—Clos, 'Mem. Acad. Toulouse,' vi, 1862, *Delphinium.*—Morren, C., 'Bull. Acad. Belg.,' xix, part ii, p. 519, *Primula.*—Caspary, 'Schrift. d. Physik. Œk. Gesell. zu Königsberg,' band ii, p. 51, tabs. ii, iii. Fleischer, 'Ueber Missbildungen Verschiedener Cultur Pflanzen.,' &c., Esslingen, 1862. Cramer, 'Bildungsabweich,' p. 68, &c. &c., *Trifolium.*—Moquin-Tandon, 'El. Terat. Veg.,' p. 206, *Cortusa.*—Guillard, 'Bull. Soc. Bot. Fr.,' 1857, vol. iv, p. 761, *Stellaria.*—Moelkenboer, 'Tijdschrift v. Natuurl. Geschied.,' 1843, p. 355, t. vi, vii, *Primula.*—Van Tieghem, 'Bull. Soc. Bot. Fr.,' 1865, p, 411, *Tropæolum.*

Phyllody in accessory organs.—In addition to the ordinary organs of the plant, what are termed the accessory organs, such as hairs, spines, &c., sometimes become foliaceous. It is not to be wondered at that spines, when they represent the framework of a leaf, become sometimes clothed with cellular tissue, and thus become indeed true leaves. This happens occasionally in *Berberis;* a similar thing occurs in the stipules of some*Leguminosæ*; the scales of some begonias; the tendrils of *Bignonia,Cobæa,* &c.

The presence of two small green laminæ on the outer side of the two posterior stamens in *Antirrhinum majus* has also been met with. The adventitious organs appeared as if they were developments from the thalamus—a kind of foliaceous disc, in fact.

[Pg 273]

FIG. 149.—Leafy petal of *Epilobium*.

FIG. 150.—Chloranthy, &c. *Epilobium hirsutum*.

Chloranthy.—The term phyllomorphy is applied to the individual parts of the flower which assume the form and appearance of leaves. By chloranthy it is to be understood that all, or the great majority of the organs of the flower assume these conditions.[280] In chloranthy, as here defined, there is no unusual number of buds, as there is in prolification, but the appearance of the flower-bud is so changed as to make it resemble more closely a leaf-bud than a flower-bud. There is not necessarily any increase in the number, or any alteration in the position of the buds, but the form and appearance of the latter differ from what is usual. Chloranthy, then, is a more complete form of frondescence. Owing to the vagueness with which the word has been applied by various authors, it becomes very difficult to ascertain whether the recorded instances of chloranthy were really illustrations of what is here meant by that term, or whether they were cases of mere virescence (green colour, without other perceptible change), or of prolification (formation of adventitious buds). It is, therefore, quite possible that some of[Pg 274] the instances to be now mentioned were not strictly cases of chloranthy.

127

FIG. 151.—*a*. Open leafy carpel of "green rose," with two deformed ovules. *b*.Ovule separate. *c*. Primine removed. *d*. Secondine and nucleus, with the bulbous end that projects through the micropyle.

Seringe[281] has described a malformation in *Diplotaxis tenuifolia* in which all the floral organs were replaced by sixteen distinct leaflets which had preserved their proper relative position. The *Cruciferæ*, of which family the last-named plant is a member, are particularly liable to this malformation, as also are the *Rosaceæ*, as will be seen from the following illustrations. Roses indeed often exhibit alterations of this kind as the commencement of prolification. There is also in cultivation a rose[282]called the green rose, "Rose bengale à fleurs vertes," in which all the parts of the flower are represented by leaves. One of the most remarkable features in this plant is, that the carpels have often two ovules on their margins. Now, Payer, in his "Organogénie," has shown that at a certain period of the development of the ordinary rose flower the ovary contains two collateral ovules, of which one[Pg 275] becomes in process of time suppressed.[283] *Geum coccineum* has been found by Wigand with its flowers in this condition.[284]

Lindley[285] figures a very interesting illustration in *Potentilla nepalensis*, in which some of the flowers have their component parts leafy, in others the receptacle lengthens, till in extreme cases the whole of the floral apparatus is represented by a branch bearing a rosette of leaves.

A particular variety of the Alpine strawberry is also described as occasionally subject to this transformation. In these flowers the calyx remains normal, while all the other parts of the flower, even to the coating of the ovule, assume a leaf-like condition.[286]

[Pg 276]

Among *Leguminosæ* a partial leafy condition (frondescence), or a more complete degree of the same change, (chloranthy) is not infrequent, particularly in *Trifolium repens*. In this species the changes are so common, so various and important, that they may be alluded to in some little detail. M. Germain de Saint Pierre,[287] in commenting on the frequency with which the flowers of this plant are more or less frondescent, remarks that although all the flowers on one plant may be affected, they are all changed in the same manner, but on different specimens different degrees of transformation are found. In all the corolla and stamens are comparatively little removed from the ordinary form, the calyx and pistil, however, have a particular tendency to assume a foliar condition. The author just cited arranges the malformations of this plant under three heads, as follows:

1. Calyx-teeth larger than usual, sometimes dentate at the margin; petals more or less regular and disposed to run away from the papilionaceous form; filaments free; anthers normal; carpel transformed into a true leaf with a long stalk provided at the base, with two stipules, terminal leaflet, solitary, green, with no trace of ovules. Sometimes a second carpellary leaf, similar to the first, is formed; in other cases the central axis of the flower is occasionally prolonged into a head of young flowers—median prolification. In some few instances the calyx is not at all altered, but the carpellary leaf is trifoliolate, or even quinquefoliolate,[Pg 277] the corolla being then absent. The heads of flowers in this first form have the aspect of little tufts of leaves.

2. Each of the teeth of the calyx is represented by a long stalk, terminated by a single articulated leaflet, the bi-labiate form of the calyx is still recognisable; the two upper petals are united, the three lower separate; the tube of the calyx is not deformed and seems to be formed of the petioles of the sepals united by their stipules. In this second class of cases the corolla is papilionaceous, the filaments free, the carpellary leaf on a long stalk provided with stipules, its blade more or less like the usual carpel, with its margins disunited or more commonly united with the ovules in the interior, sometimes represented by a foliaceous, dentate primine only. In one case the carpel was closed above, gaping below, where it gave origin to several leaflets, the lower ones oval, dentate, like ordinary leaflets, the upper ones merely lanceolate, leafy lobes, representing the primine reduced to a foliaceous condition. Inflorescence—a head with leafy flowers on long stalks, which are longer at the circumference than in the centre.

3. Calyx-teeth lance-shaped, acuminate; corolla more or less regular, arrested in its development and scarcely exceeding the tube of the calyx within which it is crumpled up;

stamens but little changed; carpellary leaf on a short stalk, not exceeding the calyx tube, but the ovarian portion very long, and provided with abortive ovules.

These three groups will be found to include most of the forms under which frondescence of the clover blossoms occurs, but there are, of course, intermediate forms not readily to be grouped under either of the above heads. Such are the cases brought under the notice of the British Association at Birmingham in 1849 by Mr. R. Austen, in some of which the petals and stamens even were represented by leaves.

Although, on the whole, chloranthy is most frequent in the families already alluded to, yet it is by no means confined to them, as the examples now to be given amply show. Specimens of *Nymphæa Lotus* have been seen in which all the parts of the flower, even to the stigmas, were leafy, while the ovules were entirely wanting.

Planchon[288] figures and describes a flower of *Drosera intermedia* that had passed into a chloranthic condition, excepting the calyx, which was unchanged; the petals, like the valves of the ovary, were provided with stipules, and were circinate in vernation.

[Pg 278]

M. A. Viaud-Grand-Marais[289] records an interesting example of chloranthy, in which the sepals, petals, pistils, and ovules of *Anagallis arvensis* were all foliaceous. Similar changes have not unfrequently been met with in *Dictamnus Fraxinella*.

M. Germain de Saint Pierre has also recorded the following deviations in the flowers of *Rumex arifolius* and *R. scutatus*; in these specimens the calyx was normal, the petals large, foliaceous, shaped like the stem-leaves, the stamens were absent, the three carpels fused into a triangular leafy pod, as long again as the perianth, the stigmas normal or wanting, the ovule represented by a thick funicle, terminated by a foliaceous appendage analogous to the primine.[290]

In grasses it frequently happens that the flowers are replaced by leaf-buds; this condition is alluded to elsewhere under the head of viviparous grasses, but in this place may be mentioned a less degree of change, and which seems to have been a genuine case of chloranthy in *Glyceria fluitans*, the spikelet of which, as observed by Wigand,[291] consisted below of the ordinary unchanged glumes, but the remaining paleæ as well as the lodicles and stamens were represented by ligulate leaves. The plant, it is stated, was affected by a parasitic fungus. On the other hand, General Munro, in his valuable monograph of the *Bambusaceæ*,[292] refers to an illustration in which "the lowest glumes generally, and the lowest paleæ occasionally, had the appearance of miniature leaves, with vaginæ, ligules and cilia, enveloping, however, perfect fertile spiculæ; as progress is made towards the top of the spike, the ligule first, then the cilia, and finally, the leaf-like extension disappears, and the uppermost glumes assume the ordinary shape and form of those organs."

General remarks on chloranthy and frondescence.—Moquin[Pg 279] remarks with justice that the position of the flowers on the axis is of importance with reference to the existence of chloranthy. Terminal flowers are more subject to it than lateral ones, and if the latter, by accident, become terminal, they seem peculiarly liable to assume a foliaceous condition. Kirschleger says, that in *Rubus* there are two sorts of chloranthy, according as the anomaly affects the ordinary flowering branches, or the leafy shoots of the year, the summits of which, instead of developing in the customary manner, terminate each in one vast and long inflorescence, very loose and indeterminate, and with axillary flowers.[293]

On the whole, taking in consideration cases of partial frondescence, as well as those in which most of the parts of the flower are affected, phyllody would seem to be most common in the petals and carpels, least so in the case of the stamens and sepals. It is more common among polysepalous and polypetalous plants than in those in which the sepals or petals are united together.

The causes assigned for these phenomena are chiefly those of a nature to debilitate or injure the plant; thus it has been frequently observed to follow the puncture of an insect. M. Guillard[294] gives an instance in *Stellaria media* where the condition appeared to be due to the attacks of an insect *Thrips fasciata*. Still more commonly it arises from the attacks of parasitic fungi, *e.g. Uredo candida*, in Crucifers, &c.

In other cases it has been observed when the plants have been growing in very damp places, or in very wet seasons, or in the shade, or where the plant has been much trampled on. This happens frequently with *Trifolium repens*. The frequency with which the change is encountered in this particular species is very remarkable; it is difficult to see why one species should be so much more subject to the kind of change than another of nearly identical conformation.

[Pg 280]It might at first be supposed that the same causes that bring about the complete substitution of leaf-buds for flower-buds (see Heterotaxy) would operate also in the partial substitution of leaves for other parts of the flower, but it will be seen that the inducing cause, whether similar or not in the two cases respectively, acts at different times; in the one case, it is not brought into play until the rudiments of the flower are already formed, whereas in the other the influence is exerted prior to the formation of the flower. So that while the formation of leaf-buds in place of flower-buds may be and generally is due to an excess of nutrition, inducing over activity of the vegetative organs, the production of phyllomorphic or chloranthic flowers may be owing rather to a perversion of development arising from injury or from some debilitating agency. The discrepancies in the assigned causes for the conditions above mentioned may, therefore, in great measure, be attributed to the different periods at which the causes in question operate.

The following list may serve as a guide to the plants most frequently the subjects of chloranthy, but reference should also be made to preceding and subsequent sections, and to that relating to prolification of the inflorescence.

- Aquilegia vulgaris.
- Chelidonium majus.
- Corydalis aurea.
- Nymphæa Lotus!
- *Brassica oleracea!
- Bunias.
- Hesperis matronalis.
- *Sinapis arvensis!
- Sisymbrium officinale.
- Erucastrum canariense.
- Diplotaxis tenuifolia.
- Lychnis dioica!
- Cerastium glomeratum!
  o   triviale.
- Stellaria media.
- Poterium polygamum.
- Torilis anthriscus.
- Seseli, sp.
- Selinum caruifolium.
- Epilobium hirsutum!
- Begonia fuchsioides.
- Gomphia, sp.
- Scabiosa Columbaria.
- Dipsacus fullonum.
- Matricaria Parthenium.
- Calendula officinalis.
- Campanula pyramidalis.

- Reseda odorata!
- Vitis vinifera.
- Dictamnus Fraxinella!
- Triumfetta, sp.!
- *Tropæolum majus!
- Rhamnus Frangula.
- *Trifolium repens!
- Lupinus, sp.
- Rosa diversifolia![Pg 281]
- Potentilla nepalensis.
- ○   argentea.
- Fragaria vesca!
- Geum rivale.
- Rubus fruticosus.
- ○   cæsius.
- Saxifraga foliosa.
- Verbascum phlomoides.
- Scrophularia nodosa.
- ○   aquatica!
- *Primula sinensis!
- Lysimachia Ephemerum.
- Anagallis arvensis.
- ○   Webbiana.
- Nicotiana rustica.
- Anchusa ochroleuca.
- Myosotis cæspitosa.
- Stachys sylvatica.
- Gilia capitata.
- Euphorbia segetalis.
- Rumex arifolius.
- ○   scutatus.
- Juncus lampocarpus.
- ○   uliginosus.

In addition to the publications before cited the following may be named as containing valuable information on the subject of this chapter.

Jæger, 'Missbild. Gewächs.,' 1814, p. 83, *Trifolium repens*. For other accounts of similar malformations in the same plant, see Schmitz, 'Linnæa,' xv, p. 268. Unger, 'Flora' (B. Z.) xxv, p. 369. Caspary, 'Schrift. der. Physik. ökon. Gesellsch. zu Königsberg,' 2, 1861, p. 51, tabs. ii, iii. Fleischer, 'Missbilld. verschied. Cult. Pflanz.,' 1862, p. 55, &c., t. v, vii, &c. For *Primula* see Brongniart, 'Ann. Sc. Nat.,' ser. 2, t. i, p. 308. A. P. and Alph. De Candolle in 'Neue Denkschrift.' Morren, C., 'Bull. Acad. Roy. Belg.,' xix, part 2, p. 539. Molkenboer, 'Tijdschr. voor Natuurl. Geschied.,' 1843, p. 355, tabs. vi, vii. Marchand, 'Adansonia,' iv, p. 167 and p. 159. *Anagallis*, p. 171, *Lonicera*, p. 83, *Juncus*. For other plants see Fresenius, 'Mus. Senk.,' 2, p. 35, &c. Norman, 'Ann. Sc. Nat.,' ser. 4, 1858, vol. ix, p. 220. Christ, 'Flora' (B. Z.) 1867, p. 376, tabs. v, vi,*Stachys*. Cramer, 'Bildungsabweich.,' p. 26, &c. Baillon, 'Adansonia,' ii, p. 300.

Moquin-Tandon, 'El. Ter. Veg.,' p. 230. Schauer's translation, p. 220. Hallier, 'Phytopathologie,' p. 160.

FOOTNOTES:

[245]Engelmann makes use of the word frondescence in the same cases. 'De Anthol.,' p. 32, § 38, while Morren adopts the term Phyllomorphy, 'Lobelia,' p. 95.

[246]See Schlechtendal, 'Bot. Zeit.,' vol. xv, 1857, p. 873; also Marchand, 'Adansonia,' iv, p. 156.

[247]For instances of similar changes in *Compositæ*, see De Candolle, 'Prod.,' t. vi, p. 571, *Centaurea Jacea phyllocephala*. Clos, 'Ann. Sc. Nat.,' ser. iii, tom. xvi, 1851, p. 41. 'Science Gossip,' 1865, p. 104, &c.

[248]Kickx, 'Bull. Acad. Belg.,' t. xviii, part 2, p. 288.

[249]Weber, 'Verhandl. Nat. Hist. Vereins. f. Preuss.,' &c., 1860, p. 381.

[250]Weber, loc. cit.

[251]Sauter, 'Flora v. Bot. Zeit.,' 1831, p. 11.

[252]'Descr. et Icon. Plant.' tab. 20.

[253]For references see p. 115; see also to Eichler, 'Excurs. Morpholog. de format. flor. Gymnosperm.,' in "Mart. Flor. Brasil," abstracted in English in 'Natural History Review,' April, 1864.

[254]"Calyx tunc plane non differt a foliis proxime ipsi præcedentibus." Wolff, 'Theor. Gener.,' § 114. Linn., 'Proleps.,' § 6. Goethe, 'Versuch.,' §§ 31–38.

[255]'Bull. Soc. Bot. France,' vol. viii, 1861, p. 697.

[256]'Organ. Véget.,' t. i, p. 492, pl. xxxii, f. 6.

[257]This distinction between laminar and vaginal venation is well seen in cases like *Mussaenda*, *Calycophyllum*, or *Dipterocarpus*, where the enlarged calycine segment has a strictly vaginal arrangement of its veins, very different from that which occurs in the true leaf-blades. These are cases, therefore, where the sheath of the leaf is unusually enlarged, and are not to be referred, as is often done, to metamorphosis of one or more sepals to perfect leaves. Prolified roses, cherries, &c., furnish frequently parallel cases. With reference to *Mussaenda*, C. Morren held the view that the petal-like sepal was really a bract adherent to the calyx, and incorporating with itself one of the calycine lobes—"soudée au calice et ayant dévorée, en englobant dans sa propre masse, un lobe calicinal." The Belgian *savant* considers this somewhat improbable explanation as supported by a case wherein there were five calyx lobes of uniform size, and a detached feather-veined leaf proceeding from the side of the ovary lower down ('Bull. Acad. Belg.,' xvii, p. 17, *Fuchsia*, p. 169).

[258]In this order *Agrostemma Githago* offers an illustration of a normally leafy calyx.

[259]'Bull. Bot.,' i, p. 6.

[260]Wolff's original opinion was that the stamens were equivalent to so many buds placed in the axil of the petals or sepals (see 'Theoria Generationis,' 1759, § 114)—an opinion which more recently has received the support of Agardh and Endlicher. Wolff himself, however, seems to have abandoned his original notion, for in his memoir, "De formatione intestinorum præcipue tum et de amnio spurio aliisque partibus embryonis gallinacei, nondum visis," &c., in 'Comm. Acad. Petrop.,' xii, p. 403, anno 1766, he considers the stamens as essentially buds. See also Linn. 'Prolepsis,' § viii; Goethe, 'Metam.,' § 46.

[261]Müller (Argov.), in 'Mém. Soc. Phys. et d'Hist. Nat. Genev.,' t. xvii.

[262]"If we keep in view the observations which have now been made, we shall not fail to recognise the leaf in all seed-vessels, notwithstanding their manifold forms, their variable structure, and different combinations."—(Goethe, 'Metam.,' § 78.) Wolff, 'N. Comm. Acad. Petrop.,' 1766, xii, p. 403, expresses precisely the same opinion as to the nature of the seed-vessel.

[263]'El. Terat. Veg.,' p. 205.

[264]'Ann. Sc. Nat.,' 4th series, vol. ix, p. 209.

[265]'Adansonia,' iv, p. 70. A similar deviation has been observed by M. van Tieghem in the ovary of *Tropæolum majus*, 'Bull. Soc. Bot. Fr.,' 1865, p. 411.

[266]Planchon et Marès, 'Ann. Sc. Nat.,' ser. 5, vol. vi, 1866, p. 228, tab. xii.

[267]'Act. Acad. Nat. Cur.,' 22, 11. 1850, p. 543, t. v, vi.

[268]'Neue Denkschrift der allg. Schweiz. Gesellsch.,' band v. p. 9, tab. 3, 4.

[269]'Ann. Sc. Nat.,' 2 ser., vol. i, p. 308, pl. ix, c.

[270]'Adansonia,' vol. iv, pp. 159, 171.

[271]'Bildungsabweichungen,' &c., tab. iv, figs. 1, 2, 21, 28, 29, &c.

[272]'Bull. Soc. Bot. France,' viii, p. 395.

[273]'Notulæ,' p. 125, atlas, pl. xxxv; and 'Journals of Travels,' 1847, p. 475, *Lonicera*.

[274]'Ann. Science Nat.,' 3rd ser., vol. ix, p. 86, tabs. 5, 6.

[275]'Comptes Rendus,' vol. xviii, March 25th, 1864, and 'Ann. Sc. Nat.,' 3 ser., vol. ii, p. 32.

[276]'Mém. Acad. Sc. Toulous.,' ser. 5, vol. iii.

[277]'Bildungsabweich. Pflanz. Famil.,' p. 89, tab. xi.

[278]'Bull. Soc. Bot. Fr.,' 1865, p. 411.

[279]Translated in 'Ann. Sc. Nat.,' 4th series, t. xiv, p. 24.

[280]The calyx is not unfrequently excepted.

[281]'Bull. Bot.,' t. i, p. 6.

[282]Lindley, 'Theor. Horticult.,' ed. 2, p. 84, f. 17.

[283]Gris, 'Bull. Soc. Bot. Fr.,' 1858, vol. v, p. 261, and 'Ann. Sc. Nat.,' ser. 4, vol. ix, p. 80. Planchon, 'Flore des Serres,' vol. i, 1856, p. 129.

[284]'Flora,' 1856, p. 711.

[285]'Theory of Horticult.,' ed. 2, p. 90, f. 25.

[286]As considerable interest attaches to the "Plymouth strawberry," and very little is known of it in this country, or on the continent, the author gladly avails himself of this opportunity of inserting an account of it, for which he is indebted to the kindness of Dr. Robert Hogg.—The Plymouth Strawberry (*Fragaria vesca fructu hispido*) is a sort of botanical Dodo upon which many have written, and which few have seen. Many years have elapsed since it was first discovered; and although a century and a half have passed since there was any evidence of its existence, it serves still as an illustration for students in morphology of one of those strange abnormal structures with which the vegetable kingdom abounds.

It is to old John Tradescant we are indebted for the earliest record of this plant. Johnson, in his edition of 'Gerard,' says; "Mr. John Tradescant hath told me that he was the first that tooke notice of this strawberry, and that in a woman's garden at Plimouth, whose daughter had gathered and set the roots in her garden, in stead of the common strawberry; but she, finding the fruit not to answer her expectation, intended to throw it away; which labour he spared her in taking it and bestowing it among the louers of such varieties, in whose garden it is yet preserved." Doubtless one of those "lovers" was his friend John Parkinson, who, in the year 1629, thus wrote concerning it: "One strawberry more I promised to shew you, which, although it be a wilde kinde, and of no vse for meate, yet I would not let this discourse passe without giuing you the knowledge of it. It is in leafe much like vnto the ordinary, but differeth in that the flower, if it haue any, is greene, or rather it beareth a small head of greene leaues, many set thicke together like vnto a double ruffe, in the midst whereof standeth the fruit, which, when it is ripe, sheweth to be soft and somewhat reddish, like vnto a strawberry, but with many small harmlesse prickles on them which may be eaten and chewed in the mouth without any maner of offence and is somewhat pleasant as a strawberry; it is no great bearer, but those it doth beare, are set at the toppes of the stalks close together, pleasant to behold, and fit for a gentlewoman to weare on her arme, &c., as a rairitie in stead of a flower."

Merret, in his 'Pinax.' published in 1667, says he found it growing in the woods of Hyde Park and Hampstead, and Zanoni was the first to figure it (with the exception of Parkinson's rude woodcut) in his 'Istoria Botanica,' published in 1675. It is mentioned by Morison and also by Ray, the latter of whom inserts it in his Synopsis, but without any habitat; though in his 'Historia Plantarum' he says: "Cantabrigiæ in horto per aliquot annos colui." From this time henceforth the Plymouth strawberry has become a botanical Dodo, nothing more having been seen or heard of it except the mere record of the name. In 1766, M. Duchesne informed the world of the generosity of "M. Monti, Docteur de Philosophie et de Médecine à Boulogne en Italie," who divided with him a dried specimen taken from his own herbarium, "Ce présent prétieux m'ôte toute incertitude sur la nature de ce Fraisier et sur ses caractères monstrueux. Il paroît ne pas avoir aujourd'hui plus d'existence."

[287]'Bull. Soc. Bot. France,' 1856, vol. iii, p. 477.

[288]'Ann. Sc. Nat.,' 3 ser., vol. ix, p. 86, tabs. v, vi.

[289]'Bull. Soc. Bot. France,' vol. viii, 1861, p. 695.

[290]Ibid., vol. iii, 1856, p. 475.

[291]'Flora,' 1856, p. 712.

[292]'Trans. Linn. Soc.,' vol. xxvi, p. 37.

[293]'Bull. Soc. Bot. France,' 1862, vol. ix, p. 36, tab. i, and also p. 291.

[294]Ibid., 1857, vol. iv, p. 761.

CHAPTER II.
METAMORPHY OF THE FLORAL ORGANS.

One of the main arguments adduced by Goethe and others in support of the now generally received doctrine of the essential morphological identity of the various whorls of the flower is derived from the frequent appearance of one organ in the guise of another. The several parts of the flower become, as it is said,[Pg 282] metamorphosed; sometimes the change is complete, while at other times there may be every conceivable intermediate condition between one form and another. The sense in which the terms metamorphosis, substitution, transformation, and the like, are herein used has already been explained. For the convenience of arrangement, metamorphosis of the parts of the flower may be divided into several subdivisions, according to the particular organ affected, and according to the special kind or degree of change manifested, the main subdivisions being here classed as Sepalody, Petalody, Staminody, and Pistillody.

Sepalody of the petals.—This change, spoken of by most authors as retrograde metamorphosis of the petals into sepals, or as a substitution of sepals for petals, is obviously a condition that is in most cases hardly distinguishable from virescence of the corolla, or from multiplication of the sepals. Nor is this of much consequence unless there are some special structural features which render the discrimination a matter of importance, in which case the difficulty is generally easily surmounted. The flower of the Saint-Valèry Apple may perhaps be cited under this head. In the flower in question there are neither stamens nor petals, unless the second or inner of sepals be considered as sepaloid petals (fig. 152).

FIG. 152.—Flower of St. Valèry apple, with sepaloid petals.

M. Alph. de Candolle[295] describes an instance in *Primula Auricula* in which the corolla had assumed the appearance of the calyx, but neither calyx nor corolla in this case possessed perfect stomata.

This malformation is much less common than the converse one of calycanthemy. Many of the recorded instances of so-called metamorphosis of the parts of[Pg 283] the flower to sepals have occurred in monocotyledonous plants, or others in which the calyx and corolla are of the same colour, and constitute what is frequently termed the perianth; and as this is usually brightly coloured (not green) it is more convenient to group the metamorphoses in question under the general term Petalody, which thus includes all those cases in which the organs of the flower appear in the form of coloured petal-like organs, whether they be true petals or segments of a coloured perianth. As the morphological difference between the organs is one of position merely, there is little objection to be raised to this course, the less so as the term petalody merely conveys an idea of resemblance and not of absolute identity.

Petaloid coloration of the ordinary leaves, or of the bracts, is mentioned under the chapter relating to colour.

Petalody of the calyx—Calycanthemy.—As with the bracts, so the calyx in certain instances is naturally coloured, as in *Delphinium*, *Tropæolum*, and others. In *Mussænda*, *Calycophyllum*, *Usteria*, &c., one or more of the calyx lobes become enlarged normally. Considered teratologically, petaloid coloration of the sepals is either general or partial; in the latter case the nerves retain their green colour longest. There is in cultivation a variety of the primrose called *Primula calycanthema*, in which the upper part of the calyx becomes coloured, so that the flower seems to have two corollas placed one within the other; a similar thing happens in *Mimulus*, in which plant, as the calyx is permanent while the corolla is deciduous, the coloured calyx is a great advantage in a horticultural point of view.

Morren[296] says that in order to produce the fine colour of the calyx of *Primula officinalis* (var. *smaragdina*) the Belgian gardeners cut away the corolla in a very early stage, and that in consequence the colouring matter[Pg 284]proper to the corolla is developed in the tube of the calyx, the edges of the limb remaining green, the middle of the limb being purple (*Primula tricolor*).

FIG. 153.—Flower of *Mimulus*, with petaloid calyx.

Under this head may be mentioned the occurrence of tubular sepals in place of the ordinary flat ones in *Helleborus olympicus*; only two of the sepals were thus affected in a specimen recently observed—a third exhibited an intermediate condition.

The normal coloration of the calyx occurs most frequently in polysepalous calyces; teratological coloration, on the other hand, occurs especially in gamosepalous flowers. This assertion is borne out by the frequency of the change in the plants already mentioned, and also in the following:—*Campanula persicifolia, Anagallis arvensis, Gloxinia, Syringa persica*,[297] *Calceolaria, &c. &c.* In the last-named plant one or more of the lobes of the calyx may frequently be seen replaced by a slipper-like petal.

[Pg 285]

Among polysepalous plants petaloid sepals have been observed in *Ranunculus auricomus, Rubus cæsius, &c.* Fleischer also describes a case of this kind in *Carum carui*.[298]

It will be seen from the above that in the majority of cases there is no real metamorphosis or substitution of petal for calyx, but simply an alteration in colour; nevertheless, a change in form may accompany a change of colour: this happens especially if there has been any displacement of organs. Thus, if, in an orchidaceous plant, a sepal be displaced from any cause, or a petal be twisted out of its natural position to occupy the place of an absent sepal, that petal will be sepal-like in form, and *vice versâ*.

Petalody of the stamens.—A petaloid condition of the stamens is one of the commonest of all malformations. A large number of so-called double flowers (flores pleni)[299] owe their peculiar appearance to this circumstance.

It is necessary to distinguish carefully this petaloid development of the stamens from the corresponding condition of the pistils, and from that kind of doubling which is a result of multiplication of the corolla, as in *Datura, Campanula, Primula*, &c. (flores duplices, triplices, &c.), or from that produced by true median prolification (flores geminati, &c.).

In cases of true petaloid development of the stamens there are usually numerous intermediate forms between that of the true petals and that of the perfect stamens; indeed, in *Nymphæa, Canna*, and in some other plants, such a transition occurs normally. Petalody of the stamens may occur either without material change in the flower or it may exist in combination or in conjunction with an increased development of parts (Multiplication), or with a similar change in the carpels, and it is either partial or complete.

[Pg 286]Among the flowers in which petaloid development of the stamens happens most frequently may be mentioned those in which the calyx is normally coloured, as in *Nigella damascena, Aquilegia*, and *Delphinium*.

M. Alph. de Candolle, in the 'Neue Denkschriften,' 1841, described and figured a singular form of *Viola odorata*, known under the name of "Bruneau," in Switzerland, in which the stamens are absent, and their place supplied by a second row of petals, within which is a third series of petals, representing, says M. de Candolle, the inner row of stamens that theory suggests should exist in the natural condition. Moreover, the carpels in this variety are five in number instead of three. In *Erica Tetralix* the corolla may not unfrequently be found divided to the base into its constituent petals, and the place of the stamens occupied by a series of petal-like structures entirely destitute of anther.

In monocotyledonous flowers, especially those with a coloured perianth, the substitution of segments of the perianth for stamens occurs not unfrequently. M. Seringe has observed this in the stamens of *Lilium Martagon*, and there is in cultivation a variety of the white lily, *Lilium candidum*, sometimes called the double white lily, in which the segments of the perianth, in place of being arranged in two rows, are greatly increased in number, and disposed in a spiral manner. In these flowers, not only are the stamens and pistils thus modified, but also the upper leaves of the stem. In so-called double tulips there is likewise a replacement of stamens by coloured segments of the perianth, but this happens generally in connection with an increase in the number of organs. Moquin-Tandon remarks having seen in a garden in the environs of Montpelier a tulip, the stamens of which showed all possible stages of transition between the form proper to them and that of the perianth. The pistil in this case was transformed into several small leaves. Similar appearances have been observed in Iris, Hyacinths, Narcissus,[Pg 287] Colchicum, and Crocus. M. Fournier[300] describes a flower of *Narcissus Tazetta* from within the normal perianth of which sprang a second one, equally provided with a cup and occupying the space usually filled by the stamens. Flowers of *Narcissus poeticus* may also be met with in which the stamens are replaced by six distinct segments exactly resembling those of the perianth in miniature.[301]

FIG. 154.—**Double columbine,** *Aquilegia*—**petalody of the filament.**

From an examination of these flowers it becomes evident that petalification is brought about in different flowers in different ways; sometimes it is the filament which becomes petaloid, sometimes the anther-lobes, while at other times it is the connective which assumes the appearance of petals.[302] For instance, in *Solanum*[Pg 288] *tuberosum, S. Dulcamara*, in *Anagallis*, in *Fuchsia*, and some other plants, the anther-lobes themselves become petaloid, while the filament remains unchanged.

In gardens two distinct varieties of Columbine are cultivated, the one in which the filaments are dilated into the form of flat petals almost entirely or quite destitute of anthers, while in the other the filament is present in its usual form, but the anther is developed in the shape of a tubular hood or spur.

De Candolle[303] observes that in the *Ranunculaceæ* the species of *Clematis* become double by the expansion of the filament, those of *Ranunculus* by the dilatation of the anther, and those of *Helleborus* by the petal-like development of both filament and anther. In some cases even on the same plant all three modifications may be seen, as in Camellias, some of which may be found with petaloid filaments with anthers on the top, others with the filaments unchanged, but supporting petaloid anthers, while in others it is the connective alone which is petal-like. Where the flower naturally contains a large number of stamens, as in Mallows, Roses, Magnolias, &c., petaloid expansion of the filament is most common, though it is by no means confined to such flowers, the change occurring in *Allamanda cathartica, Jasminum grandiflorum*, and many other flowers with few stamens. A similar change in the anther and connective takes place more frequently in flowers where the number of stamens is smaller, but there are of course numerous exceptions to this rule.

In those cases where there is more than one row of stamens, the outermost are most liable to this change: thus in *Saxifraga decipiens*, as shown by Ch. Morren,[304] the outer series of stamens—those opposite to the sepals—become first affected, and, at a more advanced stage, the inner row also; and this is the case in most[Pg 289] flowers that have their stamens in two rows. Occasionally it happens that an outer series of stamens is abortive, or wholly suppressed, while the inner row becomes petalodic; this was the case in some flowers of *Lilium auratum* lately exhibited by Messrs. Veitch.

Those flowers in which only a portion of the stamens undergo this change are called semi-double, while in other cases that will be hereafter mentioned, not only are the stamens thus rendered petaloid, but their number is also augmented, as in most double roses, pinks, anemones, poppies, &c.

In some double flowers, in which the stamens assume more or less completely the appearance of petals, a singular appearance is afforded by the presence of four wing-like processes emanating from the central filaments, two on each side, so that the arrangement may be compared to two sheets of paper folded in the centre and adherent in that situation, though perfectly separate elsewhere, except sometimes at the top, where they form a sort of hood. This change results from an imperfect petalody of the anther; the two wings on each side of the central vascular cord represent the front and back walls of an anther lobe, or rather of that portion of the anther which, under ordinary circumstances, produces pollen. In the malformed flowers no pollen is formed, at least in the more complete states of the malformation, but the walls of the anther lobe become preternaturally enlarged, and petaloid in texture and appearance. This change occurs in some semi-double rhododendrons and azaleas, in crocuses, and in a species of violet found at Mentone by Mr. J. T. Moggridge.

There are numerous intermediate forms wherein the wing-like processes may be traced all the way along the filament till they ultimately lose themselves in the anther-lobes, with which they become continuous. In some cases, as in *Crocus* and *Rhododendron*, this is shown even more clearly by the existence of two perfect pollen-sacs or quarter-anthers, the remaining portions[Pg 290] being petaloid and continuous with the dilated filament. Not unfrequently these semi-petaloid stamens adhere to the fronts of the petals, and then it appears, at a first glance, as if three organs were stuck together, one in front of another, while in reality there are but two.[305](See *antè*, p. 35, fig. 12.)

FIG. 155.—**Four-winged filaments of *Rhododendron*.**

The change in the anther, above alluded to, must not be mistaken for that far more common one in which only a small portion of the anther becomes petaloid, forming a sort of lateral wing or appendage to the polliniferous portion, as happens normally in *Pterandra*, and is common in some double fuchsias. In this latter instance there is but a single wing, and the nature of the case is obvious.

Double flowers of *Orchidaceæ* generally arise from petalification of the filaments, with or without other coincident changes. What makes double flowers in this order the more interesting is the development, in a petaloid condition, of some or all of those stamens which under ordinary circumstances are wholly suppressed, so that the morphological structure of the flower, at first a matter of theory, becomes actually[Pg 291] realised. Fig. 156 is a diagram showing the presence of two additional labella within the ordinary one in a species of *Catasetum*, and representing two petaloid stamens, thus evidently completing the outer staminal whorl, of which there is usually but a single representative (see Peloria, Multiplication, Prolification). In some of these double orchids it is, however, necessary not to confound a petaloid condition of the existing column with the development of usually suppressed stamens in a petaloid form. Thus, in *Lycaste Skinneri* the column is frequently provided with two petal-like wings, which might readily be supposed to be two stamens of the inner whorl adherent to the column; a little attention, however, to the relative position of these adventitious wings is generally sufficient to enable the observer to ascertain the true nature of the appearance.[306]

FIG. 156.—**Diagram of flower of *Catasetum*, with two labella.**

Some forms of duplicate or hose in hose corollas are apparently due, not so much to the formation of a second corolla within the first, as to the presence of an inner series of petal-like stamens, which, by their cohesion, form a second pseudo-corolla within the first. The staminal nature of this pseudo-corolla is inferred from the occasional presence of anthers on it.[307] In *Datura fastuosa*, as well as in *Gloxinia*, a pseudo-corolla of this kind sometimes occurs with the addition of a series of petaloid stamens attached to its outer surface.[308]

When the petalody specially affects the anther-lobes, as in *Arbutus*,*Petunia*, *Fuchsia*, *&c.*, the venation of the petal-like portion is very frequently laminar, thus[Pg 292] tending to show that the anther is in such cases really a modification of the blade of the leaf; but as, on the other hand, we often find petal-like filaments bearing pollen-sacs on their sides, it is clear that we must not attribute the formation of pollen to the blade of the leaf only, but we must admit that it may be formed in the filament as well.[309]

[Pg 293]

FIG. 158.—**Portion of a double columbine (*Aquilegia*), showing petalody of the connective.**

FIG. 159.—**Petaloid stamens, *Hibiscus*.**

Petalody of the connective is of less frequent occurrence than the corresponding change in the other portions of the stamen. It may be seen in some forms of double columbine,[310] in which the connective forms a tubular petal or nectary, and in double petunias and fuchsias. When it occurs, the true[Pg 294] anther-lobes are usually atrophied, and little or no pollen is formed.

An occurrence of this nature in *Tacsonia pinnatistipula*, in conjunction with the partial detachment of the stamens from the gynophore, led Karsten to establish a genus which he called *Poggendorffia*.[311]

From the subjoined list of genera in which petalody of the stamens, in some form or other, has been observed, it will be seen that it happens more often in plants with numerous distinct organs (Polypetalæ, Polyandria, Polygynia, &c.) than in other plants with a smaller number of parts, and which are more or less adherent one to the other. The tendency to petalification is, moreover, greater among those plants which have their floral elements arranged in spiral series, than among those where the verticillate arrangement exists; and in any given flower, if the stamens are spirally arranged while the carpels are grouped in whorls, the former will be more liable to petalody than the latter, and *vice versâ*. It has been before remarked, that this condition is far more common in plants whose petals, &c., have straight veins, like those in the sheath of a leaf, than in those the venation of which is reticulate, as in the blade of the leaf. It must also be remembered that in the same genus, even in the same species, different kinds of doubling occur. Familiar illustrations of this are afforded in the case of anemones, columbines, fuchsias, and other plants.

The existence of "compound stamens" in some flowers, as pointed out by Payer, and others, and the researches of Dr. Alexander Dickson, confer additional importance on the subject of petalody, and necessitate the examination of double flowers with special reference to these compound stamens, and to the order of their development.[312] The presence of these compound stamens[Pg 295] affords a satisfactory explanation of the appearance in some double *Malvaceæ*, wherein the tufts of adventitious petals are very liable to be mistaken for buds, produced by axillary prolification in the axils of the petals, but which are in reality compound and petaloid stamens. At other times, however, true axillary prolification exists in these flowers; but then the supplemental florets have always a calyx, which is wanting in the other instances.

Petalody of the stamens has been met with most frequently in the following genera:

- *Ranunculus!
- *Anemone!
- *Papaver!
- *Clematis!
- *Hepatica!
- *Ficaria!
- Thalictrum.
- *Caltha!
- *Trollius!
- *Nigella!
- *Aquilegia!
- *Delphinium!
- *Adonis!
- *Pæonia!
- *Nelumbium!
- *Nymphæa!
- *Berberis!
- *Papaver!
- *Chelidonium!

138

- Sanguinaria.
- Podophyllum.
- *Mathiola!
- *Cheiranthus!
- *Iberis!
- *Cardamine!
- *Hesperis.
- *Barbarea!
- *Sinapis!
- *Brassica!
- *Helianthemum!
- *Viola!
- *Dianthus!
- *Saponaria!
- *Lychnis!
- *Silene!
- *Sagina!
- *Hibiscus!
- *Althæa!
- *Malva!
- Æsculus!
- *Geranium!
- *Pelargonium.
- *Tropæolum!
- Oxalis!
- *Impatiens!
- *Camellia!
- Thea!
- Trifolium!
- Medicago!
- *Ulex!
- Spartianthus.
- Clitoria.
- Pisum!
- Orobus!
- Genista!
- Spartium!
- Cytisus!
- Anthyllis.
- Coronilla.
- Lotus!

- *Rosa!
- *Kerria!
- *Spiræa!
- *Fragaria!
- *Potentilla!
- *Cratægus!
- Cydonia.
- *Pyrus!
- Eriobotrya!
- *Amygdalus!
- *Prunus!
- *Myrtus!
- *Punica!
- *Philadelphus!
- *Deutzia!
- *Fuchsia!
- Godetia!
- Clarkia![Pg 296]
- Portulaca!
- Ribes!
- Saxifraga!
- Daucus.
- Ixora.
- Serissa!
- Gardenia!
- Lonicera!
- Sambucus.
- Viburnum.
- Scabiosa.
- *Campanula!
- Platycodon!
- Calluna!
- Azalea!
- Rhododendron!
- *Arbutus!
- *Erica!
- *Anagallis!
- *Primula!
- *Jasminum!
- Syringa!
- *Vinca!

- *Nerium!
- Allamanda!
- Tabernæmontana.
- *Calystegia!
- Convolvulus!
- Ipomœa.
- *Datura!
- *Petunia!
- Solanum!
- Orobanche.
- Gentiana.
- Mimulus.
- *Antirrhinum!
- Gratiola!
- *Digitalis!
- *Linaria!
- Veronica!
- Calceolaria!
- Achimenes.
- Gloxinia!
- Clerodendron!
- Bignonia.
- Cyclamen!
- Mirabilis.
- Laurus!
- Gladiolus!
- Crocus!
- Iris!
- *Galanthus!
- Leucojum!
- Sternbergia!
- Hippeastrum.
- *Narcissus!
- *Orchis!
- Catasetum!
- Hydrocharis.
- Asphodelus.
- *Tulipa!
- Scilla.
- *Convallaria!
- Fritillaria!

- *Lilium!
- *Hyacinthus!
- *Polianthes!
- *Hemerocallis!
- *Colchicum!
- *Sagittaria!
- *Tradescantia!
- Commelyna!
- Tofieldia.

Petalody of the pistils.—Taken by itself, this is much less common than the corresponding change in the stamens. It generally affects the style and stigma only, as happens normally in *Petalostylis, Iris*, &c., but this is by no means always necessarily the case. In some of the cultivated varieties of *Anemone* and *Ranunculus* all the parts of the flower remain in their normal state, except the pistils, which latter assume a petaloid appearance.

Many of the double flowers owe their peculiar appearance to the combination of the following appearances—a petal-like form of the stamens, increase in[Pg 297] the number of these organs and similar changes affecting the pistils, and is applied to several distinct conditions. If in any given flower all the stamens and all the pistils become wholly petaloid, no pollen is formed, and of course no seeds can be produced, but this very rarely happens, as usually some pollen is produced, and some ovules capable of being fertilised are developed.

In double flowers of *Primula sinensis* it frequently happens that the capsule is either partially leafy or partly petal-like; in either case the fruit is open at the extremity, and often destitute of the style and stigma. It is, however, doubtful if the ovules can be fertilised in these flowers.

The following list comprises the names of those genera in which this change has been most frequently observed, independently of corresponding alterations in the stamens, but it is more usual for both sets of organs to be similarly affected.

- *Ranunculus!
- *Anemone!
- Nigella.
- *Papaver!
- *Dianthus!
- Saponaria!
- Viola!
- Camellia!
- Alcea.
- Hibiscus!
- Amygdalus!
- Lonicera!
- Scabiosa.
- Æschynanthus!
- Primula!

Petalody of the ovules.—The principal changes which occur in the ovule have already been alluded to at pp. 262–272; it may here be stated, however, that the ovules are occasionally represented by small stalked petal-like structures. This happens with especial frequency among *Cruciferæ*.[313]

142

Petalody of the accessory organs.—A petaloid condition of the disc, of the scales, or other excrescences from the axis or from the lateral portions of the flower, is of frequent occurrence, though it is but rarely that the change is of any great importance in a morphological[Pg 298] point of view. C. Morren has given the name adenopetaly to a case wherein one of the glands at the base of the petals in *Lopezia* was replaced by a petal.[314] A similar change may be seen in the double Oleander.

Staminody of the bracts.—An instance of this has been already alluded to in *Abies excelsa*, as observed by Prof. Dickson, and in which some of the bracts were seen assuming the form and characteristic of the stamens see *ante*: p. 192. Signor Licopoli met with a similar substitution of anthers for bracts in *Melianthus major*.[315]

Staminody of the sepals and petals.—In the first named this is of very rare occurrence. M. Gris has recorded an instance in *Philadelphus speciosus*[316] which appears to be the only case on record. The corresponding change in the case of the petals is far more common. De Candolle cites in illustration of this occurrence flowers of the common haricot, in which the alæ and carina of the corolla were thus changed.[317]There is in cultivation a form of *Saxifraga granulata* wherein the petals are replaced by stamens, so that there are fifteen stamens. A similar change has been observed in *Capsella bursa-pastoris*.

Cramer figures and describes a stamen occupying the place of a petal in*Daucus Carota*.[318] Turpin[319] describes a similar occurrence in*Monarda fistulosa*, in which the lower lip terminated in an anther, but this may have been a case of adhesion. Moquin cites from Chamisso, *Digitalis purpurea*, and from Jussieu, *Asphodelus ramosus*, as having presented this change, and Wiegmann[320] has seen anthers developed on the awns of*Avena chinensis*. In semi-double flowers of *Ophrys aranifera* and *Orchis mascula*, the lateral petals[Pg 299] are occasionally partially antheroid, and others occur in which two of the outer series of stamens, which are ordinarily suppressed, are present, but in a petaloid state. Reichenbach[321] figures an illustration of this change, and also Moggridge.[322]

Staminody of the pistils.—The existence of this change has been denied by several authors, nevertheless, it is of sufficiently common occurrence. Alexander Braun notices the transformation of pistils into stamens in Chives (*Allium Scorodoprasum*), and in which three stamens appeared in the place of as many pistils, and had extrorse anthers, while the six normal anthers are introrse. In the horse-radish (*Armoracia rusticana*), two of the carpels are frequently converted into stamens, while two other organs absent from the normal flower make their appearance as carpels. Roeper has observed this phenomenon in *Euphorbia palustris*,[323] and in*Gentiana campestris*.[324] In these examples one of the carpels was apparently absent, and its place supplied by an anther. Roeper has also mentioned a balsam with a supernumerary stamen occupying exactly the position of a carpel.[325]

Agardh has observed a similar thing in a hyacinth, one half of the fruit of which contained seeds, and the other half, anthers. B. Clarke mentions an instance in *Mathiola incana* in which the carpels were disunited, and antheriferous at the margin.[326]

The passage of pistils to stamens in willows has been frequently remarked, as in *Salix babylonica, silesiaca, cinerea, Caprea* and *nigricans*. One of the most curious illustrations of this transformation in this genus is given by Henry and Macquart (Erst. Jahrb. des bot. Vereines am m. et n. Rhein., 1837). In the flowers in[Pg 300] question the series of changes were as follows:—first, the ovary opened by a slit, and then expanded into a cup; next, anther-cells were developed on the margin of the cup, with stigmas alternating with them, the ovules at the same time disappearing; lastly, the margin became divided, and bore three perfect anthers, which in the more perfect states were raised on three filaments.

Campanula persicifolia, C. rapunculoides, and *C. glomerata* have been observed to present an anther surmounting the pistil.[327] Double tulips often present this change, and a like appearance has been observed in*Galanthus nivalis*, and *Narcissus Tazetta*.

Moquin mentions the existence of this condition in a female plant of maize, some of the pistils of which were wholly or partially converted into anther-like organs. Mohl has recorded an analogous malformation in *Chamærops humilis*, and in which the three carpels were normally formed, and only differed from natural ovaries in this, that along the two edges of the ventral suture there was a yellow thickening, which a cross section of the ovary showed to be an anther-lobe filled with pollen.[328]

In *Tofieldia calyculata* a similar substitution of a stamen for a carpel has been observed by Klotsch,[329] and Weber[330] gives other instances in *Prunus* and *Pæonia*. Corresponding alterations may be met with in cultivated tulips, in the cowslip and other plants. In most of the above cases the transmutation has been perfect, but in quite an equal number of cases a portion only of the carpel is thus changed, generally the style or the stigma; thus Baillon describes the stigmas of *Ricinus communis* as having been in one instance[Pg 301] antheriferous.[331] Moggridge figures a flower of *Ophrys insectifera* in which the rostellate process was replaced by an anther.[332]

Mohl remarks that the change of pistils into stamens is more common in monocarpellary pistils than it is in those which are made up of several carpels. It seems clear that in this transformation the lobes of the anther and the development of pollen have no relation to the production of ovules.

Staminody of the accessory organs of the flower.—The scales that are met with in some plants, either as excrescences from the petals, or as imperfect representatives of stamens or other organs, are occasionally staminoid; thus the scales of *Saponaria officinalis*, of *Silene, Nerium Oleander*, the rays of *Passiflora*, the corona of *Narcissus*, have all been observed occasionally to bear anthers.[333] In the case of *Narcissus* the loose spongy tissue of the corona seems to have the nearest analogy to the anther-lobes, while the prolonged connective is more like the ordinary segments of the perianth in texture. The species in which this change may most frequently be observed are, *N. poeticus, N. incomparabilis*, and *N. montanus*.

M. Bureau found in some flowers of *Antirrhinum majus* two petal-like bodies standing up in front of, or opposite to the two petals of the upper lip,[334] and similar developments in which each of the two adventitious segments are surmounted by an anther may be met with frequently. It does not follow because these organs bear anthers that they are morphologically true stamens. They are really scales, &c., taking on themselves accidentally the characters proper to stamens.

[Pg 302]**Pistillody of the perianth.**—The passage of the segments of the perianth into carpels has been observed frequently in *Tulipa Gesneriana*, the change in question being generally attended by a partial virescence. M. Gay is said by Moquin to have observed a flower of *Crocus nudiflorus* in which the segments of the perianth were cleft and fringed at the same time, so that they presented the appearance of the stigmas.

FIG. 160.—**Flower of tulip, allowing vertical attachment of a leaf, and also the existence of ovules on the margins of the segments of the perianth. Some of the parts are removed.**

Pistillody of the sepals.—In some double flowers of the garden pea communicated by Mr. Laxton, among other peculiarities was a supernumerary 5–6-leaved calyx, some of the segments of which were of a carpellary nature, and bore imperfect ovules on their margins, while at their extremities they were drawn out into styles.[335]

[Pg 303]

Pistillody of the stamens.—This change whereby the stamens assume more or less the appearance of pistils is more commonly met with than is the metamorphosis of the envelopes of the flower into carpels. In some cases the whole of the stamen appears to be changed, while in others it is the filament alone that is altered, the anther being deficient, or rudimentary; while, in a third class of cases, the filament is unaffected, and the anther undergoes the change in question. In those instances in which the filament appears to be the portion most implicated, it becomes dilated so as to resemble a leaf-sheath rather than a leaf-stalk, as it does usually.

One of the most curious cases of this kind is that recorded in the 'Botanical Magazine,' (tab. 5160, f. 4) as having occurred in *Begonia frigida* already alluded to, and in which, in the centre of a male flower, were four free ovoid ovaries alternating with as many stamens. In the normal flowers of this plant, as is well known, the male flowers have several stamens, while in the female flowers the ovary is strictly inferior, so that, in the singular flower just described, the perianth was inferior instead of being superior, as it is usually. It should be added also that the perianth in these malformed flowers was precisely like that which occurs ordinarily in the male flowers.

FIG. 161.—Supernumerary carpels in the orange, arising from substitution of pistils for stamens.

In some varieties of the orange, called by the French "bigarades cornues," the thalamus of the flower, which is usually short, and terminated by a glandular ring-like disc, is prolonged into a little stalk or gynophore, bearing a ring of supernumerary carpels. These carpels are isolated one[Pg 304]from another, and are formed by the transformation of the filaments of the stamens.[336]

The additional carpels in the case of the apple of St. Valéry, in which the petals are of a green colour, like the sepals, are by some attributed to the transformation of the stamens into carpels. These adventitious carpels frequently contain imperfect ovules and form a whorl above the normal ones. (See *Pyrus dioica* of Willdenow.)[337] A similar change occasionally happens in the stamens of *Magnolia fuscata*, while in double tulips this phenomenon is very frequent, and among them may be found all stages of transition between stamens and pistils, and many of the parts combining the characters of both.[338] Dunal and Campdera have described flowers of *Rumex crispus*, with seven pistils, occupying the place of as many stamens.

FIG. 162.—Substitution of carpels for stamens in *Papaver*.

In *Papaver bracteatum* a considerable number of the stamens sometimes become developed into pistils,[Pg 305] especially those which are nearest to the centre of the flower, and in these flowers the filaments are said to become the ovaries, while the anthers are curled so as to resemble stigmas. A similar change is not infrequent *Papaver somniferum*. Goeppert, who found numerous instances of the kind in a field near Breslau, says the peculiarity was reproduced by seed for two years in succession.[339]Wigand ('Flora,' 1856, p. 717) has noticed among other changes the pistil of *Gentiana Amarella* bearing two sessile anthers. *Polemonium cœruleum*is another plant very subject to this change.

Brongniart[340] describes a flower of this species in which the stamens were represented by a circle of carpels united to each other so as to form a sheath around the central ovary. By artificial fertilization M. Brongniart obtained fertile seeds from the central normal ovary as well as from the surrounding metamorphosed stamens.

Cheiranthus Cheiri has long been known as one of the plants most subject to this anomaly. De Candolle even mentions it in his 'Prodromus' as a distinct variety, under the name of *gynantherus*. Brongniart (loc. cit.) thus refers to the *Cheiranthus*:—"Sometimes these six carpellary leaves are perfectly free, and in this case they spread open, presenting two rows of ovules along their inner edges, or these edges maybe soldered together, forming a kind of follicle like that of the columbine; at other times, these staminal pistils are fused into two lateral bundles of three in each bundle, or into a single cylinder which encircles the true pistil. In a third set of cases these outer carpels are only four in number, two lateral and two antero-posterior, all fused in such a manner as to form around the normal pistil a prism-shaped sheath, with four sides presenting four parietal placentæ, corresponding to the lines of junction of the staminal carpels."

[Pg 306]In the accompanying figures (fig. 163, *a-d*) the nature of this change is illustrated. In some of the specimens it is easy to see that the two shorter stamens undergo the change into carpels later and less perfectly than the four longer ones, and not infrequently the outer pair are altogether absent. In most of the flowers of this variety the petals are smaller and less perfectly developed than usual.[341]

FIG. 163.—*Cheiranthus Cheiri*, var. *gynantherus*. *a*. Sepals and petals removed to show carpellodic stamens. *b*. The same laid open. *c*. Transverse section. *d*. Plan of flower with four carpel-like stamens, &c.

In *Lilium tigrinum*, some specimens of which were gathered by Mr. J. Salter, in addition to various degrees of synanthy and other changes, some of the stamens were developed in the form of carpels, adherent by their edges so as to form an imperfect tube or sheath around the normal pistil. Fig. 164[Pg 307] shows one of the intermediate organs from these flowers, in which half the structure seems devoted to the formation of ovules, while the other half bears a one-celled anther. Lindley[342] has also described a case of this kind in a species of *Amaryllis*.

FIG. 164.—Structure half anther, half carpel, *Lilium*.

In *Saxifraga crassifolia* it sometimes happens that mixed with the stamens, and originating with them, are a number of distinct and perfectly formed carpels, wholly separated from the normal carpels, in the centre of the flower. In this particular instance there is usually no intermediate condition between the stamen and the pistil. Guillemin[343] also describes a transformation of the stamens into carpels in *Euphorbia esula*.

When the anther is involved it may be only partially so, or almost the whole organ may be transformed. As instances of very partial change may be cited the passage of the connective into a stigma in *Thalictrum minus*, or the passage of the points of the anthers into imperfect styles in some species of bamboo.[344]

In *Rosa arvensis* similar transformations have been observed of a slightly more complex character than those just mentioned, and passing into more important changes, especially to the formation of pollen within ovules, formed on the edges of an open carpellodic anther (see p. 186).

Mr. Berkeley has recorded an analogous case in a gourd in which the stamens bore numerous ovules (p. 200), and Baillon describes another gourd in which certain fleshy appendages surrounding the andrœcium were provided with ovules.[345]

[Pg 308]Payer, in his 'Organogénie,' p. 38, mentions a stamen of *Dionæa* bearing not only an anther, but likewise an ovule.

Sempervivum tectorum and *S. montanum*, have long been noticed as being very prone to present this change. Mohl[346] remarks that, in the transformation of the stamens to the pistil in the common houseleek, the filament of the stamen generally preserves its form, the anthers alone undergoing change. At other times, however, the transformation takes place at the same time, both in the filament and in the anther. When the stamens are numerous some of them remain in their normal state, while others, and especially the inner ones, undergo a change. Sometimes all the stamens are changed simultaneously, while at other times some of these organs may be found in which the anther is partially filled with ovules, and partially with pollen.

In the accompanying figures (fig. 165, *a-h*) a series of intermediate stages is shown between the ordinary stamen of *Sempervivum tectorum* and the ordinary carpel, from which it will be seen that the filament is little, if at all, affected, and that in those cases where there is a combination of the attributes of the stamen and of the pistil in the same organ the pollen is formed in the upper or inner surface of the leaf-organ, while the ovules arise from the opposite surface from the free edge, (*b, c, d, e, f, g*).

In a drawing made by the Rev. G. E. Smith of a malformed flower of*Primula acaulis*, and which the writer has had the opportunity of examining, the stamens are represented as detached from the corolla, and their anthers replaced by open carpels, with ovules arising, not only from their edges, but also from their surfaces, while the apex of the carpellary leaf was drawn out[Pg 309] into a long style, terminated by a flattened spathulate stigma.

Delphinium elatum is one of the plants in which this change has been most frequently noticed.[347]

Fig. 165.—*Sempervivum tecotorum*. *a*. Normal stamen. *b*. Normal carpel. *b, c, e, f,g*. Structure partly staminal, partly carpellary. *d*. Transverse section through *c*, showing pollen internally, ovules externally.

In willows the change of pistils into staminal organs has been frequently observed. In *Salix babylonica* Prof. Schnizlein has described various transition stages between the carpels and the stamens, and in one instance, in addition to this change, a perfect cup-shaped perianth was present, as happens normally in *Populus*[348]. Mr. Lowe also records the conversion of stamens into ovaries in *Salix Andersoniana*, and this by every conceivable intermediate gradation.[349]

[Pg 310]The following list will serve to show what plants are most subject to this anomaly. It is difficult to draw any accurate inference from this enumeration, but attention may be called to the frequency of this occurrence in certain plants, such as the *Sempervivum*, the wallflower, the poppy, and the heath. Why these plants should specially be subject to these changes cannot be at present stated.

By the student of animal physiology such a change as above described—equivalent to the substitution of an ovary or a uterus for a testis—would be looked on as next to impossible; the simpler and less specialised structure of plants renders such a change in them far more easy of comprehension.

- Thalictrum minus.
- Delphinium elatum.
- Magnolia fuscata.
- Bocconia cordata.
- *Papaver bracteatum!
  o   *somniferum!
  o   nudicaule.
- Dionæa muscipula!
- Barbarea vulgaris.
- *Cheiranthus Cheiri!
- Cochlearia Armoracia.
- Tropæolum majus.
- Citrus Aurantium.
- *Sempervivum tectorum!
  o   montanum.
- Begonia frigida!
- Cucumis, sp.
- Cucurbita Pepo.
- Pyrus Malus.
- Rosa arvensis!
- Saxifraga crassifolia!
- Myrtus, sp.
- Campanula rapunculoides.
- Polemonium cæruleum.
- Gentiana Amarella.
- *Erica Tetralix.
- Stachys germanica.
- Primula acaulis.
- Rumex crispus.
- *Salix, sp. plur.!
- Euphorbia esula.
- Glochidion.
- Asphodelus ramosus.
- Amaryllis.
- Lilium tigrinum!

- ○   longiflorum.
- •   *Tulipa Gesneriana!
- ○   var. cult. plurim.!
- •   Hemerocallis.
- •   Zea Mays.
- •   Bambusa, sp.

Pistillody of the ovule.—An instance of this extraordinary transformation in the carnation, as observed by the Rev. Mr. Berkeley, is given at p. 268.

FOOTNOTES:

[295]'Neue Denkschrift. Schweiz. Gesellsch.,' band v, p. 9.

[296]'Bull. Acad. Belg.,' xix, part 2, p. 93.

[297]Schlechtendal, 'Linnæa,' ix, p. 737.

[298]Misbilld., 'Cult. Gewachs.,' p. 32.

[299]Linn., 'Phil. Botan.,' § 120.

[300]'Bull. Soc. Bot. France,' 1859, vol. vi, p. 199.

[301]Seemann's 'Journal of Botany,' vol. iii, p. 105; also Morren, 'Bull. Acad. Belg.,' vol. xx, part 2, p. 264.

[302]Morren, 'Bull. Belg.,' xviii, p. 503.

[303]'Organ. Vég.,' t. i, p. 513.

[304]'Bull. Acad. Roy. Belg.,' tome xvii; and Lobelia, p. 65.

[305]Masters, "On Double Flowers," 'Rep. Internat. Bot. Congress,' London, 1866. p. 127.

[306]See also C. Morren, "Sur les vraies fleurs doubles chez les Orchidées," 'Bull. Acad. Roy. Belg.,' vol. xix, part ii, 1852. p. 171.

[307]C. Morren, 'Bull. Acad. Belg.,' vol. xx, 1853, part ii, p. 284 (*Syringa*).

[308]'Rep. Bot. Congress,' London, 1866, p. 135, t. vii, f. 14.

[309]Although it is generally admitted that the filament of the stamen corresponds to the stalk of the leaf, and the anther to the leaf-blade, yet there are some points on which uncertainty still rests. One of these is as to the sutures of the anther. Do these chinks through which the pollen escapes correspond (as would at first sight seem probable) to the margins of the antheral leaf, or do they answer to the lines that separate the two pollen-cavities on each half of the anther one from the other? Professor Oliver, 'Trans. Linn. Soc.,' vol. xxiii, 1862, p. 423, in alluding to the views held by others on this subject, concludes, from an examination of some geranium flowers in which the stamens were more or less petaloid, that Bischoff's notion as to the sutures of the anther is correct, viz., that they are the equivalents of the septa of untransformed tissue between the pollen-sacs. Some double fuchsias ('Gard. Chron.,' 1863, p. 989) add confirmation to this opinion. In these flowers the petals were present as usual, but the stamens were more or less petaloid, the filaments were unchanged, but the anthers existed in the form of a petal-like cup from the centre of which projected two imperfect pollen-lobes (the other two lobes being petaloid). Now, in this case, the margins of the anther were coherent to form the cup, and the pollen was emitted along a line separating the polliniferous from the petaloid portion of the anther. This view is also borne out by the double-flowered *Arbutus Unedo*, and also by what occurs in some double violets, wherein the anther exists in the guise of a broad lancet-shaped expansion, from the surface of which project four plates (fig. 157), representing apparently the walls of the pollen-sacs, but destitute of pollen; the chink left between these plates corresponds thus to the suture of the normal anther.

FIG. 157.—Petaloid stamen of *Viola*, with four projecting plates.

The inner or upper portion of the anther-leaf is that which is most intimately concerned in the formation of pollen; it comparatively rarely (query ever) happens that the back or lower surface of the antheral leaf is specially devoted to the formation of pollen. On the other hand, in cases like those of the common houseleek, where we meet with petaloid organs combining the attributes of anthers and of carpels, we find the inner layers devoted to the production of pollen, the outer to the formation of ovules.

That the pollen-lobes are not to be taken as halves of a staminal leaf, but rather as specialised portions of it, not necessarily occupying half its surface, is shown also in the case of double-flowered *Malvaceæ*, in which the stamens are frequently partly petal-like, partly divided into numerous separate filaments, each bearing a one-, or it may be even a two-lobed anther. This circumstance is confirmatory of the opinion held by Payer, Duchartre, Dickson, and other organogenists, as to the compound nature of the stamens in these plants. The stamens are here analogues not of a simple entire leaf, but of a lobed, digitate, or compound leaf, each subdivision bearing its separate anther. On this subject the reader may consult M. Müller's paper on the anther of *Jatropha Pohliana, &c.*, referred to at page 255.

[310]See C. Morren, "On Spur-shaped Nectarines," &c., 'Ann. Nat. Hist.,' March, 1841, p. 1. tab. 11.

[311]Karsten, 'Flor. Columb. Spec.,' tab. xxix.

[312]See Dickson, "On Diplostemonous Flowers," 'Trans. Bot. Soc. Edin.,' vol. viii, p. 100; and on the Andrœcium of *Mentzelia, &c.*, in Seemann's 'Journal of Botany,' vol. iii, p. 209, and vol. iv (1866) p. 273 (*Potentilla,&c.*).

[313]See Baillon, 'Adansonia,' iii, p. 351, tab. 12, *Sinapis.*

[314]'Bull. Acad. Belg.,' xvii, part i, p. 516, c. tab., and '*Lobelia*,' p. 83.

[315]Cited in 'Bull. Soc. Bot. France,' xiv, p. 253 ('Rev. Bibl.').

[316]'Bull. Soc. Bot. Fr.,' 1858, p. 331.

[317]'Mem. Legum.,' p. 44.

[318]'Bildungsabweich, 'Pflanz. Fam.,' tab. 8, f. 12.

[319]'Atlas de Göthe' p. 55, t. 4, f. 18.

[320]Wiegmann, 'Bot. Zeit.,' 1831, p. 5, tab. i.

[321]'Ic. Flor. Germ.,' xiii, tab. 112, cccclxiv, f. 2.

[322]Seemann's 'Journal of Botany,' 1867, p. 317, t. 72, A (*Ophrys*).

[323]'Enum. Euphorb.' p. 53.

[324]'Linnæa.' i, p. 457.

[325]'De Balsam,' p. 17.

[326]B. Clarke, 'Arrangement of Phænog. Plants,' p. 23.

[327]See 'Engelmann,' p. 26, tab. 3, f. 10, 11, 14.

[328]'Ann. Sc. Nat.,' ser. 2, t. viii, 1837, p. 58.

[329]'Bot. Zeit.,' 4, 1846, 889.

[330]'Verhandl. Nat. Hist. Ver. Preuss. Rheinl. und Westph.,' 1858, 1860, p. 381. Cramer also, 'Bildungsabweich,' p. 90, cites a case in *Pæonia* where the carpel was open and petaloid, and bore an anther on one margin, and four ovules on the other.

[331]'Euphorbiaceæ,' p. 205.

[332]Seemann's 'Journ. Bot.,' iv, p. 168, tab. 47, f. 1.

[333]Moquin-Tandon, l. c., 220, *Passiflora.* Masters, 'Journ. Linn. Soc.,' 1857, p. 159, *Saponaria.* Seemann's 'Journ. Botany,' vol. iii, p. 107,*Narcissus.*

[334]'Bull. Soc. Bot. Fr.,' 1857, p. 452.

[335]'Gardeners' Chronicle,' 1866, p. 897.

[336]Maout, 'Leçons Element.,' vol. ii, p. 488.

[337]Poiteau and Turpin, 'Arb. Fruit,' t. 37, and Trécul, 'Bull Soc. Bot. France,' vol. i. p. 307.

[338]Clos, 'Mem. Acad. Toulouse,' 5 ser., vol. iii.

[339]'Bot. Zeit.,' 1850, t. viii, pp. 514, 664. 'Flora,' (B. Z.) 1832, t. xv, p. 252; also cited in 'Ann. des Serres et des jardins,' vi, pp. 241–5. See also Schlechtendal, 'Bot. Zeit.,' 1845, t. 3, p. 6.

[340]'Bull. Soc. Bot. France,' t. viii, p. 453.

[341]See also Allmann, 'Rep. Brit. Assoc.,' July, 1851.

[342]'Theory of Horticulture,' ed. 2, p. 82.

[343]'Mém. Soc. Hist. Nat. Paris.' i, 16.

[344]Gen. Munro, 'Trans. Linn. Soc.,' xxvii, p. 7.

[345]'Bull. Soc. Bot. Fr.,' 1857, p. 21.

[346]'Ann. Scienc. Nat.,' t. viii, 1837, p. 50, and 'Bot. Zeit.' (R.), 1836, t. xix, p. 513, &c. See also MM. Sourd Dussiples and G. Bergeron, 'Bull. Soc. Bot. France,' viii, p. 349; Von Schmidel, 'Icon. plant. et Anal. part.' 1782, p. 210, fig. 54.

[347]Godron, 'Bull. Soc. Bot. Fr.,' xiii, p. 82, Rev. Bibl.

[348]Cited in Henfrey, 'Bot. Gazette,' iii, p. 12.

[349]'Ann. Nat. Hist.,' September, 1856, p. 56. See also Kirschleger, 'Flora (Bot. Zeit.),' xxiv, 1841, p. 340, *Salix alba*. Henschel, 'Flora (Bot. Zeit.),' 1832, t. xv, p. 253, *S. cinerea*. Hartmann, 'Flora (Bot. Zeit.),' xxiv, p. 199, *S. nigricans*. Meyer, C. A., 'Bull. Phys. Math.,' t. x, *S. alba*.

[Pg 311]

PART IV.
HETEROMORPHY.

There are certain malformations that have little in common beyond this, that they cannot readily be allocated in either of the great groups proposed by writers on teratology. There are also deformities which, unlike the majority of deviations from the ordinary structure, are absolute and not relative. While the latter are due to an exaggeration, or to an imperfection of development, or, it may be, to a partial perversion in organization, the former differ from the normal standard, not merely in degree, but absolutely. This is often the case when disease or injury affects the plant; for instance, in the case of galls arising from insect-puncture the structure is rather a new growth altogether, than dependent on mere hypertrophy of the original tissues. These absolute deformities arising from the causes just mentioned belong rather to pathology than to teratology strictly so called; but, under the head of deformities, may be mentioned sundry deviations not elsewhere alluded to.

CHAPTER I.
DEFORMITIES.

The special meaning here attached to the term deformity is sufficiently explained in the preceding paragraph; it remains to give a few illustrations, and to refer to other headings, such as Heterotaxy, Hypertrophy,[Pg 312] Atrophy, &c., for malformations capable of more rigid classification than those here alluded to.

FIG. 166.—Portion of the under surface of a cabbage-leaf, with horn-like excrescences projecting from it.

Formation of tubes.—The production of ascidia or pitchers from the cohesion of the margins of one or more leaves has been already alluded to (see pp. 21, 30), but there is another class of cases in which the tubular formation is due, not so much to the union of the margins of a leaf as to the disproportionate growth of some portions as contrasted with others, whence arises either a depressed cavity, as in the case of a leaf, or[Pg 313] an expanded and excavated structure, when the stem or some portion of it is affected.

The fruit of the rose, the apple, the fig, and many others, is now generally admitted to be composed externally of the dilated end of the flower-stalk in which the true carpels become imbedded. Between such cases and that of a peltate leaf with a depressed centre, such as often occurs, to some extent, in *Nelumbium*, there is but little difference.

In cabbages and lettuces there not unfrequently occurs a production of leaf-like processes projecting from the primary blade at a right angle (see Enation). Sometimes these are developed in a tubular form, so as to form a series of little horn-like tubes, or shallow troughs, as in *Aristolochia sipho*. At other times the nerves or ribs of the leaf project beyond the blade, and bear at their extremities structures similar to those just described.

FIG. 167.—Lettuce leaf, bearing on the back a stalked cup, arising from the dilatation of the stalk (?).

[Pg 314]

In a variety of *Codiæum variegatum* a similar formation may be seen to a minor extent. Even the common *Scolopendrium vulgare* occasionally produces small pitchers of this character, as in the varieties named *perafero-corautum*, Moore, and *peraferum*, Woll.[350]

In carnations leaves may sometimes be seen from both surfaces, from which project long, sharp-pointed tubular spurs at irregular intervals. A very singular illustration of this is figured by Trattinick,[351], in which the leaves, epicalyx, sepals, and petals, were all provided with tubular spurs.

In *Cephalotus follicularis* rudimentary or imperfect pitchers may be frequently met with, in which the stalk of the leaf is tubular and bears at its extremity a very small rudimentary leaf-blade. It is not in all cases easy to trace the origin and true nature of the ascidium, as the venation is sometimes obscure. If there be a single well-marked midrib the probability is that the case is one of cohesion of the margins of the leaf; but if the veins are all of about equal size, and radiate from a common stalk, the pouch-like formation is probably due to dilatation and hollowing of the petiole. Again, when the result of a union of the margins of the leaf, the pitcher is generally less regular than when formed from the hollowed end of a leaf-stalk. Further information is especially needed as to the mode of development and formation of these tubular organs, so as to ascertain clearly when they are the result of a true cupping process, and when of cohesion of the margins of one or more leaves. (See Cohesion, p. 31. For bibliographical references consult also A. Braun, 'Flora v. Bot. Zeit.,' 1835, t. xviii, p. 41, *Aristolochia.*)

Tubular formations in the flower.—A similar formation of tubes happens in some double flowers; for instance, it is not infrequent in double flowers of *Primula sinensis*, in which tubular petal-like structures are[Pg 315]attached to the inner surface of the corolla; sometimes these petaloid tubes replace the stamens, while at other times they appear to have no relation to those organs. In the particular flowers now alluded to the tubular form seems due to a dilatation, and not to a cohesion of the margins. (See Cohesion, p. 23.) These tubular petals resemble in form and colour almost precisely the normal corolla in miniature, but are not surrounded by a calyx, nor do they contain stamens, while the less perfect forms show clearly their origin from a single tube-like organ.

FIG. 168.—Corolla of *Primula sinensis* turned back to show a tubular petal springing from it. One only is shown for the sake of clearness; they are generally numerous.

The formation of spurs or spur-like tubes in a quasi-regular manner has been spoken of under the head of Irregular Peloria, p. 228, but we occasionally meet with tubular processes which seem to occur in an irregular manner, and to have no reference to the symmetrical plan of the flower, and which are due probably to the same causes as those which induce hypertrophy. Such spurs have frequently been seen on the corolla of *Digitalis purpurea, Antirrhinum majus,*[352] *Tulipa Gesneriana,* and occasionally on the sepals of[Pg 316] *Fuchsia.* They are very frequent in some seasons in the corolla of certain calceolarias (*C. floribunda*). By Morren this production of adventitious spurs was called "Ceratomanie."

FIG. 169.—Corolla of *Calceolaria*, showing irregular tubular spurs projecting from the lower lip.

Similar processes may sometimes be seen in the capsules of *Linaria vulgaris,* as also in the fruits of some of the Solanums, quite without reference to the arrangement of the carpels, so that their production seems to be purely irregular.

Morren, as previously remarked, gave the name "Solenaidie" to tubular deformities affecting the stamens, a term which has not been generally adopted; the deformity in question is by no means of uncommon occurrence in some double or partially pelorised flowers, as *Antirrhinum,Linaria,* &c. A similar formation of conical out-growths may frequently be met with in the fruits quite irrespectively of any disjunction of the carpels.

Contortion.—An irregular twisting or bending of the stem or branches is by no means of uncommon occurrence, the inducing causes being often some restriction to growth in certain directions, or the undue or disproportionate growth in one direction, as contrasted with that in another. Hence it may arise from insect-puncture, parasitic growth, or any obstacle to the natural development. Frequently it exists in conjunction with fasciation, the ends of the branches being curved round like a shepherd's crook, from the growth on one side being so much greater than on the other. Sometimes it is a mere exaggeration of a normal condition; thus, in what are termed flexuose stems the stem twists alternately to one side or another, frequently in association[Pg 317] with an oblique form of the leaf. This state

151

is sometimes present to an extreme degree, as in some varieties of shrubs (*Cratægus*, *Robinia*, &c.) cultivated for their singularly tortuous branches.

FIG. 170.—Portion of the culm of a *Juncus*, bent irregularly.

FIG. 171.—Portion of a branch of *Cratægus oxyacantha*, var. *tortuosa*.

Such cases as those just mentioned, however, are but slightly irregular compared to others in which the deformity exists to such an extent that the traces of the ordinary mode of growth are almost obliterated.[Pg 318] M. Moquin-Tandon[353] alludes to a case of this kind in a species of pine (*Pinus*), in which a branch ended in four unequal divisions, which were strongly curved from without inwards, then became united in pairs, these latter in their turn blending into a single mass.

In the case of some beeches growing in the forest of Verzy, near Rheims, the trunks of the trees are contorted in every direction, and, at a height of from fifteen to twenty feet, a number of branches are also given off, also much contorted, and occasionally intergrafted, so that it seems as if a heavy weight had been placed on the trees and literally flattened them. Similar malformations may occasionally be met with in the branches of the oak, and commonly in the weeping ash.

M. Fournier[354] mentions the stems of *Ruscus aculeatus* rolled in a circle, others twisted spirally.

The phenomenon is not confined to woody plants, but has been met with in chicory, in *Antirrhinum*, and other herbaceous species.

It is very difficult in some cases to separate these instances of irregular torsion from those in which the twisting takes place in a more or less regular spiral direction. In the former case the fibres of the plant are only indirectly involved, but in the latter the fibres themselves are coiled spirally from right to left, or *vice versâ* (spiral torsion), while not unfrequently both conditions may be met with at the same time.

The leaves also are subject to similar deformities, of which a notable illustration has been recorded in the case of the date palm, *Phœnix dactylifera*, originally observed by Goethe, and figured and described by Jaeger;[355] the leaves are folded and twisted in every direction, in consequence of the fibrous band or cord which surrounds the leaves, and which generally breaks[Pg 319] as the leaflets increase in size, remaining from some cause or other unbroken, and thus serving to restrain the growth.

A similar irregularity of growth occurs, not unfrequently, in the case of crocus leaves, when in the course of their growth, as they push their way through the soil, their progress becomes checked either by a stone or even by frost.

Spiral torsion.—Growth in a spiral direction, and the arrangement of the various organs of the plant in a spiral manner, are among the most common of natural phenomena in plants.[356] Fibres are coiled spirally in the minute vessels of flowering plants, and are not wholly wanting even among fungi. The leaf-organs are very generally spirally arranged; the leaf-stalks are often so twisted as to bring leaves on one plane which otherwise would occupy several. In the leaf itself we have a spiral twist taking place constantly in *Alstrœmeria*, in *Avena*, and other plants. A similar tendency is manifested in the flower-stalks, as in *Cyclamen* and *Vallisneria*, and the whole inflorescence, as in *Spiranthes*. Even the bark and wood of trees is often disposed spirally. This is very noticeable in some firs, and in the bark of the sweet chestnut (*Castanea*), of *Thuja occidentalis*, and other trees. The knaurs or excrescences which are sometimes found on the roots or stems of trees afford other illustrations of this universal tendency. These bodies consist of a number of embryo buds, which, from some cause or other, are incapable of lengthening. On examination every rudimentary or undeveloped bud may be seen to be surrounded by densely crowded fibres arranged spirally.

The axes of nearly all twining plants are themselves twisted, and twisted in a direction corresponding to the spontaneous revolving movement exhibited by these plants, as in the hop, the convolvulus, passion flower,[Pg 320]&c., the degree of twisting being dependent to a great extent on the roughness of the surface around which the stem twines[357].

Considered as an exceptional occurrence, it occurs frequently in certain plants, and, when it affects the stem or branches, necessarily causes some changes in the arrangement of the parts attached to them; thus, spiral torsion of the axial organs is generally accompanied by displacement of the leaves, whorled leaves becoming alternate, and opposite or whorled leaves becoming arranged on one side of the stem only. Frequently also this condition is associated with fasciation, or, at least, with a distended or dilated state. An illustration of this in *Asparagus* has been figured at p. 14.

Very often the leaves are produced in a spiral line round the stem, as in a specimen of *Dracocephalum speciosum* described and figured by C. Morren. The leaves of this plant are naturally rectiserial and decussate, but, in the twisted stem the leaves were curviserial, and arranged according to the 5/13 plan. Now, referring to the ordinary notation of alternate leaves, we shall have the first leaf covered by the fifth, with two turns of the spiral; since decussate leaves result from two conjugate lines, the formula will be necessarily 2/5. The fraction 5/13 hence comes regularly into the 2/5 series (2/5, 3/8, 5/13). Thus, the leaves in assuming a new phyllotaxy, take one quite analogous to the normal one.

One of the most curious instances that have fallen under the writer's own observation occurred in the stem of *Dipsacus fullonum*. (See 'Proceedings of[Pg 321] the Linnean Society,' March 6, 1855, vol. ii, p. 370). The stem was distended, and hollow, and twisted on itself; its fibres, moreover, were arranged in an oblique or spiral direction; the branches or leaf-stalks, which usually are arranged in an opposite and decussate manner, were, in this case, disposed in a linear series, one over the other, following the line of curvature of the stem. When the course of the fibres was traced from the base of one of the stalks, upward around the stem, a spiral was found to be completed at the base of the second stalk, above that which was made the starting point. Now, if opposite leaves depend on the shortened condition of the internode between the two leaves, then, in the teazel-stem just described, each turn of the spiral would represent a lengthened internode; and, if the fibres of this specimen could be untwisted, and made to assume the vertical direction, and, at the same time, the internodes were shortened, the result would be the opposition of the branches and the decussation of the pairs; this explanation is borne out by the similar twisting which takes place so frequently in the species of *Galium* and other *Rubiaceæ*.

FIG. 172.—Twisted stem of *Dipsacus fullonum*.

G. Franc[358] was one of the first to notice this twisting in *Galium*, and M. Duchartre,[359] in mentioning a similar instance, gives the following explanation of the appearance which will be found to apply to most of these cases. In the normal stem of *Galium Mollugo* the branches[Pg 322] are opposite in each verticil and crossed in the two successive ones. The stem is four-angled, each angle having a nerve. Each of these nerves, springing from the origin of a branch in one whorl, terminates in the interval which separates the point of origin of the two branches in the whorl next above it. In the deformed stem one of the nerves corresponds to the insertion of a branch, its neighbour is in the adjoining vacant space; hence it results that four nerves correspond to two branches and to two consecutive interspaces, and hence the analogy between a single normal internode provided with its two branches and its four nerves. What confirms this inference is that the nerve, which begins at the point of origin of a branch, after making one spiral turn round the stem, terminates in the interval that separates the two following branches, just as in a branch of the normal stem it ends in the upper whorl between the two next branches. The torsion, then, in this *Galium* caused the separation of the two opposite branches of the same verticil, and placed them one above another, and this being reproduced in all the whorls, all the branches come to be arranged on the same longitudinal line. The leaves are susceptible of the same explanation; they are inserted in groups of three or four in one arc round the origin of each branch. In the malformation each series or group of four leaves, with its central branch, is equivalent to half a whorl of the natural plant with its axillary branch. In other words, the malformation consists in a torsion of the stem, which separates each whorl into two distinct halves; these half-whorls, with their axillary branches, are placed on a single longitudinal series one above another. This case is quoted at some length, as it is an admirable example of a very common form of malformation in these plants.

In some parts of Holland where madder is cultivated a similar deformation is particularly frequent. The leaves, however, are not always grouped in the way in which they were described by M. Duchartre,[Pg 323] but more commonly form a single continuous line; when arranged in leaf-whorls it generally happens that some of the leaves are turned downwards, while others are erect. It has been said that this condition occurs particularly frequently in plants growing in damp places. It is certainly true that spiral torsion of the stem is specially frequent in the species of *Equisetum*, most of which grow in such spots. In these plants either the whole of the upper part of the stem is thus twisted, or a portion only: thus Reinsch[360] cites a case in *Equisetum Telmateia*, where the upper and lower portions of the stem were normal, while the intermediate portion was twisted spirally. In this instance the whorl next beneath the spiral had twenty-eight branchlets, and that immediately above it thirty. Along the course of the spire there were two hundred and three; dividing this latter number by the mean of[Pg 324] the two preceding, it was seen that the spire included the constituents of seven ordinary verticils.

FIG. 173.—Stem of *Galium* spirally twisted. From a specimen communicated by Mr. Darwin.

Here also may be mentioned a curious bamboo, the stem of which is preserved in the British Museum, and in which the internodes, on the exterior, and the corresponding diaphragms and cavities within are spiral or oblique in direction.

The root is also subject to the same malformation, the inducing cause being usually some obstruction to downward growth, as when a plant has been grown in a small pot, and becomes, as gardeners say, pot-bound.

FIG. 174.—Showing "pot-bound" root twisted spirally (from the 'Gard. Chron.,' 1849).

The axial portion of the flower, the thalamus, is also occasionally twisted in a spiral direction, the lateral parts of the flower being in consequence displaced.[Pg 325] Morren spoke of this displacement of the floral organs as "speiranthie."[361]

Morren draws a distinction between spiral-torsion or spiralism and the less regular torsion spoken of in the preceding section; in the former case not only is the axis twisted, but its constituent fibres also. The condition in question in some cases seems to be inherited in the seedling plants.

The following is a list of the plants in which spiral torsion of the stem or branches has been most frequently observed. (See also under Fasciation and Contortion.)

- Hesperis matronalis.
- Dianthus barbatus.
- Pyrus Malus.
- torminalis.
- Cercis siliquastrum!
- Punica Granatum.
- Robinia pseudacacia!
- Rubia tinctorum.
- Dipsacus fullonum!
- pilosus.
- Gmelini.
- Scabiosa arvensis.
- *Valeriana officinalis!
- dioica!
- Galium aparine!
- *Mollugo!

- o   verum!
- Hippuris vulgaris!
- Veronica spicata.
- o   longifolia.
- Hyssopus officinalis.
- Thymus Serpyllum.
- Lamium purpureum!
- Dracocephalum speciosum.
- Mentha aquatica.
- Mentha viridis.
- Fraxinus vulgaris!
- Sambucus nigra.
- Zinnia.
- Phylica.
- Beta.
- Rumex, sp.
- Ulmus campestris.
- Casuarina rigida.
- Abies excelsa!
- Lilium Martagon!
- o   candidum.
- *Asparagus officinalis!
- Sagittaria sagittifolia.
- Epipactis palustris.
- Triticum repens!
- Lolium perenne!
- Phleum pratense.
- Juncus conglomeratus!
- Scirpus lacustris.
- Equisetum Telmateia.
- o   limosum.
- o   fluviatile.
- o   arvense!

Among the more important papers relating to this subject may be mentioned:
Moquin-Tandon, 'El. Ter. Veg.,' p. 181. Kros, 'De Spira in plantis conspicua.' Morren, 'Bull. Acad. Roy. Belg.,' 1851, tom. xviii, part i, p. 27. Milde, 'Nov. Act. Acad. Leop. Carol. Nat. Cur., 1839. Ibid., vol. xxvi, part ii, p. 429, *Equisetum*. Irmisch, 'Flora,' 1858, t. ii, *Equisetum*. Vrolik, 'Nouv. Mem. Instit. Amsterdam,' *Lilium*. Schlechtendal, 'Bot. Zeit.,' xiv, p. 69, et v, p. 66. De Candolle, 'Organ.[Pg 326] Veget., t. i, p. 155, tab. xxxvi, *Mentha, &c.* Alph. de Candolle, 'Neue Denkschr. Allg. Schweiz. Gesellschft.,' band v, tab. vi, *Valeriana*. Duchartre, 'Ann. Sc. Nat.,' ser. 3, vol. i, p. 292. 'Gardeners' Chronicle,' July 5, 1856, p. 452, *c. ic. xylogr.*, spiral branches from Guatemala—tree not known.

Spiral twisting of the leaf is scarcely of so common occurrence as the corresponding condition in the stem. In *Alstræmeria* it occurs normally, as also in some grasses. In the variety *annularis* of *Salix babylonica* the leaf is constantly coiled round spirally. A

155

similar contortion occurs in a variety of *Codiæum variegatum* lately introduced from the islands of the South Seas by Mr. J. G. Veitch.

Fern fronds are occasionally found twisted in the same manner, *e.g. Scolopendrium vulgare* var. *spirale.*[362]

Adventitious tendrils.—Under ordinary circumstances tendrils may be described as modifications of the leaf, the stipule, the branch, or of the flower stalk, so that it is not a matter of surprise to find tendrils occasionally springing from the sepals or petals, as indeed happens normally in *Hodgsonia, Strophanthus, &c.*

M. Decaisne[363] found a flower of the melon in which one of the segments of the calyx was prolonged into a tendril, and Kirschleger records a similar instance in the cucumber, while Mr. Holland ('Science Gossip,' 1865, p. 105) mentions a case in which one of the prickles on the fruit of a cucumber had grown out into a tendril.

In *Cobæa scandens* the foliar nature of the tendril is shown by the occasional presence of a small leaflet on one of the branches of the tendril, and a similar appearance may frequently be seen in *Eccremocarpus scaber.* On the other hand, in the vine, the axial nature of the tendril is revealed by the not infrequent presence of flowers or berries on them, as also in *Modecca* and some *Passifloraceæ.*

[Pg 327]

Darwin, speaking of the tendrils of *Bignonia capreolata*, says it is a highly remarkable fact that a leaf should be metamorphosed into a branched organ, which turns from the light, and which can, by its extremities, either crawl like a root into crevices, or seize hold of minute projecting points, these extremities subsequently forming cellular masses, which envelope by their growth the first fibres and secrete an adhesive cement.

Interrupted growth.—This term is here used in the same sense as in ordinary descriptive botany, as when an "interruptedly pinnate" leaf is spoken of. A similar alternation may be observed occasionally as a teratological occurrence, though it is not easy to account for it.

FIG. 175.—Interrupted growth of Radish (from the 'American Agriculturist.')

FIG. 176.—Interrupted growth in Apple.

Fig. 175 shows an instance of the kind in a radish, and fig. 176 a similar deformity in the case of an apple, the dilatation of the flower-stalk below the ordinary fruit producing an appearance as if there were two fruits one above another.

In leaves this peculiar irregularity of development is more common.

[Pg 328]

In some varieties of *Codiæum variegatum* the leaves resemble those of *Nepenthes*, as the basal portion is broad, and terminates in a projecting midrib destitute of cellular covering, and this again terminates in a small pouch or pitcher. Somewhat similar variations may be found in ferns, especially *Scolopendrium vulgare.*

Instead of the pouch there is formed sometimes in the plant last mentioned a supplementary four-lobed lamina, the four lobes being in two different planes, and diverging from the midrib, so that the section would resemble [symbol: Sideways X], the point of intersection of the x representing the position of the midrib. This four-winged lamina is thus very similar to the four-winged filaments described and figured at p. 289, and to the leaf-like anther of *Jatropha* described by M. Müller, p. 255.

Cornute leaves (*Folia cornuta*).—The condition to which this term applies is that in which the midrib, after running for a certain distance, generally nearly to the point of the leaf, suddenly projects, often in a plane different from that of the leaf, and thus forms a small spine-like out-growth. Should this happen to be terminated by a second laminar portion, an interrupted leaf would be formed. In *Scolopendrium vulgare* and other ferns this condition has been noticed, as also in some of the varieties of *Codiæum variegatum* already referred to.

Flattening.—There are some plants whose stem or branches, instead of assuming the ordinary cylindrical form, are compressed or flattened; such are some species of *Epiphyllum, Coccoloba, Bauhinia,* &c. The same thing occurs in the leaf-like branches

156

of *Ruscus*, the flower-stalks of *Xylophylla*, *Phyllanthus*, *Pterisanthes*. Martins proposes to apply the word 'cladodium' to such expansions, just as the term phyllodium is applied to the similar dilatation of the leaf-stalks. If we exclude[Pg 329] instances of fasciation, *i.e.* where several branches are fused together and flattened, we must admit that this flattening does not occur very often as a teratological appearance.

Mr. Rennie figures and describes a root of a tree which had become greatly flattened in its passage between the stones at the bottom of a stream, and had become, as it were, moulded to the stones with which it came into contact.[364]

The spadix of *Arum*, as also of the cocoa-nut palm, has been observed flattened out, apparently without increase in the number of organs.

When the blade of the leaf is suppressed it often happens that the stalk of the leaf is flattened, as it were, by compensation, and the petiole has then much the appearance of a flat ribbon (phyllode). This happens constantly in certain species of *Acacia*, *Oxalis*, &c., and has been attributed, but doubtless erroneously, to the fusion of the leaflets in an early state of development and in the position of rest.[365]

In some water plants, as *Sagittaria*, *Alisma*, *Potamogeton*, &c., the leaf-stalks are apt to get flattened out into ribbon-like bodies; and Olivier has figured and described a *Cyclamen*, called by him *C. linearifolium*, in which, owing to the suppression of the lamina, the petiole had become dilated into a ribbon-like expansion—déformation rubanée of Moquin.

FOOTNOTES:

[350]Moore, 'Nature Printed Ferns,' 8vo edition, vol. ii, p. 154, et p. 173.

[351]'Flora (B. Z.),' 1821, vol. iv, p. 717, c. tab.

[352]Chavannes, 'Mon. Antirrh.'

[353]'Bull. Soc. Bot. France,' t. vii, 1860, p. 877.

[354]Ibid., t. iv, 1857, p. 759.

[355]Jaeger, "De monstrosa folii *Phœnicis dactyliferæ* conformatione a Goetheo olim observata," 'Act. Acad. Leop. Car. Nat. Cur.,' vol. xvii, suppl., p. 293, c. tab. color. iv.

[356]See Goethe, 'Ueber die spiral Tendenz.'

[357]See Darwin "On Climbing Plants," 'Journ. Linn. Soc. Botany,' vol. ix, p. 5.

[358]'Ephem. Nat. Cur.,' dec. 2, ann. 1, 1683, p. 68, fig. 14.

[359]'Ann. des Scienc. Nat.,' third series, vol. i, 1844, p. 292.

[360]'Flora' Feb. 4, 1858, p. 69, tab. ii, f. 3, and also 'Flora,' 1860, p. 737, tab. vii, f. 9.

[361]'Bull. Acad, Belg.,' t. xvii, p. 196, "Lobelia," p. 53, c. tab.

[362]Moore, 'Nature-printed Ferns,' 8vo edition, vol. ii, p. 183.

[363]'Bull. Soc. Bot. Fr.,' 1860, vol. vii, p. 461. See also Naudin, 'Ann. Sc. Nat.,' 4 ser., t. iv, p. 5. Clos, 'Bull. Soc. Bot. Fr.,' t. iii, p. 546.

[364]London's 'Magazine Nat. Hist.,' vol. ii, p. 463.

[365]C. Morren, 'Bull. Acad. Belg.,' 1852, t. xix, part iii, p. 444.

CHAPTER II.

POLYMORPHY.

Usually the several organs of the same individual plant do not differ to any great extent one from another. One adult leaf has nearly the same appearance and[Pg 330] dimensions as another; one flower resembles very closely another flower of the same age and so on. Nevertheless it occasionally happens that there is a very considerable difference in form in the same organs, not only at different times, but it may also be at the same time. Descriptive botanists recognise this occurrence in the case of leaves, and apply the epithet heterophyllous to plants possessed of these variable foliar characters. In the case of the flower, where similar diversity of form occasionally exists, the term dimorphism is used.

As these phenomena appear constantly in particular plants, they are hardly to be looked on, under such circumstances, as abnormal, but where they occur in plants not usually polymorphic, they may be considered as coming within the scope of teratology.

Heterophylly.—As a general rule, the leaves or leaf-organs in each portion of a plant, from the rhizome or underground axis, where it exists, to the carpellary leaf, have their own special configuration, subject only to slight variations, dependent upon age, conditions of growth, &c. The cotyledons are very uniform in shape in each plant, and are scarcely ever subject to variation. The leaves near the base of the stem, the root-leaves as they are not unfrequently called, sometimes differ in form from the stem-leaves; these again differ from the bracts or leaves in proximity to the flower. The floral envelopes themselves, as well as the bud-scales, all have their own allotted form in particular plants, a form by which they may, in most cases, be readily recognised. Hence, then, in the majority of plants there is naturally very considerable difference in the form of the leaf-organs, according to the place they occupy and the functions they have to fulfil; but, in addition to this, it not unfrequently happens that the leaf-organs in the same portion of the stem are subject to great variation in form. This is the condition to which the term heterophylly properly applies. The variation in form is usually[Pg 331] dependent on a greater or less degree of lobing of the margin of the leaf; thus, in the yellow jasmine, almost every intermediate stage may be traced from an ovate entire leaf to one very deeply and irregularly stalked. *Broussonettia papyrifera*, and *Laurus Sassafras*, and the species of *Panax*, may be mentioned as presenting this condition. Sometimes in the last-named genus, as also in *Pteridophyllum*, every gradation between simple and compound leaves may be traced. The horse-radish (*Cochlearia Armoracia*) may also be instanced as a common illustration of polymorphism in[Pg 332] the leaves. In ferns it is likewise of frequent occurrence, markedly so in *Scolopendrium D'Urvillei*, in which plant every gradation from a simple oblong frond to an exceedingly divided one may be found springing from the same rhizome at the same time.

FIG. 177.—*Syringa persica laciniata*, showing polymorphous leaves.

A similar protean state, but little less remarkable, occurs in many of our British ferns, notably in *Scolopendrium vulgare*, of which Mr. Moore enumerates no fewer than 155 varieties,[366] many of the forms occurring on the same plant at the same time. Cultivators have availed themselves of this tendency to produce multiform foliage, not only for the purposes of decoration or curiosity, as in the many cut-leaved or crisped-leaved varieties, but also for more material uses, as, for instance, the many varieties of cabbages, of lettuces, &c. Most of these variations are mentioned under the head of the particular morphological change of which they are illustrations.

The effect of a change in the conditions of growth in producing diversity in the form of the leaf may be here alluded to. *Ficus stipulata*, a plant used to cover the walls of plant-stoves in this country, and growing naturally on walls in India, like ivy, produces leaves of very different form, size, and texture, when grown as a standard, from what it does when adhering to a wall. *Marcgraavia umbellata* furnishes another example of a similar nature, as indeed, to a less extent, does the common ivy.

Allusion has been already made to the occasional persistence of forms in adult life, which are commonly confined to a young state, as in the case of some conifers which present on the same plant, at the same time, two different forms of leaves. Mention has also been made of the presence of adventitious buds on leaves and in other situations. The leaves that spring from these buds are usually of the same form as the other leaves of the plant, but now and then they differ. Of this a remarkable illustration is afforded by a fern,[Pg 333] *Pteris quadriaurita*, in which the fronds emerging from an adventitious bud are very different from the ordinary fronds.

FIG. 178.—Portion of a frond of *Pteris quadriaurita*, with an adventitious bud, the form of the constituent foliage of which is very different from that of the parent frond.

Dimorphism.—This term, applied specially to the varied form which the flowers or some of their constituent elements assume on the same plant, is an analogous phenomenon to what has been above spoken of as heterophylly, and, like it, it cannot, except under special circumstances, be considered as of teratological importance. A few illustrative cases, however, may here be cited.

Sir George Mackenzie describes a variety of the potato[367] (*Solanum tuberosum*), which produces first double and sterile flowers, and subsequently single fertile ones; the other portions of the plant do not differ much.

[Pg 334]

Stackhousia juncea, according to Clarke, has mixed with its perfect flowers a number of apetalous blossoms destitute of anthers.[368]

This peculiarity is well exemplified in the tribe *Gaudichaudieæ* of the order *Malpighiaceæ*. A. de Jussieu, in his monograph, speaks of these flowers as being very small, green, destitute of petals, or nearly so, with a single, generally imperfect anther; the carpels also are more or less imperfect, but not sufficiently so to prevent some seeds from being formed. A similar production of imperfect flowers has been noticed in many other

orders, *e.g. Violaceæ, Campanulaceæ*, &c. In some cases these supplementary blossoms are more fertile and prolific in good seeds than are the normally constructed flowers. M. Durieu de Maisonneuve alludes to a case where flowers of this description are produced below the surface of the ground. The plant in question is *Scrophularia arguta*, and it appears that towards the end of the summer the lowest branches springing from the stem bend downwards, and penetrate the soil; the branches immediately above the lowest ones also bend downwards, but do not always enter the earth. These branches bear fertile flowers: those which are completely below the soil are completely destitute of petals; those which are on the surface have a four-lobed corolla whose divisions are nearly equal, like those of *Veronica*.[369]

To Sprengel, and specially to Darwin, physiologists are indebted for the demonstration of the relation of di- and trimorphic flowers to fertilisation. In certain genera of orchids, such as *Catasetum*, &c., flowers of such different form are produced that botanists, without hesitation, considered them as belonging to different genera, until the fact of their occasional production on the same plant showed that they were not of even specific importance. It was reserved for Mr. Darwin to show experimentally that these very different flowers[Pg 335] are really sexual forms of one and the same species, ordinarily occurring on different plants, i.e. diœcious, but occasionally formed on the same spike. The same excellent observer has demonstrated that the di- and trimorphic forms of *Primula*, of *Linum,Lythrum*, and other plants—forms differing mainly in the relative length of the stamens and styles, are also connected with striking differences in the number of perfect seeds produced. The most perfect degree of fertility is obtained when the stigma of one form is fertilised by the pollen taken from stamens of a corresponding height. On the other hand, when the union is, as Mr. Darwin states, illegitimate, that is, when the pollen is taken from stamens not corresponding in length to the style, more or less complete sterility ensues in the progeny, sometimes even utter infertility, such as happens when two distinct species are crossed, so that, in point of fact, the offspring of these illegitimate unions correspond almost precisely to hybrids.[370]

Mere variations of form arising from hybridisation or other causes hardly fall within the limits of this work, though it is quite impossible to say where variations end and malformations begin. There are, however, two or three cases cited by Mr. Darwin[371] from Gallesio and Risso to which it is desirable to allude. Gallesio impregnated an orange with pollen from a lemon, and the fruit borne on the mother tree had a raised stripe of peel like that of a lemon both in colour and taste, but the pulp was like that of an orange, and included only imperfect seeds. Risso describes a variety of the common orange which produces "rounded-oval leaves, spotted with yellow, borne on petioles, with heart-shaped wings; when these leaves fall off they are succeeded by longer and narrower leaves, with undulated margins, of a pale green colour, embroidered with yellow, borne on foot-stalks without[Pg 336] wings. The fruit whilst young is pear-shaped, yellow, longitudinally striated and sweet; but, as it ripens, it becomes spherical, of a reddish-yellow, and bitter."

Sports or bud variations.—These curious departures from the normal form can only be mentioned incidentally in this place, as they pertain more to variation than to malformation.

The occasional production of shoots bearing leaves, flowers, or fruits of a different character from those found on the normal plant, is a fact of which gardeners have largely availed themselves in the cultivation of new varieties. The productions in question have been attributed to various causes, such as cross-breeding, grafting, budding, dissociation of hybrid characters, or reversion to some ancestral form, all of which explanations may be true in certain cases, but none of them supply the clue to the reason why one particular branch should be so affected, and the rest not; or why the same plant, at the same time, as often happens in Pelargoniums, should produce two, three, or more "sports" of a different character.

These bud variations may be perpetuated by grafts or by cuttings, sometimes even by seed. With reference to cuttings a curious circumstance has been observed, viz., that if taken from the lower part of the stem, near the root, the peculiarity is not transmitted, but the young plant reverts to the characters of the typical form (Carrière). This circumstance, however, is not of universal occurrence.

For further particulars on this interesting subject the reader is referred to Darwin's 'Variation of Animals and Plants,' i, p. 373, where numerous references are given, and wherein certain well-known and highly remarkable instances, such as the *Cytisus Adami*, the trifacial orange, &c., are discussed.

FOOTNOTES:

[366]'Nature-printed Ferns,' 8vo edition, vol. ii, p. 197.

[367]'Gard. Chron.,' 1845. p. 790.

[368]'A New Arrangement of Phænog. Plants,' p. 36.

[369]'Bull. Soc. Bot. France,' 1856, t. iii, p. 569.

[370]The reader will find an abstract of Mr. Darwin's views in his work on the 'Variation of Animals and Plants,' vol. ii, p. 181.

[371]Loc. cit., i, 336.

[Pg 337]

CHAPTER III.
ALTERATIONS OF COLOUR.[372]

Changes in the colour of the several organs of plants are more often either pathological or the result of variation than of malformation properly so called.

Alterations in colour arise from a diminished or an increased amount of colouring matter, or from an unusual distribution of the solid or fluid matters on which the colour depends. The superposition of cells containing colouring material of different tints produces naturally a very different set of hues from those which are manifested when the colours are not blended. Referring the reader to the ordinary text-books on vegetable physiology and chemistry for details as to the nature and disposition of colouring materials in plants under natural circumstances, it will only be necessary to cite a few instances of deviation from the general colour of plants or their organs.

Albinism.—This change is due to the deficient formation of green colouring matter or chlorophyll, and is more a pathological condition than a deformity.

It seems necessary to draw a distinction between this state and ordinary blanching or etiolation. In the former case chlorophyll seems never to be formed in the affected parts, even if they be exposed to light, while an etiolated organ, when placed under favorable circumstances, speedily assumes a green colour. In *Richardia æthiopica* one or more leaves become occasionally as white as the spathe is usually.

[Pg 338]

Virescence.—Engelmann[373] pointed out that, so far as flowers were concerned, there are two ways in which they assume a green colour, either by a simple development of chlorophyll in place of the colouring matter proper to the flower, or by an actual development of leaf-like organs in the room of the petals—frondescence. Morren[374] judiciously proposed to keep these two conditions separate, calling the one virescence, the other frondescence (see p. 241).

Many of the cases recorded as reversions of the parts of the flower to leaves are simply instances of virescence; indeed, it is not in all cases easy to distinguish between the two states. The examination of the arrangement of the veins is often of assistance in determining this point; for instance, if, under ordinary circumstances, the venation of the petal be such as is characteristic of the sheath of the leaf, while in the green-coloured flower of the same species the venation is more like that which belongs to the blade of the leaf, the inference would, of course, be that the green colour was due to frondescence or phyllody.

The persistence or duration of petals is often increased when they are subject to this change; instead of falling off speedily they become persistent when so affected.

Some flowers are more liable to virescence than others. The common honeysuckle, *Lonicera Periclymenum*, is one of these, and it is noticeable in this plant that the calyx remains unaffected—a circumstance which Morren says shows the distinctness of virescence from frondescence; for, in this instance, we have the most foliaceous portion of the flower remaining unchanged, while the corolla and other organs, usually less leaf-like in their nature, assume a green colour; but this may rather be attributed to the axial nature of the so-called adherent calyx. The stamens in these green-flowered honeysuckles are usually green also, but with[Pg 339] abortive anthers, and the pistil also is in a rudimentary condition. *Umbelliferæ* are not unfrequently subject to this change, *e.g., Torilis Anthriscus, Daucus Carota, Heracleum Sphondylium, Carum carui,* &c. *Primulaceæ*, again, are frequently subject to virescence. Among *Compositæ* the following species are recorded as having had green flowers—*Cirsium tricephalodes,Senecio vulgaris, Calendula officinalis, Pyrethrum Parthenium, Carduus crispus, Hypochæris radicata, Hieracium prealtum, Cirsium arvense,Coreopsis Drummondi.*[375] In *Ranunculaceæ* virescence has been observed in *Delphinium elatum, crassicaule* and *Ajacis, Anemone hortensis* and *nemorosa, Aquilegia vulgaris, Ranunculus Philonotis.*

Many of these cases, and others that might be cited, are probably instances of frondescence or phyllody (see p. 241).

Chromatism.—This term is here intended to apply specially to those cases in which any organ of a plant assumes a colour approximating to that of the petals, or in which the normal green is replaced by tints of some other colour. To a certain extent the change in question is the same as that spoken of under the head of petalody (see p. 283), but there are cases in which, while the ordinary situation and form are those of leaves, the coloration is that of the petals. Such was the case in the *Gesnera*mentioned by Morren (see p. 88), and in which a leaf occupied the position of an inflorescence, and became brightly coloured. In tulips the presence of a highly coloured leaf on the flower-stalk, below the flower, is not uncommon. So also the bracts or leaves below the perianth in*Anemone coronaria* and *hortensis* not unfrequently assume the coloration usually confined to the parts of the perianth. A similar illustration has presented itself, as this sheet is passing through the press, in which two of the leaflets of the compound leaf of a rose were brightly coloured like[Pg 340] the petals, the others being of their ordinary green colour.

The occurrence of coloured bracts, as in *Poinsettia, Bougainvillea,* &c., is very common under natural conditions, and need not here be further alluded to.

Increased intensity of colour often accompanies teratological changes; an instance has just been alluded to in the *Gesnera*; the feather hyacinth,*Muscari comosum*, furnishes another illustration, the adventitious pedicels being brightly coloured.

In fasciated stems, also, of herbaceous plants, it not unfrequently happens that the upper portions of the stem are brightly coloured.

The occurrence of flowers or fruits of different colours on the same plant, or even in the same cluster, is a phenomenon which does not come within the scope of the present book; the reader may, however, be referred to the excellent summary on this subject published by Mr. Darwin in his work on the 'Variation of Animals and Plants under Domestication.'

FOOTNOTES:

[372]These deviations are treated of under the head of alterations of form, because they are not, in a teratological point of view, of sufficient importance to demand a specific heading, while they appeal to the sight in the same way as the deviations from the customary forms of organs.

[373]'De Antholys,' p. 32, § 38.

[374]'Bull. Acad. Belg.,' xvii, part 2, p. 131, c. tab.

[375]See Cramer, 'Bildungsabweich,' pp. 17, 55, 82, 65. See also Lucas, 'Verhandl. des Bot. Vereins. Brandenb.,' heft 1, 2, *Anchusa*. Christ, 'Flora,' 1867. pp. 376, tab. 5, 6, *Stachys.*

[Pg 341]

BOOK III.
DEVIATIONS FROM THE ORDINARY NUMBER OF ORGANS.

To a certain extent the number of the organs of a plant is of even greater consequence for purposes of classification than either their form or their arrangement; for instance, the number of cotyledons in the embryo is made the chief basis of separation between the two great groups of flowering plants, the monocotyledons and the dicotyledons. In the one group, moreover, the parts of the flower are arranged in groups or whorls of five; in the other the arrangement is ternary. In mosses the teeth of the peristome are arranged in fours, or in some multiple of that number. So far as the larger groups are concerned, and also in cases where the actual number of parts is small, the numerical relations above described are very constant; on the other hand, in the minor subdivisions, and especially where the absolute number of parts is large, considerable variation may occur, so that descriptive botanists frequently make use of the term indefinite, and apply it to cases where the number of parts is large and variable, or, at any rate, not easy to be estimated.

Considered teratologically, the changes, as regards the number of organs, are readily grouped into those[Pg 342] consequent on a decreased and into those resulting from an increased development. The alteration may be absolute or relative. There may be an actual deficiency in the number of parts or an increase in their number, but in either case the change may be simply a restoration of the primitive number, a species of peloria, in fact. An increased number of parts, moreover, may depend not so much on the formation of additional parts as on the subdivision of one.

It seems also desirable to treat separately those cases in which there is an increased number of buds either leaf-buds or flower-buds, as the case may be, as happens in what is termed prolification. This formation of buds occurring, as it does, often in unwonted situations is treated of under the head of alterations of arrangement, the mere increase in number being considered of subordinate importance as contrasted with the altered disposition (see p. 100).

[Pg 343]

PART 1.
INCREASED NUMBER OF ORGANS.

An augmentation in the number of parts may arise from several causes, and may sometimes be more apparent than real. True multiplication exists simply as a result of over-development; the affected organs are repeated sometimes over and over again each in their proper relative position, and without any transmutation of form.

Metamorphy, on the other hand, often gives rise to the impression that parts are increased in number, when it may be that the stamens and pistils, one or both, are not so much increased in number as altered in appearance. The double anemones and ranunculus of gardens, amongst many other analogous illustrations, may be mentioned. In these flowers, owing to the petalody of the stamens and pistils, one or both, an impression of exaggerated number is produced, which is by no means necessarily a true one. Fission or lateral subdivision also gives rise to an apparent increase in number; thus, some so-called double flowers, the elements of which appeared to be increased in numbers, owe the appearance merely to the lacination or subdivision of their petals.

The French botanists, following Dunal and Moquin, attribute an increase in the number of whorls in the corolla, and other parts of the flower, to a process which they call chorisis, and they consider the augmentation to be due to the splitting of one petal, for instance, into several;—somewhat in the same manner as one may separate successive layers of talc one from the other.

[Pg 344]

English botanists, on the other hand, have been slow to admit any such process, because, in most instances, no alteration in the law of alternation takes place in these double flowers, and in those few cases where the law is apparently infringed, the deviation is explained by the probable suppression of parts, which were they present would restore the natural arrangement of the flower; and, that this is no imaginary or purely theoretical explanation, is shown by some of the *Primulaceæ*, wherein a second row of stamens is occasionally present in the adult condition, and renders the floral symmetry perfect.

The double daffodil, where there are from forty to fifty petaloid organs instead of fifteen, and wherein each piece exhibits a more or less perfect coronal lobe at the junction of the claw and the limb, has been cited as an objection to chorisis, though it is difficult to see on what grounds.

In *Delphinium*, as shown by Braun,[376] the stamens and carpels are members of a continuous spiral series, and in the double balsam an extra corolline whorl is produced, without the suppression of the stamens, in the following manner: the ordinary stamens are replaced by petals, the carpels by stamens, while an additional whorl of carpels is produced at the summit of the axis. In this instance, therefore, the doubling is distinctly referrible to an absolute increase in the number of whorls, and not to chorisis.[377]

On the other hand, it must be admitted that there are many cases which are not to be explained in any other way than that suggested by the French botanists before alluded to. Probably, the main difficulty in the way of accepting the doctrine of chorisis is the unfortunate selection of the word used to designate the process; this naturally suggests a splitting of an organ already perfectly formed into two or more portions, either in the same plane as the original organs,[Pg 345] "parallel chorisis;" or at right angles to it "collateral chorisis." Indeed, before so much attention had been paid to the way in which the floral organs are developed, it was thought that an actual splitting and dilamination did really take place; Dunal and Moquin both assert as much. The truth would rather seem to be that, in the so-called parallel chorisis at least, the process is one of hypertrophy and over-development rather than of splitting. The adventitious petal or scale is an excrescence or an outgrowth from the primary organ, and formed subsequently to it.

In the case of "compound stamens" the original stamens are first developed each from its own cellular "mamelon," or growing point; and, after a time, other secondary growing points emerge from the primary one, and in this way the stamens are increased in number, without reference, necessarily, to the so-called law of alternation. Outgrowths from leaves, multiplying the laminar surface, are alluded to under the head of hypertrophy, and it is probable that some of the cases of duplication of the flower, or of the formation of adventitious segments outside the ordinary corolla as alluded to in succeeding paragraphs (see Pleiotaxy of the corolla), are due to a similar process.[378]

The formation of parts in unwonted numbers may be merely a reversion to what is supposed to have been the original form, and in this way there may be a restoration of parts that are usually undeveloped or suppressed. There can be little or no doubt that there are in reality six stamens in *Orchidaceæ*, of which one only, under ordinary circumstances, is developed. When the numerical symmetry is restored, as it sometimes is, it is obvious that the augmentation that occurs is of a different character from that arising from[Pg 346] a repetition or renewed development of organs. When the increased number arises from multiplication proper, or from repetition, the ordinary laws of alternation are not interfered with, but if from chorisis or "dédoublement," it may happen that the normal arrangement is disturbed.

Without studying the mode of development, it is not in all cases possible to tell under which of the above categories any particular instance should be placed; hence, in the following sections, except where otherwise stated, the cases are grouped according to the appearance presented in the adult condition, rather than to the way in which the changes from the typical condition are brought about. With reference to the foliar organs it is necessary to distinguish those cases in which there is, from any cause, an augmentation in the number of component parts of a whorl, from those in which the increase takes place in the numbers of the whorls themselves.

FOOTNOTES:

[376]Braun, 'Pringsheim Jahrbuch f. Wiss. Bot.,' 1858, 1, p. 307, tab. 22, 23.

[377]Henfrey, 'Jour. Linn. Soc. Bot.,' vol. iii, p. 159.

[378]On the subject of chorisis or dédoublement the reader may profitably consult Moquin-Tandon, 'Ess. sur les Dédoublements,' and the same author in 'Ann. Sc. Nat.,' t. xxvii, p. 236. and 'El. Ter. Veget.,' p. 337. Dunal, 'Consid. Org. Fleur.,' Montpell., 1829, p. 32, note 3. A. de St. Hilaire in 'Ann. Sc. Nat.,' ser. 3, t. iii, p. 355, adnot. Lindley, 'Elements of Botany,' p. 76. Asa Gray. 'Botanical Text Book.'

CHAPTER I.
MULTIPLICATION OF AXILE ORGANS, INFLORESCENCE, ETC.

By Linné an undue number of branches was designated as "plica," from the analogy with the disease of the hair known as plica polonica: "*Plicata dicitur planta, cum arbor vel ramus excrescit minimis intertextis ramulis, tanquam plica polonica ex pilis, ceu instar nidi Picæ, quod vulgo a genio ortum arbitratur; frequens apud nos in Betula, præsertim Norlandiæ, in Carpino Scaniæ, nec infrequens in Pinu.*"[379]

By some of the older authors this condition was called polyclady. In some cases, it would seem to[Pg 347] be due to fungi as in the witches' brooms (hexenbesen) of the German forests; in other instances, it is a result of mutilation as after the operation of pollarding.

Moquin-Tandon[380] mentions a case in a grafted ash in the botanic garden of Toulouse, where below the graft there was a large swelling, from which proceeded more than a thousand densely-packed, interlacing branches.

This must have been similar to the condition so commonly met with in the birch, and frequently in the hornbeam and the thorn, and which has prompted so many a schoolboy to climb the tree in quest of the apparent nest. It is probable that some of the large "gnaurs" or "burrs," met with in elms, &c., also in certain varieties of apples, are clusters of adventitious buds, some of which might, and sometimes do, lengthen out into branches.

An increased number of branches also necessarily arises when the flower-buds are replaced by leaf-buds.

FIG. 179.—Flower stalks of *Bellevalia comosa*, nat. size, after Morren.

Occasionally, a great increase in the number of pedicels, or flower-stalks, may be met with in conjunction[Pg 348] with a decreased number of flowers, as in the wig-plant (*Rhus Cotinus*), or the feather-hyacinth (*Bellevalia comosa*). In these cases the supernumerary pedicels are often brightly coloured. To this condition Morren gave the name mischomany, from μίσχος, a pedicel, a term which has not generally been adopted.[381]

FIG. 180.—Tuft of branches at the end of the inflorescence of *Bellevalia comosa*, enlarged after Morren.

M. Fournier[382] describes a case in the butcher's broom (*Ruscus aculeatus*), wherein from the axil of the minute leaf subtending the flower a secondary flattened branch proceeded.

Duchartre[383] cites the case of a hyacinth which, in addition to the usual scape, had a second smaller one by its side terminated by a solitary flower; indeed, such an occurrence is not uncommon.

Some tulips occasionally present three or four, or more, flowers on one inflorescence, but whether from a branching of the primary scape, or from the premature development of some of the axillary bulbils into flowering stems which become adherent to the primary flower-stalk, cannot, in all cases, be determined. Certainly,[Pg 349] in some cases examined by me the latter was the case.[384]

Under this head, too, may be included those cases wherein an ordinarily spicate inflorescence becomes paniculate owing to the branching of the axis and the formation of an unwonted number of secondary buds. Instances of this kind may be met with in willows, hazels, alders, and other amentaceous plants. In the case of the hazel the unusual development of male catkins sometimes coincides with an alteration in their position, instead of being placed near the axil of a leaf; they become terminal. Jaeger figures and describes a bunch of *Pinus sylvestris* bearing in one case seventy minute cones, and in another fifty-nine. These cones preserved the same spiral arrangement among themselves which is proper to the leaves. These latter, indeed, replaced the strobili above.[385]

FIG. 181.—Increased number of male catkins in the hazel *Corylus avellana*.

M. Reichardt describes an analogous case in the same species, and attributes the inordinate number of cones to a fungus (*Peridermium pini*). In this case[Pg 350] there were no less than 227 cones, but each one half the size of the ordinary cones.[386]

Of a similar character is the many-headed pineapple. Among grasses such a branching of the inflorescence is exceedingly common,—which is the more readily understood as the normal inflorescence is in so many cases paniculate. Cultivators have, in some instances, availed themselves of this peculiarity, as in the Egyptian wheat or corn of abundance (*Triticum compositum*), certain varieties of Maize, etc. Similar exuberant growths occur in *Orchidaceæ*, in *Cyperaceæ*, e.g. *Carex*, in *Restiaceæ*, and indeed they may be found in any plant with a similar form of inflorescence. In all these cases the branching begins at the lower part of the spike, and extends from below upwards in an indefinite manner, even although the primary inflorescence be definite.

Among the *Equisetaceæ* a similar plurality of spikes occurs often as a result of mutilation.[387] The deviation in question might in some instances be turned to good account, as in the *Triticum* before mentioned or as in the broccoli shown at fig. 182, though it must be added that the apparent advantages are often counterpoised by some undesirable qualities or by some circumstance which prevents us availing ourselves of the new condition. **Multiplication of Bulbs.**—This occurrence has been briefly alluded to previously (see p. 84). The most curious cases are those in which one bulb is placed on the top of another as happened in some bulbs of *Leucoium æstivum* described by M. Gay.[388] Irmisch described a similar phenomenon in *L. vernum*; and Mr. Moggridge has communicated drawings of a similar formation in the same species grown in the neighbourhood of Mentone.

[Pg 351]

From the instances cited it is clear that branching of the inflorescence occurs most frequently in those plants naturally characterised by a dense compact mode of growth, whether that be definite or indefinite, as in spikes, umbels, capitula, &c.; so that compound spikes, umbels, &c., are formed in the place of simple ones (see also prolification of the inflorescence, p. 102).

FIG. 182.—Broccoli, with six perfect heads on one stalk ('Gard. Chron.,' 1856, Oct. 25).

Increased number of florets in the individual spikelets of grasses is also met with under some circumstances. I have seen this in *Hordeum* and *Lolium*, and an instance is figured in *Avena* by Dr. Wiegmann.[389] M. Duval Jouve[390] records a similar occurrence in *Catabrosa aquatica*, the spikelets of which contained from two to seven flowers.[391]

FOOTNOTES:

[379]'Phil Bot.,' § 274.

[380]'El. Ter. Veget.,' p. 392.

[381]'Bull. Acad. Belg.,' xvii, part ii, p. 38.

[382]'Bull. Soc. Bot. Fr.,' vol. iv, 1857. p. 760.

[383]Ibid., vol. viii, 1861, p. 159.

[384]See 'Gard. Chron.,' July, 1866, p. 656, and Clusius, 'Plant. Rar.,' lib. 2, p. 143, *Tulipa serotina* πολυκλαδης, *minor, &c.* Hort. Eysttett. Plant. Vern.,' fol. 12.

[385]'Jaeger de Pini sylvestris monstrositate,' Stuttgardt, 1828.

[386]Cited in 'Bull. Soc. Bot. Fr.,' xiv, p. 265.

[387]Duval Jouve, 'Hist. Nat. Equiset. Fr.,' tab. 8, also Milde, 'Nov. Act. Acad. Nat. Cur.,' t. xxvi, part 2. For branched inflorescence of orchids, see 'Reichenbach Proc. Lond. Bot. Congress,' 1866, p. 121.

[388]'Bull. Soc. Bot. Fr.,' vi, 266, vii, 457. Irmisch, 'Knollen und Zwiebelgew.,' tab. 7, figs. 10, 11.

[389]'Flora,' 1831, p. 5, tab. i; see also Hanstein, 'Flora,' 1857, p. 513. Schlechtendal, 'Bot. Zeit.,' xviii, p. 381.

[390]'Bull. Soc. Bot. Fr.,' ix, p. 8.

[391]It will be seen, from what has been just said, that in some of the cases where the axile organs, branches, &c., appear to be multiplied, the increased number is due to subdivision rather than to renewed formation (see Fission). Of this last description is an instance which came under the writer's notice after the section relating to that subject was in

print, and which may therefore here be alluded to. The instance is that of the subdivision of the leaf-like organs of *Sciadopitys verticillata*. In one instance the pseudo leaf divided, and from the division proceeded a little axis, bearing at its summit a verticil of pseudo leaves. This division and formation of new axes and verticils affords ample confirmation of the opinion thrown out by Professor Alexander Dickson, that the apparent leaves of this plant were really branches: see 'Revue Horticole,' 1867, and 'Report. Bot. Congress,' London, 1866, p. 124.

[Pg 352]

CHAPTER II.
MULTIPLICATION OF FOLIAR ORGANS.

The cases referrible to this head may be ranged under two sections according as the increase is due to plurality of ordinarily single organs, or to an increase in the number of verticils or whorls.

When, in place of a single leaf organ two or more are really or in appearance present the occurrence may be due to one of several causes; among them may be mentioned an actual formation of parts in unwonted number, hypertrophy or enation, chorisis or fission, disjunction, adhesion of one leaf to another or to the stem, as in some of the leaves called "geminate," wherein the two leaves, though apparently in juxtaposition, yet originate from different parts of the stem, but by coalescence or lack of separation produce the impression as if they sprang from the same node. In the adult state it is not always possible to ascertain with certainty to which of these causes the increase in the number of leaves is due, though a clue to the real state of things may be gained from attention to the distribution of the veins, to the arrangement or phyllotaxy of the leaves, the size and position of the supernumerary organs, &c.

The term "phyllomania," as ordinarily used, is applied to an unwonted development of leafy tissue, as in some begonias where the scales or ramenta are replaced by small leaflets, or as in some cabbage leaves, from the[Pg 353] surface of which project, at right angles to the primary plane, other secondary leafy plates; but these are, strictly speaking, cases of hypertrophy (see Hypertrophy).

Those instances in which the actual number of leaves is increased, so that in place of one there are more leaflets, may be included under the term "pleiophylly," which may serve to designate both the appearance of two or more leaves in the place usually occupied by a single one, and also those normally compound leaves in which the number of leaflets is greater than usual.

The increased number of leaves in a whorl may well be designated as "polyphylly," using the word in the same sense as in ordinary descriptive botany, while "pleiotaxy" may be applied to those cases in which the number of whorls is increased.

FIG. 183.—Supernumerary leaflet, *Ulmus campestris*.

Pleiophylly.—As above stated, this term is proposed to designate those cases in which there is an absolute increase in the number of leaves starting from one particular point, as well as those in which the number of leaflets in a compound leaf is preternaturally increased. The simplest cases are such as are figured in the adjacent cuts, wherein, in place of a single leaf, two are produced in the elm. In the one case the new leaflet springs from the apex of the petiole and partially fills[Pg 354] the space consequent on the obliquity of the base of the leaf. In the other it would seem as if two distinct leaves emerged from the stem in juxtaposition. This is probably due to a lateral chorisis or subdivision of the primitive tubercle or growing point, followed by a like subdivision of the vascular bundle supplying it. There are certain varieties of elm that very generally present this anomaly on their rank, coarse, growing shoots. In these cases the new growths have the same direction as the primary one, but in other cases the supplementary production is exactly reversed in direction. Thus, in the common hazel (*Corylus*) a second smaller leaf proceeding from the end of the leaf-stalk at the base of the primary one may frequently be seen. M. Germain de Saint Pierre records an instance in a mulberry leaf, from the base of which proceeded a large leafy expansion divided into two[Pg 355] tubular, horn-like projections, and in the centre a thread-like process representing the midrib and terminated by a small two-lipped

166

limb.[392] Dr. Ferdinand Müller speaks of a leaf of *Pomaderris elliptica* as bearing a secondary leaf on its under surface.[393]

FIG. 184.—Supernumerary leaf, *Ulmus montana.*

FIG. 185.—Supernumerary leaf of hazel.

The leaves of *Heterocentron macrodon* have likewise been observed occasionally to produce leaflets from their upper surface.

To this production of leaves from leaves the late Professor Morren applied the term "autophyllogeny."[394] The Belgian botanist figures a small perfect leaf springing from the nerves of the upper surface of the primary leaf in a species of *Miconia*. As in the hazel, the direction of the adventitious leaf is inversely that of the primary one, the upper surface of the supernumerary leaflet being turned towards the corresponding surface of the normal leaf. A similar occurrence took place in *Gesnera zebrina*, but the new growth in this case sprang from the lower face of the leaf. Morren explains the appearances in question by supposing that the supplementary leaf is one of a pair belonging to a bud borne on a slender stalk. This stalk and one of the bud-leaves are supposed to be inseparably united[Pg 356] with the primary leaf. But there is no reason at all for supposing the existence of adhesion in these cases; no trace of any such union is to be seen. A much more natural explanation is that, from some cause or another, development at the apex of the petiole or on the surface of the nerves, instead of taking place in one plane only, as usual, takes place in more than one, thus showing the close relationship, if not the intrinsic identity, between the leaf-stalk and its continuation, the midrib, with the branch and its subdivisions. The form of the leaf-stalk and the arrangement of the vascular bundles in a circle in the case of the hazel, before alluded to, bear out this notion. Such cases are significant in reference to the notion propounded by M. Casimir de Candolle, that the leaf is the equivalent of a branch in which the upper portion of the vascular circle is abortive.[395]

Compound leaves, as has been stated, occasionally produce an extra number of leaflets; one of the most familiar illustrations of this is in the case of the four-leaved shamrock (*Trifolium repens*), which was gathered at night-time during the full moon by sorceresses, who mixed it with vervain and other ingredients, while young girls in search of a token of perfect happiness made quest of the plant by day. Linné, who in this matter, at any rate, had less than his usual feeling for romance, says of the four-leaved trefoil that it differs no more from the ordinary trefoil than a man with six fingers differs from one provided with the ordinary number. It should be stated that five and six adventitious leaflets are found almost as frequently as four.

Walpers describes a case where the leaf of *T. repens* bore seven leaflets. Schlechtendal alludes to a similar increase in number in *Cytisus Laburnum*, and many other instances might be cited.

For figures or descriptions of four-leaved shamrocks the reader is referred to Lobel, 'Stirp. Advers.,' Nov., p. 382. Tabernæmontanus 'Krauterbuch,' S. 222. Schlechtendal, 'Bot. Zeit.,' ix, p. 583, xiv, p. 71.[Pg 357] Maugin, 'Bull. Soc Bot. Fr.,' 1866, t. xiii, p. 279. See also Cramer, 'Bildungsabweich,' p. 92. Walpers, 'Linnæa,' 1840, p. 362 (7-leaved). Schlechtendal, 'Bot. Zeit.,' 1844, p. 457, *Cytisus*. Wigand, 'Flora,' 1856, p. 706.

Frondiferous leaves have much the appearance of branches provided with leaves, and they may be compared with those instances in which an adventitious bud is placed on the surface or edges of the leaves, as in *Gesnera, Cardamine*, &c. In truth, the two conditions merge one into the other, as in some begonias, where the ramenta often become leaf-like and bear small bulbils in the axil.

When frondiferous leaves die the appendages die also, but when a true bud has been formed on a leaf it does not of necessity die with the leaf that bears it, but separates from it and continues to grow independently.

Increased number of stipules, spathes, &c.—Seringe relates the occasional presence of two or three additional stipules upon the leaf-stalks of *Salix fragilis*, and even makes a variety (*Salix pendula*, var. *multistipulata*).

167

An increase in the number of the spathes has been often noticed in Arads[396]. Prof. Alex. Braun has studied this subject in some detail[397]. In *Calla palustris* the shoot which continues the growth of the plant proceeds from the axil of the last leaf but one; the very last leaf producing no bud, but if accidentally a shoot is developed in this latter situation it produces flowers at once. No leaves are formed, but, on the contrary, two or three spathes surround the spadix, so that the presence of an increased number of spathes in this plant is associated with the development of a side shoot from the axil of the last leaf, the situation whence, under natural circumstances, no shoot at all issues. The supernumerary spathes are not always on the same level, but may be separated by a considerable interval. They vary very much in size, and sometimes assume the form and appearance of leaves. Similar anomalies[Pg 358] occur in other Arads as *Arum maculatum*, *Richardia æthiopica*, and *Anthurium Scherzerianum*, frequently combined with a leaf-like appearance of the spathes and sometimes with a subdivision of the spadix into two or three branches.

Engelmann relates the occurrence of an increased number of glumes in *Bromus velutinus* associated with suppression of the flowers.

Polyphylly.—As previously explained, this term is here applied to those cases in which the members of any particular whorl are increased in number, the whorls themselves not necessarily being augmented.

The simplest cases of this kind are those in which we meet with an unusual number of leaves in a whorl.

Increased number of leaves in a whorl.—This may arise from actual multiplication, or from lateral chorisis, or fission. The true nature of the case may usually be ascertained by an examination of the distribution of the veins of the leaves, or of the fibrous cords of the stem, by the relative position of the supernumerary organs, &c.

Among plants with normally opposite leaves the following occasionally produce them in whorls of three:—*Lonicera brachypoda*, *L. Xylosteum*, *Weigela rosea*, *Cornus mas*, *Vinca minor*, &c. *Paris quadrifolia* may frequently be met with five leaves in its whorl, or even six.[398]

Increased number of bracts.—This is not of infrequent occurrence; one of the most curious instances is that recorded by Mr. Edwards[399] in *Cerastium glomeratum*, where, in place of the usual pair of bracts at the base of the head of flowers, there was a whorl of six or eight, forming an involucre. The flowers in this case were apetalous and imperfect.

Polyphylly of the calyx.—This may occur without any[Pg 359] other perceptible change, while at other times the number of the other parts of the flower is proportionately increased. In a flower of a plum six sepals in place of five sometimes exist; a precisely similar occurrence in the flowers of the elder (*Sambucus*), the *Fuchsia*, and of *Œnanthe crocata*, may occasionally be met with. In the latter case, indeed, there are sometimes as many as ten segments to the calyx, and this without the other parts of the flower being correspondingly augmented. Among monocotyledons a similar increase is not uncommon, as in *Tulipa*, *Allium*, *Iris*, *Narcissus*, &c.

In some plants there seems to exist normally much variation in the number of parts; thus in some species of *Lacistema* in adjacent flowers the calyx may be found with four, five, or six segments.

Most of these cases of polyphylly affecting the calyx may be explained by lateral chorisis or fission.

Polyphylly of the corolla.—This may happen in connection with similar alterations in the calyx and stamens, or sometimes as an isolated occurrence. In the latter case it may be due to lateral chorisis, to substitution, or to the development of organs usually suppressed; thus, when in aconites we meet with four or five horn-like nectaries (petals) instead of two only, as usual, the supernumerary ones are accounted for by the inordinate development of parts which ordinarily are in an abortive or rudimentary state only. This is borne out by what happens in *Balsamineæ*. In the common garden balsam the fifth petal is occasionally present, while in *Hydrocera triflora* this petal is always present.

In a flower of a *Cyclamen* recently examined there were ten petals in one series, the additional five being evidently due to the subdivision of the five primary ones; the natural circular plan of the flower was here replaced by an elliptical one. A similar occurrence takes place in the flowers of maples (*Acer*), which sometimes show an increased number of parts in their[Pg 360] floral whorls and an elliptical outline. Whether the additional organs in this last case are the result of complete lateral chorisis or of multiplication proper I do not know.

Orchids are very subject to an increase in the number of their labella. As illustrations may be cited an instance recorded by Mr. J. T. Moggridge in a flower of *Ophrys insectifera*, and in which there were two labella without any other visible deviation from the ordinary conformation.[400]

I am indebted to Mr. Hemsley for the communication of a similar specimen in *O. apifera*, in which there were two divergent lips, each with the same peculiar markings. One of the sepals in this flower was adherent to one of the lateral petals. This augmentation of the labella depends sometimes on the separation, one from the other, of the elements of which the lip is composed, at other times on the development, in the guise of lips, of stamens which are usually suppressed (see p. 380).

The following enumeration will suffice to show the genera in which an increased number of petals or perianth-segments in any given whorl most frequently occurs.

- Anemone!
- Ranunculus!
- Aconitum!
- Raphanus.
- Bunias.
- Saponaria.
- Dianthus!
- Pelargonium!
- Hibiscus.
- Fuchsia.
- Sarothamnus!
- Lotus!
- Ulex!
- Prunus!
- Trifolium.
- Œnanthe and Umbellif. pl.!
- Sambucus!
- Bryonia.
- Campanula.
- Solanum.
- Veronica.
- Cyclamen!
- Primula!
- Anagallis!
- Plumbago.
- Jasminum.
- Syringa!
- Tradescantia.
- Iris.
- Tigridia.
- Narcissus.

- Tulipa.
- Convallaria!
- Paris!
- Hyacinthus!
- Allium!
- Ornithogalum.
- Orchideæ, sp. pl.!

[Pg 361]

For other illustrations see multiplication of whorls, petalody; see also Moquin, loc. cit., p. 350. Engelmann, loc. cit., p. 20, § 18. Cramer, loc. cit., p. 25.

Polyphylly of the andrœcium.—An increased number of stamens frequently accompanies the corresponding alterations in other whorls, and seems, if anything, to be more frequent among monocotyledonous plants than among dicotyledonous ones; thus, we occasionally find tetramerous flowers in *Crocus, Hyacinthus, Tulipa, Iris, Tigridia,* &c., and more rarely in *Yucca* (*Y. flexilis*[401]).

The increased number of stamens in a single whorl may result from a development of organs usually suppressed, and constitute a form of regular peloria as in *Linaria,* wherein a fifth stamen is occasionally met with. Among normally didynamous plants such numerical restitution, so to speak, is not unusual; thus, in *Veronica* four and five stamens occur. Fresenius has seen five stamens in *Lamium, Mentha, Chelone*;[402]Bentham in *Melittis,* and other instances are cited under the head of peloria. Chorisis may also serve to account for some of these cases; thus, Eichler[403] figures a flower of *Matthiola annua* with five long stamens instead of four; one of the long pairs of stamens has here undergone a greater degree of repetition than usual. De Candolle[404] cites and figures a curious form of *Capsella Bursa-pastoris* sent him by Jacquin, and which was to some extent reproduced by seed. In the flowers of this variety there were no petals, but ten stamens; hence De Candolle inferred that the petals were here replaced by stamens, but Moquin[405] objects, and with justice, to this view, as the ten stamens are all on the same line; he considers the additional stamens to be the result of chorisis. Buchenau[406] mentions the presence[Pg 362] of seven stamens in another Crucifer, *Ionopsidium acaule.* Here the supernumerary organ was placed between two of the long stamens. The effect of chorisis in producing an augmentation of parts is well seen in some plants that have some of their flowers provided with staminodes or abortive stamens, and others with clusters or phalanges of perfect stamens. Thus, in the female flowers of *Liquidambar* there are five small staminodes without anthers, whereas in the male flower the stamens are numerous and grouped together in phalanges, so that the relation of simple to compound stamens is in this case readily seen, as also in many*Malvaceæ, Sterculiaceæ, Byttneriaceæ, Tiliaceæ,* and *Myrtaceæ.* It is probably the idea of splitting or dilamination involved in the word chorisis that has led many English botanists to hesitate about accepting the notion. Had they looked upon the process as identical with that by which a branched inflorescence replaces an unbranched one, or a compound leaf takes the place of a simple one, the objections would not have been raised with such force. The process consists, in most cases, not so much in actual cleavage of a pre-existing organ as in the development of new-growing points from the old ones.

An illustration given by Moquin from Dunal[407] goes far to support the notion here adopted. The majority of the stamens of laurels (*Laurus*) have, says M. Dunal, on each side of the base of their filaments a small glandular bifid appendage; these excrescences are liable to be changed into small stamens. The male flowers have a four-leaved calyx, and sometimes eight stamens, each with two glands, four in one row, opposite to the sepals, four in a second series alternating with the first. More generally two of the stamens are destitute of glands, but have in their place a perfectly developed stamen, so that in these latter flowers there are twelve stamens.

[Pg 363]

M. Clos[408] mentions a flower of rue (*Ruta*) wherein there were two stamens joined together below and placed in front of a petal, as in *Peganum*.

Buchenau[409] mentions a flower of *Lotus uliginosus* in which there were eleven stamens, namely, two free and nine monadelphous; and Hildebrand describes an analogous increase in a flower of *Sarothamnus scoparius* in which, in conjunction with a seven-toothed calyx, there were two carinas and fourteen stamens. It would seem probable in this case that there was a coalescence of two flowers at an early date and consequent suppression of some of the parts of the flower. Whether this was the case or not in this particular illustration, it is nevertheless certain that many of the recorded instances of increased number in the organs of a flower are really the results of a fusion of two or more flowers, though frequently in the adult state but few traces of the coalescence are to be seen.

Polyphylly of the gynœcium.—Moquin[410] remarks that, as the pistils are, generally speaking, more or less subject to pressure, owing to their central position, and it may be added owing to their later development, than the other parts of the flower, they are more subject to suppression than to multiplication; nevertheless, augmentation in the number of carpels does occasionally take place, especially when the other parts of the flower are also augmented in number. Sometimes this increase in the number of carpels is due to pure multiplication, without any other change. At other times the increase is due to a substitution of stamens or other organs for carpels (see Substitutions). In other cases the augmentation seems to be due to the development of parts usually suppressed; for instance, in *Antirrhinum*, where there are usually only two carpels[Pg 364] present, but where, under peculiar circumstances, five may be found—thus rendering the symmetry complete.[411] In *Papilionaceæ*, wherein usually only one carpel is developed, we occasionally find two, or even more, as in *Wistaria, Gleditschia, Trifolium*, &c. In *Prunus* and *Amygdalus* from two to five carpels are occasionally to be found,[412] in *Mimosa* five, in *Umbelliferæ* three to five; in some composites, *e.g. Spilanthes*, five carpels have also been noticed; in *Cruciferæ* three and four, in grasses three.[413] The double cocoa-nut affords an illustration of the development of two carpels out of three, one only generally arriving at perfection. Triple nuts (*Corylus*) also owe their peculiarity to the equal development of all three carpels which exist in the original flower, but of which, under ordinary circumstances, two become abortive. It is necessary, however, to distinguish these cases from those in which two embryos are developed in one seed.

The following list may serve to show in what genera this change has been most frequently noticed, and it may be said in general terms that *Cruciferæ, Umbelliferæ*, and *Liliaceæ*, are the orders most frequently affected. Cases of peloria are not included in the subjoined list.

- Nigella.
- Aquilegia.
- Pæonia!
- Delphinium!
- Iberis.
- Diplotaxis.
- Lunaria.
- Ricotiana.
- Octadenia.
- Draba!
- Lepidium.
- *Cheiranthus!
- Dianthus.
- Brassica!

- Parnassia.
- *Acer!
- Ptelea.
- Citrus!
- Philadelphus.
- Prunus!
- Amygdalus!
- Cratægus!
- Fuchsia!
- Trapa!
- Cassia.
- Cercis.
- Medicago.
- *Phaseolus!
- Wistaria.
- Gleditschia.
- Affonsea.
- Trifolium![Pg 365]
- Archidendron.
- Mimosa.
- Robinia.
- Diphaca.
- Cœsalpinia.
- Vicia.
- Anthyllis.
- Cucurbita.
- Passiflora!
- Sambucus!
- *Œnanthe!
- Daucus!
- Angelica!
- Heracleum!
- Silaus.
- Carum.
- Thysselinum.
- Campanula!
- Spilanthes.
- Chrysanthemum.
- Anagallis.
- Primula!
- Fraxinus!

- Lycium.
- Cobæa.
- Datura!
- Solanum!
- Sesamum.
- Sideritis.
- Coleus.
- Veronica!
- *Digitalis!
- Antirrhinum!
- Linaria.
- Gloxinia!
- Symphytum.
- Anchusa.
- Polygonum.
- Euphorbia.
- Cneorum.
- Mercurialis!
- Chenopodium.
- Suæda.
- Beta.
- Corylus!
- Lambertia.
- Cocos!
- Tigridia.
- Tulipa!
- Iris!
- Narcissus!
- Allium!
- Ornithogalum.
- Gagea!
- Tradescantia!
- Schœnodon.
- Bambuseæ.

A few additional references may here be given to papers where an increased number of carpels is described:—Engelmann, 'De Antholys,' § 17, p. 19. Bernhardi, 'Flora,' 1838, p. 129. Schkuhr., 'Bot. Handb.,' t. 179. Godron, 'Ann. Sc. Nat.,' ser. 5, vol. ii, p. 280, tab. xviii,*pluricarpellary Crucifers.* Weber, 'Verhandl. Nat. Hist. Vereins. Rhein. Pruss.,' &c., 1860, *Cerasus*, &c., &c. Baillon, 'Adansonia,' iv, p. 71,*Trifolium.* Schlechtendal, 'Bot. Zeit.,' xv, p. 67, *Datura*, three-celled fruit; 'Bot. Zeit.,' xiii, p. 823, *Phaseolus*, double pistil—a common case. Cramer, 'Bildungsabweich,' p. 99, reference to several leguminous plants with polycarpellary pistils. Munro, Gen., 'Linn. Trans.,' vol. xxvi, p. 26,*Bambuseæ.* Alph. de Candolle, 'Neue Denkschrift,' *Cheiranthus.* Schimper, 'Flora,' 1829, ii, p. 433. Wigand, 'Bot. Untersuch.' Fleischer, 'Missbild. Cultur Pfl.' Cramer, 'Bildungsabweich,' p. 65, *Umbelliferæ.*

Polyphylly of the flower in general.—Although, for the sake of convenience, multiplication has here been treated of as it affects the members of individual whorls of the flower, yet it must be remembered that, in general, the augmentation is not confined to one whorl, but affects several; thus, if the sepals are increased, the[Pg 366] petals are likely to be so likewise, and so forth. One of the most curious illustrations of this is that recorded by Mr. Berkeley[414] in a plum, wherein there was an increased number of sepals, a corresponding augmentation in the petals, while the pistil was composed of two and sometimes three carpels distinct from the calyx and from each other. In the flowers there did not appear to be any definite relation in the position of the parts either with reference one to another or to the axis.

FIG. 186.—Plum. Increased number of parts in the calycine, corolline, and carpellary whorls respectively.

In *Primulaceæ* this general augmentation has been frequently noticed.[415]

Among *Orchideæ* the instance related by Dr. Seubert is worth alluding to here. This botanist observed and figured a flower of *Orchis palustris* with tetramerous arrangement of parts, that is to say there were[Pg 367] four outer segments to the perianth, four petals, of which two were lip-like, four stamens, three of which were rudimentary, and an ovary with four parietal placentæ.[416]

The following list will serve to show in what plants this general augmentation of parts has been observed most frequently:

- Ranunculus.
- Clematis!
- Delphinium.
- Brassica!
- Ruta.
- Acer!
- Prunus!
- Rosa!
- Rubus.
- Philadelphus!
- Chrysosplenium.
- Umbelliferæ, sp. pl.!
- *Fuchsia!
- Œnothera.
- Adoxa.
- Bryonia.
- Cucumis!
- Campanula!
- Sambucus!
- *Primula!
- Anagallis!
- Lycium.
- Solanum.
- Symphytum.
- Syringa!

174

- Linaria.
- Chenopodium.
- *Paris!
- Convallaria!
- Allium.
- *Lilium!
- *Tulipa!
- Ornithogalum.
- *Gagea!
- Tradescantia!
- Orchideæ, sp. pl.!

Increased number of ovules or seeds.—This appears not to be of very frequent occurrence, at least in those plants where the number of these organs is normally small; where, as in *Primula*, the ovules and seeds are produced in large quantities, it is not practicable to ascertain whether the number be augmented or not in any particular case. Very probably, the attachment or source of origin of the ovules determines, in some measure, their number. Thus, in the case of marginal placentation the number must be limited by the narrow space from which they proceed, whereas in parietal and free central placentation the ovules are generally numerous. In the latter case, however, it will be remembered that solitary ovules are not rare. An increased number of ovules is generally remarked in conjunction with some other change, such as a foliaceous[Pg 368] condition of the carpel, in which the margins are disunited. In such cases the ovules may occupy the margin or may be placed a short distance within it, as in the case of some open carpels of *Ranunculus Ficaria*,[417] and in which two ovules were borne in shallow depressions on the upper or inner surface of the open carpel and supplied with vascular cords from the central bundle or midrib. The outer coating of the ovule here contained barred or spiral fusiform vessels derived from the source just indicated.

In the very common cases where the pistil of *Trifolium repens* becomes foliaceous (see Frondescence), the outer ovules are generally two or more instead of being solitary. So, also, in the Rose with polliniferous ovules (see p. 274). Among *Umbelliferæ* affected with frondescence of the pistil a similar increase in the number of ovules takes place. It will be borne in mind that in most, if not all, these cases the structure of the ovule is itself imperfect.[418]

What are called in popular parlance double almonds or double nuts (*Corylus*) are cases where two seeds are developed in place of one.

In the 'Revue Horticole,' 1867, p. 382, mention is made of a bush which produces these double nuts each year—in fact, it never produces any single-seeded fruit. The plant was a chance seedling, perhaps itself the offspring of a double-seeded parent. It would be interesting to observe if the character be retained by the original plant, and whether it can be perpetuated by seed or by grafting.

It is necessary to distinguish in the case of the nut between additional seeds or ovules, as just described, and the double, triple, or fourfold nuts that are occasionally met with, and which are the result either of actual multiplication of the carpels or of the continued development of some of the carpels which, under ordinary[Pg 369] circumstances cease to grow (see ante, p. 364). In the case of a ripe nut with two seeds it might be impossible to tell whether the adventitious seed were the product of multiplication, or whether it belonged, in the first instance, to the same carpel as that producing the fellow-seed, or to a different and now obliterated ovary. In all probability, however, the second seed would be accounted for by the development of two seeds in one carpellary cavity.

There is still another condition occasionally met with in the almond, and which must be discriminated from the more common multiplication of the seed, and which is the multiplication of the embryos within the seed, and which furnishes the subject of the succeeding paragraph.

Increased number of embryos.—A ripe seed usually contains but a single embryo, although in the ovular state preparation is commonly made for more; and, indeed, in certain natural orders plurality of embryos in the same seed does occur, as in *Cycadeæ* and *Coniferæ*. In the seeds of the orange (*Citrus*), in those of some *Euphorbiaceæ*, &c., there are frequently two or more additional embryos. A similar occurrence has been recorded in the mango, for a specimen of which I am indebted to the Rev. Mr. Parish, of Moulmein.[419]

Plurality of embryos has also been observed in—

- Raphanus sativus.
- *Citrus Aurantium!
- Diosma, sp.
- Hypericum perforatum.
- Triphasia aurantiaca.
- *Æsculus Hippocastanum!
- Euonymus latifolius.
- *Mangifera indica!
- Eugenia Jambos.
- Amygdalus vulgaris!
- Vicia, sp.
- Cassia, sp.
- *Viscum album!
- Daucus Carota.
- Ardisia serrulata!
- Cynanchum nigrum.
- ○ fuscatum.
- Euphorbia rosea.
- Cœlebogyne ilicifolia.
- Allium fragrans.
- Funckia, sp.
- Carex maritima.
- Zea Mays.

[Pg 370]

See Schauer's translation of Moquin-Tandon, 'El. Terat. Veget.,' p. 245, adnot., and 'Al. Braun Polyembryonie.'

Increased number of the cotyledons.—Although the presence of one or of two cotyledons in the embryo is generally accepted as a valuable means of separating flowering plants into two primary groups, yet, like all other means of discrimination, it occasionally fails, and, indeed, almost always requires to be taken in conjunction with some other character. There are cases among flowering plants where the embryo is homogeneous in its structure, there are others in which the number of the cotyledons is more than two. Thus, in some seeds of *Cola acuminata* the cotyledons vary in number from two to five. I have not been able to ascertain precisely whether this multiplication of the cotyledons is characteristic of all the seeds of particular trees, or whether some only are thus affected. Some fruits that I examined bore out the latter view, as in the same pod were seeds with two, three, and four cotyledons respectively.

I have also seen three cotyledons present in embryo-plants of *Correa*, *Cratægus Oxyacantha*, *Dianthus sinensis*, *Daucus Carota*, *Cerasus Lauro-cerasus*. De Candolle alludes to a case

176

of the kind in the bean, and figures a species of *Solanum* with three cotyledons.[420] Jaeger alludes to a similar instance in *Apium Petroselinum*;[421] Ehrenberg to one in the marigold (*Calendula*);[422] Reinsch to an analogous appearance in the beech (*Fagus*), associated with a union of the margins of two out of the three cotyledons, and of those of two out of the three leaves next adjacent.[423] This fusion seems frequently to accompany increase in the number of cotyledons. It was so in the *Correa*, and in the *Cratægus* previously mentioned. Some of these cases may be accounted for by chorisis or by a cleavage of the original cotyledons, as happens, according to Duchartre,[424] in some[Pg 371] Coniferæ, which he considers to be improperly termed polycotyledonous. Whether this holds good in the Loranths, where (*Nuytsia, Psittacanthus*) an appearance of polycotyledony exists, is not stated. In the case of the rue (*Ruta*) figured by M. A. de Jussieu[425] this splitting of one cotyledon into two is sufficiently evident, as is also the case in the sycamore (*Acer pseudo-platanus*), seedlings of which may often be met with divided cotyledons.

In other instances a fusion of two embryo plants may give rise to a similar appearance, as in the *Euphorbia* and *Sinapis* found by M. Alph. de Candolle (see ante, p. 56).

Pleiotaxy or multiplication of whorls.—In the preceding section notice has been taken of the increased number of parts in a single whorl, but an augmentation of the number of distinct whorls is still more frequently met with. Many of the so-called double flowers owe their peculiarity to this condition. The distinction between the two modes in which the parts of the flower are increased in number has been pointed out by Engelmann, Moquin, and others, and the two seem to require distinctive epithets; hence the application of the terms polyphylly and pleiotaxy, as here proposed.

Pleiotaxy in the bracts.—An increase in the number of bracts has been met with very constantly in a species of *Mæsa*, and in a peculiar variety of carnation, called the wheat-ear carnation.[426] In some of these cases the increase in the number of bracts is attended by a corresponding suppression in the other parts of the flower. Such a condition has been frequently met with in *Gentiana Amarella*, where the bracts are increased in[Pg 372] number, coloured purple, and destitute of any true floral organs. A similar condition exists in some varieties of *Plantago major* (var.*paniculata*), as has been previously stated, p. 109.

FIG. 187.—**Wheat-ear carnation. The appearance is due to the multiplication of the bracts and the suppression of the other parts of the flower.**

It has been noticed also in the common pea, *Pisum sativum*, and M. Lortet[427] records a case of the kind in *Erica multiflora*, the flowers of which, under ordinary circumstances, are arranged in clusters, but in this case the pedicels were more closely crowded than[Pg 373] usual, and were covered for their whole length with small rose-coloured bracts arranged in irregular whorls, the upper ones sometimes enclosing imperfect flowers. In the 'Gardeners' Chronicle,' 1865, p. 769, is figured a corresponding instance of*Delphinium Consolida*, in which the bracts were greatly increased in number, petaloid, and, at the same time, the central organs of the flower were wholly wanting.

FIG. 188.—*Delphinium Consolida*. **Multiplication of bracts at the expense of the other parts of the flower.**

FIG. 189.—**Multiplication of bracts, &c.,** *Pelargonium*.

In flowers of *Pelargonium* may occasionally be seen a repetition of the whorls of bracts, in conjunction with suppression and diminished size of some of the other portions of the flower (fig. 189).

The common foxglove (*Digitalis purpurea*) has likewise occasionally been observed subject to a similar malformation.

[Pg 374]

Cornus mas and *C. suecica* sometimes show a triple involucre.[428]Irmish[429] records an analogous case in *Anemone Hepatica*, wherein the involucre was doubled. Similar augmentation occurs in cultivated Anemone. In addition to the plants already mentioned, Engelmann[430]mentions as having produced bracts in unwonted numbers, *Lythrum Salicaria, Plantago major, Veronica spicata, Echium vulgare, Melilotus arvensis*, and *Rubus fruticosus*.

177

It must here be remarked that this great number of the bracts occurs naturally in such plants as *Godoya*, in which the bracts, or, as some consider them, the segments of the calyx, are very numerous, and arranged in several overlapping segments.

In some of the cultivated double varieties of *Nigella* the finely divided involucral bracts are repeated over and over again, but on a diminished scale, to the exclusion of all the other parts of the flower.

Pleiotaxy or repetition of the calyx.—The true calyx is very seldom affected in this manner, unless such organs as the epicalyx of mallows,*Potentilla*, &c., be considered as really parts of the calyx.

In *Linaria vulgaris* Rœper observed a calyx consisting of a double series, each of five sepals, in conjunction with other changes.[431] It is also common in double columbines, delphiniums, nigellas, &c.

In the 'Revue Horticole,' 1867, p. 71, fig. 9, is described and figured by M. B. Verlot a curious variety of vine grown for years in the Botanic Garden at Grenoble, under the name of the double-flowered vine. The place of the flower is occupied by a large number of successive whorls of sepals disposed in regular order, and without any trace of the other portions of the flower. It is, in fact, more like a leaf-bud than a[Pg 375] flower. The outermost whorls of this flower open at the time when the ordinary flowers of vines do; the second series are gradually produced, and expand about the time when the ovaries of the normal flowers begin to swell; a third series then gradually forms, and so on, until frost puts a stop to the growth. This malformation, it appears, is produced annually in certain varieties of vine, and may be perpetuated by cuttings.

The flower of the St. Valèry apple, already alluded to under the head of sepalody, might equally well be placed here. It is not very material whether the second whorl of organs be regarded as a repetition of the calyx or as a row of petals in the guise of sepals.

Engelmann[432] cites the following plants as occasionally presenting a repetition of the calyx, in most cases with a suppression of the other floral whorls:—*Stachys lanata, Myosotis palustris, Veronica media, Aquilegia vulgaris, Nigella damascena, Campanula rapunculoides.*

Pleiotaxy in the perianth.—Increase in the number of whorls in the perianth is common in lilies, narcissus, hyacinths, &c. It may be also met with occasionally among orchids. The lily of the valley (*Convallaria maialis*) seems also to be particularly subject to an increase in the number of parts of which its perianth consists, the augmentation being due partly to repetition or pleiotaxy, partly to the substitution of petaloid segments for stamens and pistils.[433]

In this place may also be mentioned the curious deviation from the ordinary structure occasionally met with in *Lilium candidum*, and known in English gardens as the double white lily. In this case there are no true flowers, but a large number of petal-like segments[Pg 376] disposed in an irregular spiral manner at the extremity of the stem, some of the uppermost being occasionally verticillate.[434]

FIG. 190.—**Double white lily. Multiplication of perianth-segments and other changes.**

Pleiotaxy of the corolla.—With reference to double flowers, it was remarked by Linné that polypetalous flowers were, as he said, multiplied, while monopetalous flowers were duplicated, or triplicated, as the case may be,[435] a statement that is true in the main, though it[Pg 377] requires modification. In the case of polypetalous, or rather dialypetalous flowers, the petals may be very largely increased by multiplication, as in roses, anemones, pinks, &c. In the last-named genus the number is often so much increased that the calyx splits from the tension exercised on it by the increasing mass within. This multiplication may happen without any metamorphy or substitution of petals for stamens, though, in the majority of cases, it is associated with such a change. It is curious to observe in some of these flowers that the total number of parts is not greatly increased; thus, in some of the double-flowered *Leguminosæ*, such as *Ulex europæus* and *Lotus corniculatus*, the petals are repeated once or twice, the stamens are petalodic, but reduced in number, while the carpels are usually entirely wanting. Thus, owing to the diminished number of parts in the inner

178

whorls of the flower, these very double-looking blooms do not contain any greatly increased number of parts.[436]

Flowers that, under ordinary circumstances, are gamopetalous, become, in some instances, multiplied by the formation of additional segments, just as in the case of polypetalous corollas; but in these cases the corollas become polypetalous, their petals do not cohere one with another. Among double flowers of this character may be mentioned *Campanula rotundifolia*,*Gardenia* sp., *Nerium Oleander*, *Serissa* sp., *Arbutus Unedo*, &c. The change is associated with petalody of the stamens and pistils.

A more frequent change among the monopetalous orders is the duplication or triplication of the corolla, in consequence of which there appear to be a series of corollas enclosed one within the other, the lobes of which generally alternate with one another, but which sometimes are superposed. This happens occasionally in the primrose (*Primula acaulis*), and constitutes the variety called by the gardeners "hose in hose."

[Pg 378]

The same condition occurs frequently in some species of *Datura* and*Campanula*.

FIG. 191.—*Campanula rotundifolia*. "Double flowers" resulting from dialysis and multiplication of the petals.

In *Antirrhinum majus* double flowers of this character sometimes occur; the outermost corolla is normal, the succeeding ones usually have their petals separate one from the other; the stamens are sometimes present, sometimes absent, and at other times petalodic. Similar occurrences may be met with in labiates and jasmines, and in *Erica hyemalis*.

Mr. W. B. Hemsley has kindly furnished me with flowers of a similar kind occurring in wild specimens of[Pg 379] *Epacris impressa*,[437] and there are analogous phenomena in the common honeysuckle (*Lonicera Periclymenum*), in which three corollas and no stamens often occur.

This duplication may either be accounted for on the theory of chorisis above alluded to, or by supposing that the extra corolline whorl is due to a series of confluent petalodic stamens; that the latter is the true explanation, in certain cases at least, is shown by some flowers of *Datura fastuosa*, in which the second corolla was partially staminal in its appearance, and bore nearly perfect anthers, in addition to the five ordinary stamens, which were unaltered either in form or position. Some partially virescent honeysuckle flowers have a similar structure.

There are other cases of apparent multiplication or duplication, due, probably, rather to the formation of outgrowths from the petals than to actual augmentation of their number. These excrescences occur sometimes on the inner surface of the petals, or of the corolla; at other times on the outer surface, as in some gloxinias, &c. This matter will be more fully treated of under the head of hypertrophy and enation.

Pleiotaxy of the andrœcium.—An increase in the number of whorls in the stamens is very common, especially in cases where the number of circles of stamens is naturally large. The augmentation of the number of stamens is still more frequent where these organs are arranged, not in verticils, but in one continuous spiral line.

In *Cruciferæ* there is always an indication of two whorls of stamens, and this indication is rendered even more apparent in some varieties accidentally met with. So in *Saponaria*, in *Dianthus*, and other*Caryophylleæ*, three and four verticils of stamens have been met with. In*Lonicera Periclymenum* a second whorl of stamens more or less petalodic sometimes occurs.

Moquin mentions a variety of *Rubus fruticosus* in[Pg 380] which nearly 900 petaloid organs existed in the place of the twenty-five or thirty stamens natural to the plant, the other organs of the flower being in their ordinary condition, with the exception of the pistil, which did not attain its full size. Baillon records the occasional existence of two rows of stamens in *Ditaxis lancifolia*.

Increased number of stamens in orchids, &c.—Various deviations from the ordinary type of orchid structure have been already alluded to under the head of displacement, fusion, peloria, substitution, &c., but the alterations presented by the andrœcium in this family are so important in reference to what is considered its natural conformation, that it seems desirable, in this place, to enter upon the teratological appearances presented by the andrœcium in this order, in somewhat greater detail than usual. The ordinary structure of the flower with its three sepals, two petals, labellum, column; and inferior ovary, is well known. Such a conformation would be wholly anomalous and inexplicable were it not that the real number and arrangement of parts have been revealed by various workers labouring to the same end in different fields. Thus, Robert Brown, Link, Bauer, Darwin, and others, paid special attention to the minute anatomy and mode of distribution of the vessels; Irmisch, Crueger, Payer, and others, to the evolution of the flower; Lindley, St. Hilaire, and Reichenbach, to the comparison of the completed structures in the various genera and species; while the teratological observers have been numerous, as will be seen from the selected references cited at the end of this paragraph and in other places. The result of this manifold study has been a pretty general agreement that the structure of the order (omitting minor details) is as follows:—A six-parted perianth in two rows, the outer three (sepals) generally regular and equal in shape; of the inner three (petals or tepals) two are regular, and one, the labellum very[Pg 381] irregular, consisting not only of a petal, but of two abortive stamens incorporated with it. The column is considered to be made up of one perfect and three abortive stamens, in inseparable connection with three styles. By some, however, it is supposed that all the stamens are confluent with the column and none with the lip.

FIG. 192.—Diagram showing the arrangement of parts in an orchid flower. According to Crüger, the stamens A 2, A 3, should be distinct from the lip. The uppermost figure 2 should have been 1. (See text.)

In either case it is admitted that there are six stamens in two rows. The first row consists of one posterior stamen, which is generally perfect, and two abortive stamens incorporated with the labellum. The second row also consists of three stamens, all of which are usually abortive and inseparable from the column. Traces of them may occasionally be met with in the form of tubercles or wing-like processes from the column. In *Cypripedium*, while the ordinary stamen of the outer row is deficient, two of the inner series are present. The diagram, fig. 192, will serve to show the arrangement of the parts as above described. + represents the situation of the stem or axis; on the opposite side is the bract; between these are placed the sepals, one posterior or next the axis (incorrectly numbered 2 in the plan), two lateral 1, 1; next in order follow the petals, 2, 2, 2, two lateral and somewhat posterior, one larger (the lip), anterior; the outer series of stamens are represented by A 1, A 2, A 3, the two latter being fused with the labellum; *a* 1, *a* 2,[Pg 382] *a* 3 represent the position of the inner verticil of stamens, while s, s, s denote the three carpels. It is foreign to the purpose of this book to detail the varied evidence in support of this explanation of the homologies of orchid flowers.[438] All that can be done in these pages is to set forth the evidence furnished by teratology as to this matter—evidence for the most part accumulated and recorded without any special reference to any theory of orchid structure.

The following details all refer to flowers in which the number of stamens in orchidaceous plants was increased beyond what is necessary. They are arranged with reference to the number of adventitious organs, beginning with those in which the number was smallest, and proceeding thence to those in which it was greatest. In some cases it has not been possible to ascertain whether the adventitious organs were really restorations of the numerical symmetry, substitutions of one part for another, stamen for petal, &c., or wholly adventitious productions. Unless otherwise stated, the interpretation put upon the facts thus recorded is that of the present writer, and not necessarily that of the original observer.

Mr. J. T. Moggridge has described and figured a flower of *Ophrys insectifera* in which there was a vestige of a second stamen present, probably one of the inner series fig. 192 (*a²*).[439] The same observer also records the presence of a second anther between the lobes of the normal one. This can hardly be referred to either of the typical stamens, but would seem to be a perverted development of the rostellum.[440]

Rœper is stated by Cramer[441] to have seen a specimen of *Orchis morio* with two stamens.

In a flower of *Habenaria chlorantha*, described by the late Professor Henslow,[442] the outer three stamens are suppressed, while two of the inner group are present, as happens normally in *Cypripedium*.[Pg 383]

A flower of *Cattleya violacea* afforded a similar illustration; but in this case only one of the inner stamens was developed, and this in the form of a small petal, partly adherent to the column.

In *Dendrobium normale*, Falconer, not only is the perianth regular, but the column is triandrous,[443] the three stamens (according to the diagram of its structure given by Lindley) pertaining to the outer row.

In a specimen of *Dendrobium hæmoglossum* kindly forwarded from Ceylon by Mr. Thwaites there were three stamens present, of which one posterior belonged to the outer series A 1, and two lateral to the inner *a* 1,*a* 2, fig. 192.

M. His observed, several years in succession, some flowers of a species of *Ophrys* with three sepals, no lateral petals, one lip, and three perfect stamens. In this case probably the two supernumerary stamens were petals which had assumed an anther-like character.

Wydler describes a flower of *Ophrys aranifera* in which one outer and two inner stamens were present.[444] I have myself met with three such flowers in the same species. The stamens present were A 1, *a* 1, *a* 2.

Dr. J. E. Gray exhibited at the Botanical Society of London, in August, 1843, a specimen of *Ophrys apifera* with a triandrous column, the supernumerary anthers belonging, apparently, to the inner whorl.

In his 'Catalogue of the Plants of South Kent,' p. 56, tab. iv, f. 16, the Rev. G. E. Smith describes and figures a flower of *O. aranifera* with a triandrous column, seemingly of the same kind as that spoken of by Dr. Gray.

Mr. Moggridge met with a triandrous flower in the same species, and refers the appearance to "a fusion of two flowers, accompanied by suppression and modification."[445] As, however, no details are given in support of this opinion, it may be conjectured that the two additional stamens were members of the inner whorl *a* 1, *a* 2, and thus the conformation would be the same as in the flowers just mentioned. The figures given by Mr. Moggridge bear out this latter view, while they lend no support to the hypothesis advanced by him. Nevertheless, no decided opinion can be pronounced by those who have not had the opportunity of examining the flowers in question.

Alphonse de Candolle[446] figures a flower of *Maxillaria* in exactly the same condition, so far as the stamens are concerned, as in the Ophrys flowers just mentioned. It is curious to observe that in many of these cases the two lateral petals are suppressed.

Von Martius mentions the occurrence of three anthers (*naturaliter*[Pg 384]*conformatæ*) in *Orchis morio*.[447] Richard, as cited by Moquin-Tandon, Lindley, and others, describes and figures a peloria of *Orchis latifolia* with regular triandrous flowers.[448]

The writer has examined, in the Royal Gardens at Kew, a flower of *Cattleya crispa* in which were three stamens, the central one normal; the two lateral ones, belonging probably to the inner whorl, were in appearance like the lateral petals, and one of them was adherent to the central perfect column. Duchartre[449] mentions a flower of *Cattleya Forbesii* in which there were two labella in addition to the ordinary one, the column being in its normal condition. From the analogy of other cases it would appear as if the additional labella in this instance were the representatives of two stamens of the outer whorl. Beer likewise has put on record the existence of a triandrous *Cattleya*.[450]

A specimen of *Catasetum eburneum* forwarded by Mr. Wilson Saunders was normal so far as the sepals and two lateral petals were concerned, but the anterior petal or labellum was flat and in form quite like the two lateral ones; the column was normal and in the situation of the two anterior stamens of the outer series A 2, A 3, were two labella of the usual form (fig. 156, p. 291). Perhaps the *Oncidium* represented at p. 68, fig. 29, may also be explained on the supposition that the two lateral lobes of the labellum in this flower were the representatives of stamens.

In Fig. 193 is shown the arrangement of parts in a flower of *Ophrys aranifera*. Here there were three sepals, two lateral petals, one of which was adherent to the side of the column; the central labellum was seemingly deficient, but there were two pseudo-labella placed laterally in the position of the two antero-lateral stamens of the outer series (A 2, A 3). Within these was another perfect stamen occupying the position of the anterior stamen of the inner series (a 3). In another flower of the same species, gathered at the same time (fig. 194), there were three sepals not at all different from those of the normal flower. The three petals next in succession were also, in form and position, in their ordinary state. In colour, however, the two upper lateral petals differed from what is customary, in having the same purplish-brown tint which characterises the lip. Within these petals, at the upper part of the flower, there was the ordinary column, and at the opposite side, alternating with the petals before mentioned, two additional lip-like petals, one provided with a half-anther containing a single perfectly formed pollen-mass (A 2, A 3). It is, perhaps, worthy of notice that the arrangement[Pg 385] of the coloured spots on the true labellum, and that on the adventitious lips, replacing the two lower of the outer stamens, were not of a similar character. The supernumerary lips had the π-shaped marking which is so common in this species, while the true lip was, as to its spots, much more like *O. apifera*. Alternating with this last whorl were three columns, all apparently perfectly formed and differing only from the ordinary one in their smaller size and corresponding to *a* 1, *a* 2, *a* 3. The ovary in this flower was two-celled, with four parietal placentas, thus giving an appearance as though there had been a fusion of two or more flowers associated with suppression and other changes. The position of the supernumerary organs and the absence of any[Pg 386] positive sign of fusion in the bracts or other part of the flower, seemed, however, to negative the idea of fusion.[451]

FIG. 193.—Diagram showing the arrangement of parts in a malformed flower of*Ophrys aranifera* (see p. 384).

FIG. 194.—Malformed flower of *Ophrys aranifera* with two supernumerary lips and three additional stamens.

A similar illustration, for a knowledge of which the writer is indebted to the kindness of Professor Asa Gray and Mr. Darwin, occurred in some specimens of *Pogonia ophioglossoides* collected by Dr. J. H. Paine in a bog near Utica, New York. It will be seen from the following description that these flowers presented an almost precisely similar condition to those of the *Ophrys aranifera* just mentioned. "The peculiarities of these flowers," writes Professor Gray, "are that they have three labella, and that the column is resolved into small petaloid organs. The blossom is normal as to the proper perianth, except that the labellum is unusually papillose, bearded almost to the base. The points of interest are, first, that the two accessory labella are just in the position of the two suppressed stamens of the outer series, viz. of A2 and A3, as represented in the diagram, fig. 192; and there is a small petaloid body on the other side of the flower, answering to the other stamen, A1. Secondly, in one of the blossoms, and less distinctly in another, two lateral stamens of the inner series (*a*1 and*a*2) are represented each by a slender naked filament. There are remaining petaloid bodies enough to answer for the third stamen of the inner series and for the stigmas, but their order is not well to be made out in the dried specimens." It may here be mentioned that *Isochilus* is normally triandrous.

A tetrandrous flower of *Cypripedium* has also been recorded.

In *Isochilus*, according to Cruger, there are often five stamens, and[Pg 387] there are several, besides those already mentioned, in which six more or less perfect stamens have been seen—of these the following may be taken as illustrations. A hexandrous flower of *Orchis militaris* has been recorded by Kirschleger,[452] and in the accompanying diagram (fig. 195), from Cramer,[453] of a monstrous flower of *Orchis mascula*, there is one perfect stamen of the outer row and two lip-like stamens of the same series, while the inner verticil comprises one perfect and two abortive stamens.

FIG. 195.—Diagram of flower of *Orchis mascula* with two additional lips, two perfect and two imperfect stamens (after Cramer).

Morren[454] describes some flowers of *Orchis morio* in which there were three sepals, three petals, and within the latter two other ternary series of petals; this would seem to be a case of petalody of all six stamens. Morren, however, seems to have considered the additional segments as repetitions of the corolline whorl, though he describes a central mass as the column bearing a "*souvenir* of the anther." Nevertheless, there is no decisive evidence either in his figure or his description in support of his opinion as to the nature of the central mass, which might be a distorted condition of the styles, or, as is more probable, a rudimentary and irregular flower. Morren also describes another flower of the same plant in which there were three sepals, two lateral petals partially lip-like in aspect, a third labellum normal, two additional labella representing the two anterior stamens of the outer whorl, while more or less developed rudiments of the remaining four stamens also exist.

While, in most cases, the supernumerary stamens can, by reason of their relative position, their complete or partial antheriferous nature, be safely referred to one or other of the six stamens, making up a typical orchid flower, there are other specimens in which the additional stamens are altogether adventitious, and do not admit of reference to the homologue. Thus it was in a specimen of *Odontoglossum Alexandræ* examined by the writer, and in which, within a normally constructed perianth, there were six columns, all polliniferous, but arranged in so confused and complicated a manner that it was impossible to make out any definite relation in their position. There was nothing to indicate a fusion of flowers, but rather an extension of the centre of the flower, and consequent displacement of the stamens, &c. Again, the existence of adventitious stamens does not necessarily imply the development of organs usually suppressed, inasmuch as they may result from the assumption by the lateral petals of staminal characteristics.

Nevertheless, as far as teratology is concerned, specimens may be found in which some or all of the usually suppressed stamens of *Orchidaceæ* may be found. These stamens may be all perfect (polliniferous), or, as is more frequently the case, more or less petal-like. Moreover,[Pg 388] when the stamens are petalodic, the form assumed is usually that of the labellum.

The presence of stamens in undue numbers in orchids is very generally, but not always, attended by some coincident malformation, of which the most frequent is cohesion of two or more sepals, and consequent displacement or adhesion of one petal to the side of the column. Petalody of the styles and median prolification are also sometimes found in association with an augmented number of stamens.

FIG. 196.—**Increased number of carpels, tulip.**

FIG. 197.—**Fruit of St. Valery apple cut lengthwise.**

Pleiotaxy of the gynœcium.—An increase in the number of whorls of which the pistil consists is not of very frequent occurrence. Generally after the formation of the whorl of carpels, the energy of the growing point ceases, or if by chance it be continued, the result is more generally the production of a new flower-bud (median prolification) than the repetition of the carpellary series. It is necessary also to distinguish between the veritable augmentation of the pistil and the semblance of it, brought about by the substitution of carpels for some other organs, as pistillody of the stamens, and even of the segments of the perianth, is not very unfrequent, as has already been stated under the head of substitution. Again, the increased number of carpels which is sometimes met with in such flowers, as *Magnolia* or *Delphinium*, where the ovaries are arranged[Pg 389] in spiral series, is not strictly referable to the present category.

The orange is one of the plants most frequently subject to an augmentation in the number of carpellary whorls; sometimes this is due to the stamens assuming the guise of carpels, but at other times the increase occurs without any alteration in the stamens or other organs. If the adventitious carpels be exposed, they are covered with yellow rind, while those portions that are covered by the primary carpels are destitute of rind. Some varieties of the double tulip are very subject to a similar change, but, in this case, the petals and the stamens very frequently become more or less carpellary in their nature. Fig. 196 represents an

183

increased number of whorls of carpels in the variety called "rex rubrorum," the segments of the perianth having been removed.

In the St. Valery apple, already referred to, there is a second whorl of carpels above the first, a fact which has been made use of to explain the similar structure of the pomegranate.

The tomato (*Lycopersicum esculentum*) is another plant in which an adventitious series is frequently produced, and generally in combination with the primary series.

In the Chinese primrose (*Primula sinensis*) a supernumerary whorl is frequently met with, generally associated with other changes in the construction and arrangement of the parts of the flower.

M. de Candolle[455] mentions a flower of *Gentiana purpurea* with four carpels in one series, and five others in the circle immediately above them. Wigand[456] alludes to an instance wherein there was a second pair of carpels above the first in *Vinca herbacea*. Dr. Sankey has forwarded flowers of a *Pelargonium* having a double series of carpels, eight in the outer row, five in the inner, and this condition is stated to exist in the flowers[Pg 390] of the same plant for two years consecutively. In *Aquilegia* I have met with a similar increase in the whorls of carpels.[457] Meissner records a similar augmentation in *Polygonum orientale*.[458]

Wigand[459] describes and figures a flower of *Vinca minor*, in which there were two carpels intervening between the ordinary pair, and a similar illustration has been observed by the writer in *Allamanda cathartica*. Eichler[460] has put on record a similar case in a capparid.

Marchand[461] mentions a polycarpellary berberid (*Epimedium Musschianum*). The supernumerary carpels in this flower were placed on a short axis, which originated in the axils of the stamens, and as these latter organs were present in their usual number and position, the adventitious carpels could not be considered as resulting from a transformation, or substitution of carpels for stamens.

Lastly, the instance cited by Dr. Allman[462] in *Saxifraga Geum* may be alluded to. Here there was a row of adventitious carpels between the stamens and pistils, the backs of the carpels being turned towards the axis of the flowers. Dr. Allman explains the presence of the supernumerary parts by the supposed production of a whorl of secondary axes between the stamens and the centre of the flower. These axes are further supposed to bear imperfect flowers, of which the additional carpels are the only traces, but this explanation seems forced.

In addition to the references already cited the following may be given:

Duchartre, 'Ann. Sc. Nat.,' 4 ser., vii, p. 23 (Tulip).

Ferrari, 'Hesperides,' pp. 271, 395, 405. Duchartre, 'Ann. Sc. Nat.,'[Pg 391] 4 ser., 1844, vol. i, p. 294. Maout, 'Leçons Elément.,' vol. ii, pp. 488–9. Clos, 'Ann. Sc. Nat.,' 1865, p. 317 (*Citrus Aurantium*).

Clos, 'Bull. Soc. Bot. Fr.,' vol. xiii; 'Rev. Bibl.,' p. 75. Pasquale, 'Reddicont Accad. Sc. Fis. e Math. Napoli.' Octr. 1866 (*Solanum Lycopersicum*).

On the general subject of multiplication, in addition to previous citations, the reader may be referred to A. P. de Candolle, 'Théorie Elément. Bot.,' ed. 3, p. 89.

Increased number of flowers in an inflorescence.—This happens generally as a result of over luxuriant growth, and scarcely demands notice here, being rather referable to variation than to malformation. The increased number of florets in the spikelets of some grasses has already been alluded to (p. 351). Thus spikelets of wheat occasionally produce more than the three florets which are proper to them.[463] It will be remembered that in this as in many other grasses there are rudimentary florets, and it is no matter for surprise that these florets should occasionally be fully developed.

FOOTNOTES:

[392]'Bull. Soc. Bot. Fr.,' vol. vii, 1860, p. 587.
[393]'Fragment. Phyt. Austral.,' part xx, p. 270.
[394]'Bull. Acad. Belg.,' xvi, pt. i, p. 60, "Fuchsia," p. 125, c. ic.
[395]'"Théorie de la feuille," 'Arch. des Sciences Bibl. Univers.,' 1868.
[396]See Engelmann, 'De Antholysi,' p. 16, section 12.
[397]Verhandl. des Botanisch. Vereins Brandenburg,' 1859, 1 heft.
[398]See Henslow. 'Mag. Nat, Hist.' 1832, vol. v, p. 429.

184

[399]'Phytologist,' September, 1857.

[400]Seemann's 'Journal of Botany,' iv, p. 168, t. 47, f. 3.

[401]'Illust. Hortic.,' 1866, misc., p. 97.

[402]See Fresenius, 'Mus. Senkenb.,' bd. 2, p. 43. Schlechtendal, 'Bot. Zeit.,' iv, pp. 403, 492, *Veronica tetrandra.*

[403]'Flora,' 1865, tab. 6, fig. 8.

[404]'Org. Veget.,' t. i, p. 497, pl. 42, f. 3.

[405]'El. Ter. Veg.,' p. 354.

[406]Cited in "Rev. Bibl." of 'Bull. Soc. Bot. Fr.,' 1866, p. 171.

[407]Loc. cit., 351.

[408]'Mém. Acad. Toulous.,' vi, 1862, ex 'Bull. Soc. Bot. Fr.,' "Rev. Bibl.," vol. ix, 1862. p. 127.

[409]'Flora.' 1857. p. 289.

[410]L. c., p. 354.

[411]Giraud, 'Ed. Phil. Mag.,' Dec., 1839.

[412]See *Cerasus Caproniana*, D. C. 'Plant. Rar. Hort. Genev.,' tab. 18.

[413]Nees, 'Linnæa,' v, p. 679, tab. 11 (*Schœnodorus*).

[414]'Gard. Chron.,' 1852, p. 452.

[415]See Cramer, 'Bildungsabweich.' pp. 16, 24.

[416]'Linnæa,' 1842, p. 389, c. ic.

[417]Seemann's 'Journal of Botany,' 1867, vol. v, p. 158.

[418]Cramer, 'Bildungsabweich,' p. 66, *Astrantia major, Eryngium*, to which may be added *Daucus, Heracleum*, &c.

[419]See also Reinwardt, 'Nov. Act. Acad. Nat. Cur.,' 12, 1, 37; and Masters, 'Journ. Linn. Soc.,' vi, p. 24.

[420]'Organog. Veget.,' tab. 53.

[421]'Missbild.,' p. 206.

[422]Ehrenberg, 'Flora,' 1846, p. 704.

[423]'Flora,' 1860, tab. 7.

[424]'Ann. Sc. Nat.,' 3 ser., t. x, p. 207.

[425]'Mem. Mus.,' xii. t. 17.

[426]'Nov. Act. Acad. Nat. Cur.,' xv, tab. xxviii, f. 3; 'Bot. Mag.,' t. 1622. "Caryophyllus spicam frumenti referens." A similar malformation in *Dianthus barbatus* is not uncommon. It has lately been introduced into gardens under the name of *Dianthus* "*mousseux*," but is not likely to find favour with gardeners.

[427]'Bull. Soc. Bot. France,' t. vi, 1859. p. 268.

[428]Weber, 'Verhandl. Nat. Hist. Vereins. Rhein. Pruss.,' 1860.

[429]'Bot. Zeit.,' 1848, p. 217.

[430]'De Anthol.,' p. 17, § 12.

[431]'Linnæa,' vol. ii, 1827, p. 85.

[432]'De Antholysi,' p. 17, tab. iii, f. 15, 16; Weinmann, 'Phytanth. iconogr.,' nro. 292.

[433]See Hildebrand, 'Bot. Zeit.,' 1862, p. 209, tab. viii; Cramer, 'Bildungsabweich.,' p. 7, tab. xiii; Engelmann, 'De Antholysi,' p. 18, &c. For similar changes in *Gagea arvensis* see Wirtgen, 'Flora,' 1838, t. xxi. p. 350, and 'Flora.' 1846, p. 353. Some of these are cases of synanthy.

[434]Schlechtendal, 'Bot. Zeit.,' xx, 1862, p. 301.

[435]'Phil. Bot.,' § 126.

[436]C. Morren, 'Bull. Acad. Belg.,' xix, part ii, p. 17.

[437]'Seemann's Journal of Botany,' iii, p. 354.

[438]On this point the reader will find an excellent summary in Lindley's 'Vegetable Kingdom,' cd. iii, p. 183a, and in Darwin, 'Fertilisation of Orchids,' p. 292. See also Crüger,'Journ. Linn. Soc.,' t. viii, p. 134.

[439]'Seemann's Journal of Botany,' vol. iv, p. 168, tab. 47.

[440]Ibid., t. iv. 1866, p. 168, t. xlvii, f. 1.

[441]'Bildungsabweich,' p. 8; see also 'Bot. Zeit.,' 1852, p. 425.

[442]'Journ. Linn. Soc.,' t. ii, p. 104. tab. 1, fig. B.

[443]Lindl., "Orchid. Ind.," 'Jour. Linn. Soc.,' iii, p. 9.

[444]'Arch. Bot.,' ii, p. 300, tab. xvi, f. 11.

[445]'Seemann's Journal of Botany,' v, p. 318, tab. lxxii, figs. A 4, 4 *a.*

[446]"Monstr. Veg.," in 'Neue Denkschrift,' p. 17, tab. vii.

[447]'Flora,' t. viii, 1825, p. 736.

[448]'Mem. Soc. d'Hist. Nat.,' ii, 1, p. 212, tab. iii.

[449]'Bull. Soc. Bot. Fr.,' t. vii, 1860, p. 26.

[450]'Beitr. Morphol. und Biol. Orchid.,' quoted by Cramer; 'Bildungsabweich,' p. 9.

[451]Masters, 'Journ. Linn. Soc.,' viii, p. 207. See also Rodigas, 'Bull. Soc. Bot. Belg.,' iv, p. 266, for similar changes in *Cypripedium Hookeræ.*

[452]Kirschleger, 'Flora,' 1844, p. 131.

[453]'Bildungsabweich,' p. 11, tab. xiv, f. 3.

[454]'Bull. Acad. Roy. Belg.,' t. xix, part 2, p. 171.

[455]'Organogr. Végét.,' t. i, p. 509, tab. 40, figs. 6, 7.

[456]'Flora,' 1856, p. 715.

[457]'Linn. Trans.,' t. xxiii, p. 364, tab. 34, fig. 5.

[458]'Monog. Polygon,' pl. 3, K. f. 12.

[459]'Flora,' 1856, tab. viii.

[460]Ibid., 1865, tab. ix, f. 6.

[461]'Adansonia,' vol. iv, 1864, p. 127.

[462]'Ann. Nat. Hist.,' 1845, vol. xvi, p. 126.

[463]See Schlechtendal, 'Bot. Zeit.,' t. xviii, p. 381 (*Triticum*); also 'Flora,' t. xiv, 1831, p. 5 (*Avena*).

[Pg 392]

PART II.
DIMINISHED NUMBER OF ORGANS.

A diminution in the number of parts is generally due to suppression, using that word as the equivalent of non-development. It corresponds thus in meaning with the *Fehlschlagen* of the Germans, the *avortement complète* of Moquin and other French writers. It differs from atrophy, or partial abortion, inasmuch as the latter terms apply to instances wherein there has been a partial development, and in which evolution has gone on to a certain extent, but has, from some cause or other, been checked. These cases will be found under the head of diminished size of organs. As the word abortion is used by different authors in different ways, it is the more necessary to be as precise as possible in the application of the term. In the present work abortion is used to apply to cases wherein parts have been formed, but wherein growth has been arrested at a certain stage, and which, therefore, have either remained *in statu quo,* while the surrounding parts have increased, or have, from pressure or other causes, actually diminished in size.

In practice, however, it is not always possible to discriminate between those instances in which there has been a true suppression, an absolute non-development of any particular organ, and those in which it has been formed, and has grown for a time, but has afterwards ceased to do so, and has been gradually[Pg 393] obliterated by the pressure exercised by the constantly increasing bulk of adjacent parts, or possibly has become incorporated with them. In the adult flower the appearances are the same, though the causes may have been different.

CHAPTER I.
SUPPRESSION OF AXILE ORGANS.

Absolute suppression of the main axis is tantamount to the non-existence of the plant, so that the terms "acaulescent," "acaulosia," etc, must be considered relatively only, and must be taken to signify an atrophied or diminished size of the stem, arising from the non-development of the internodes.

The absence of lateral branches or divisions of the axis is of frequent occurrence, and is dependent on such causes as the following:—deficient supply of nutriment, position against a wall or other obstacle, close crowding of individual plants, too great or too little light, too rich or too poor a soil, &c.

Probably the absence of the swollen portion below the flower in the case of many proliferous roses, double-flowered apples, as already referred to, may be dependent on the non-development of the extremity of the peduncle or flower-stalk. Thus, in a double-flowered apple recently examined, there was a sort of involucel of five perfect leaves, then five sepals surrounding an equal number of petals, numerous stamens, and five styles, but not a trace of an expanded axis, nor of any portion of the carpels, except the styles. The views taken as to the nature of this and similar malformations must depend on the opinion held as to the nature of inferior pistils, and on the share, if any, that the expanded axis takes in their production. As elsewhere said, the[Pg 394] evidence furnished by teratology is conflicting, but there seems little or nothing to invalidate the notion that the end of the flower-stalk and the base of the calyx may, to a varying extent, in different cases, jointly be concerned in the formation of the so-called calyx-tube and of the inferior ovary. Obviously it is not proper to apply to all cases where there is an inferior ovary the same explanation as to how it is brought about.

As these pages are passing through the press, M. Casimir de Candolle has published a different explanation as to the nature of the hip of the rose, having been led to his opinion by the conclusion that he has arrived at, that the leaf is to be considered in the light of a flattened branch, whose upper or posterior surface is more or less completely atrophied.

According to M. de Candolle, the calyx-tube, in the case of the rose, is neither a whorl of leaves, nor a concave axis in the ordinary sense in which those terms are used, but is rather to be considered as a ring-like projection from an axis arrested in its ulterior development. The secondary projections from the original one correspond to an equal number of vascular bundles, and develope into the sepals, petals, stamens, and ovaries. If these organs remained in a rudimentary condition, the tube of the calyx would be reduced to the condition of a sheathing leaf. The rose flower, then, according to M. de Candolle, may be considered as a sheathing leaf, whose fibro-vascular system is complete, and from which all possible primary projections are developed.[464]

If, as M. de Candolle considers, the leaf and the branch differ merely in the fact that the vascular system is complete in the latter, and partly atrophied in the former, it would surely be better to consider the "calyx-tube" of the rose as a concave axis rather than as a leaf, seeing that he admits the fibro-vascular system to be complete in the case of the rose.

[Pg 395]

With reference to this point the reader is referred to Mr. Bentham's account of the morphology and homologies of the *Myrtaceæ* in the 'Journal of the Linnean Society,' vol. x, p. 105. See also *ante*, pp. 71, 77.

Some doubts also exist as to the nature of the beak or columella of such fruits as those of *Geraniaceæ, Malvaceæ, Umbelliferæ, Euphorbiaceæ,* &c. The nature of the organ in question may probably be different in the several orders named; at any rate the subject cannot be discussed in this place, and it is mentioned here because, now and then, it happens that the organ in question is completely wanting, and hence affords an illustration of suppression.

FOOTNOTES:

[464]'Théorie de la feuille.' p. 24.

CHAPTER II.
SUPPRESSION OF FOLIAR ORGANS.

This subject may be considered, according as the separate leaves of the stem or of the flower are affected, and according as either the number of members of distinct whorls, or that of the whorls themselves, is diminished.

The terms aphylly, meiophylly, and meiotaxy may be employed, according as the individual leaves are altogether wanting, or with reference to the diminished number of parts in a whorl, or a decrease in the verticils.

Aphylly.—Entire suppression of the leaves is a rare phenomenon. Under ordinary circumstances it occurs in most *Cactaceæ*, in some of the succulent Euphorbias, and other similar plants, where the epidermal layers of the stem fulfil the functions of leaves. But even in these plants leaf-like organs are present in some stage or another of the plant's life.

[Pg 396]

Partial suppression of the leaf occurs sometimes in compound leaves, some or other of the leaflets of which are occasionally suppressed. Sometimes, as Moquin remarks, it is the terminal leaflet which is wanting, when the appearance is that of *Cliffortia*, at other times the lateral leaflets are deficient, as in *Citrus* or *Phyllarthron*. *Ononis monophylla* and *Fragaria monophylla* may be cited as instances of the suppression of the lateral leaflets. If the blade of the leaf disappears entirely, we have then an analogous condition to that of the phyllodineous acacias.

With reference to the strawberry just mentioned, Duchesne, 'Hist. Nat. Frais.,' p. 133, says that this was a seedling raised from the *fraisier des bois*, and the characters of which were reproduced by seed, and have now become fixed. The monophyllous condition has been considered to be the result of fusion of two or more leaflets, but however true this may be in some cases, it is not the case with this strawberry. M. Paillot states that he has found the variety in a wild state.[465]

In like manner varieties of the following plants occur with simple leaves,*Rosa berberifolia* (*Lowea*), *Rubus Idæus*, *Robinia pseudacacia*, *Fraxinus excelsior*, *Sambucus nigra*, *Juglans nigra*, &c.

In one instance seen by the writer every portion of the leaf of a rose was deficient, except the stipules and a small portion of the petiole. (See abortion.)

Meiophylly.—A diminished number of leaves in a whorl occasionally takes place; thus, in some of the *Stellatæ*, and frequently in *Paris quadrifolia*, the number of leaves in the verticil is reduced. Care must be exercised in such instances that an apparent diminution arising from a fusion of two or more leaves be not confounded with suppression.

Meiophylly of the calyx or perianth.—A lessened number[Pg 397] of sepals is not a very common occurrence among dicotyledonous plants. Seringe figures a proliferous flower of *Arabis alpina* with two sepals only, and a similar occurrence has been noticed in *Diplotaxis tenuifolia*.

In *Cattleya violacea* the writer has met with a flower in which the uppermost sepal was entirely wanting, while two of the lateral petals were fused together. Moquin records that in some of the flowers of*Chenopodiaceæ*, in which the inflorescence is dense, a suppression of two or three sepals sometimes occurs. The species mentioned are *Ambrinaambrosioides*, *Chenopodium glaucum*, and *Blitum polymorphum*.

Meiophylly of the corolla.—Suppression of one or more petals is of more frequent occurrence than the corresponding deficiency in the case of the sepals.
Among *Caryophyllaceæ* imperfection as regards the numerical symmetry of the flower is not uncommon, as in species of *Cerastium*,*Sagina*, *Dianthus*, &c. In *Ranunculaceæ* the petals are likewise not unfrequently partially or wholly suppressed. A familiar illustration of this is afforded by *Ranunculus auricomus*, in which it is the exception to find the corolla perfect.[466] Some varieties of *Corchorus acutangulus* in west tropical Africa are likewise subject to the same peculiarity. Amongst*Papilionaceæ* absence of the carina or of the alæ is not uncommon, as in*Trifolium repens*, *Faba vulgaris*, &c.

Moquin relates a case of the kind in the haricot bean, in which the carina was entirely absent, and another in the pea, where both carina and alæ were missing, thus reducing the flower to the condition that is normal in*Amorpha* and *Afzelia*. Suppression of the upper lip in such flowers as*Calceolaria* has been termed by Morren "apilary."

[Pg 398]

In *Orchidaceæ* entire absence of the labellum, frequently without any other perceptible change, is of common occurrence. The writer has seen numerous specimens of the kind in *Ophrys apifera* and *O. aranifera*; also in *Dendrobium nobile*, *Ærides odoratum*, *Cypripedium villosum*, *Listera ovata*, &c. Morren[467] mentions analogous deficiencies in *Zygopetalum maxillare*, *Calanthe* sp., and *Cattleya Forbesii*. In most of these there was also a fusion of the two lower sepals, which were so twisted out of place as to occupy the situation usually held by the labellum. At the same time the column was partially atrophied. To this deficiency of the lip the author just quoted proposed to apply the term acheilary, α-χειλαριον. Mr. Moggridge has communicated to the author an account of certain flowers of *Ophrys aranifera*, in which the petals were deficient, sometimes completely, at other times one or two only were present.

Meiophylly of the andrœcium.—Suppression of one or more stamens, independently of like defects in other whorls, is not uncommon, even as a normal occurrence, *e.g.* in *Carlemannia*, where the flower, though regular, has only two stamens, and other similar deficiencies are common in Dilleniads.

Seringe relates the occurrence of suppression of some of the stamens in *Diplotaxis tenuifolia*,[468] St. Hilaire in *Cardamine hirsuta*, others in *C. sylvatica*.

In *Caryophyllaceæ* suppression of one or more stamens has been observed in *Mollugo cerviana*, *Arenaria tetraquetra*, *Cerastium*, &c.[469] Among violets the writer has observed numerous flowers in which two or three stamens were suppressed. Chatin[470] alludes to a similar reduction in *Tropæolum*, while in flowers that are usually didynamous absence of two or more of the stamens is not unfrequent, *e.g.* in *Antirrhinum*, *Digitalis*,[Pg 399]while in a flower of *Catalpa* a solitary perfect stamen, and a complete absence of the sterile ones usually present, have been observed. This might have been anticipated from the frequent deficiencies in the staminal whorl in these plants under what are considered to be normal conditions. Reduction of the staminal whorl is also not unfrequent in *Trifolium repens* and *T. hybridum*, and has been seen in *Delphinium*, &c.[471]

Meiophylly of the gynœcium.—Numerical inequality in the case of the pistil, as compared with the other whorls of the flower, is of such common occurrence, under ordinary circumstances, that in some text-books it is looked on as the normal condition, and a flower which is isomerous in the outer whorls is by some writers not considered numerically irregular if the number of the carpels does not coincide with that of the other organs.

But in this place it is only necessary to allude to deviations from the number of carpels that are ordinarily found in the particular species under observation. As illustrations the following may be cited:—*Arenaria tetraqueta*, which has normally three styles, and a six-valved capsule, has been seen with two styles, and a four or five-valved capsule. Moquin relates an instance in *Polygala vulgaris* where there was but a single carpel, a condition analogous to that which occurs normally in the allied genus *Mozinna*. *Reseda luteola* occasionally occurs with two carpels only, while Aconites, Delphiniums, Nigellas, and Pæonies frequently experience a like diminution in their pistil.

In a flower of *Papaver Rhœas* the writer has recently met with an ovary with four stigmas and four parietal placentæ only, and to Mr. Worthington Smith he is indebted for sketches of crocus blooms with two, and in one instance only a solitary carpel.

Moquin cites the fruit of a wild bramble (*Rubus*)[Pg 400] in which all the little drupes which go to make up the ordinary fruit were absent, except one, which thus resembled a small cherry. In *Cratægus* the pistil is similarly reduced to a single carpel, as in *C. monogyna*. The writer has on more than one occasion met with walnuts (*Juglans*) with a single valve and a single suture.[472] If the ovary of *Juglans* normally consisted of two valvate carpels, the instances just alluded to might possibly be explained by the suppression of one carpel, but the ovary in *Juglans* is at first one-celled according to M. Casimir de Candolle.

Among monocotyledons *Convallaria majalis* may be mentioned as very liable to suffer diminution in the number of its carpels, either separately or in association with other changes.[473]

Meiophylly of the flower as a whole.—In the preceding sections a reduction in the parts of each individual whorl has been considered without reference to similar diminution in neighbouring verticils. It more commonly happens, nevertheless, that a defect in one series is attended by a corresponding imperfection in adjoining ones. Thus trimerous fuchsias and tetramerous jasmines may frequently be met with, and Turpin describes a tetramerous flower of *Cobæa scandens*. Perhaps monocotyledonous plants are more subject to this numerical reduction of the parts of several verticils than are other flowering plants. Thus, in both *Lilium lancifolium* and *L. auratum* the writer has frequently met with pentamerous flowers. In *Convallaria maialis* a like deviation not unfrequently occurs.[474] M. Delavaud has recorded a similar occurrence in a tulip.[475]

Dimerous crocuses may also sometimes be met with. In one flower of this nature the segments of the perianth were arranged in decussating pairs, and the [Pg 401] four stamens were united by their filaments so as to form two pairs.

189

M. Fournier mentions something of the same kind in the flower of an *Iris*.[476]

Orchids seem peculiarly liable to the decrease in the number of their floral organs. Prillieux[477] mentions a flower of *Cattleya amethystina* wherein each whorl of the perianth consisted of two opposite segments.

The same observer has put on record instances of a similar kind in*Epidendrum Stamfordianum*. In one flower of the last-named species the perianth consisted of one sepal only, and one lip-like petal placed opposite to it.[478] Morren[479] describes a flower of *Cypripedium insigne*, in which there were two sepals and two petals. Of a similar character was the flower found by Mr. J. A. Paine, and described in the following terms by Professor Asa Gray in the 'American Journal of Science,' July, 1866:—"The plant" (*Cypripedium candidum*) "bears two flowers: the axillary one is normal; the terminal one exhibits the following peculiarities. The lower part of the bract forms a sheath which encloses the ovary. The labellum is wanting; and there are two sterile stamens, the supernumerary one being opposite the other, *i.e.* on the side of the style where the labellum belongs. Accordingly the first impression would be that the labellum is here transformed into a sterile stamen. The latter, however, agrees with the normal sterile stamen in its insertion as well as in shape, being equally adnate to the base of the style. Moreover, the anteposed sepal is exactly like the other, has a good midrib and an entire point. As the two sterile stamens are anteposed to the two sepals, so are the two fertile stamens to the two petals, and the latter are adnate to the style a little higher than the former. The style is longer than usual, is straight and erect; the broad, disciform stigma therefore[Pg 402] faces upwards; it is oval and symmetrical, and a light groove across its middle shows it to be dimerous. The placentæ, accordingly, are only two. The groove on the stigma and the placentæ are in line with the fertile stamens.

Here, therefore, is a symmetrical and complete, regular, but dimerous orchideous flower, the first verticil of stamens not antheriferous, the second antheriferous, the carpels alternate with these; and here we have clear (and perhaps the first direct) demonstration that the orchideous type of flower has two stamineal verticils, as Brown always insisted."

FIG. 198.—**Regular dimerous flower of** *Calanthe vestita*.

FIG. 199.—**Regular dimerous flower of** *Odontoglossum Alexandræ*.

Dr. Moore, of Glasnevin, kindly forwarded to the writer a flower of*Calanthe vestita* (fig. 198), in which there were two sepals only, anterior and posterior, and two petals at right angles to the two sepals. The lip was entirely wanting, but the column and ovary were[Pg 403] in their usual condition. In *Odontoglossum Alexandræ* a similar reduction of parts has been observed by the author (fig. 199).

It is curious to observe in these flowers how precisely one sepal occupies the position of the labellum, and how the lateral petals are displaced from the position they usually occupy, so as to form a regular flower, the segments of which decussate, thus giving rise to a species of regular peloria.

The genus *Mælenia* was established on a malformed flower of *Orchis* of similar character to those above mentioned.

Meiotaxy of the calyx.—As already mentioned, this term is here employed to denote those illustrations in which entire whorls are suppressed. Complete deficiency of the calyx in a dichlamydeous flower seems seldom or ever to occur; the nearest approach to it would be in those cases where the calyx is, as it is termed, "obsolete," but here it is chiefly the limb of the calyx which is atrophied, the lower portion being more or less adherent to the ovary. In what are termed monochlamydeous flowers both calyx and corolla are wanting, as in *Salicineæ* and many other orders.

Meiotaxy of the corolla.—Deficiency of the entire corolla occurs in conjunction with similar reductions in other organs, or as an isolated phenomenon in the many apetalous varieties of plants recorded in books. Deficiency of the corolla was observed in *Campanula perfoliata* and*Ruellia clandestina* by Linné, who calls such blooms *flores mutilati*.[480]Drs. Hooker and Thomson relate a similar occurrence in *Campanula canescens* and *C. colorata*. Some plants seem as a normal occurrence to produce flowers of different construction, and are hence termed dimorphic, as in many *Malpighiaceæ*, *Violaceæ*, *Oxalidaceæ*, in some of the flowers of which the petals are altogether wanting, while in others the[Pg 404] corolla is developed as usual. This deficiency of the corolla is frequently, but not invariably, associated with an increased fertility. Thus, in some violets the flowers produced in summer, and in which the petals are either entirely suppressed or are more or less atrophied, are always fertile, while the blossoms developed in spring, and in which the petals are always present, are much less fertile. In *Oxalis Acetosella* there are two forms of flower, the one with, the other without, petals, but both seem equally fertile. Linné remarks that many plants which, in warm latitudes, produce a corolla, do not do so when grown in colder climates. Thus, certain species of*Helianthemum* are apetalous in Lapland. In the Pyrenees, according to Bentham, the flowers of *Ajuga iva* are constantly deprived of their corolla.[481]

Apetalous flowers have been noted most frequently in the following plants:

- Aconitum, sp. pl.!
- Cardamine impatiens.
- Cheiranthus Cheiri!
- Viola odorata!
- Cerastium vulgatum!
- Alsine media.
- Stellaria.
- Lychnis dioica!
- Dianthus barbatus, and other Caryophylleæ.
- Helianthemum, sp.!
- Oxalis Acetosella.
- Balsamineæ.
- Malpighiaceæ.
- Rosa centifolia.
o   arvensis!
- Cratægus!
- Medicago lupulina.
- Melilotus officinalis.
- Ononis minutissima.
- Saxifraga longifolia.
- Verbascum Thapsus.
- Ajuga iva.
- Teucrium Botrys.
- Lamium purpureum!
o   amplexicaule.
- Polemonium cæruleum.
- Campanula, sp. pl.!
- Ruellia clandestina.
- Lonicera Periclymenum!
- Tradescantia, sp.!
- Hymenocallis.

The following references apply some to apetalous and others to dimorphic flowers, but it must be remembered that the latter plants are not necessarily wanting in petals or stamens, &c., though the functional activity of the parts may be impaired:

191

A. de Jussien, 'Monogr. Malpigh.,' pp. 82, 334. Torrey, 'Fl. New York,' i, p. 428. Hooker and Thomson, 'Journ. Linn. Soc.,' ii, p. 7, Guillemin, 'Archiv. de Botan.,' i, p. 412. Michalet, 'Bull. Soc. Bot. Fr.,' vii. p. 465. Müller, 'Bot. Zeit.,' 1857, p. 729. 'Natural History Review,' July, 1862, p. 235.

[Pg 405]

Meiotaxy of the andrœcium.—Complete suppression of the stamens occurs normally in the female flowers of unisexual plants, and, as an accidental occurrence, is not very uncommon. *Erica Tetralix* is one of the plants in which this is said to happen. The variety *anandra* is said to have been known in France since 1635. Cornuti speaks of it in his 'Enchiridion.' In 1860 M. du Parquet discovered it in peaty woods near Nangis (Seine et Marne).

Many *Umbelliferæ*, such as *Trinia vulgaris*, present a like deficiency, while it is of common occurrence among *Rosaceæ* and *Pomaceæ*. In the latter group the St. Valery apple, so often referred to, is an illustration. To obtain fruits from this variety it is necessary to apply pollen from another flower, a proceeding made the occasion of festivity and rejoicing by the villagers in some parts of France. In some of the *Artemisias*, especially in *Artemisia Tournefortiana*, all the florets have been noticed to be female, owing to the suppression of the stamens, and this suppression is associated with a change in the form of florets.[482] Mr. Moggridge has communicated to the author flowers of *Thymus Serpyllum* from a plant in which all the stamens were deficient, the flower being otherwise normal.

M. Dupont has given a list of nineteen species of *Chenopodiaceæ* in which female flowers are occasionally produced, owing to the entire suppression of the staminal whorl.[483]

Flowers the subjects either of regular or irregular peloria, *q. v.*, are often destitute of some or all their stamens, *e.g. Calceolaria, Linaria, Viola,* &c., while in cases of synanthy suppression of some of the parts of the flower, and specially of the stamens, is of very common occurrence.

Suppression of the andrœcium as a teratological occurrence has been most frequently noticed in the[Pg 406] following plants, omitting members of those families whose floral construction is normally incomplete in the majority of instances, and exclusive also of cases of substitution. See also under Heterogamy.

- Ranunculus Ficaria!
- o   auricomus!
- o   bulbosus!
- Cruciferæ, sp. pl.
- Violaceæ, sp. pl.
- Honckenya peploides.
- Stellaria.
- Caryophyllaceæ, sp. pl.
- Malpighiaceæ, sp. pl.
- Tropæolum majus!
- Fragaria vesca!
- Rubus, sp.
- Pyrus Malus.
- Agrimonia vulgaris.
- Rosaceæ, sp. pl.
- Trifolium hybridum.
- o   repens.
- Umbelliferæ, sp. pl.

192

- Onagraceæ, sp. pl.
- Hippuris vulgaris.
- Callitriche vernalis.
o   autumnalis.
- Lonicera Periclymenum.
- Erica Tetralix.
- Thymus Serpyllum.
- Calceolaria.
- Compositæ, sp. pl.
- Chenopodiaceæ, sp. pl.
- Stratiotes aloides.

Meiotaxy of the gynœcium.—Complete suppression of the pistil is of more frequent occurrence than that of the stamens, hence more flowers become accidentally unisexual by suppression of the pistil than by deficiency of the stamens.

In many *Umbelliferæ*, e.g. *Torilis Anthriscus, Cicuta virosa*, the central flowers are often male, owing to the suppression of the pistil. In many double flowers, owing to the excessive multiplication of petaloid stamens, the pistil is suppressed, in which cases it often happens that the flower is depressed in the centre, as in some garden varieties of *Ranunculus*. Schlechtendal, in describing a flower of *Colchicum autumnale*, in which the perianth was virescent, says that, although the stamens were present, the pistil was absent.

In proliferous flowers the pistil is often completely defective, its place being occupied by the adventitious bud or axis.

As in other cases of like nature, suppression of the pistil is very frequently consequent on fusion of flowers or other changes. Thus Morren relates an instance of synanthy in the flowers of *Torenia scabra*, accompanied by resorption or disappearance of some parts[Pg 407] and spiral torsion of others. The pistil was entirely absent in this instance.[484]

M. Gaetano Licopoli places on record an instance where the petals and carpels of *Melianthus major* were suppressed.[485]

On the whole, the pistil seems less subject to changes of this character than the andrœcium.

Suppression of the pistil has been most frequently recorded in flowers (normally bisexual) of—

- Ranunculus!
- Aconitium!
- Delphinium!
- Pæonia.
- Caryophylleæ!
- Umbelliferæ.
- Trifolium repens.
o   hybridum.
- Compositæ, sp. pl.
- Datura.
- Torenia asiatica.
- Colchicum autumnale.

Suppression of ovules,—abortion of seeds.—The two cases are taken together, as the effects are similar, though it must be remembered that in the one case the ovules at any rate have been formed, but their development has been arrested, while in the other they have never existed. The precise cause that has determined the absence of seed cannot in all cases

193

be ascertained in the adult condition, hence it is convenient to treat the two phenomena under one head.

Many plants in other than their native climates either produce no fruit at all, or the fruits that are produced are destitute of seed, *e.g. Musa, Artocarpus,* &c. Some of the cultivated varieties of the grape and of the berberry produce no seeds.

Suppression or abortion of the seed is frequently associated with the excessive development either in size or number of other portions of the plant, or with an altered condition, as when carpels become foliaceous and their margins detached. Hybridisation and cross fertilisation are also well-known agents in diminishing the number and size of seeds.

[Pg 408]

Meiotaxy of the parts of the flower in general.—In the preceding sections suppression has been considered as it affected individual members of a whorl or separate whorls. It rarely happens, however, that the suppression is limited in this way. More generally several of the parts of the flower are simultaneously affected in the same manner. A few illustrations are all that is necessary to give as to this point.

One of the most familiar instances is that of the cauliflower or broccoli, where the common flower-stalk is inordinately thickened and fleshy, while the corolla and inner parts of the flower are usually entirely suppressed; the four sepals can, however, generally be detected.

Maximowicz describes a *Stellaria* (*Kraschenikovia*) in which the upper flowers are male only, while the lower ones, which ultimately become buried in the soil, have neither petals, stamens, nor styles, but the walls of the capsule are fleshy, and enclose numerous seeds.[486]

Kirschleger[487] mentions a variety of *Lonicera Caprifolium,* which was not only destitute of petals but of stamens also.

In some species of *Muscari* and *Bellevalia* the uppermost flowers of the raceme show more or less complete suppression of almost all the part of which the flower normally consists. In those cases where an imperfect perianth exists, but in which the stamens and pistils are entirely suppressed, Morren applies the term Cenanthy, κενος, empty.

Complete suppression of the flower.—It is not necessary in this place to allude to that deficient production of flowers characteristic of what is termed by gardeners a "sky bloomer." In such plants often the requisite conditions are not complied with, and the skill of the[Pg 409] gardener is shown in his attempt to discover and allow the plant to avail itself of the necessary requirements. We need here only allude to those instances in which provision is made for the production of flowers, and yet they are not produced. A good illustration of this is afforded by the feather-hyacinth, *Hyacinthus comosus,* in which the flowers are almost entirely suppressed, while the pedicels are inordinately increased in number, and their colour heightened. Something similar occurs in several allied species, and in *Bowiea volubilis.* The wig plant (*Rhus Cotinus*) affords another illustration of the same thing. Some tendrils also owe their appearance to the absence of flowers, being modified peduncles; proofs of this may frequently be met with in the case of the vine.

In *Lamium album* I have seen one of the verticillasters on one side of the stem completely wanting, the adjacent leaf being, however, as fully formed as usual.

General remarks on suppression.—On comparing together the various whorls of the flower in reference to suppression, and, it may be added, to atrophy, we find that these phenomena occur most rarely in the calyx, more frequently in the corolla, and very often in the sexual organs and seeds; hence it would seem as if the uppermost and most central organs, those most subject to pressure and latest in date of development—formed, that is, when the formative energies of the plant are most liable to be exhausted—are the most prone to be suppressed or arrested in their development. When the plants in which these occurrences happen most frequently are compared together, it may be seen that partial or entire suppression of the floral envelopes, calyx, and corolla, is far more commonly met with in the polypetalous and hypogynous groups than in the gamopetalous or epigynous series.

The orders in which suppression (speaking generally) occurs most often as a teratological occurrence are the[Pg 410] following:—

Ranunculaceæ, Cruciferæ, Caryophyllaceæ, Violaceæ, Leguminosæ, Onagraceæ, Jasminaceæ, Orchidaceæ. It will be observed that these are all orders wherein suppression of the whole or part of the outer floral whorls takes place in certain genera as a constant occurrence.

Again, it may be remarked that many of these orders show a tendency towards a regular diminution of the assumed normal number of their parts; thus, among *Onagraceæ*, *Circæia* and *Lopezia* may be referred to, the former normally dimerous, the latter having only one perfect petal. So in fuchsias, a very common deviation consists in a trimerous and rarely a dimerous symmetry of the flower.

Although, if the absolute number of genera or orders be counted, there appears to be little difference in the frequency of the occurrence of suppression in irregular flowers as contrasted with regular flowers, yet if the individual instances could be counted in the two groups respectively it would be found that suppression is more common among irregular than in regular flowers. Thus, the number of individual instances of flowers in which the perianth is defective is comparatively large among *Violaceæ*, *Leguminosæ*, and *Orchidaceæ*. This statement hardly admits of precise statistical proof; still, it is believed that any observer who pays attention to the subject must come to the same conclusion. This is but another illustration of the fact that conditions which are abnormal in one plant constitute the natural arrangement in others.

As to the suppressions that occur in the case of the sexual organs, and the relations they bear to dimorphism, diclinism, &c., but little stress has been laid on them in this place, because their chief interest is in a physiological point of view, and is treated of in the writings of Mohl, Sprengel, Darwin, Hildebrand, and others. All that need be said here is, that teratology affords very numerous illustrations of those intermediate conditions which are also found, under[Pg 411] natural circumstances, between the absolutely unisexual flowers, male or female, and the structurally hermaphrodite ones. Rudimentary stamens or pistils are of very common occurrence in monstrous flowers. See Chapter on Heterogamy, &c.

FOOTNOTES:

[465]'Rev. Hortic.,' 1866, p. 467.

[466]De Rochebrune, 'Bull. Soc. Bot. Fr.,' ix, p. 281. The author points out seven grades between complete absence of petals and their presence in the normal number in this plant. See also Gaudin, in 'Koch. Fl. Helv.;' Koch. 'Synops. Fl. Germ.;' Cramer, 'Bildungsabweich,' p. 85.

[467]'Bull. Acad. Belg.,' t. xix, part 1, p. 255.

[468]'Bull. Bot.,' i, p. 7, tab. i, f. 7.

[469]See Gay, 'Ann. Sc. Nat.,' iii, p. 27.

[470]'Ann. Sc. Nat.,' 4 ser., v, p. 305.

[471]Cramer, 'Bildungsabweich,' p. 90.

[472]See also Clos, 'Bull. Soc. Bot. Fr.,' xiii, p. 96, adnot.

[473]See Cramer, 'Bildungsabweich,' p. 7. Hildebrand, 'Bot. Zeit.,' xx, 1862, p. 209.

[474]See Hildebrand, 'Bot. Zeit.,' xx, 1862, p. 209.

[475]'Bull. Soc. Bot. Fr.,' viii, p. 287.

[476]'Bull. Soc. Bot. Fr.,' vol. viii, 1861, p. 152.

[477]Ibid., ix, p. 275.

[478]Ibid., 1861, vol. viii, p. 149.

[479]'Lobelia,' p. 55.

[480]'Phil. Bot.,' p. 119.

[481]'Cat. Plant. Pyr,' p. 58.

[482]Moquin-Tandon, loc. cit., p. 328.

[483]For other instances see Chatin in 'Ann. Sc. Nat.,' 4 ser., vol. v, p. 305.

[484]See also Morren. 'Bull. Acad. Belg.,' xv, Fuchsia, p. 67.

[485]Cited in 'Bull. Soc. Bot., France,' t. xiv ("Rev. Bibl."), p. 253.

[486]'Primit. Flor. Amurens.' p. 57.

[487]'Flora.' 1848. p. 484.

[Pg 412]

[Pg 413]

BOOK IV.
DEVIATIONS FROM THE ORDINARY SIZE AND CONSISTENCE OF ORGANS.

In the animal kingdom the entire adult organism, as well as each of its separate parts, has certain dimensions, beyond which, under ordinary circumstances, it does not pass, either in the one direction or the other. It may not be easy or possible to state what the limits are, but, practically, this inability to frame a precise limitation is productive of no inconvenience. It is universally admitted that a certain animal attains such and such dimensions, and that one organ has a certain proportionate size as contrasted with another. The same rules hold good in the case of plants, though in them it is vastly more difficult to ascertain what may be called the normal dimensions or proportions. Nevertheless observation and experience soon show what may be termed the average size of each plant, and any disproportion between the several organs is speedily detected.

When there is a general reduction in size throughout all the organs of a plant, or throughout all the nutritive organs, stem, leaves, &c., and the several portions participate in this diminished size, we have what are generally termed "dwarf varieties," dwarf in comparison, that is, with the ordinary condition of the plants; on the other hand, if the entire plant, or, at least, if the[Pg 414] whole of one set of organs be increased in size beyond the recognised average, we have large varieties, often qualified by such terms as *macrophylla, longifolia, macrantha*, &c. &c. In all these cases either the entire plant or whole series of organs are alike increased or diminished beyond average limits; and such variations are often very constant, and are transmitted by hereditary transmission. It may be supposed that such deviations may have originated, in the first instance, either from excessive use, or from disuse, or from the agency of certain conditions promoting or checking growth, as the case may be; but whether or no, it is certain that these variations often persist under different conditions, and that they often retain their distinctive characters side by side with plants presenting the normal average dimensions. In other cases the variations in size are of a less general character, and affect certain organs of a whorl in a relative manner, as, for instance, in the case of didynamous or tetradynamous stamens, where two or four stamens are longer than their fellows, the long or short stamens and styles of di- and tri-morphic flowers, &c. These differences are sometimes connected with the development of parts in succession, and not simultaneously.

Teratological deviations of size differ from those of which mention has just been made chiefly in this, that they are more limited in their manifestations. It is not, as a rule, the whole plant, or the whole series of nutritive or of reproductive organs, that are affected, but it is certain parts only; the alteration in size is more a relative change than an absolute one.

For convenience sake the teratological alterations of size may be divided into those which are the result of[Pg 415] increased growth and those which arise from diminished action. It will be seen, therefore, that in these instances it is the bulk of the organs that is increased, not their number; moreover, their development or metamorphosis is not necessarily altered. In connection with increased size an alteration of consistence is so frequent that the two phenomena are here taken together. It will be borne in mind that the changes of consistence from membranous to succulent or woody are very frequent in the ordinary course of development. They may also occur as accidental phenomena, or the normal conditions of any particular flower or fruit may be exactly reversed, the usually succulent fruit becoming dry and capsular, and so forth.

[Pg 416]
PART I.
HYPERTROPHY.

The term hypertrophy may serve as a general one to comprise all the instances of excessive growth and increased size of organs, whether the increase be general or in one direction merely. General hypertrophy is more a variation than a deformity, unless indeed it be caused by insect puncture or the presence of a fungus, in which case the excessive size results from a diseased condition. For our present purpose hypertrophy may be considered as it affects the axile or the foliar organs, and also according to the way in which the increased size is manifested, as by increased thickness or swelling—intumescence, or by augmented length-elongation, by expansion or flattening, or, lastly, by the formation of excrescences or outgrowths, which may be classed under the head of luxuriance or enation.

As size must be considered in this place relatively, it is not possible to lay down any precise line separating what are considered to be the normal dimensions from those which are abnormal.

In practice no inconvenience will be found to accrue from this inability to establish a fixed rule, and we may say that an hypertrophied organ is one which, from some cause or other, attains dimensions which are not habitual to the plant in its usual, healthy, well-formed state.

It will be seen that under this general head of hypertrophy, increase of size, however brought about, is included; thus, not only increase in length, but also in thickness; alterations of substance or consistence, no less than of dimensions, are here grouped together.[Pg 417] The alterations of consistence resulting from an inordinate development of cellular, fibrous, or ligneous tissue, are, of course, strictly homologous with the similar changes which occur, under ordinary circumstances, during the ripening of fruits or otherwise.

Hypertrophy, whatever form it may assume, may be so slight as not perceptibly to interfere with the functions of the part affected, or it may exist to such an extent as to impair the due exercise of its office. It may affect any or all parts of the plant, and is generally coexistent with, if not actually dependent on, some other malformation. Thus, the inordinate growth of some parts is most generally attended by deficiency in the size and number of others, as in the peripheral florets of *Viburnum* or*Hydrangea*, where the corollas are relatively very large, and the stamens and pistils abortive.

CHAPTER I.

ENLARGEMENT.

A swollen or thickened condition (*renflement*) is usually the result of a disproportionate formation of the cellular tissue as contrasted with the woody framework of the plant. We see marked instances of it in cultivated carrots and turnips, the normal condition of the roots or root-stocks in these plants being one of considerable hardness and toughness, and their form slender, tapering, and more or less branched.

The disproportionate development of cellular tissue is also seen in tubers and bulbs, and in the swollen stems of such plants as *Echinocactus,Adenium obesum*, some species of *Vitis*, &c. So, too, the upper portion of the flower-stalk occasionally becomes much dilated,[Pg 418] so as ultimately to form a portion of the fruit. But it is not necessary to give farther illustrations of this common tendency in some organs to become hypertrophied. As a result of injury from insects or fungi, galls and excrescences of various kinds are very common, but their consideration lies beyond the scope of the present work.

FIG. 200.—*Pelargonium*, one branch of which was hypertrophied.

Enlargement of axile organs.—All the species of *Pelargonium,Geranium, Mirabilis,* as well as those of *Caryophylleæ* and other orders, have tumid nodes as a normal occurrence. In the genus *Pelargonium* this swelling is sometimes not confined to the nodes, but[Pg 419] extends to the interspaces between them, *e.g. P. spinosum*. This condition, which happens as a natural feature in the species just named, may also occur as an exceptional thing in others. The author is indebted to Dr. Sankey for a branch of *Pelargonium* which was thus thickened, the remaining branches not being in any way affected. The leaves on the swollen branch were smaller than the others, and their stalks more flattened. There was, in this instance, no trace of fungus or insect to account for the swelling of a single branch, which might, therefore, be due to bud-variation, perhaps to reversion to some ancestral form. The repeated cross fertilisations to which Pelargoniums have been subjected render this hypothesis not an improbable one.

As an accompaniment to a spiral torsion of the woody fibres, this distension of the stem is frequently met with, as in *Valeriana, Dipsacus,*&c. (See Spiral Torsion.)

Knaurs.—On certain trees, such as the oak, the hornbeam, some species of *Cratægus*, &c., hard woody lumps may occasionally be seen projecting, varying greatly in size, from that of a pea to that of a cocoa-nut. They are covered with bark, and consist in the interior of very hard layers of wood disposed irregularly, so as to form objects of beauty for cabinetmakers' purposes. From the frequent presence of small atrophied leaf-buds on their surface, it would seem as if the structures in question were shortened branches, in which the woody layers had become inordinately developed, as if by compensation for the curtailment in length.[488] The cause of their formation is not known, but it has been ascertained that they are not due to insect agency. Knaurs may occasionally be used for purposes of propagation, as in the case of[Pg 420] the "uovoli of the olive" and the "burrs" that are formed on some varieties of apple, from which both roots and leaf-shoots are produced in abundance.

A distinction must be drawn between those instances in which the swelling is solid throughout from the excessive formation of cellular tissue, and those wherein it is hollow from the more rapid growth of the outer as contrasted with the inner portions. These latter cases might be classed under the head of distension.

FIG. 201.—Formation of tubers or hypertrophied buds in the axils of leaves in the potato.

Enlargement of the buds may be seen in the case of bulbs and tubers. Occasionally these organs are developed in the axils of leaves, when their nature[Pg 421] becomes apparent. A swollen bud or bulbil in this situation is not uncommon in some cultivated tulips and lilies. The presence of small tubers in the axils of the leaves in the potato, as shown in fig. 201, is also not unfrequent.

FIG. 202.—Inflorescence of ash (*Fraxinus*), with hypertrophied pedicels, flowers absent.

Enlargement of the flower-stalk.—The cauliflower and broccoli afford familiar illustrations of hypertrophy of the flower-stalk, accompanied by a corresponding[Pg 422] defective development of the flowers. In the case of the ash the terminal pedicels occasionally become swollen and distorted, while the flowers are completely deficient, as shown in the adjacent cut (fig. 202).

In grapes a similar condition may occasionally be met with in which the terminal pedicels become greatly swollen and fused into a solid mass. It would seem probable that this change is due to insect puncture, or to the effect of fungus growth at an early stage of development, but as to this point there is at present no evidence.[489]

FIG. 203.—Monstrous pear, showing extension and ramification of the succulent floral axis. The bases of the sepals are also succulent.

In the apple a dilatation of the flower-stalk below the ordinary fruit may occasionally be observed, thus giving rise to the appearance of two fruits superposed and separated one from the other by a constriction.[Pg 423] (See fig. 176, p. 327.) The lower swelling is entirely axial in these cases, as no trace of carpels is to be seen. M. Carrière[490] mentions an instance wherein from the base of one apple projected a second smaller one, destitute of carpels, but surmounted by calyx-lobes as usual. The direction of this supernumerary apple was the exact opposite of that of the primary fruit.

FIG. 204.—Monstrous pear, showing extension and swelling of axis, &c.

In pears, quinces, and apples, a not uncommon deviation is one in which the axis is prolonged beyond the ordinary fruit, like which it is much swollen. Occasionally the axis is not only prolonged, but even ramifies, the branches partaking of the succulent character of the ordinary pome. Such instances are frequently classed under the head of prolification, but they have in general no claim to be considered in this light, for the reasons already given in the chapter relating to that subject. (See p. 135.)[491]

[Pg 424]

A very curious illustration of hypertrophy of the flower-stalk is recorded and figured by M. Carrière[492] in the cherry. The calyx in these fruits was completely superior, the succulent portion of the fruit being made up of the dilated extremity of the peduncle, and possibly in part of the base of the calyx. The general appearance was thus that of a crab-apple. There was no stone in the interior, but simply a rudimentary kernel or seed.[493]

Moquin-Tandon records an instance in which the stamens of each individual flower in the inflorescence of a vine were hypertrophied, the sepals, petals, and other organs of the flower, being proportionately diminished.[494]

In this place may also be mentioned the hypertrophied condition of the placenta observed by Alphonse de Candolle in a species of *Solanum*, and also in a species of *Melastoma*. Not only was the placenta unusually large in these flowers, but it also protruded beyond the ovary.[495] A similar state of things in *Lobelia* and *Cuphea* has already been alluded to under the head of Alterations of Direction (p. 210).

The following singular growth in a tomato is described[Pg 425] by the Rev. M. J. Berkeley in the 'Gardeners' Chronicle' for 1866, p. 1217, and appears to have been an extension of the placenta:—"On the first glance it seemed as if an unusually large grape-stone had accidentally fallen on the upper surface of the fruit, and was attached by the narrow base. The process was, however, five lines long, and much narrowed below, besides which, though it was pale green above, the base was coral-red, like the tomato itself. It grew on a narrow and shallow crack on the surface of the fruit, and was found below to communicate directly with a fibro-vascular bundle, which entered into the composition of a portion of the placenta. On making a vertical section, instead of being succulent, as I expected, it was white and spongy within, with several lacunae, and one or two irregular fibro-vascular bundles, with highly developed spiral vessels threading the centre. These vessels, moreover, were tinged with brown, as in many cases of diseased tissues. There was not the slightest appearance of placentæ or anything indicating an abortive fruit. On closer examination the cuticle was found to consist of thick-walled cells, exactly like those of the tomato, while the spongy mass consisted of a similar tissue to the fleshy portion of the fruit, but with far less wrinkled walls, and more indistinct intercellular spaces. The most striking point, however, was the immense quantity of very irregular and unequal starch-grains with which they were gorged, which gave a peculiar sparkling appearance to them when seen *en masse*. I am inclined to regard the body rather as an abortive axis than an undeveloped fruit. In almost all, if not all, these cases of abnormal growth, whether from leaves, petioles, fruit, or other portions of the plant, we find an immediate connection with one or more spiral vessels, which if not existent at first are developed sooner or later. In the present case the connection of the fibro-vascular tissue of the fruit and abnormal growth was plain enough, but whether it existed when the body was[Pg 426] first given off I am unable to say, as it was fully developed when the fruit was brought to me."

Enlargement of the leaves.—Increase in the size or substance of leaves takes place in several ways, and affects the whole or only certain portions of them. The simplest form of this malformation is met with in our cabbages, which, by the art of the gardener, have been made to produce leaves of greater size and thickness than those which are developed in the wild form. In such instances the whole substance of the leaf is increased in bulk, and the increase affects the fibrous framework of the leaves as well as the cellular portions, though the exaggerated development of the latter is out of proportion to that of the former.

In some species of *Podocarpus* there may occasionally be seen at the base of the branchlets a dozen or more fleshy scales, of a rose colour, passing gradually into the ordinary leaves of the plant, and evidently analogous to the three fleshy confluent bracts which surround the ripe fruit.

In other instances, while the fibrous framework of the leaf retains its usual degree of development, the cellular parenchyma is developed in excess, and, if the increase is so arranged that the number of superposed layers of the cellular tissue is not increased, or their thickness exaggerated, then we get such leaves as those of the "kail," or of the "Savoys" leaves, which are technically called by descriptive botanists "folia bullata." In such leaves the disc of the leaf, rather than the margin, is increased and its surface is thrown up into little conical projections, which are hollow on the under side.

But leaves may increase beyond their usual size without such grave alterations of form as those to which allusion has just been made. It is well known that if a tree be cut down and new shoots be sent out from the stump, the leaves formed on these shoots very often greatly exceed the ordinary ones in dimensions.[Pg 427] Such cases as this hardly come under the head of malformations. But where one part only of the leaf is excessively developed, the other portion remaining in its ordinary condition, there can be no hesitation in ranking the phenomenon as teratological.

Thus, Moquin says that the median nerve may be prolonged beyond the blade of the leaf in the form of a short strap or ribbon-like excrescence, while, at other times, the lateral parts of the leaf are subjected to undue development. He refers to a case cited by Schlotterbec[496] in which each side of the leaves of a yellow "violier" (wallflower) was dilated into a kind of projecting lobe on either side of the true apex of the leaf, thus rendering it in appearance three-lobed. M. Delavaud[497] puts on record a case of hypertrophy in the leaves of the common elm, resulting in the formation of an additional lobe and a return to the tricostate type. A leaf so affected is stated to have presented the appearance of a fusion of two leaves. (See also Multiplication of leaves, p. 353.)

The hypertrophied and coloured leaf of *Gesnera* occupying the place of the absent inflorescence has been previously alluded to under the head of displacement (p. 88).

In some instances hypertrophy is the opposite of suppression; as in the case previously mentioned, where the stipule in the inflorescence of a pea, which is usually undeveloped and rudimentary, was developed in the form of a leafy cup or pitcher.

Another instance of the development of parts usually suppressed, is afforded by the bud-scales of *Magnolia fuscata*, which may sometimes be found with small but perfect leaves projecting from them, the leaf in this case being the lamina which is ordinarily abortive, while the scales are the representatives of the stipules. This condition is said by Hooker and Thomson ('Flora Indica,' p. 73) to be constant in *Magnolia Campbelli*.

[Pg 428]

Enlargement of the perianth, &c.—One or all the segments of the perianth may be subjected to hypertrophy; thus, the utricle of *Carex vulpina* may frequently be observed to attain four or five times its usual size, the contained ovary remaining unaffected. This condition is generally the result of insect puncture. The growth of parasitic fungi will produce a similar result, as is often seen in the common shepherd's purse, *Thlaspi bursa pastoris*, and other *Cruciferæ*. The perianth of *Rumex aquaticus* has been also observed to be occasionally hypertrophied in conjunction with a similar condition of the pistil and with atrophy of the ovules.

Moquin relates having found flowers of *Salsola Kali* and of *Chenopodium murale* in which some of the segments of the perianth were five or six times larger than they should be.

FIG. 205.—Hypertrophy of the perianth in *Cocos nucifera*.

The adjoining woodcut represents a singular condition of some cocoa-nuts in the Kew Museum, the[Pg 429] appearance of which is due apparently to an hypertrophied condition of the segments of the perianth, which have not only increased in length as the central nut has ripened, but have developed in their tissues that fibrous tissue which ordinarily is found in the pericarp only. This view of the structure of these nuts is borne out by the fact that, under normal circumstances, the base of the perianth contains a considerable amount of fibrous material. In the present case this has increased to such an extent that the fruit appears surrounded by a double husk, by an inner one as usual, and by an outer six-parted one.

It will be remembered that in some of the *Cinchonaceæ*, e.g. *Mussænda*,*Pinckneya*, *Calycophyllum*, one or more of the calycine lobes are normally dilated and petaloid, the others remaining small and comparatively inconspicuous. Inequality in size is, indeed, a common occurrence in the sepals of many natural orders— *Polygaleæ*, *Leguminosæ*, *Labiatæ*, &c. The flowers of a rose are mentioned by Moquin as having presented an enlargement of the calyx without any other alterations in form. Schlechtendal has noticed the same thing in *Papaver Rhœas*, Reichenbach in *Campanula persicifolia*, and A. de Candolle in *C. Rapunculus*. M. Brongniart also has recorded[498] a remarkable variety of *Primula sinensis*cultivated in the Jardin des Plantes at Paris, wherein the calyx is enormously developed. MM. Fournier and Bonnet have described flowers of *Rubus* with hypertrophied calyx in conjunction with atrophy and virescence of the petals and other changes.[499]

200

The corolla may be hypertrophied in some cases, though the change is more rare than in most other organs. Moquin-Tandon mentions as subject to this anomaly species of *Galeopsis, Prunella, Scabiosa*, and *Dipsacus*, and also mentions a remarkable variety of *Viola odorata* cultivated in the neighbourhood of[Pg 430] Toulouse. The same learned author also alludes to the so-called double Composites, viz. those in which the usually tubular florets of the disc assume the form and proportions of those of the ray, but these are hardly cases of hypertrophy.

Enlargement of the andrœcium.—Dunal[500] alludes to a curious instance in a species of *Verbascum*, the lower flowers of which had hairy stamens as usual, but the filaments of the topmost flower were quite destitute of hairs, and dilated like a flat ribbon.

Moquin relates having found in the neighbourhood of Toulouse a plant of *Solanum Dulcamara* in which all the upper flowers had two or three stamens of larger dimensions than the others. This happens habitually in *Solanum tridynamum* and *S. Amazonicum*, and to a less extent in *S. vespertilio* and *S. cornutum*; also in some species of *Hyoscyamus*. These cases show the close affinity between the *Solanaceæ* and the *Scrophulariaceæ*.

Enlargement of the gynœcium.—In some flowers which have become accidentally female the pistil becomes unusually large, and even to such an extent as to prevent the passage of the pollen. Moquin remarks having seen this enlargement in the pistils of *Suæda fruticosa* and *Kochia scoparia*. The flowers of these Chenopods, under these circumstances, resemble the female flowers of some nettles. The styles of *Anemone* are also much enlarged as the result of cultivation, and from their petaloid appearance resemble those of the *Iris* (Goethe). MM. Seringe and Heyland[501] have figured some anomalous flowers of *Diplotaxis tenuifolia* in which the pistil, more or less distended and deformed, was considerably elongated below, so that it seemed to be borne upon a long stalk, analogous to that of fruits of Capparids. Dr. Klinsman[502] mentions an instance of a similar kind combined[Pg 431] with hypertrophy of the sepals and pistils; indeed, the alteration is not uncommon among Crucifers. *Pyrethrum inodorum* is very subject to hypertrophy. The styles of its radial florets become elongated without any other alteration; at the same time the small corollas become green, and show a tendency to assume a foliaceous condition. Sometimes the hypertrophy affects also the styles of the central florets, and these also become enlarged to double or treble their usual dimensions.

Linné has remarked that the ovary of *Tragopogon* sometimes assumes very large dimensions, as also does the pappus. He mentions a double-flowered variety, the ovaries of which become ten or twelve times larger than ordinary. M. Clos[503] records an instance in *Rumex scutatus* wherein the pistil was hypertrophied or club-shaped, and open at the top, or in other cases funnel-shaped, three-lobed at the summit, each lobe terminated by a style. One of the most frequent causes tending to the hypertrophy of the pistil is attributable to the puncture of insects; thus, when the ovary of *Juncus articulatus* is thus punctured, it acquires a size two or three times larger than ordinary, becoming at the same time sterile.[504]

Occasionally the enlargement may be due to a fusion or incorporation of other elements; thus, M. Lemaire describes an instance in which the style of *Sinningia purpurea* was much larger than ordinary, tubular, bearing three small lobes, and altogether bearing much resemblance to the column or "gynoseme" of Orchids. This appearance was due to the cohesion and intimate union of the styles with three abortive stamens.[505]

Enlargement of the fruit.—Most cultivated fruits are in a state of true hypertrophy. Girod de Chantrans, after many trials, succeeded in producing a peculiar variety[Pg 432] of pea with pods double the ordinary size.[506] M. Clos[507] mentions a case wherein the carpels of *Delphinium dictyocarpum* were hypertrophied. The change in size may or may not be attended by a difference in form; thus, in certain *Leguminosæ*, as *Medicago lupulina, Melilotus leucantha*, the carpels are sometimes hypertrophied and elongated, so as to resemble a claw or hook.[508]

The fruit of the common groundsel (*Senecio vulgaris*) is in its normal condition two or three times shorter than the involucre, and cylindrical for its whole length, but it frequently happens that the fruits become as long as the involucre itself, and taper from the base upwards, so as to become beaked. Under this head may also be mentioned the fleshy bulbils that are found in the capsules of *Crinum, Amaryllis*, and *Agave*. These are true seeds

201

enormously dilated.[509] In these seeds the outer coating becomes very thick and fleshy, and is traversed by spiral vessels.

It is obvious that very important results in a practical point of view may be and have been arrived at by cultivators availing themselves of this tendency of plants to increase in dimensions under certain circumstances. It is needless to do more than refer to the many fruits, vegetables, and cereals, which have thus become enlarged and improved by careful selection and rearing.

Alterations of consistence often accompany changes in size. The change may be one whereby the tissues become unusually hardened, by the excessive formation of secondary woody deposits, or softer and more succulent than ordinary, from the formation of an inordinate amount of loose cellular tissue. Generally[Pg 433] speaking, the appearances presented in such cases are not sufficiently striking to demand notice other than as regards their size. One illustration, however, may be cited from its singularity. This was the case of a dahlia, in which the centre of the flower was occupied by a projecting knob as large as a walnut, brown in colour, and very hard in texture. This knob was nothing but the enlarged and indurated extremity of the common receptacle, destitute of the scales and florets which usually spring from it. No insect-puncture could be detected, and no other reason for this peculiarity could be ascertained.

FOOTNOTES:

[488]On the subject of knaurs, the reader is referred to Trécul, 'Ann. Sc. Nat.,' 3 ser., vol. xx, p. 65; Lindley, 'Theory of Horticulture;' Rev. M. J. Berkeley, 'Gardeners' Chronicle,' 1855, p. 756.

[489]Jaeger, 'Flora.' 1860. p. 49, tab. i.

[490]'Revue Horticole,' 1868, p. 110, figs. 12, 13.

[491]The reader may also refer for further information on the subject of malformed pears to Irmisch. 'Flora,' 1858, p. 38, tab. i; Lindley, 'Theory of Horticulture'; Caspary, 'Bull. Soc. Bot. France,' vol. vi, 1859 (Rev. Bibl.), p. 235; Duhamel, 'Phys. Arbr.,' liv. iii, cap. 3. p. 393, fig. 308; Bonnet, 'Recherch. Us. feuilles,' tab. xxvi, fig. 2; Moquin-Tandon, 'El. Ter. Veg.,' p. 384, &c. Some of the cases recorded are, however, instances of true prolification.

[492]'Revue Horticole' 1868, p. 310.

[493]The interest of this accident is great, as showing how an habitually superior ovary may become inferior—a change so rare in its occurrence that its existence has been denied, and thus forming a marked contrast with the frequency with which the converse change of an inferior ovary to a superior one, from want of union with the calyx or from imperfect development of the peduncle, may be observed. It is also interesting as showing how the peduncle may become swollen, and at the same time how the woody deposit of the endocarp may, as if by compensation, be deficient. And, again, the malformation is not without significance in regard to the relationship between the drupaceous and the pomaceous subdivisions of *Rosaceæ*. The case would fitly be included under alterations of position, but the sheets relating to that subject were printed off before the publication of M. Carrière's notice.

[494]'Bull. Soc. Bot. France,' 1860, vol. vii, p. 881.

[495]"Monstr. Veget.," in 'Neue Denkschrift.'

[496]"Sched. de Monst. Plant." in 'Act. Helvet.,' t. ii, pl. ii, f. 14.

[497]'Bull. Soc. Bot. France,' vol. viii, 1861, p. 144.

[498]'Ann. Sc. Nat.,' sér. 2, t. i, p. 308, pl. ix *c*, fig. 1.

[499]'Bull. Soc. Bot. France,' 1862, t. ix, p. 37.

[500]'Consid. org. Fleur.,' Montpell., 1829, 25, 26, pl. ii, f. 18 and 19.

[501]'Bull. Bot.,' t. i, p. 7, tab. 1.

[502]'Linnæa,' vol. x, p. 604, tab. 5.

[503]'Mém. Acad. Sc. Toulouse,' 5 ser., vol. iii.

[504]'Ré. nosol. Végét.,' pp. 342.

[505]'Illustr. Hortic.,' 1868, Misc., p. 62.

[506]'Ann. Soc. Linn.,' Paris, t. i, p. 139.

[507]'Mém. Acad. Toulouse,' t. 6, 1862.

[508]'D. C. Prod.,' ii, pp. 172, 187.

[509]Richard, "Obs. sur les bulbilles des Crinum;" 'Ann. Sc. Nat.,' t. ii, p. 12. pl. i, fig. 1, 2. See also A. Braun, "Mémoire sur les graines charnues des Amaryllidèes," &c.; 'Ann. Sc. Nat.,' 1860, vol. xiv, p. 1, tab. 1.

CHAPTER II.

ELONGATION.

The class of cases coming under this head are sufficiently indicated by the name. There are many instances of this phenomenon occurring under different conditions, which, though unusual, can hardly be called abnormal, such, for instance, as the great lengthening of roots in their search for water, the excessive elongation that takes place in plants when grown at a distance from the light, in their endeavour to attain to which they become, as gardeners phrase it, "drawn." A similar result is brought about in forests or plantations, where long spars are required, by allowing the trees to grow very close to each other, so as to prevent the lateral extension of the branches. When plants grow in running water their roots, stems, and sometimes their leaves, become excessively elongated, as in *Ranunculus fluitans*, the flower-stalks of *Valisneria spiralis*, &c. These are cases of variation rather than of malformation, but are none the less curious, or sometimes perplexing; thus, Lapeyrouse described, in[Pg 434] his 'Supplement à la flore des Pyrénées,' p. 27, under the name *Potamogeton bifolium*, a plant which Mr. Bentham subsequently discovered to be nothing but a flowerless variety of *Vicia Faba* distorted by its growth in water.[510]

Elongation of the root.—This, as already remarked, is more often a variation than a malformation, and is usually due to the presence of water at a distance necessitating growth at the extremities of the root, or to the presence of some obstacle, such as a stone, to avoid which the root elongates till it has passed the obstruction. Occasionally in Crocus corms some of the fibrils may be met with much lengthened and thickened, and invested with a fleshy sheath. It is not certain, however, that these structures are roots; possibly, nay probably, they may be processes from the stem thrust downwards into the soil, similar to the formations already described in the tulip (p. 85, fig. 39).

Elongation of the inflorescence.—Under this heading it is necessary to consider lengthening of the common rachis in the case of an aggregate inflorescence, and lengthening of the individual flower-stalks, whether they be solitary or portions of a multiple inflorescence. The two phenomena may occur together, but they are quite as often independent one of the other. Thus, among *Umbelliferæ* the umbels are occasionally met with supported on unusually long stalks, while the pedicels of the individual flowers may or not be increased in length; so also with some of the Composites, or the heads of flowers of some *Leguminosæ*, *Trifolium repens*, &c. &c.

Another illustration of the sort is that recorded by M. Fournier, wherein the usually umbellate inflorescence of *Pelargonium* was, through the lengthening of the main stalk, transformed into a raceme. Among Composites a similar change may sometimes be met with.

[Pg 435]

MM. Clos and De Schönefeld have recorded the existence of a variety of the sweet chestnut (*Castanea*)in which the female catkins were as long, and bore nearly as many flowers, as the male spikes. This is stated to be of constant occurrence in some localities, and to be accompanied by a diminished size of the fruits. A similar elongation has been observed in the case of the walnut, catkins of which have been seen bearing thirty to thirty-five large nuts.[511]

In the strobile of the hop, *Humulus Lupulus*, a like elongation may sometimes be met with, generally in association with a more or less leafy condition of some of the scales.

Of a similar character, but complicated with extrusion or eversion of an ordinarily concave axis, is the fig described by Zuccarini,[512] and from the appearances presented by which that author draws the inference that the peculiar appearance of the fig is due to the formation of a large number of small bracts blended together for the greater part of their length, and accompanied by the suppression of the internodes, and consequent shortening of the axis. In the monstrous fruit the axis is prolonged, and forms a kind of raceme or catkin, surrounded at the base by numerous bracts, as in many *Amentaceæ*. (See p. 204, figs. 105, 106.)

A lengthening of the axis of the female strobiles of *Coniferæ* is not of infrequent occurrence in *Cryptomeria japonica, Larie europæa*, &c., and this is usually associated, as has been before stated, with a leaf-like condition of the bracts, and sometimes even with the development of leaf-bearing shoots in place of the scales. (See under Prolification of Inflorescence and Phyllomorphy, and for references, p. 115.)

Elongation of the secondary flower-stalks.—In the previous section the effect of elongation of the main rachis has been considered. A corresponding deviation occurs in[Pg 436] the peduncles or pedicels, and sometimes alters the general character of the inflorescence very considerably, converting a spike into a raceme, a raceme into a corymb, a capitulum into an umbel, and so forth. A few such cases may here be alluded to. Fig. 206 represents a specimen of *Ranunculus acris*, in which the lower and lateral flower-stalks were not only increased in number, but so much lengthened as to form a flat-topped inflorescence—a corymbose cyme. In many leguminous plants, as in *Trifolium repens, Lotus corniculatus*, &c., what is usually a compact spike, or head[Pg 437] of flowers, becomes a raceme from the elongation of the pedicels. In *Umbelliferæ* a similar change occurs, by virtue of which sometimes the umbels themselves, and at other times the florets, are raised on unusually long stalks, as in *Angelica Razoulzii, Carum Carui, Thysselinum palustre*.[513]In *Compositæ*, when affected by an analogous change, the capitulum assumes the appearance of a simple umbel, as in *Hypochæris radicata, Senecio vulgaris*, and other plants.

FIG. 206.—Inflorescence of *Ranunculus acris*, with secondary peduncles lengthened.

In some of the double-flowered apples which have been previously alluded to, the flower-stalk is inordinately long when compared with the adjacent ones. Possibly in some of these cases the absence of the usual swelling of the upper part of the peduncle may be connected with its increased length. One of the most striking instances of lengthened flower-stalk occurred in an apple flower, wherein there was no swelling beneath the calyx, while the latter was represented by five perfect stalked leaves.

Elongation of the leaves.—In the case of water plants this change keeps pace with the corresponding growth of the stem, *e.g. Ranunculus fluitans*, and in terrestrial plants there are varieties termed longifoliar, from the unusual length of the leaves. A similar lengthening occurs in the involucral leaves of *Umbelliferæ* and *Compositæ*, changing very materially the general aspect of the inflorescence. Occasionally, also, the leaf-lobes of parsley (*Apium Petroselinum*) and other crested-leaved plants may be observed to lose their ordinary wavy form, and to be lengthened into flat riband-like segments, as shown in fig. 207.

The only further illustrations that it is requisite to give of such changes in this place are those occurring in lobed or compounded leaves, which, from a lengthening of the midrib or central stalk, convert a digitate or palmate leaf into a pinnate one. In these instances[Pg 438] the lobes or leaflets become separated one from another by a kind of apostasis. This change may be frequently seen in the horse-chestnut, particularly in the young shoots formed after the trees have been pruned or pollarded. In the adjoining cut the intermediate stages between a palmate or digitate leaf to a pinnate one may be seen. The specimens from which the drawing was made were taken from the same tree at the same time.

FIG. 207.—Portion of leaf of parsley, showing the change from short wavy to long flat leaf-lobes.

In the white clover, *Trifolium repens*, a similar transition may often be observed, as also in some species of *Potentilla*.[514]

Elongation of the parts of the flower.—The only circumstance that needs especial mention under this section is the great lengthening that sometimes takes place in[Pg 439] the carpels, sometimes as a result of injury from insects or fungus, at other times without assignable cause.

FIG. 208.—Leaves of horse-chestnut, *Æsculus*, showing passage from digitate to pinnate leaves.

204

In the case of inferior ovaries this lengthening is, perhaps, even more common, as in *Umbelliferæ, Compositæ,* &c. The common groundsel (*Senecio vulgaris*) is especially liable to this form of enlargement of the[Pg 440]pistil, either in association with a leafy condition of the pappus or without any such change.

Elongation of the thalamus, placenta, &c.—In some plants, as in*Magnolia* or *Myosurus,* the thalamus becomes much elongated, and bears the carpels disposed spirally around it. A similar lengthening occurs in malformed flowers, usually in association with a similar change in the lower or outer part of the flower, by virtue of which the whorls become separated from each other (Apostasis). Elongation and protrusion of the placenta have been already alluded to at p. 119, and also at p. 125. In some of these cases the elongated placenta has taken the form of a leaf-bearing shoot.[515]

Apostasis.—Engelmann made use of this term to express the separation of parts one from another by the unusual elongation of the internodes.[516]He drew a distinction between the separation of individual organs one from the other, and the corresponding displacement of whorls. The subject has already been, to a considerable degree, treated of in these pages under the head of dialysis, displacement, and prolification, and but little need here be added. With reference to the distance between one whorl and another, it will be remembered that, although in the majority of cases the floral whorls are packed closely together, yet in other instances the floral axis becomes elongated, and thus separates the whorls one from another, by structures such as the gynophores, androphores, &c., of *Passifloreæ,Caryophylleæ, Capparideæ,* &c. &c.

A similar elongation of the thalamus, bringing about the separation of the floral whorls, or of their constituent parts, is very commonly met with in association with median prolification. Where the individual floral elements are thus thrown out of their usual verticillate arrangement, they naturally assume a spiral disposition,[Pg 441] and are, in some cases, united by their margins, so that a spiral sheet or tube is formed, surrounding the axis. This frequently occurs in double flowers of the Chinese primrose, *Primula sinensis.*

Engelmann[517] figures a case wherein the calyx of *Anagallis phœnicea*was separated by a rather long internode from the corolla, and a like illustration in *Torilis Anthriscus.*

FIG. 209.—Flower of *Delphinium,* showing apostasis of carpels, from lengthening of the thalamus, &c. (Cramer.)

[Pg 442]

A frequent change in Crucifers is due to the formation of a long stalk bearing the pod, and thus giving rise to the appearance met as a constant occurrence in Capparids.

In *Tropæolum majus* a similar elevation of the pistil may occasionally be seen.

The adjacent figure of a monstrous *Delphinium* taken from Cramer illustrates well the elongation of the floral axis and the apostasis of the carpels. In this instance the axis is terminated by a second flower (median prolification).

One of the best-marked illustrations of these changes occurs in a permanent malformation of *Epilobium hirsutum,* specimens of which were originally obtained from the late Professor Henslow. The several floral parts are here, some virescent, others truly foliaceous, and each whorl is separated from its neighbour by a rather long internode. In *Fuchsia* and*Campanula* a like change may occasionally be observed.

Engelmann, in addition to those previously mentioned, cites the following plants as having manifested this change:

*Convallaria majalis!, *Tulipa Gesneriana!, Veronica Chamædrys,Orobanche gracilis, Solanum Lycopersicum, Gentiana campestris,Hypericum, Helleborus fetidus, Caltha palustris, Brassica oleracea! and many *Rosaceæ, Caryophylleæ, Cruciferæ,* and *Ranunculaceæ.* (See Dialysis, Median Prolification, &c.)

Apostasis of the sub-floral or involucral leaves is not of infrequent occurrence in malformations affecting *Compositæ* and *Umbelliferæ.* In the following genera it has been observed with especial frequency:—*Torilis Anthriscus, Eryngium, Athamanta Cervaria, Leontodon, Tragopogon pratense!, Wedelia perfoliata!* In garden anemones, also, it is a common deviation.

FOOTNOTES:

[510]'Cat. Plant.,' Lang., p. 113.

[511]'Bull. Soc. Bot. France,' t. i, 1854, p. 173, and t. xiii, p. 96.

[512]'Abhandl. Math. Phys. Class.,' Band. iv, Abhandl. i, tab. i.

[513]See Cramer, 'Bildungsabweich,' pp. 62–79, and Fleischer, 'Missbild, der Culturpflanzen.'

[514]Schlechtendal, 'Bot. Zeit.,' 1844, p. 457; 'Linnæa,' xi, p. 301, xiv, p. 363; 'Bot. Zeit.,' 1856, p. 72; Masters, 'Rep. Brit. Assoc.,' Manchester, 1861; Coultas, 'What may be learnt from a tree,' p. 118.

[515]For further details refer to the chapter on Displacements, p. 86.

[516]'De Antholysi,' p. 42, § 49.

[517]Loc. cit., tab. 2, f. 6.

[Pg 443]

CHAPTER III.
ENATION.

Under the above heading are included certain forms arising from excess not of growth, but of development, and consisting in the formation of supplementary lobes or excrescences from various organs.

The new formations are not due either to a repetition or to a partition of any organ, but are out-growths from others previously formed.

In prolification and in multiplication the adventitious structures are of independent origin. In fission the new developments grow simultaneously with the older ones, of which, indeed, they are mere repetitions. Moreover, in fission the supplementary lobes do not, in general, project a plan different from that of the original structure, at least in the first instance, though their direction may ultimately become changed.

In enation the new growth projects from a previously formed organ after it has attained to considerable size, or even after its ordinary proportions have been attained, and it sprouts out from the beginning in a plane which is at a considerable angle to that of the parent organ, and it is sometimes of a different structure from it, and has different functions to fulfil.

Many of the instances that occur of scales projecting from petals, as in *Caryophylleæ*, *Sapindaceæ*, &c., the coronal filaments of passion-flowers, the cup of *Narcissus*, the appendages that beset the segments of the perianth in *Lilium lancifolium*, and other similar growths, may be referred to a like process. In many cases this has been proved by a study of the development of the flower, from which it appears that the growths in question are developed subsequently to the formation of the ordinary floral whorls. It is requisite, however, to be cautious in pronouncing upon the exact[Pg 444] nature of these bodies, in the absence of a knowledge of their period and mode of formation. They may be mere outgrowths from one or other of the customary whorls, or they may represent abortive stamens or petals, &c. Where circumstances prevent the course of development from being traced, something may be inferred as to their real nature from their position in regard to the other parts of the flower, from their anatomical structure, and from analogy or comparison with like organs in other plants. The period of their formation is, perhaps, of less importance than was at one time supposed, since it is well ascertained that, in some cases, the formation of the parts of the flower, e.g. the stamens of mallows, follows a centrifugal rather than a centripetal order.

In the case of monstrous developments of this nature too much care can hardly be exercised, and the observer should rarely venture on an explanation of the nature of the case from the evidence afforded by the monstrous growth apart from that to be derived from the study of the development and organization of the normal flower and from analogous formations in allied plants.

Excrescences from axile organs—Warts.—In a preceding paragraph the formation of gnaurs has been alluded to. There are other outgrowths, called warts, occasionally met with in trees, and which are more closely connected with the central tissues of the stem, while at the same time they are not provided with buds, in which two particulars warts differ from gnaurs.

Excrescences of this kind often attain a very large size, and may be seen on old elms and other trees, but, as their formation is probably more pathological than teratological, no further notice of these structures need here be given. No special notice need here be taken of the tubercles on the roots of so many *Leguminosæ*, nor of the peculiar excrescences on the roots of *Taxodium distichum*, as these appear to be normal formations. But it may be well to mention in this[Pg 445] place an anomalous development which occurs occasionally in *Ruscus aculeatus*, and in which, from the upper surface of the ordinary flattened leaf-like branch, projects at right angles a second similar branch, so that in section the appearance would be like that of the inverted letter t; thus, [symbol: Inverted upper-case T].

Enation from foliar organs—Leaves.—The development of adventitious lobes from leaves may take place either from their surfaces or their margins. A few illustrations may be given of each. In cabbage leaves a formation of adventitious laminæ projecting at right angles from the primary one may frequently be observed. In the instance figured (fig. 210) the new growths proceeded almost exclusively from the thick midrib, which, in the figure, is shown cut through just above the base. Not only is the ordinary semilunar band of vascular tissue to be here seen, but a similar broken line of vessels exists on the upper side of the leaf-stalk; thus the whole structure resembles that of a stem or a branch as much as that of a true leaf.

FIG. 210.—**Section through base of midrib of cabbage leaf, showing supplementary laminæ, &c.**

The development of secondary leaves from the surfaces of primary ones (phyllomania, autophyllogeny) has already been alluded to at p. 355.

[Pg 446]

Some of the cases wherein a leaf seems to have a double lamina may be alluded to here, though possibly they would more properly be referred to fission. The appearance presented is as if four wings projected from the midrib, so that a cross section would be nearly in the form of [Symbol:)O(turned 90 degrees.]. In an orange leaf presenting this appearance the lower surface of one lamina was, as usual, dull in colour, while the upper surface of the subjacent lamina was likewise dull; hence the impression might arise that this was an instance of the adhesion of two leaves back to back, but the petioles were not twisted, as they must have been had two leaves thus been united, and neither in the petiole nor in the midrib was there the slightest indication of fusion, the vascular bundles being arranged in a circular manner, not in a horseshoe-like arrangement, as would have been the case had adhesion taken place.[518] (See p. 33.)

[Pg 447]

Such leaves as those of the hedgehog holly, *Ilex Aquifolium*, var. *feroæ*, and, to a less extent, bullate leaves, may also be mentioned here as illustrations of hypertrophy or enation.

FIG. 211.—*Nephrodium molle.* **Ordinary frond and forked and crested varieties of the same, the crest arising from the inordinate development of the margins of the pinnules.**

When the increased development occurs at the margin of the leaves, especially, the result is a wavy or crisped appearance, "folia undulata, *vel*crispa."[519] These[Pg 448] conditions occur normally in such leaves as those of*Rumex crispus, Malva crispa*, &c., and are developed to an extreme degree in garden varieties of parsley, some kails, &c., as well as in many ferns, but these are probably cases rather of fission than enation as here understood.[520]

Enation from the sepals.—The basal lobes of the calyx in *Campanula Medium*, under normal circumstances, may be referred to in illustration of this occurrence, while the adventitious spurs on the calyx of some monstrous flowers seem due also to a like cause. These have already been alluded to at p. 315.

Enation from the corolla.—The instances of this are more frequent than in the case of the calyx, and admit of classification according as they occur in polypetalous or gamopetalous flowers, on the outer or inner surface of the petals, &c. Under natural circumstances the formation of scales, lobes, &c., from the petals, as in some *Caryophylleæ, Sapindaceæ,* &c. &c., may be explained, as already remarked, by this process, rather than by fission, chorisis, or by substitution of petals for stamens, &c. Each case must, however, be examined on its own merits, as it is not safe to decide upon the arrangement of parts in one flower by simply referring to the analogy of others. In the following illustrations the course of development has not, in all cases, been observed, and hence the explanation here given must be taken with some reserve; for should it prove that the adventitious lobes, &c., are formed simultaneously with the ordinary petals, the case will be one of chorisis rather than of enation, as here understood. Again, it may be that the supernumerary organs really represent petals or stamens in disguise, though this hypothesis demands the further assumption (in order to account for the interference with the law[Pg 449] of alternation) that suppression of certain organs has taken place.

Taking first those instances in which the supplementary petals appear on the inner surface of the corolla, as being at once the most frequent, and as presenting the closest analogy, with similar conformations, under natural circumstances, certain double-flowered varieties of the Chinese primrose,*Primula sinensis,* may be mentioned. In these flowers the calyx is normal, the tube of the corolla is traversed by ten vascular bundles, and the limb is divided into ten fimbriated lobes. About halfway up the tube, on the inner surface, are given off five supernumerary petals, opposite to as many lobes of the corolla. Some of the supplementary petals have a stamen in front of them, in the same relative position as in the normal flower. In some cases the back or outer surface of the supplementary petal is turned towards the inner or upper surface of the primary corolla, thus [Symbol: ((turned 90 degrees cw]; while, in other instances, the front of the adventitious lobe is directed towards the corresponding surface of the original petal, thus [Symbol: () turned 90 degrees]. Whether these supernumerary petals are formed by chorisis or by enation cannot, with certainty, be determined without examining the early stages of development.

FIG. 212.—*Datura fastuosa.* **True corolla turned back to show the supernumerary corolla with the petal-like segments attached to its outer surface (reduced).**

Of more interest are those instances where the adventitious growth is on the outside of the corolla; thus in a garden azalea there was intermediate between the calyx and the corolla, both of which were normal, a series of five petalodes, alternating with the sepals, and, therefore, opposite to the lobes of the corolla, and adherent with them at the very base, though elsewhere detached. These petalodes were concave on the surface looking towards the calyx, and were there brightly coloured, while the tint of the opposite surface looking towards the corolla was of a duller hue, corresponding with that of the outside of the corolla-tube. This arrangement of the colour was thus precisely similar to that which occurred in the four-winged leaves[Pg 450] already referred to at p. 446. In some flowers of*Datura fastuosa* a similar series of excrescences was observed; the calyx and the corolla were normal within the latter, intervening between it and the stamens was a second corolla produced by duplication, and adherent to the inner surface of this latter were five stamens. So far there was nothing very peculiar; it remains to say, however, that on the outer surface of the second corolla were five petal-like lobes closely adherent to it below, but partially detached above. The colour of the adventitious segments was paler on the outside than on the inner surface, as in the corolla itself. The position of the several parts was such that they were opposite one to the other; hence, while the lobes of the inner corolla were opposite to those of the outer one, the intermediate petalodes were opposite to both; thus:

```
    S  S  S  S    ------------------------    P  P  P  P  P   | X  X
X X X   |------------------------   | P  P  P  P  P   |st st st st st
```
[Pg 451]

The X indicating the position of the petalodes.

FIG. 213.—**Gloxinia, with supernumerary segments on the outside of the true corolla.**

A still more singular case is that of a variety of the Gloxinia, described originally by Professor Edouard Morren,[521] but which is now becoming common in English gardens.

When first observed these flowers were observed to produce petaloid segments outside the ordinary corolla, and partially adherent to (or rather, not completely separated from it) much as in the azalea before mentioned, the outer surface being brightly coloured, like the inner surface of the corolla in ordinary gloxinias. Being encouraged and tended by gardeners, in course of time, instead of a series of petalodes, more or less distinct from one another, a second corolla or "catacorolla" was formed outside the primary one, so that a hose in hose flower was produced, but, in this case, the supplementary flower was formed on the outside and not within the ordinary corolla. Moreover, the disposition of the colour was reversed, for in the outermost corolla the richest hues were on the outer surface, while in the inner or true corolla they were on the inside.

[Pg 452]

Professor Morren considers the adventitious petalodes as rudiments of so many supplementary flowers, axillary to the calyx, and adnate to the corolla; each lobe then would, in this view, represent an imperfect flower, and the completed catacorolla would be formed of a series of confluent flowers of this description. But this view involves the assumption of the suppression of all the parts of the flower, except the lobes in question.

FIG. 214.—"Catacorolla" of *Gloxinia*, formed from the union of adventitious petalodes on the outside of the true corolla (after Morren).

The view here propounded that the lobes in question are enations from the true petals, which become confluent, so as to form the catacorolla, is surely more simple, involves no assumptions of suppression of parts; and moreover, is borne out by the examination of some flowers, where the production of these adventitious[Pg 453] lobes from the outside of the minute partially developed petals could be distinctly seen.

Enation from the stamens.—An illustration of this process occurred in some double-flowered rhododendrons, which presented the following arrangement of parts:—calyx and corolla normal; within the latter eight petal-like stamens, forming a pseudo-corolla. The appearance presented by the petaloid filaments and anthers was as if they were adnate to the centre of the petals, but, on closer examination, it appeared that the petaloid expansion to which the dilated filament was apparently attached, was equally a part of the stamens; in other words, that the filament was provided with four petal-like wings, two on each side [Symbol: 00 topped by (turned cw 90°, an o above and another (turned cw above that]. This disposition was well seen in the anther, half of which was, in some cases, petaloid like the filament; in fact, the inner wing of the latter was directly continuous with the petal-like expansion from the anther. A section through the latter showed, going from within outwards, the cut edges of two perfect polliniferous lobes in the centre; and on either side the petaloid wing representing the remaining anther-lobe; outside these were the edges of the remaining wings, one on each side. (See p. 290, fig. 155.)

Enation from the carpels.—The only instances of this that need be referred to are such cases as those in which spur-like projections, horns, tubercles, or winged expansions, are formed from the surface of the ovary during the course of its development. The extraordinary cornute oranges described and figured by Ferrari, Gallesio, and other writers on the genus*Citrus*, may be mentioned under this head. A similar formation occurs in the fruit of some species of *Solanum*. (See p. 316.)

FOOTNOTES:

[518]It is desirable in this place to allude to a singular case of fissiparous division of a leaf of *Prunus Laurocerasus* described by Prof. Alexander Dickson ('Seemann's Journ. Botany,' vol. v, 1867, p. 323), and which did not come under the writer's notice till after the sheet relating to fission, p. 61, had been sent to press. Dr. Dickson thus speaks of this abnormal leaf:—"The petiole (unchanged) supported two laminæ, placed back to back, and united by their midribs (*i.e.* not separated) to within about an inch from their extremities, which were perfectly free from each other. These laminæ stood vertically, their edges being directed towards and away from the axis; and as they were placed back to back, the shining surfaces, corresponding in structure to the normal upper leaf-surface, were directed laterally outwards. In the axil of this abnormal leaf were two axillary buds. The existence of two leaf-apices and two axillary buds shows that this was not due to an accidental exuberance of development,

but to fissiparous division, which, had it been complete, would have resulted in the replacement of a single leaf by two leaves. The arrangement in Prof. Dickson's leaf may be thus represented: [symbol:)OO(with X above]. The nature of the case may be even better seen by comparison with the normal arrangement, which would be [symbol: (OX turned 90 degrees ccw], while in those cases where the fission of the leaf occurs in the same plane as that of the primary lamina, as where a leaf splits into two lobes at the apex, with a midrib to each, the arrangement is as follows: [symbol: OX turned 90 degrees ccw, with 2 arcs below], the X in all cases representing the position of the axis, the O that of the axillary bud, and the [symbol: (turned 90 degrees ccw] that of the laminæ."

[519]Linn., 'Phil. Bot.,' § 274. The term "*crispa*" is surely preferable to that of Ré, "phyllorhyseme."

[520]See C. Morren, "Consid. sur les déformations," &c., in 'Bull. Acad. Belg.,' 1852, tom, xix, part 3, p. 444; and as to ferns, see Moore, 'Nature-Printed British Ferns,' 8vo ed., where numerous illustrations are given.

[521]'Bull. Acad. Belg.,' t. xix, p. 224, tab. i; and 'Gardeners' Chronicle,' 1865, p. 865.

[Pg 454]

PART II.
ATROPHY.

Under the head of atrophy are included those cases wherein the organs affected are actually present, but in a dwarfed and stunted condition as compared with surrounding parts.

The diminished size is, in such instances, obviously due to a partial development and to an arrest of growth at a certain stage, from the operation of various causes, either external or inherent to the organization itself. It may affect any part of the plant, and exists, in very varying degree, in different instances, being sometimes so slight in amount as not to preclude the exercise of the functions of the part; while in others, the structure is so incomplete that the office cannot be performed. These differences depend, of course, upon the stage of development which the organ had reached when its growth was checked. For practical purposes atrophy may be distinguished from suppression by the fact that in the latter case a certain element of the flower or plant which, under ordinary circumstances, is present, is entirely wanting, while, in the former class, it exists but in a rudimentary condition.

Again, atrophy is to be separated from that general diminution in the size of the whole plant or of distinct parts of that plant which is comprised under the term "nanism." Thus the several dwarf varieties of plants (var.*nanæ*), or those in which the leaves or flowers are smaller than usual (var.*parvifoliæ*, v. *parvifloræ*), are truly regarded as variations, and not as malformations properly so called.

[Pg 455]

Atrophy is partial and special in its operation, nanism is general.

Under ordinary circumstances atrophy is exemplified by the presence of rudimentary or imperfect organs, as, for instance, in *Pentstemon,Scrophularia,* &c., where one stamen is atrophied.

For convenience sake atrophy may be divided into abortion and degeneration, the first including cases where, from arrest of development occurring at an early stage, organs are present; but in a much smaller and more rudimentary condition than usual, their form and general appearance, except so far as regards their dimensions, not being materially altered. On the other hand, in cases of degeneration, development is not entirely checked, but rather perverted, so that not only the dimensions are lessened, but the form is altered.

CHAPTER I.
ABORTION.

The sense in which this term is here understood has been explained in the preceding paragraph. It is only necessary to say further, that cases of abortion are to be distinguished from those of suppression, on the one hand, and those of degeneration on the other. In suppression there is from the first an absolute deficiency of a particular organ. In degeneration the part is present, but in a diminished and perverted condition. In abortion it exists, but in a stunted and dwarfed, but not otherwise permuted state.

Abortion of axile organs.—When the main stem is arrested in its growth, the habit and general appearance of the plant are materially altered, as in the so-called stemless plants, *plantæ acaules*. In these the internodes[Pg 456] are so slightly developed that the leaves are closely crowded in tufts or rosettes. When this shortening of the stem (acaulosia) occurs, without other considerable change in other organs, the deviation is classed under the head of variation rather than of monstrosity; and, indeed, in very many plants, this arrested growth of the axis is the rule rather than the exception. When occurring in an abnormal manner, atrophy of the stem is most frequently attended by other more or less grave alterations in other structures; thus Moquin-Tandon[522] cites an instance of *Camphorosma monspeliaca*, wherein the stems presented the form of very short, hard, woody tubercles, thickly clothed with deformed leaves, and invested by a vast number of hairs, longer and more dense than usual. A similar deformity sometimes occurs in an Indian species of *Artabotrys*; in these specimens the branchlets are contracted in length, and bear numerous closely packed scaly leaves, densely hairy, and much smaller than ordinary.

Spines and thorns may he looked on as atrophied branches, and seem to result from poorness of soil, as the same plants, which, in hungry land, produce spines, develop their branches to the full extent when grown under more favorable conditions.[523]

In the birch an arrest of development in some of the branches is of common occurrence. The branch suddenly ceases to grow in length; at the same time it thickens at the end into a large bulbous knob, from which are developed a profusion of small twigs, whose direction is sometimes exactly the reverse of that of the main branch. (See p. 347.)

The branches of the common spruce fir, especially the lateral ones, when attacked by a particular species of aphis, are very apt to be developed into a cone-like excrescence.[524] [Pg 457]

A shortened condition of the flower-stalks occurs occasionally, greatly altering the general character of the inflorescence. This has been observed in pelargoniums and in the Chinese primrose, in both of which the effect was to replace the umbellate form of inflorescence by a capitate one.

Abortion of the receptacle.—Here may be mentioned those cases of flowers with habitually inferior ovary (real or apparent), in which the receptacle fails, from some cause or other, to dilate as usual. This has already been alluded to under the head of Prolification, Displacements, &c. (pp. 78, 130, &c., figs. 35–37, 64, &c.), and hence requires only incidental comment in this place. There are, however, certain other cases of a similar nature which may here be referred to; such as the abortive condition of the inferior ovary, or rather of the receptacle, that usually encircles the ovary in *Compositæ* and *Umbelliferæ*. In the former natural order the following plants have been met with in this condition:—*Tragopogon pratense!*, *Cirsium arvense*, *Hypochæris radicata*, *Senecio vulgaris!*, *Coreopsis Drummondi*. In the latter order, *Daucus Carota! Œnanthe crocata!* and *Thysselinum palustre*, seem most frequently to have been observed in this state.[525] In some gourds the receptacle may be seen[Pg 458] partially developed only, and forming a kind of cup, from which the true carpels protrude.

Abortion of the leaves.—Arrest of growth in the leaves occurs in different ways; sometimes the whole leaf is smaller than usual; at other times certain parts only are reduced in size; while, in a third class of cases, portions of the leaf are entirely suppressed.

Moquin[526] mentions having seen the leaves of *Chenopodium vulvaria*, and of *Diplotaxis muralis* reduced to a fourth of their natural size; and he alludes to other cases of the same nature, seen by other observers, in *Hypericum perforatum* and *Blitum polymorphum*.

Nicandra physaloides[527] has also been met with in a similar condition, which, indeed, is a common result of insect-puncture, and of fungous growth in plants. Those instances in which the leaf is diminished in size, without any attendant malformation in other organs, may be regarded rather as variations than as monstrosities, as in the case of the entire-leaved varieties of those plants which ordinarily have cut or divided leaves, e.g. *Plantago Coronopus*, var. *integrifolia*, *Papaver Rhœas integrifolia*, &c. &c. The same remark may be made of those specimens in which one part of the leaf is developed to a less extent than another, as happens in the submerged leaves of such plants as *Ranunculus aquatilis*, *Cabomba aquatica*, the spiney leaves of *Berberis*, the fenestrated leaves of *Ouvirandra*, &c. In the illustrations last cited the relative deficiency of one portion, as contrasted with another, takes place as a constant occurrence, and is uniform and regular throughout the whole leaf. When, on the other hand, the deficiency in question happens accidentally and irregularly, the change may be considered as a malformation. One side of the blade of the leaf is frequently affected in this manner, the other portions remaining unaffected. It would appear as if any plant might be[Pg 459] thus altered, but the following species appear to be particularly subject to this change:*Æsculus Hippocastanum, Digitalis purpurea, Morus alba, Fagus silvatica contracta* (hort.), *Codiæum variegatum* var. *erosum* (hort.),*Broussonettia papyrifera, Scolopendrium vulgare,* &c.

Frequently this irregular diminution in proportion is coexistent with an unusual degree of cleavage or laciniation of the margin, as in *Acer platanoides laciniatum, Tilia asplenifolia, Alnus imperialis* (hort.), *Fagus silvatica* var. (hort.), &c.

In the case of what are sometimes termed interrupted leaves, the laminar portions of the leaf are here and there deficient on both sides of the midrib, leaving small portions of the latter, as it were, denuded and connecting the segments of the laminæ one with the other. This has been observed amongst other plants in *Veronica latifolia, Broussonettia papyrifer,Codiæum variegatum* var. *interruptum* (hort.), *Scolopendrium vulgare,* &c.[528] (See p. 328.)

In some of the leaves which have been already referred to in illustration of the inordinate growth of the cellular portions, the increased development of parenchyma is associated with a contracted state of the midrib and its branches, producing a puckered appearance of the leaf, an exaggerated degree of that change which produces what are termed "folia bullata." In illustration may be cited various species of *Mentha, Perilla, Coleus, Fagus silvatica crispa, Cytisus, Laburnum* var., and other forms, cultivated in gardens for their singularity.

Entire absence of the stalk of the leaf occurs normally in sessile leaves; on the other hand the blade of the leaf is only occasionally developed in the phyllodineous Acacias, in some species of *Oxalis, Indigofera, Lebeckia,Ranunculus, Bupleurum,* &c.

[Pg 460]

De Candolle,[529] from a consideration of *Strelitzia juncea,* in which the petiole alone is developed, was led to the inference that in many monocotyledonous plants the blade of the leaf was never developed, the portion present being the sheath or stalk, unprovided with limb. The correctness of this inference is shown, amongst other things, by the occasional presence of a leaf-blade in *Strelitzia juncea* itself.

Occasionally the laminar portions of the leaf are completely wanting, leaving only the main ribs, as in the case of *Berberis,* while the adjoining figure (fig. 215) represents an instance of a cabbage wherein the innermost leaves are represented by thick fleshy cylindrical bodies corresponding to the midribs of the ordinary leaves. There is in cultivation a variety of the cabbage which constantly presents this peculiarity.

FIG. 215.—Inner leaves of cabbage reduced to their midribs.

The suppression of one or more leaflets of a compound leaf has already been referred to at p. 396.

Abortion of the perianth, calyx, and corolla.—Illustrations of partial development in these organs are not rare, under ordinary circumstances, as for instance the "obsolete" calyx of Umbellifers. In the cauliflower the branches of the inflorescence are contracted in length, while their succulence is much increased; at their[Pg 461] extremities they bear crowds of imperfect flowers, in which the calyx only is visible, and that only in a rudimentary and partially developed condition. Imperfect development of the whole or of some of the constituent parts is more common in the case of the corolla than in that of the calyx. In *Arenaria serpyllifolia* the petals, especially in autumn, are only one fourth the length of the sepals.*Anagallis phœnicea, Honckenya peploides, Arabis alpina, Ranunculus auricomus, Rubus fruticosus,* and *Geranium columbinum,* also frequently afford illustrations of this circumstance.

FIG. 216.—Abortion of four out of five petals, *Viola tricolor,* side and front views.

At fig. 216 is represented a pansy in which four of the five petals were very small and colourless, while the lower spurred petal was of the usual size and colour. In this flower the stamens and pistils were wholly suppressed, and the flower-stalk, instead of being bent near the flower, retained its primary straight direction. Similar atrophic conditions of the corolla occur habitually among *Violaceæ.*

The diminished size of the petals sometimes coexists with an increase in their number, as in a flower of *Streptocarpus Rexii*, mentioned by Bureau.[530]

Among monocotyledons this partial development seems to be even more frequent than in dicotyledons. In addition to the well-known cases of certain species of *Bellevalia* and *Muscari*, wherein the uppermost flowers of the raceme are more or less atrophied (see[Pg 462] p. 347, fig. 179), a few less common illustrations may be cited. In crocuses it is not a very uncommon circumstance to find the three inner segments of the perianth smaller than natural, and generally unequal in size. This occurs without any other perceptible change in the flower.

Schlechtendal[531] mentions a flower of *Fritillaria imperialis* in which the perianthial leaves were relatively very small, and destitute of the usual nectary, while the stamens, on the other hand, were of their natural size and appearance. Fresenius[532] records a similar occurrence in the same plant.

Morren[533] gives details of like appearances in *Hymenocallis americana*, and Delavaud[534] in *Tigridia pavonia*.

In certain orchids an arrested development of the perianth is habitual, as in *Oncidium abortivum* (fig. 217), where, on a large branching panicle, numerous abortive, but few perfect, flowers are produced. In a similar way the petals and labellum of *Odontoglossum Uro-Skinneri* have been found reduced to filamentous processes.

FIG. 217.—**Flower of *Oncidium abortivum*, magnified.**

[Pg 463]

Abortion of the stamens.—Atrophy of one or more stamens is of very common occurrence, as a general rule, in many genera of plants, *e.g.* *Scrophularia, Erodium*, many *Restiaceæ*, &c. &c. As a strictly teratological condition atrophy of the stamens is more rare than complete suppression. It has been noticed in *Arabis alpina, Cerastium glomeratum, C. tetrandrum, Rhamnus catharticus, Anemone, Hepatica*, &c. It happens frequently among Orchids both wild and cultivated. In the *Hymenocallis* flowers described by the elder Morren, four out of five stamens were atrophied. In other flowers, otherwise perfectly formed, one abortive stamen was found bearing a spherical indehiscent anther. All these atrophied anthers of *Hymenocallis* were found to contain pollen, differing at first sight but little from what is usual, but presenting this important peculiarity, that while the normal pollen does not burst until it comes into contact with the stigma, in the abnormal flowers the outer coat of the pollen-grains split while still within the anther, from which latter, indeed, they could not escape, owing to the indehiscent nature of the latter. Again, the pollen-tube of the abnormal grains cracked, in its turn, on mere exposure to the air, and liberated the fovilla, so that the pollen of these atrophied anthers was necessarily impotent, because it opened before it could be applied to the stigma, even had that been rendered possible by the opening of the anther.

An abortive condition of the stamens and of the pollen, is of very common occurrence among hybridised plants. Gaertner and other writers have spoken of this defective condition as contabescence.[535] It forms one reason for the sterility so frequently observed in the case of true hybrids. In some hybrid passion-flowers, while all other parts of the flower were apparently perfect, even to the ovules, the stamens were[Pg 464] atrophied, and distorted, and contained little or no pollen; the few grains of the latter being smaller than usual. (See under Heterogamy, pp. 193–196, and p. 398.)

Abortion of the pistil, fruit, &c.—Traces of the carpels occur in many male flowers of unisexual plants, *e.g. Sterculiaceæ, Euphorbiaceæ, Restiaceæ*, &c. &c., and in some natural orders there appears to be a tendency towards a diœcious condition, *e.g. Caryophylleæ*, as in *Lychnis dioica, Silene otites, Arenaria tetraquetra*, &c. The last-named plant is stated to have, in some cases, imperfect pistils; in others, rudimentary stamens; while a third set of flowers are hermaphrodite.[536] The ovary of aconites, according to Moquin, is very subject to atrophy.

FIG. 218.—**Bladder plum.**

During the maturation of the pistil, and its passage to the fruit, great changes of consistence frequently[Pg 465] take place, owing to the development of cellular tissue, or of woody matter, according as the fruit is succulent or woody. It sometimes happens that,

213

owing to some disturbing causes, the changes that usually occur fail to do so; thus, the stone of plums is occasionally deficient, as in what are termed bladder-plums (fig. 218); some of these, consisting merely of a thin bladder, are curiously like the pods of *Colutea*.[537]

MM. Fournier and Bonnet[538] describe a fruit of a *Rubus*, with perfectly dry fruits, like those of a *Geum*, and this form was considered by Steudel to form a distinct species. It is, however, merely a variety in which the fruits have not become succulent.[539]

Schlechten'dal describes[540] the ordinarily baccate fruit[Pg 466] of a vine as becoming dry, and even dehiscing by valves like a capsule.

In maize it occasionally happens that one or two of the longitudinal series of fruits become abortive, leaving a smooth furrow, at first of a greenish colour, but ultimately of a reddish yellow. Often a second row of fruits, opposite to the first, is also atrophied, so that the whole spike changes its cylindrical form for a flattened one.[541] See also under Heterogamy, Meiophylly, &c.

Abortion of the ovules.—In the case of a pluri-ovulate ovary it rarely happens that all the ovules attain to maturity, some never get fertilised, others, pressed on by their neighbours on either side, become impeded in their development, and finally disappear, or remain as rudiments.[542] This is the case, under ordinary circumstances, and still more so in the case of hybrid plants, or of monsters. Where the outer coats of the ovule become more or less leafy in appearance (see p. 262), the inner investments become more or less atrophied, or are even more frequently entirely suppressed, as is also the nucleus.

In other cases, a simple arrest of development takes place; the ovule, for instance, which should be anatropal, remains straight, while the integuments, checked in their development, form imperfect sheaths from which the shrivelled nucleus protrudes.

Depauperated Ferns.—The preceding illustrations have been taken from flowering plants chiefly, but a similar defective development is manifested in cryptogamous plants. The contraction and imperfect development of the fronds of some varieties of ferns, hence called depauperated, may receive passing notice, as also the cases in which the sori or clusters of spore cases are denuded of their usual covering, owing to the abortion[Pg 467] or imperfect development of the indusium, as in what are termed exindusiate varieties.[543]

General remarks on abortion, coincident changes, &c.—Reference has already been made, while treating of hypertrophy, suppression, &c., to certain other changes affecting the flower at the same time. Atrophy of one organ or set of organs, for instance, is frequently accompanied by a compensating hypertrophy or by an increased number of other parts. In the feather-hyacinth, *Muscari comosum*, var., *monstrosum*, the absence of flowers is compensated for by the inordinate formation of brightly coloured threads which appear to be modified pedicels (see pp. 347, 348); so also in the wig plant, *Rhus Cotinus*. So the atrophy of the stamens, in some flowers, is coincident with the hypertrophy of the pistil. Thus, Unger, 'Denkschr. d. Kais. Acad. der Wissensch. Math. Nat. Classe,' Mai 25, 1848, p. 103, tab. ix, describes a case wherein the corolla and stamens of *Desmodium marylandicum* were atrophied, while the calyx and legume, on the other hand, were hypertrophied.

Fusion of the members of one whorl with one another, or with the components of an adjacent series, often entails atrophy or suppression, either in the united organs themselves, or in adjacent ones. A foliaceous condition of the outer portions of a flower is very generally attended by atrophy or complete suppression of the inner portions.

From this point of view the observations of Morren[544] on the different degrees of atrophy up to complete suppression, observable in the flowers of *Bellevalia comosa*, are of importance. According to this observer, the most highly differentiated parts, such as the stigmas, the ovules, and the anthers, are the first to disappear,[Pg 468] the filaments often being developed without anthers. Ultimately a deformed and empty perianth alone remains. In the ordinary course of things the mouth of the perianth is open, but in some of these malformations it is closed, and when that happens, the effects of atrophy are the more observable in the stamens and pistils.

The impotence of the pollen in certain atrophied flowers, as noticed by the same observer, is of much interest, especially in reference to the sexual relationship between the different forms in polymorphic flowers as studied by Mr. Darwin.

A change in direction may also be noted as a common accompaniment of atrophy or suppression; thus, in a capsule of *Veronica Beccabunga*, which was one-celled by the abortion of one carpel, the style was lateral instead of terminal.

As to the causes of these structural deviations but little is known; certain of them have been already alluded to. In some cases atrophy and suppression maybe regarded as permanent states of a condition usually transitory, but this is clearly not always the case. Among external causes anything bringing about an enfeebled condition might be supposed to lead to atrophy, or suppression of some parts.

Gaertner[545] attributes the arrested development and fall of flowers to some among the following causes:—1. non-application of the pollen of the same variety, and consequent imperfect fertilisation; 2. any considerable injury to the calyx, &c.; 3. destruction of the style or stigma before the fertilisation of the ovary; 4. application to the stigma of imperfect or heterogeneous pollen or indifferent pulverulent matter; 5. defective conceptive power in the ovary.

Abortion of the ovules is considered by the same authority to be due to—1. deficiency of heat; 2. excess of moisture; 3. peculiar formation of the ovary; 4. over-luxuriant development of roots or buds; 5. peculiar[Pg 469]conditions of cultivation; thus, cuttings and layers produce sterile and abortive seeds much more frequently than plants of the same species raised from seed; 6. abortion of the seed is often combined with luxuriant development of the walls of the fruit.

Temperature and climatal changes in general seem not to be without effect, as has been already mentioned in the case of *Arenaria tetraquetra*, which is polygamous when growing in mountain districts. Other illustrations of a similar character are mentioned under the head of Heterogamy (p. 196).

Pressure has been already alluded to as one of the most obvious of the inducing causes of atrophy and suppression.

In the case of *Ranunculus auricomus* before cited, in which the petals are rarely perfect, M. de Rochebrune considers that the deficiencies in question depend, in great measure, on the amount of moisture in the localities where the plant grows. In most places the flowers and carpels are apt to become more or less abortive, while the leaves are luxuriant; while, in dry places, the foliage is small, but the flowers are more perfect. This is quite consonant with other facts relating to the development of flowers or of leaves in general.

But while external agencies undoubtedly play some part in bringing about these changes, it is almost certain that internal causes inherent to the organization of the plant are more important. Mr. Darwin[546] accounts for the existence of rudimentary organs by the operation of the general rule of inheritance, and explains their stunted condition as the effect of disuse, not so much, of course, in the particular flower as in its predecessors. This disuse may be the result of the superior efficacy of foreign pollen as contrasted with that formed in the individual flower itself. In this way many hermaphrodite flowers tend to become diœcious, as in *Caryophyllaceæ*, *Orchidaceæ*, *Plantaginaceæ*, *Primulaceæ* and other orders.

[Pg 470]

Although many of the circumstances above mentioned apply to plants whose structure is habitually rudimentary, there is no reason why they may not, under due restrictions, be applied to plants whose organs are only occasionally defective.

For further remarks on the subject of Abortion, the reader is referred to the sections relating to suppression, etc., also to Moquin-Tandon, 'El. Terat. Veget.,' p. 120; C. Morren, "De l'atrophie en général," in 'Bull. Acad. Belg.,' t. xviii, 1851, part i, p. 275.

FOOTNOTES:

[522]'El. Ter. Veg.,' p. 132.

[523]*Spinosæ arbores cultura sæpius deponunt spinas in hortis,* 'Linn. Phil. Bot.,' § 272.

[524]Mr. Selby, in his 'History of British Forest Trees,' p. 465, gives the following account of the formation of this peculiar growth:—"In the autumn the parent aphis deposits her eggs at the base of the embryo leaves, within the bud destined to produce the shoots of the following year. When these begin to burst and expand in spring, the leaves, at whose bases the eggs have been deposited, instead of increasing in length, enlarge at the base, and form a cell or cyst whose mouth is at first closed by a red velvety-looking substance. If

opened in this state a nest of small greenish aphides is distinctly visible, and at a certain period, or when they have acquired maturity, which is towards the end of the summer, the mouth of the cell opens and the insects fly off to inflict a similar injury upon the nascent buds of the year. In some instances the leaves of only a portion of the circumference of a shoot are affected, in which case, though a slight distortion may take place, the branch is not prevented from elongating; but in others, where the whole of the leaves around the shoot are converted into nidi, elongation is prevented and distortion to a great extent takes place."

[525]See Cramer, 'Bildungsabweich.,' pp. 53, 64, for further references.

[526]'El. Ter. Veg.,' p. 124.

[527]Schlechtendal, 'Bot. Zeit.,' 1857, vol. xv, p. 67.

[528]On the subject of this paragraph the reader may consult A. Braun, "Ueber abnorme Blattbildung," &c., in 'Verhandl.,' d. 35, 'Naturforscherversammlung;' Jaeger, 'Flora,' 1850. p. 481, tab. 4, *Digitalis*.

[529]'Org. Veget.,' i. p. 286.

[530]'Bull. Soc. Bot. France, vol. viii, 1861, p. 710.

[531]'Linnæa,' 1830, vol. v, p. 492.

[532]'Mus. Senkenb.,' ii. p. 45.

[533]'Bull. Acad. Roy. Belg.,' 1851, t. xviii. part i, p. 275.

[534]'Bull. Soc. Bot. France,' vol. viii, 1861, p. 147.

[535]See Darwin, 'Variation of Domest. Anim. and Plants,' ii, 165.

[536]Gay, 'Ann. Sc. Nat.,' ser. i, 1824, t. iii, p. 44.

[537]See De Candolle, 'Mem. Legum.,' tab. 3, f. 1; Wyville Thomson, 'Trans. Bot. Soc. Edinb.,' 1851, July 10th; Berkeley, 'Gardeners' Chronicle,' June 22nd, 1867, p. 654. A similar case is described by Dr. Robb, in Sir W. Hooker's 'Journal of Botany,' 1841, vol. iii, p. 99, with illustrative figures. The specimens there described were produced at New Brunswick, where plum trees flower very freely, but seldom produce ripe fruit. Dr. Robb's account is as follows:—"In the summer of 1839 I had an opportunity of watching the process of destruction among the plums, and it was as follows—Before or soon after the segments of the corolla had fallen off, the ovarium had become greenish yellow, soft, and flabby. As the fruit continued to increase in magnitude, its colour grew darker and of a more ruddy yellow, and at the end of a fortnight or three weeks the size of the abortive fruit rather exceeded that of a ripe walnut. In fact, an observer might imagine himself to be walking amongst trees laden with ripe apricots, but, like the fabled fruit on the banks of the Dead Sea, these plums, though tempting to the eye, when examined, were found to be hollow, containing air, and consisting only of a distended skin, insipid, and tasteless. By-and-bye a greenish mould is developed on the surface of the blighted fruit; then the surface becomes black and shrivelled, and at the expiration of a month from the time of flowering the whole are rotten and decomposed. The flower appears about the beginning of June, and before August there is hardly a plum to be seen. It is curious that where two flower-stalks arise from one point of the branch, one will often go on to ripen in the normal way, while the other will become abortive, as above described."

In a specimen described by Mr. Berkeley there were two distinct ovules of equal size close to the apex of the fruit, connected with the base by vessels running down the walls. It should be observed that there is a worthless variety of plum, Kirke's stoneless, or Sans Noyau, in which the kernel is not surrounded by any bony deposit.

[538]'Bull. Soc. Bot. Fr.,' 1862, vol. ix, pp. 37 et 291.

[539]Carl Schimp, 'Fl. Friburg,' vii, p. 745; Hook, fil., 'Journ. Linn. Soc.,' vi, p. 9.

[540]'Linnæa,' vol. v, 1830, p. 493.

[541]Moquin-Tandon, 'El. Ter. Veg.,' p. 325.

[542]Alph. De Candolle states that the position of the abortive ovules affords a good character for discriminating between certain species of *Quercus*, 'Bibl. Univ. Genev.,' 1862, t. xv, p. 929.

[543]See Moore, 'Nature-Printed Ferns,' 8vo, for numerous illustrations both of depauperate and exindusiate ferns. *Scolopendrium vulgare* seems to be one of the ferns most commonly affected in this way. Moore, loc. cit., vol. ii, pp. 135, 147, 159, 165, &c.

[544]'Bull. Acad. Belg.,' t. xvii, p. 38, t. 1; Lobelia, p. 85.

[545]Cited in 'Henfrey's Botanical Gazette,' i, p. 179.

[546]'Origin of Species,' p. 450.

CHAPTER II.
DEGENERATION.

While the terms atrophy and abortion apply in the main to a mere diminution of size, as contrasted with the ordinary standard, degeneration may be understood to apply to those cases in which not only is the absolute bulk diminished, but the whole form is altered and depauperated. Degeneration, thus, is the result not so much of a deficiency in growth as of a perversion of development.

Under natural, *i.e.* habitual circumstances, the formation of pappus in place of a leafy calyx may be considered as an illustration of degeneration. It is evident, however, that no very decided line of demarcation can be drawn between cases of perversion and of arrest of development.

Formation of scales.—These may be mere epidermal excrescences, or they may be the abortive rudiments of leaves. Of this latter nature are the "cataphyllary" leaves which invest the root stocks of so many perennial plants, the perulæ of leaf-buds, or the paleæ on the common receptacle of composite flowers. Other illustrations of a like character are to be met with in the[Pg 471] membranous scales that represent leaves in *Ruscus, Asparagus,Pinus,* &c. Similar productions are met with within the flower, where they may occur as the representatives of sepals, petals, stamens, or pistils, or as mere excrescences. (See Enation.) Whole families of plants, *e.g.Sapindaceæ*, are characterised by the presence of these organs, which are often of great interest to the morphologist as indicating the true symmetry of the flower, while they have acquired fresh importance since the publication of Mr. Darwin's work on the 'Origin of Species,' wherein we are taught to regard these rudiments as, in many cases, vestiges of organs that were more completely developed in the progenitors of the present race of plants, and the exercise of whose functions, from some cause or other, having been rendered impossible, the structures become, in process of time, proportionately stunted.

Thus, in diœcious plants we frequently find traces of stamens in the female flowers, and rudiments of the pistil in the male flower, indicating, according to the Darwinian hypothesis, that the ancestors of these plants were hermaphrodite (see Heterogamy).

Mr. Darwin has also shown that, in some cases, the utmost degree of fertility is attained, not from the action of the pollen on the stigma of the same flower, but on the influence of the male element of one blossom upon the female organs of another flower on another individual plant.

Hence, in such plants there is a tendency to a separation of the sexes, while, from what has been before stated, it might be expected that rudiments of the male or female organs would be found, and also as a result of the operation of the law of inheritance. On the same principles it is easy to understand the occasional presence of the perfect in place of the rudimentary organs, as in *Dianthus*.

In some instances the assumption of a scale-like form by any organ is attended by a change in texture, the organs becoming dry and scarious, or fleshy.[Pg 472] Moquin cites in illustration of the first phenomenon the flower of a*Vicia*, in which the petals were thick and fleshy, like the scales of a bulb; and of the second the leaves of a *Chrysanthemum*, which were replaced by small, glossy scales, like those which invest ordinary leaf-buds. Sometimes the entire flower is replaced by accumulations of small, acute, green scales. Cases of this kind, wherein the flowers of a pea and of the foxglove were replaced by collections of small ovate green scales packed one over the other till they resembled the strobile of a hop, have been already alluded to. Most of these scales are represented as having had other accumulations of scales in their axils.

Similar collections of scales may frequently be met with in the birch and in the oak, and probably represent abortive leaf-buds. Other cases of a like kind in *Gentiana Amarella*, where the scales are coloured, are mentioned elsewhere.

In some kinds of *Campanula* a similar change is not uncommon.

Formation of hairs, spines, &c.—The adventitious production of hairs is likewise frequently due to an arrested growth, in some cases arising from pressure impeding the proper development of the organ. In other cases the formation of hair seems to accompany the diminished development of some organ, as on the barren pedicels of the wig plant, *Rhus Cotinus*. A similar production of hair may be noticed in many cases where the development of a branch or of a flower is arrested, and this occurs with especial frequency where the arrest in growth is due to the puncture of an insect, or to the formation of a gall. In such cases the hairs are mere excrescences from the epidermis.

Prickles differ but little from hairs save in their more woody texture, but true spines or thorns are modifications either of a leaf or of a branch. Their presence seems often dependent on the soil in which the plants grow, or on other external circumstances.

[Pg 473]

They occur normally in the sepals of *Paronychia serpyllifolia* and other plants.

Formation of glands.—Under this name are associated a number of (generally) rudimentary organs very different in their morphological nature and significance, and also in their functions. Some are truly glandular or secreting organs, while others have no visible office. Anything like a complete account of these structures would be out of place, and reference is only made to them here on account of the occasional existence of intermediate forms, which throw light on the morphological significance of these structures. Thus, in *Passiflora* and *Viburnum Opulus*, the so-called glands on the sides of the petiole appear to represent leaflets, and are not unfrequently developed as such.

M. Dunal observed a flower of *Cistus vaginatus* in which some of the stamens were replaced by an hypogynous disc.[547] Moquin has seen similar instances in the flowers of a Rose, *Hypericum*, and Poppy.

M. Planchon[548] gives an account of some very curious malformations in *Drosera intermedia*, which go to show that the ovules are homologous with the glandular hairs on the margins of the leaves of these plants, an opinion corroborated by the researches of MM. Grönland and Trécul.[549]

Dr. Hooker shows that the pitcher of *Nepenthes* is due to a modification of a gland placed at the extremity of the midrib.[550]

Formation of tendrils.—These are of very varied morphological import; sometimes they are degenerated peduncles, as in passion-flowers, or vines; at other times they are of foliar origin; or, again, they may proceed from the segments of the perianth, as in [Pg 474] *Hodgsonia* and some other cucurbitaceous plants. From their very different origin in different plants it is necessary to study the development in each case, and not apply to the generality what may be peculiar to one. In any case this formation in question generally belongs more to general morphology than to teratology.[551]

Kirschleger, however, has recorded the existence of a cirrhose sepal in *Cucurbita Pepo*.[552]

FOOTNOTES:

[547]'Consid. Org. Fleur.,' p. 44, pl. ii, fig. 23.

[548]'Ann. Sc. Nat.,' 3 ser., Bot. ix, pl. 6, ff. 1, 2.

[549]'Ann. Sc. Nat.,' 3 ser., Bot. 1855, pp. 297, et 303.

[550]'Trans. Linn. Soc.,' xxii, p. 415.

[551]See Darwin, "On Climbing Plants," 'Journal of Linnean Society,' vol. ix, p. 1.

[552]'Flora,' 1845, p. 615.

[Pg 475]

GENERAL CONCLUSIONS.

At the end of many of the preceding sections, and whenever the requirements of the case demanded it, a brief summary of the main facts and of the inferences to be derived from them has been given. It may be useful to give in conclusion a few general remarks on the whole subject.

It will be seen from the numerous facts herein cited, that the so-called monstrous formations (excluding morbid growths the result of disease or injury) present no peculiarities absolutely foreign to the normal organisation of plants. The difference between the natural and monstrous development is one of degree and frequency of occurrence, not of kind.

Deviations from the customary form have been shown to arise from excessive or diminished growth, or from arrested or exalted development. Even in those instances where, for convenience' sake, the term perverted development has been used, it must be understood as applying only to the particular plant or organ under consideration, as the form assumed is perfectly in accordance with the ordinary conformation of some other plant or group of plants.

The period at which malformations occur is a matter of some importance; this is, indeed, implied in the term arrest of development; evolution goes on with[Pg 476] growth up to a certain point and is then stopped, and thus changes are brought about in the part affected of a different nature from those dependent on non-development or suppression.

Some malformations are congenital, therefore, while others are acquired—in the former instance the disturbance is coeval in origin, and contemporaneous in its growth and development, with those of the affected part; in the latter case the organ may have attained its ordinary degree of perfection, or at least may have advanced some way towards it, before any deviation shows itself. True chorisis or fission, for instance, is usually a congenital affection, arising at a very early period of development, while enation takes place from structures which are all but complete as to their organisation, even though they may not have attained their full dimensions. The date of appearance is also of consequence in determining the true nature of some changes; it does not always follow, for instance, that because one organ occupies the position of another, it is of the same nature as the one whose place it fills. The presence of anthers on petals or on such organs as the corona of *Narcissus* does not necessarily constitute those parts actual stamens, but rather staminodes. The true stamens are either wanting, or if present, they are in advance of their imitators as regards their development.

General morphology of the leaf and axis. Homology. Since the time when Goethe's generalisations were adopted by A. P. De Caudolle, special attention has been given to the form and mode of development of the leaf-organ; for as it was well said by Wolff, if once the course of evolution and the structure of the leaf were[Pg 477] known, those of the parts of the flower would follow as a matter of course.

It is not necessary, in this place, to pursue the subject of the development and construction of the leaf further than they are illustrated by ordinary teratological phenomena.

From this point of view perhaps the most interesting circumstance is the part that the sheath of the leaf plays.[553] In many cases of so-called metamorphosis, it is the sheath of the leaf that is represented and not the blade. In normal anatomy the sepals, petals, carpels, and even the stamens, as a general rule, correspond to the sheath rather than to the blade of the leaf, as may be seen by the arrangement of the veins. The blade of the leaf seems to be set apart for special respiratory and absorbent offices, while the sheath is in structure, if not in office, more akin to the stem. It would not be easy apart from their position to distinguish between a tubular sheathing leaf and a hollow stem. The development of adventitious growths by chorisis or enation has been frequently alluded to in the foregoing pages, and many illustrations have been given of the power that leaves have of branching in more than one plane, owing to the projection of secondary growing-points from the primary organ. These new centres of development are closely connected with the fibro-vascular system of the leaf, so that no sooner does a new growing point originate, than vessels are formed to connect the new growth with the general fibrous cord, see pp. 355, 445. This leads M. Casimir De Candolle to consider the entire leaf as a composite structure. The morphological unit, says he, is the cellular protrusion or growing point (*saillie*) and its corresponding fibro-vascular bundle.[554]

The identity, in a morphological point of view, of the leaves and the lateral parts of the flower is so[Pg 478] thoroughly recognised that little need be said on that score, save to repeat that the homology of the floral organs is usually not so much with the entire leaf as with its sheath.

The most singular instances of morphological identity are those relating to the sexual organs. We have seen the gradual transition of stamens to pistils, and of pistils to stamens, the development of ovules on the edges of the anther, the co-existence of pollen with ovules on an antheroid body, and, stranger still, the actual development of pollen within the tissues of the ovule itself. From such facts, in addition to what we know of the relative position, internal structure, and mode of development of the organs, it is impossible to avoid coming to the conclusion that, however distinctly these parts may, under ordinary circumstances, be set apart for the performance of distinct functions, morphologically they are homologous.

These ideas may be carried yet farther—the same sort of evidence, which is adduced in support of the morphological identity of leaves with the parts of the flower, may be advanced in confirmation of the opinion, that, morphologically, there is no distinction between axis and leaf. The leaf, according to this view, is a specialised portion of the axis set apart to do certain work, just as the petals, stamens, &c., are leaves told off for distinct uses. It is unnecessary to refer to the intermediate productions linking the leaf-form to that of the axis, all that is requisite here is to point out the facts that teratology lends in support of these views. These may be summed up by the statement that almost all those attributes which morphologists recognise as peculiar to one or the other organ respectively, may be and are manifested by both. We have the stem acquiring the characters of the leaf, and the leaf those of the stem. Thus we have seen leaves, leaf-buds, branches, and flower-buds springing from leaves or leaf-organs;[555] see pp. 174, 177, 445, &c. The structure that we[Pg 479] are apt to associate exclusively with one is found to pertain to the other. The arrangement of the vascular cords in the leaf-organ finds its counterpart in the axis, generally, it is true, modified to suit altered circumstances or diverse purposes. In some cases the disposition is absolutely indistinguishable in the two organs. It may then be said that the distinctions usually drawn between axis and leaf are not absolute, and that, however necessary such a separation may be for descriptive or physiological purposes, morphologically the two organs are identical. Again, it may be said that leaf and axis are two phases of the same organ,—an organ capable of existing in its undifferentiated state in the form of a thallus among Cryptogams, but which in the higher groups of plants becomes marked out into separate portions, each portion having its own distinct functions to fulfil for the common benefit of the whole organisation.[556]

Special morphology.—Under this heading brief reference may be made to some of the organs whose morphological nature has been, and still is, much contested. It is clear that for the due elucidation of these matters, development and the comparative investigation of similar structures in different plants must be studied. Teratological data by themselves can no more be trusted to give a correct solution of any particular question, than the evidence furnished by other departments of botanical science taken separately. With this statement by way of caution, allusion may be made to some of the organs whose morphological construction is illustrated by the facts recorded in the present volume.

[Pg 480]

Calyx-tube.—In descriptive botany it is the common practice to speak of a calyx-tube, by which is meant a tubular or sheathing portion at the base of the flower, below the sepals or calyx-lobes, and distinct or inseparable from the ovary. The question morphology has to solve is whether this tubular structure is to be considered as a portion of the axis, or whether it is to be regarded as composed of the confluent bases of the sepals.

Mr. Bentham, who has recently reviewed the evidence as to the nature of the calyx-tube in his paper on *Myrtaceæ*,[557] still holds to the notion that the "calyx-tube" or "hypanthium" is formed from the concretion of the basal portions of the sepals. He founds his conclusions upon such facts as the following: the circumstance that the point of origin of the leaf is not always the same as the point of disarticulation or separation from the axis, inasmuch as the basal portion of the leaf is often adherent to the stem for some distance, though still recognisable as foliar not axial in its nature. In the same manner, the corolla and andrœcium may be concrete at the base, so that the stamens are for convenience' sake described as inserted into the tube of the corolla, though it is generally admitted that both stamens and petals are really hypogynous, and it is not usual to consider the corolla-tube up to the divergence of the stamens as part of the receptacle. A similar remark applies to the carpels and placentas. Mr. Bentham further considers that the gradual disconnection of the various whorls, that may be traced in many plants, is a further proof of concretion, rather than of expansion of the axis, but this argument may fairly be met by the consideration that the several whorls emerge at different heights.[558]

Organs originally free and distinct become ultimately combined at the base by the gradual protrusion from[Pg 481] the receptacle of a ring or tube under them, as in the

stamens of *Leguminosæ*; yet, says Mr. Bentham, no one would propose to describe the staminal tube of monadelphous *Leguminosæ* as part of the receptacle and not of the stamens. Perhaps not, for descriptive purposes, but morphologically it would not be easy to separate such a tube from the receptacle. The principal kinds of malformation which have a bearing on this subject are mentioned at pp. 77–81 and 247, from which it may be seen that the evidence furnished by teratology is conflicting. It would seem, indeed, that while in some families of plants there may be a real calyx-tube, in others the tubular portion is a sheath-like prolongation of the axis. In *Primula* or *Pedicularis*, where the venation is clearly laminar, the tubular portion is distinctly calycine. In other cases the so-called calyx-tube seems as certainly to be an expansion of the receptacle, as
in *Rosaceæ, Myrtaceæ, Melastomaceæ, Passiflora*,[559] &c.

Where the petals and stamens are described as being inserted into the throat of the calyx, or are perigynous, it may be assumed as a general rule, subject to but few exceptions, that the so-called calyx-tube is really a portion of the receptacle.[560] After all, this is very much a question of words, and for the following reasons,—very often the base of the calyx does evidently form a tube, and no one can say where the calyx ends and the receptacle begins. Again, many leaves are known to originate in the form of a ring-like protrusion from the axis, and from this primary ring originate secondary developments. Thus the asserted difference between a leaf, with such a history of development, and an axial structure becomes obliterated. From this point of view, peltate leaves like those
of*Tropæolum* or *Nelumbium* become very significant. In both the leaf-stalk is cylindrical and traversed, as in the case of all cylindrical[Pg 482] leaf-stalks, by a circle of fibro-vascular cords, as in a branch, and which radiate in all directions in the blade of the leaf. Now, if (as often happens to a slight extent) the central portion of the leaf were much depressed, owing to the disproportionate growth of the peripheral, as contrasted with the central portions, we should have a funnel-like or tubular formation, precisely similar to many of the so-called calyx-tubes. And, if we further suppose new growths to originate from the sides of this funnel or tube, by chorisis or enation, we should have the homologue of a tubular calyx, to the inner surface of which are attached petals, stamens, &c. From the consideration of circumstances such as these just detailed, together with that of the arrangement of the vascular cords, M. Casimir De Candolle arrives at the conclusion that the calyx-tube is a ring-like projection from an axis whose further direct development is arrested. The secondary projections or growing-points correspond to the several fibro-vascular cords of the primary ring, and are ultimately developed into sepals, petals, stamens and ovaries (see pp. 394, 509).

Andrœcium.—The main points of morphological interest relating to the andrœcium, referred to in this volume, are those concerning the structure of the anther (see p. 292), the compound nature of the stamens in some orders (see pp. 294, 345), and the nature of the andrœcium in orchids (see p. 380).

Inferior ovary.—Is the pistil always foliar in its morphological nature, or is it, in some cases, as Schleiden taught, formed from the axis alone? To a great extent the reply to this question is dependent on the conclusions that may be arrived at as to the true nature of the calyx-tube. Considered from a teratological point of view, there is no reason for considering the inferior ovary to be purely axial. On the contrary, the evidence derived from this source supports the ordinary opinion[Pg 483] that the carpels are invaginated within the expanded top of the flower-stalk and more or less adherent to it. Some of the gourds afford good illustrations of this, the upper part of the carpels in these fruits projecting beyond the axial portion. But this matter loses much of its importance if the morphological identity of axis and leaf-organ be conceded. The carpels in inferior ovaries seldom or never correspond to the lamina of the leaf, and between the vaginal portion of the carpellary leaf, and the axis who shall draw the distinction?

Placentation.—Some botanists have considered the placentas to be portions of the carpel, and have compared the production of ovules on them to the formation of buds on the leaf of *Bryophyllum*. Others have been led to see in each placenta, even when it is, to all outward appearance, a portion of the carpellary leaf, a direct prolongation from the axis, adherent to the leaf. Teratology shows that ovules may be formed indifferently on leaf-organs or on stem-organs. Sutural, parietal, axile, free-central placentation, and, if there be more forms, all may be met with even in the same ovary (see pp. 96, 508). Now, if there were such special tendencies in the axis, as contrasted with the leaf, to produce ovules, it is hardly likely that such anomalous arrangements as those just mentioned would be as frequent as they are. But as leaves produce other leaves, from their edges or their surfaces, and as they form buds in the same situations, just as axial organs do,[561] there is surely little ground for considering the placentas, or ovuliferous portions of the plant, to be of necessity axial. Here again, much of the difficulty vanishes if the morphological[Pg 484] identity of the leaf-form and of the stem-form be admitted.

Structure of the ovule.—The nature of the ovule and of its coverings has been a fertile source of controversy. The teratological data bearing on this subject have been given at pp. 262–272. These data strongly support the notion of the foliar nature of the coatings, and of the axial nature of the nucleus, taking leaf and axis either in the ordinary sense, or as modifications one of the other. It has been shown that the ovular coats may themselves become carpels, and that ovules may be developed upon ovules, p. 268. Whether the intra-carpellary siliques of *Cheiranthus*, not uncommonly met with (p. 182), are instances of ovular transmutation may be open to doubt.

The axial nature of the nucleus has been inferred from its position, mode of growth, and from its occasionally lengthening into a leafy or even a floriferous shoot. Probably it may occasionally be invested by sheathing coats, more analogous to tubular processes from the receptacle, than to foliar organs, as is the case in *Welwitschia*. The discussion of this matter, however, pertains rather to normal morphology than to teratology.

Morphology of conifers.—The nature of the pseudo-leaves of *Sciadopitys*, and probably of other Conifers, is illustrated by teratology, as also is the true constitution of the scale of the cone (see pp. 192, 245, 352), though it must be admitted that little or no light is thrown on that much-contested point—the true nature of the ovule of Gymnosperms.

Relative position of organs.—When organs are considered, not separately, but in their relations to each other, the appearances presented are referable to similar causes. Thus, the separation of parts usually united has been shown to depend on an excess of[Pg 485] development, the persistent union of parts, usually separate in the adult state, has been traced to an arrest of the process of development, by no means necessarily coexistent with diminished growth. The diminished or increased number of parts is, in like manner, attributable to analogous causes, as also are the variations in arrangement and form, spoken of under the heads of Displacement, Peloria, Substitution, &c.

In the instance of displacements, it has been shown how slight a change is required to transform the so-called inferior ovary into a superior one. A defective development of the top of the flower-stalk in some cases, in others a lack of union between the tube of the receptacle or of the calyx (comprising in those terms not only the apex of the receptacle, but the base of the sepals) and the carpels, suffice to bring about this change in a character which for systematic purposes is of great value.

Law of alternation.—The circumstances that interfere with the law of alternation may be briefly alluded to. The deviations from the customary arrangement have been very generally attributed to suppression, or to chorisis. It is unquestionable that either of these affords an efficient explanation of the arrangement in question, as also does that modification of chorisis, as it may be considered, which has been treated of under the head of Enation. Spiral torsion of the axis would likewise bring about analogous results. Still, it is quite conceivable that opposition or superposition of organs may occur without the intervention of any such operations. This will be the more readily conceded when it is remembered that the phyllotaxis of leaves not unfrequently varies on different branches of the same individual tree, and that a similar variation in the flower would at once disturb the customary alternate arrangement. Coalescence of the vascular bundles in an unusual manner, and an irregular disposition[Pg 486] of these cords have also been considered to bring about deviations from the rule of alternation, but in general the formation of the cords is subsequent to that of the growing points or mamelons.

Adhesions, accompanied by displacements, occasionally produce similar deviations, the nature of which is usually easily detected.

Co-relation.—The importance of this subject first prominently brought into notice by Geoffroy St. Hilaire gains in force daily. Rarely is a malformation an isolated phenomenon, almost always it is associated, from the operations of cause or effect, with some others. Instances of this co-relation have been cited in the preceding pages, and many more might have been mentioned, had the consideration of the relationship between form and function formed part of the plan of this volume. A change in itself slight, often acquires importance from its association with other alterations. This is particularly well seen in the case of the receptacle. Let an ordinarily concave thalamus remain, from defective development, flat, and how great the change in the appearance of the flower. Let the usually contracted receptacle be lengthened, and the whole aspect of the flowers so affected is altered to such an extent that, were their history not known, botanists would have no hesitation in assigning them to widely separate groups in their schemes of classification. Peloria, too, of either form, affords excellent illustrations of the co-existence of one changed condition with another. Not only is the form of one set of organs altered, but the number, the relative proportion, and the direction of the other organs of the flower are altered likewise.[562] Not only is the whole symmetry changed, but the physiological operations carried on in the flower undergo corresponding alterations.

[Pg 487]

There are certain co-relations which do not appear to have hitherto attracted the attention they merit; such, for instance, is that which exists between the particular period at which an organ is developed and its position and form. In normal morphology this has, to some extent, been worked out, as in the case of definite and indefinite, centrifugal and centripetal inflorescences, and in the definite or indefinite formation of shoots, &c.

Other instances may be cited in the frequent co-existence of regular flowers and definite inflorescence, the terminal position of many peloriated flowers, the relationship between indefinite inflorescence and prolongation of the axis, &c.

Again, the simultaneous evolution of the parts of the flower and their consequent verticillate arrangement, are often associated with the production of different forms from those characteristic of organs developed in succession, and, in consequence, arranged spirally. In the case of simultaneous development we meet with a repetition of whorls, as in what are termed hose-in-hose flowers (flores duplicati, triplicati, &c.), and also with cases of peloria. In instances where the organs are formed successively in spiral order, we meet with such changes as median prolification, petalody, and phyllody. All these are alterations which we might anticipate from the activity of the growing point being checked at a certain stage in the one case, while it is continuous in the other. This relationship between the definite and indefinite modes of growth and the form of the several organs of the flower, is more constant in reality than it may appear to be from a perusal of the lists of genera in the foregoing pages, in which it was not possible to show sufficiently well the comparative frequency of any given changes in individual plants. Had it been possible to give statistics setting forth the frequency of certain deviations in plants or groups having a particular organisation, as compared with the rarity of their occurrence in other plants of a different[Pg 488]conformation, these co-relationships would have been rendered much more evident. A hundred different plants, for instance, may be named in any particular list, of which fifty shall be of one type of structure, and the remainder of another. And the co-relative changes in each fifty may appear to be evenly balanced, but so far is this from being the case, that the frequency of the occurrence of a particular change, in one species in the list, may be so great as far to exceed the instances of its manifestation in all the rest put together. This difficulty is only very partially obviated by the addition of the * to signify especial frequency of occurrence of any given malformation in the plants to whose names it is affixed.

Compensation.—But little further need be said on this head. An atrophied condition of one part is generally associated with an hypertrophied condition of another, and scarcely a change takes place in one direction, but it is associated with an inverse alteration in some other. This principle is not universal, and its application must not be unduly strained. It requires specially to be considered in reference to differences in the degree or kind of functional activity exercised by the organs implicated—points beyond the scope of the present volume.

Teratology and classification.—Lastly, there remain to be mentioned the bearings of teratology on systematic botany. There are those who would entirely exclude teratology from such matters. It may be expedient to do so when the object sought is one of convenience and facility of determination only, but when broader considerations are concerned, teratology must no more be banished than variation. In most instances the one differs but in degree from the other. If variation affords aid in our speculations as to the affinities and genealogical descent of species and other groups, so does teratology, and in a far higher degree.

[Pg 489]

Take the characters of exogens as distinct from endogens; even under ordinary circumstances, no absolute distinction can be drawn between them. There are plants normally of an intermediate character, while, to take exceptional instances, there are exogens with the leaves and flowers of endogens, and endogens whose outward organisation, at any rate, assimilates them to exogens. Diclinous or monochlamydeous plants owe their imperfect conformation to suppression, and may become structurally complete by a species of peloria. Structurally hermaphrodite flowers become unisexual by suppression, or are rendered incomplete by the non-development of one or more of their floral whorls. Hypogynous flowers become perigynous by adhesion, or by lack of separation; perigynous ones become hypogynous by an early detachment from the receptacle that bears them, or by the arrested development of an ordinarily cup-like receptacle.

How the relative position of the carpels and the calyx may be altered has already been alluded to, as has also the circumstance that while it is common to find an habitually inferior or adherent ovary becoming superior or free, it is much more rare to find the superior ovary adherent to the receptacle or to the calyx.[563] Regular and irregular peloria, too, serve to show how slight are the boundaries, not only between different genera, but also between different families.

While, therefore, teratology may be an unsafe guide in strictly artificial schemes, it is obvious that its teachings should have great weight in all philosophical systems of classification.

The questions will constantly arise, does such and such a form represent the ancestral condition of certain plants? Is it a reversion to that form? or is it, on the other hand, the starting point of new forms?

[Pg 490]

Such questions cannot receive at present any satisfactory answer, but the evidence we have seems to indicate that pre-existing forms were simpler, and less specialised in structure than those now existing, and hence if we meet with malformations of a simple kind, we may consider them as possible reversions; while, if they present features of increased complexity, and more sharply defined differentiation, we may assume them to be evidences of a progressive rather than of a retrogressive tendency.

That monstrosities so called may become the starting points of new forms is proved by circumstance that, in many cases, the peculiarities are inherited so that a new "race" is produced and perpetuated: and if a new race, why not a new species? The difference is one of degree only.

FOOTNOTES:

[553]See Clos., 'Bull. Soc. Bot. Fr.,' 1856, vol. iii, p. 679.

[554]'Théorie de la Feuille,' p. 26.

[555]An additional illustration of this may be cited, which has been brought under the notice of the writer by Dr. Welwitsch recently, and in which some of the leaflets of the pinnate leaf of a species of *Macrolobium* were absent, and their place supplied by flowers arranged in cymes.

[556]The presence of a bud at the extremity once considered to be an absolute distinction between branch and leaf, which latter never forms a bud exactly at the apex—is invalidated by the case of the Nepaul barley, p. 174.

[557]'Journ. Linn. Soc.,' vol. x, p. 103 *et seq.*

[558]See also the receptacular tube (ovary?) of *Bæckea* bearing stamens, see p. 183. It would be natural to see stamens springing from the receptacle but not from the ovary.

[559]In *Passiflora* the organogeny of the flower clearly shows the truth of this assertion, as was indeed shown by Payer and Schleiden.

[560]See Payer, 'Organ. Veget.'

[561]It must, however, be borne in mind that no true leaf-organ has yet been seen with a bud at its exact apex (unless it be the nepaul barley), while in the case of an axial organ such a position of the bud is constant. The nearest approach is in the case of impari-pinnate leaves in which the terminal leaflet is jointed to the common rachis, and in the leaves of some *Meliaceæ* which continue to push forth new leaflets even after the leaf has attained maturity.

[562]A singular instance of co-relation was shown by Mr. Saunders at the Scientific Committee of the Royal Horticultural Society, February 16th, 1868, in a hyacinth with perfectly green, long, tubular, erect, not horizontally spreading flowers.

[563]An illustration of this latter nature in the case of a cherry, which was surmounted by the calyx lobes, precisely as in the case of a pomaceous fruit, has been given at p. 424, *adnot.*

[Pg 491]

APPENDIX
DOUBLE FLOWERS.[564]

In ordinary language, the epithet double flowers is applied to flowers of very varied structural conformation. The most common conditions rendering a flower double, in the popular acceptation of the term, are substitutions of petals or petal-like bodies for stamens and pistils, one or both. (See Petalody, p. 283.) Another very common mode of doubling is brought about by a real or apparent augmentation in the number of petals, as by multiplication, fission, or chorisis. (See pp. 66, 343, 371, 376.) Sometimes even the receptacle of the flower within the outer corolla, divides, each subdivision becoming the centre of a new series of petals, as in some very luxuriant camellias and anemones. The isolation of organs which, under ordinary circumstances, are united together, is another circumstance, giving rise, in popular parlance, to the use of the term double flower. (See Adesmy, Solution, pp. 58, 76, 82.) Prolification is another very frequent occurrence in the case of these flowers, while still other forms arise from lacination of the petals, or from the formation of excrescences from the petals or stamens, in the form of supplementary petal-like lobes. (See Enation, p. 443.)

As these matters are all treated of under their respective headings, it is not necessary to allude to them again in detail. It may be well, however, to allude, in general terms, to the causes which have been assigned by various writers for their formation, and to the means which have been adopted by practical experimenters to secure the production of the flowers often so much esteemed by the florist. It must be admitted that, in spite of all that has been written on the subject, but very little is known about these matters. In the case of the stock the following means have been adopted by cultivators in order to[Pg 492] obtain plants bearing double instead of single flowers. There is first the crossing of single flowers with double ones, effected by planting a double-flowered plant in proximity to a single-flowered one; but this, it is obvious, could lead to no important results, since the double flowers, having no pollen, could not possibly influence the seed, which is borne only by the single-flowered plants. Another plan is the degustation of the buds, that is to say, the chewing of the well-formed buds; it is held that the single plants can be recognised by their sweeter taste and greater consistence, and may thus be weeded out; but there is at least the disadvantage attending this method, that the plants, single as well as double, must all be grown up to the period when these buds are tolerably well advanced. A third method which has been adopted is, that of sowing the seeds at a particular lunar epoch, great confidence being placed in the plan of planting them during the last quarter of the moon, but such confidence is found to be misplaced. The plan of removing the stamens has had its supporters, but as this must be done at an early stage of development, and could only influence the result by diverting the vital force which would be expended in the maturation of the pollen, to the perfecting of the seeds, it is obvious that the plan is impracticable for all ordinary purposes, even if in any degree efficient, which from the plasticity of vegetable development, and the faculty of doubling which is inherent in the stock family, is not at all improbable. Still another mark, the presence of a fifth petal in the single or seed-bearing flower, has been held to indicate the assurance of obtaining a crop of double-flowered plants from seeds saved from flowers possessing this peculiarity. To a certain extent, doubtless, this expectation would be realised, owing to the plasticity and inherent quality just alluded to, but the proportion would be too small for any useful practical purpose.

"The gardeners of Erfurt," observes M. Chaté, who has written a book[565] on the subject, in which he makes known a means of obtaining double-flowered stocks founded on more than fifty years' practice in his family, "have, for a long time, to a certain extent monopolised the sale of seeds of these plants. To obtain these seeds, the Erfurt gardeners cultivate the flowers in pots, and place them on shelves in large greenhouses, giving them only sufficient water to prevent them from dying. So cultivated the plants become weakened, the pods shortened, and the seeds less numerous, and better ripened; and these seeds give from 60 to 70 per cent. of double flowers.

"The seeds from these plants are said to be mostly of an abnormal shape, which is so striking that experienced cultivators are able to separate those which would furnish double flowers from those which would produce single ones."

[Pg 493]

M. Chaté's method, which he calls the French one, gives still greater results, viz.: 80 per cent. of double flowers, and these produced by very simple means. "When my seeds," he observes, "have been chosen with care, I plant them, in the month of April, in good dry mould, in a position exposed to the morning sun, this position being the most favourable. At the time of flowering I nip off some of the flowering branches, and leave only ten or twelve pods on the secondary branches, taking care to remove all the small weak branches which shoot at this time. I leave none but the principal and the secondary branches to bear the pods. All the sap is employed in nourishing the seeds thus borne, which give a result of 80 per cent. of double flowers. The pods under this management are thicker, and their maturation is more perfect. At the time of extracting the seeds the upper portion of the pod is separated and placed aside, because it has been ascertained that the plants coming from the seeds situated in this portion of the pod, give 80 per cent. of single flowers. They yield, however, greater variety than the others. This plan of suppressing that part of the pod which yields single flowers in the largest proportion, greatly facilitates the recognition of the single-flowered plants, because there remains to be eliminated from among the seedlings only from 10 to 15 per cent.

This separation of the single from the double-flowered plants, M. Chaté tells us is not so difficult as might be supposed. The single stocks, he explains, have deep green leaves (glabrous in certain species), rounded at the top, the heart being in the form of a shuttlecock, and the plant stout and thickset in its general aspect, while the plants yielding double flowers have very long leaves of a light green colour, hairy, and curled at the edges, the heart consisting of whitish leaves, curved so that they enclose it completely. Such is the substance of M. Chaté's method of securing so large a proportion of double-flowered plants, and then of separating them from the remaining single ones—a method which commends itself to the good sense of the intelligent cultivator."[566]

Signor Rigamonti, a great cultivator of pinks, asserted that he was able to distinguish double from single-flowered pinks, in the seedling state. According to this gentleman, those seedlings which produce three cotyledons in a whorl in place of two, form double flowers. In the case of*Primula sinensis* the same results occurred. Some had three leaves in a ring, others two; most had the leaves standing one over the other as usual. These were divided into three sets, and when they flowered, the first lot were all double, the second semi-double, the third single. But these statements have not been confirmed by other observers; and the writer can safely assert that seedling pinks occasionally[Pg 494] produce three cotyledons, and subsequently single flowers. He has never observed a double flower under these circumstances, though it is true his experience in this matter has been but small.

A writer in Otto's 'Gartenzeitung,' considers that double flowers are a consequence of dryness of soil and atmosphere, and not of a luxurious soil, rich in nutritious matter, having arrived at this conclusion from an observation of the following circumstances:

226

"Fifty years ago we saw *Kerria japonica* in a hothouse with single flowers. Twenty years later we met with it in several gardens, in the open air, but always with double flowers. At this time we were assured that single-flowered plants were no more to be found in the whole of Europe, and botanists forming herbaria offered considerable sums for a branch of *K. japonica* with single flowers. We were requested to take the plant in hand for the purpose of inducing it to produce single flowers. We were advised to plant it out in a rich soil, which was done, but, by chance, the situation was sloping, consequently it did not retain moisture, and all the flowers produced for several years in succession were double. Shortly after, the captain of an English ship again brought plants bearing normal flowers from Japan, which were soon spread over the continent, and of which we received one plant. After three years all the young plants raised from cuttings were double-flowered.

"In the year 1820 we several times visited a garden in the neighbourhood of Vienna, well known on account of its plant culture. The gardener there possessed an immense plant of *Camellia japonica* with single flowers, and some small plants raised from this by cuttings, but no other variety of camellia. He fertilised the flowers with their own pollen, harvested seeds, which he sowed, and the plants raised from them were placed in an extremely dry, lofty conservatory, where, after some years, instead of producing single flowers, they all produced double ones. The seedlings and mother plant were planted in one and the same kind of earth, and some of the flowers on the old plant also showed an inclination to become double.

"This, at that time, to us, enigmatical phenomenon, was kept in mind until we had an opportunity of instituting comparisons between the climate of Japan and China and our own, and we then concluded that in the case of a plant imported from thence, and exposed to such different climatical influences, the origin of the greater or less imperfection of its sexual organs was probably owing to this change, as we had experienced in *Kerria* and *Camellia*; and that the sterility of many other exotic plants might be attributed to the same cause. The difference in the climatical relations of Japan and Europe is very considerable. In Japan, previous to the new growth of *Kerria* and *Camellia*, a rainy season of three months' duration prevails; in Europe, on the contrary, dry winds prevail especially in the eastern part, where our plains are[Pg 495] often transformed into deserts. Is it, therefore, remarkable that a plant introduced from Japan into Europe, exposed to the influences of this great diversity of climate, should produce imperfect sexual organs incapable of further propagating the plant from seeds? A rich soil, with the necessary amount of moisture, will never engender double flowers."[567]

Mr. Darwin[568] describes a peculiar form of *Gentiana Amarella*, in which the parts of the flower were more or less replaced by compact aggregations of purple scales in great numbers. A similar condition is, indeed, not uncommon in this plant, and, as Mr. Darwin also remarked, on hard, dry, bare, chalky banks, thus bearing out the views expressed by the writer in the 'Gartenzeitung' just cited. Some double flowers of *Potentilla reptans* found growing wild near York, and transmitted to the writer by a correspondent, were observed growing along a high wall, in a dry border, close to a beaten path, bordering on a gravel pit, others were found on a raised bank, which, from its elevation and exposure to the sun, was particularly dry.

On the other hand, the double-flowered *Cardamine pratensis*, which is occasionally found in a wild state, always grows in very wet places.

Of late years a remarkable double-flowered race of *Primula sinensis* has been obtained. In particular, Messrs. Windebank and Kingsbury, of Southampton, have succeeded in raising a set of plants in which the flowers are very double and very attractive in a florist's point of view. The corollas in these flowers are not merely duplicated, but from their inner surface spring, in some cases, funnel-shaped or tubular petals (p. 315), so regular in form as quite to resemble a perfect corolla. These tubes are attached to the inner side of the tube of the corolla, in the same way as are the stamens, these latter organs being, it appears, absent. The carpels are present, but open at the top, and bear numerous ovules, hence it was at first surmised that these plants were obtained and perpetuated, by the application of pollen from single flowers to these double-flowered varieties.

The raisers of this fine race however assert that "the double kinds are all raised from the seed obtained from *single* flowers; the double blooms do not produce seed, as a rule, and even if they did yield seed, and it were to germinate, the plants so raised would simply produce single flowers." Semi-double flowers will produce seed, but it is necessary that they should be fertilised with the pollen from the single blooms. They rarely, however, if ever, produce really double flowers when so fertilised, and the number of semi-double flowers, even, is always small, the remainder, and, consequently, the larger part, proving single. To obtain double varieties, the raiser fertilises certain fine and striking single flowers, with the pollen of other equally fine[Pg 496] single blooms, and the desired result is obtained. This is Messrs. Windebank and Kingsbury's *modus operandi*, the exact process or mode of accomplishment being, however, a professional secret.[569]

From what has been said, as well as from other evidence which it is not necessary to detail in this place, it may be seen that the causes assigned by physiologists, and the plans proposed by cultivators for the production of double flowers, are reducible to three heads, which may be classed under Plethora, Starvation, and Sterility. These three seem inconsistent one with the other, but are not so much so as they at first sight appear to be.

Tho advocates of the plethora theory have much in their favour: for instance, the greater frequency of double flowers among cultivated plants than among wild ones. The great preponderance of double flowers in plants derived from the northern hemisphere, when contrasted with those procured from the southern, as alluded to by Dr. Seemann, seems also to point to the effect of cultivation in producing these flowers. Now, although this is, to a large extent, due to the selection that has been for so long a period practised by gardeners, still that process will not account for the appearance of double flowers where no such selection has been exercised; as in the case of wild plants. Some double peas, observed by Mr. Laxton, appeared suddenly; they had not been selected or sought for, but they were produced, as it would appear, as a result of high cultivation, and during the period when the plant was in greatest vigour; and as the energies of the plant failed, so the tendency to produce double flowers ceased. Indeed, in reference to this subject, it is always important to bear in mind the time at which double flowers are produced; thus, an annual plant subjected to cultivation, will, it may be, produce single flowers for the firet year or two, then a few partially double flowers are formed, and from these, by careful selection and breeding, a double-flowered race may be secured. Sometimes, as in the peas before alluded to, in the same season the earlier blossoms are single, while later in the year double blossoms are produced. This happens, not only in annuals, but also in perennials, and is not infrequent in the apple; an illustration of this occurrence in this tree is given in the 'Gardeners' Chronicle' for 1865, p. 554.[570] Sometimes the flowers on a particular branch are double, while those on the rest of the plant are single.[571] On these points, the evidence furnished by a double white hawthorn in the Royal Botanic Gardens at Edinburgh is important. Professor[Pg 497] Balfour kindly wrote as follows in reply to an inquiry respecting this plant:—"A double white hawthorn in the Royal Botanic Gardens produced double flowers in spring. It retained its leaves during autumn and winter, until the following spring. It then flowered in the second spring, but produced weak single flowers only, and has continued to do so ever since. The flowering has been always weak, since this change of flowers from double to single. Mr. M'Nab attributes the change in the duration of the leaves to the filling up of the ground round the tree, to the height of a foot and a half on the stem. He is now trying the effect of extra manure in giving extra vigour to the plant." Here, at least, the production of single flowers would seem to be the result of debilitating causes, connected with the unusual persistence of the leaves, &c., for while the tree was healthy, double flowers were produced.

A similar illustration came under the writer's own notice. Some seedling balsams, of a strain which from long selection and hereditary tendency produces, year after year, double flowers were, in the spring (of 1866), allowed to remain in the seed-pans for many weeks after they were ready to be potted off; they were hence partly starved, and when they bloomed, they produced single flowers only. But these same plants, when more liberally treated, produced an abundance of double flowers. Moreover, other seedlings of the same batch, but sown later, and potted off at the usual time, produced double flowers as usual. Of a like character is the fact that the double *Ranunculus asiaticus* loses its doubleness if the roots are planted in a poor soil.

On the other hand, the way in which double stocks are stated to be produced at Erfurt, viz.: by giving the plants a minimum supply of water, and the other circumstances alluded to as showing the connection between the production of double flowers, and a deficiency of water, as well as the experiments of Mr. Monro, go to show that, so far from plethora, the inducing cause must be more nearly allied to inanition, though the impoverishing process is, to a certain extent, counteracted by only allowing a few of the seed-pods to ripen, and thus concentrating in a small number of flowers the nutriment intended for many.

Professor Edward Morren ('Bull. Acad. Roy. Belg.,' 2me ser., vol. xix, p. 224) considers the existence of true variegation in leaves, and the production of double flowers, as antagonistic one to the other; the former is a sign of weakness, the latter of strength. But it would seem that the exceptions are so numerous—so many cases of the co-existence of variegated leaves, and double flowers are known, at least in individual plants if not in species—that no safe inferences can be drawn as to this point. Since the above remarks were printed, Professor Morren has published a second paper on the subject, upholding his former views as to the incompatibility of variegated foliage (not mere colouration) and double flowers. In this paper he criticises the objections[Pg 498] raised by the present writer and others, and examines some of the alleged exceptions. Some of these the Belgian savant finds to prove his rule, inasmuch as although there is a co-existence of variegated foliage and double flowers in these illustrations, yet the plants are weakly, the flowers ill formed, or fall off before expansion. Admitting all this, there still remain cases in which double flowers and variegated foliage do exist in conjunction, and where the plants are vigorous and the flowers well developed. Instances of this are known to cultivators in species of *Dianthus, Hemerocallis, Althœa, Pœonia, Rosa, Ranunculus, Serissa, Saponaria*, etc., and probably the art of the cultivator would speedily be successful in raising other examples, were it a matter of importance or interest to them to do so. At any rate, the existence of a few unimpeachable illustrations is sufficient to support the opinion of the present writer, and objected to so strongly by M. Morren that, in the present state of our knowledge, "no safe inferences can be drawn" from the facts alluded to by the Belgian professor.[572]

Mr. Darwin[573] has thrown out the suggestion that the cause for the appearance of double flowers may be sought for in some previous state of things, bringing about sterility or imperfect formation, or functional activity of the genitalia of the flower, and consequent compensatory increase of the petaline element, either in the form of an increased number of bracts, petals, &c., or in the substitution of petals for stamens and pistils, &c.

In considering these points the question arises whether they can be reconciled one with another. And there is little doubt but that they may be. The production of a flower is preceded by an arrest of vegetation; this is obvious: the current of the plant's life becomes changed, the growth of the leaves is checked, the lengthening of the branches is arrested as the flower-bud forms; moreover, there is a close relationship in a large majority of flowers between the outer envelopes of the flower and the scales of a leaf-bud; this is especially so in regard to the venation, and is admitted by all morphologists. So far, then, it may be said that the production of a flower, like that of a bud, is due to a diminution of vegetative action; and as in double flowers we have, for the most part, merely a repetition and exuberant formation of floral envelopes, so we may attribute their formation to a continuance of the same feeble vegetative action as that which produced the first or normal series. How, then, can a copious supply of rich food, such as is provided by cultivation, produce double flowers? To this question, according to our theory, the reply would be that the quantity of food is excessive, more than the plant can properly digest; and hence vegetative[Pg 499] action is stopped, at least partially—pretty much as it would be if the plant were placed in the opposite condition of starvation. The effect of supplying a plant (or an animal) with an excessive supply of food, which it cannot assimilate, is in many respects similar to that which results from partially cutting off the supplies. And the same reasoning applies to sterility. If by high culture, or the supply of an undue quantity of nourishment, the constitution of the plant be impaired, or if the plant be pampered, it is no wonderful thing that sterility should ensue. Hence, then, may it not be asserted as a general principle that in the production of double flowers a partial arrest of development, if not of growth, however produced, is an essential preliminary? All the attendant phenomena, such as the obliteration of the stamens, the augmentation in the number of floral whorls, the occurrence of prolification, are consistent with the supposition of a primary arrest of development, more or less complete, as the case may be: at one time permanent, at another time relaxed and intermittent, or in a third set of cases the vegetative activity or power of growth may be restored, and from the centre of the flower may spring a perfect branch with perfect leaves, the production of sheaths only being superseded by the development of leaves, in which all the parts—sheath, stalk, and blade—are present.

When once the disposition to form double flowers is established, that tendency becomes hereditary: there are races of single Stocks in which, out of hundreds of plants, scarcely one double-flowered form is met with; but when the tendency to produce double blooms is set up, single flowers become the exception: thus, in the Balsams, before mentioned, not one in fifty now produces single flowers, and the seeds of these double Balsams produce double-flowered seedlings, with scarcely a "rogue" among them.

The following list of plants producing double flowers of any kind is taken from that given in 'Seemann's Journal of Botany,' vol. ii, p. 177, and to which some additions have been made. Miscalled double flowers, such as those of the *Compositæ*, *Viburnum Hydrangea*, &c., are excluded.

RANUNCULACEÆ.

- Clematis Viticella, *Linn.*, S. Europe.
- ○   florida, *Thunb.*, Japan.
- ○   Fortunei, *Moore*, Japan.
- ○   patens, *Desne*, Japan.
- Anemone japonica, *Sieb. et Zucc.*, Japan.
- ○   coronaria, *Linn.*, S. Europe, Asia Minor.
- ○   hortensis, var. *Linn.*, S. Europe.
- ○   palmata, *Linn.*, N. Africa, Spain, Portugal.
- ○   nemorosa, *Linn.*, Europe, N. America, Siberia.
- ○   sylvestris, *Linn.*, S. Europe, Siberia.[Pg 500]
- Hepatica triloba, *Chaix.*, Europe.
- Ranunculus bulbosus, *Linn.*, Europe, N. Amer.
- ○   repens, *Linn.*, Europe, Siberia, N. Amer.
- ○   acris, *Linn.*, Europe, Siberia.
- ○   aconitifolius, *Linn.*, Europe.
- ○   gramineus, *Linn.*, Italy, France, Portugal, Switzerland.
- ○   bullatus, *Linn.*, S. Europe.
- ○   asiaticus, *Linn.*, The East.
- Ficaria ranunculoides, *Mœnch.*, Europe.
- Thalictrum anemoides, *Michæ.*, N. America.
- Caltha palustris, *Linn.*, Europe, Asia, N. America.
- Trollius europæus, *Linn.*, Europe.
- ○   nepalensis, Himalaya.
- Nigella damascena, *Linn.*, Mediterranean.
- Aquilegia vulgaris, *Linn.*, Europe.
- ○   canadensis, *Linn.*, N. America.
- Delphinium Ajacis, *Linn.*, S. Europe.
- ○   grandiflorum, *Linn.*, Siberia, N. America.
- ○   Consolida, *Linn.*, Europe, N. America.

- ○   cheilanthum, *Fisch.*, Siberia.
- ○   elegans, *D. C.*, North America.
- ● Adonis autumnalis, *Linn.*, Europe.
- ○   vernalis, *Linn.*, Europe, Asia.
- ● Pæonia Moutan, *Sims*, China, Japan.
- ○   officinalis, *Retz.*, Europe.
- ○   tenuifolia, *Linn.*, Tauria.
- ○   albiflora, *Pall.*, Siberia.
- ○   paradoxa, *Andr.*, S. Europe.

NYMPHÆACEÆ.

- ● Nelumbium speciosum, *Willd.*, Africa, Asia.

BERBERIDACEÆ.

- ● Berberis, *sp. cult.*

PAPAVERACEÆ.

- ● Papaver Rhœas, *Linn.*, Europe.
- ○   bracteatum, *Lindl.*, Russia.
- ○   somniferum, *Linn.*, S. Europe, Asia Minor, Egypt.
- ● Chelidonium majus, *Linn.*, Europe, Asia.
- ● Sanguinaria canadensis, *Linn.*, N. America.
- ● Podophyllum peltatum, *Linn.*, N. America.

CRUCIFERÆ.

- ● Mathiola incana, *R. Br.*, Mediterranean.
- ○   glabrata, *D. C.*
- ○   annua, *Sweet.*, South Europe, Syria.
- ● Cheiranthus Cheiri, *Linn.*, Europe.
- ● Iberis umbellata, *Linn.*, Europe.
- ○   amara, *Linn.*, Europe.
- ● Cardamine pratensis, *Linn.*, Europe, Asia, Africa, America.
- ● Hesperis matronalis, *Linn.*, Europe, Siberia.
- ● Barbarea vulgaris, *R. Br.*, Europe.[Pg 501]
- ● Sinapis arvensis, *Linn.*, Europe.
- ● Brassica oleracea. *Linn.*, Europe.

CISTACEÆ.

- ● Helianthemum vulgare, *Spach.*, Europe, N. Africa.

VIOLACEÆ.

- ● Viola odorata, *Linn.*, Europe, Siberia.
- ○   grandiflora, *Linn.*, Europe,
- ○   tricolor, *Linn.*, Europe.

CARYOPHYLLEÆ.

- ● Dianthus barbatus, *Linn.*, France, Germany.
- ○   chinensis, *D. C.*, China.
- ○   Poiretianus, *Seringe*, ?
- ○   Caryophyllus, *Linn.*, France, Italy.
- ○   arboreus, *Linn.*, Crete.
- ○   hybridus (*gardens*).
- ○   corymbosus, *Sibth.*, Asia Minor.

○   plumarius, *Linn.*, Europe, Siberia, N. America.

○   deltoides, *Linn.*, Europe.

● Saponaria officinalis, *Linn.*, Europe.

● Lychnis sylvestris, *Schkr.*, Europe.

○   vespertina, *Linn.*, Europe.

○   flos cuculi, *Linn.*, Europe.

○   Viscaria, *Linn.*, Europe.

○   chalcedonica, *Linn.*, Japan, Asia Minor.

● Silene inflata, *Sm.*; *var.* maritima, *D. C.*, Europe.

ALSINEÆ.

● Sagina procumbens, *Linn.*, Europe.

MALVACEÆ.

● Hibiscus Rosa sinensis, *Linn.*, E. Indies.

○   flavescens, *Cav.*, China.

○   alba, *Hook.*, China.

○   syriacus, *Linn.*, Syria, Carniola.

● Althæa rosea, *Cav.*, Caucasus, &c.

● Malva rotundifolia, *Linn.*, Europe.

○   moschata, *D. C.*, Europe.

HIPPOCASTANEÆ.

● Æsculus Hippocastanum, *Linn.*, Europe, N. America.

GERANIACEÆ.

● Geranium pratense, *Linn.*, Europe, Siberia.

○   sylvaticum. *Linn.*, Europe.

● Pelargonium zonale, *Willd.*, S. Africa.

● Tropæolum majus, *Linn.*, Peru.

○   minus, *Linn.*, Peru.[Pg 502]

● Oxalis cernua, *Thunb.*, S. Africa.

● Impatiens Balsamina, *Linn.*, E. Ind.

TERNSTRÖMIACEÆ.

● Camellia reticulata, *Lindl.*, China.

○   Sasanqua, *Thunb.*, China.

○   japonica, *Linn.*, Japan.

● Thea maliflora, *Seem.*, Japan.

AURANTIACEÆ.

● Citrus Aurantium, *Linn.*, Asia, South Europe.

PAPILIONACEÆ.

● Trifolium repens, *Linn.*, Europe, S. America.

● Medicago sp., ?., Europe.

● Ulex europæus, *Link.*, Europe.

● Spartianthus junceus, *Linn.*, S. Europe.

● Clitoria Ternatea, *Linn.*, E. India.

● Orobus viscoides, *D. C.*, Croatia, &c.

○   vernus, *Linn.*, Europe.

● Genista tinctoria, *Linn.*, Europe.

- ○   sibirica, *Linn.*, Siberia.
- ○   scoparia, *Lam.*, Europe.
- • Cytisus albus, *Link.*, Portugal.
- • Anthyllis Vulneraria, *Linn.*, Europe.
- • Coronilla Emerus, *D. C.*, Europe.
- • Lotus corniculatus, *Linn.*, Europe.

ROSACEÆ.

- • Rosa lutea, *Mill.*, Europe.
- ○   cinnamomea, *Linn.*, Europe, N. America.
- ○   spinosissima, *Linn.*, Central Asia.
- ○   Carolina, *Linn.*, N. America.
- ○   villosa, *Linn.*, Europe, Central Asia.
- ○   centifolia, *Linn.*
- ○   damascena, *Linn.*, Syria.
- ○   rubiginosa, *Linn.*, Europe, Asia, N. America.
- ○   moschata, *Ait.*, Madeira, N. Africa.
- ○   canina, *Linn.*, Europe.
- ○   alba, *Linn.*, Europe, Caucasus.
- ○   indica, *Linn.*, China.
- ○   nivea, *D. C.*, China.
- ○   Eglanteria, *Linn.*, Europe.
- ○   gallica, *Linn.*, Europe, Caucasus.
- ○   pimpinellifolia, *Linn.*, Europe, Central Asia.
- ○   Banksiæ, *R. Br.*, China.
- ○   sulphurea, *Ait.*, East.
- • Rubus fruticosus, *Linn.*, Europe.
- ○   rosifolius, *Linn.*, Mauritius, E. India.
- ○   corylifolius, *Smith*, Europe.
- ○   cæsius, *Linn.*, Europe.
- • Kerria japonica, *D. C.*, Japan.[Pg 503]
- • Spiræa Filipendula, *Linn.*, Europe.
- ○   Ulmaria, *Linn.*, Europe.
- ○   prunifolia, *Sieb. et Zucc.*, Japan.
- ○   Reevesii, *Lindl.*, China.
- ○   strobilacea, *Sieb. et Zucc.*, Japan.
- • Fragaria vesca, *Linn.*, Europe, N. America.
- • Potentilla alpestris, *Hall. f.*, Europe.
- ○   reptans, *Linn.*, Europe, Asia.
- ○   Tormentilla, *Schrank*, Europe, Asia.
- ○   anserina, *Linn.*, Europe.
- • Geum rivale, *Linn.*, Europe.

POMACEÆ.

- • Cratægus Oxyacantha, *Linn.*, Europe.
- ○   Crus galli, *Linn.*, N. America.
- • Cydonia japonica, *Pers.*, Japan.
- • Pyrus communis, *Linn.*, Europe.

○   Malus, *Linn.*, Europe.

● Eriobotrya japonica, *Lindl.*, Japan.

AMYGDALEÆ.

● Amygdalus Persica, *Linn.*, Persia.

○   communis, *Linn.*, Mauritania.

● Prunus domestica, *Linn.*, Europe.

○   spinosa, *Linn.*, Europe, N. America.

○   avium, *Linn.*, Europe.

○   Cerasus, *Linn.*, Europe.

○   Kerii, *Steud.*, Japan.

○   japonica, *Thunb.*, China, Japan.

○   insititia, *Linn.*, Europe.

○   triloba, *Lindl.*, China.

MYRTACEÆ.

● Myrtus communis, *Linn.*, S. Europe.

● Punica Granatum, *Linn.*, S. Europe, Marocco.

PHILADELPHACEÆ.

● Philadelphus Coronarius, *linn.*, S. Europe.

● Deutzia Crenata, *sieb. Et Zucc.*, Japan.

ONAGRACEÆ.

● Fuchsia globosa, *Lindl.* (and var. hort. pl.), Mexico.

● Epilobium tetragonum, *D.C.*, Europe.

● Clarkia pulchella, *Pursh.*, California.

○   elegans, *Douglas*, N. America.

PORTULACACEÆ.

● Portulaca grandiflora, *Hook*, Chili.

GROSSULARIACEÆ.

● Ribes sanguineum, *Pursh.*, N. America.[Pg 504]

SAXIFRAGACEÆ.

● Saxifraga granulata, *Linn.*, Europe.

UMBELLIFERÆ.

● Daucus Carota, *Linn.*, Europe.

RUBIACEÆ.

● Ixora grandiflora, *De Cand.*, E. India.

● Serissa fœtida, *Comm.*, China, Japan.

● Gardenia Fortuniana, *Hook.*, China.

○   florida, *Linn.*, China, E. India.

○   radicans, *Thunb.*, Japan.

CAPRIFOLIACEÆ.

● Lonicera Periclymenum, *Linn.*, Europe.

● Sambucus nigra, *Linn.*, Europe.

CAMPANULACEÆ.

● Campanula latifolia, *Linn.*, Europe, Asia.

○   Tenorei, *Morett*, Naples.

○   Trachelium, *Linn.*, Europe.

○   Vidallii, *H. C. Wats.*, Europe.

234

- pyramidalis, *Linn.*, S. Europe.
- rotundifolia, *Linn.*, Europe, N. America.
- persicifolia, *Linn.*, Europe.
- glomerata, *Linn.*, Europe, Asia.
- Medium, *Linn.*, Europe.
- rhomboidea, *Linn.*, Europe.
- Platycodon grandiflorum, *D. C.*, Siberia.

ERICACEÆ.

- Calluna vulgaris, *Linn.*, Europe, N. America.
- Rhododendron indicum, *Sweet.*, E. India.
- ponticum, *Linn.*, Asia Minor.
- Azalea nudiflora, *Linn.*, N. America.
- glauca, *Lam.*, N. America.
- Arbutus Unedo, *Linn.*, S. Europe.
- Erica Tetralix, *Linn.*, Europe.
- cinerea, *Linn.*, Europe.
- hyemalis, gardens.

EPACRIDACEÆ.

- Epacris impressa, *R. Br.*, Australia.

PRIMULACEÆ.

- Primula villosa, *Jacq.*, Europe.
- Auricula, *Linn.*, Europe.
- denticulata, *Smith*, E. India.
- acaulis, *Jacq.*, Europe.
- elatior, *Jacq.*, Europe.
- prænitens, *Ker.* = sinensis, *Lindl.*, China.[Pg 505]
- Lysimachia Nummularia, *Roem et Schult.*, Europe.
- Anagallis tenella, *Linn.*, Europe.

JASMINACEÆ.

- Jasminum officinale, *Linn.*, S. Europe.
- Sambac., *Ait.*, E. India.
- hirsutum, *Hook.*, China.
- grandiflorum, *Lindl.*, S. Europe.

OLEACEÆ.

- Syringa persica, *Linn.*, Persia.
- vulgaris, *Linn.*, Europe, Persia.

APOCYNEÆ.

- Vinca minor, *Linn.*, Europe.
- major, *Linn.*, Europe.
- Nerium odorum, *Ait.*, E. India.
- Oleander, *Linn.*, S. Europe.
- Tabernæmontana coronaria, *Willd.*, E. India.
- Allamanda cathartica, *Aubl.*, S. America.

CONVOLVULACEÆ.

- Calystegia sepium, *R. Br.*, Europe, America, Asia.
- pubescens, *Lindl.*, China.

- Convolvulus tricolor, *Linn.*, S. Europe.
- Ipomœa pandurata, *Meyer*, S. America.

SOLANACEÆ.

- Datura cornigera, *Hook.*, Peru.
- fastuosa, *Linn.*, S. America, Egypt.
- arborea, *Linn.*, S. America.
- chlorantha, *Hook.*
- humilis, *Desf.*
- Petunia nyctaginiflora, *Juss.*, S. America.
- violacea, *Hook*, S. America.
- Solanum Dulcamara, *Linn.*, Europe.

GENTIANACEÆ.

- Gentiana Amarella, *Linn.*, Europe.

OROBANCHACEÆ.

- Orobanche sp.

SCROPHULARIACEÆ.

- Mimulus luteus, *Linn.*, Chili.
- Antirrhinum majus, *Linn.*, S. Europe.
- Digitalis purpurea, *Linn.*, Europe.
- Linaria vulgaris, *Mill.*, Europe, N. America.
- Veronica, sp.
- Calceolaria, var. cult.[Pg 506]

GESNERACEÆ.

- Achimenes longiflora, *D. C.*, Mexico.
- Gloxinia var. hort.

VERBENACEÆ.

- Clerodendron fragrans, *Willd.*, Japan.
- Verbena var. hort.

NYCTAGINEÆ.

- Mirabilis Jalapa, *Linn.*, Trop. America.

LAURINEÆ.

- Laurus nobilis, *Linn.*, S. Europe.
- Sassafras, *Linn.*, N. America.

IRIDACEÆ.

- Gladiolus tristis, *Linn.*, Cape of Good Hope.
- Crocus aureus, *Sibth*, Europe, Asia Minor.
- Susianus, *Curt.*, Asia Minor.
- pusillus, *Tenore*, Italy.
- vernus, *Smith*, S. Europe.
- Iris sibirica, *Linn.*, Europe.
- Iris Kæmpferi, *Siebold*, Japan.

AMARYLLIDACEÆ.

- Galanthus nivalis, *Linn.*, Europe.
- Leucoium vernum, *Linn.*, Europe.
- Sternbergia lutea, *Gawl.*, Europe, Asia Minor.

236

- Hippeastrum equestre, *Herb.*, S. America.
- Narcissus cernuus, *Salisb.*, S. Europe.
  - Telamonius, *Schult.*, Europe.
  - lobularis, *Schult.*
  - concolor, *Schult.*, Portugal.
  - biflorus, *Curt.*, Europe.
  - italicus, *Ker.*, Italy.
  - incomparabilis, *Curt.*, Italy.
  - Cypri, *Haw.*, Cyprus.
  - Pseudo-Narcissus, *Linn.*, Europe.
  - poeticus, *Linn.*, Europe.
  - Jonquilla, *Linn.*, S. Europe, East.
  - Tazetta, *Linn.*, S. Europe.
  - poculiformis, *Salisb.*, S. Europe.

ORCHIDACEÆ.

- Orchis Morio, *Linn.*, Europe.
  - mascula, *Linn.*, Europe.
  - pyramidalis, *Linn.*, Europe.
- Ophrys fucifera, *Linn.*, Europe.
- See also pp. 380, 509.

HYDROCHARIDACEÆ.

- Hydrocharis Morsus ranæ, *Linn.*, Europe.[Pg 507]

ASPHODELEÆ.

- Asphodelus luteus, *Linn.*, S. Europe.

LILIACEÆ.

- Tulipa Gesneriana, *Linn.*, Asia Minor.
  - sylvestris, *Linn.*, S. Europe.
- Scilla autumnalis, *Linn.*, Europe.
  - nutans, *Smith*, S. Europe.
- Convallaria majalis, *Linn.*, Europe, America.
  - Polygonatum, *Linn.*, Europe.
- Trillium grandiflorum, *Spreng.*, America.
- Fritillaria Meleagris, *Linn.*, Europe.
  - imperialis, *Linn.*, Persia.
- Lilium Martagon, *Linn.*, Europe.
  - candidum, *Linn.*, Syria, Persia.
- Hyacinthus orientalis, *Linn.*, East.
- Polianthes tuberosa, *Linn.*, E. India.
- Hemerocallis disticha, *Don.*, Nepal.
  - Kwanso, gardens.
  - fulva, *Linn.*, S. Europe.

COLCHICACEÆ.

- Colchicum autumnale, *Linn.*, Europe.
- Tofieldia calyculata, *Wahl.*, Europe.

BUTOMACEÆ.

- Sagittaria latifolia, *Willd.*, N. America.
o   sagittifolia, *Linn.*, Europe, Asia, America.

COMMELYNACEÆ.

- Tradescantia virginica, *Linn.*, N. America.
o   alba, gardens.

FOOTNOTES:

[564]This appendix forms a portion of a paper published in the 'Proceedings of the International Botanical Congress,' London, 1886, p. 127, and which it has been deemed advisable to reproduce with sundry additions and modifications.

[565]'Traité des Giroflées,' per E. Chaté.

[566]Leading Article in the 'Gardeners' Chronicle,' p. 74, 1866.

[567]Otto's 'Gartenzeitung,' 1866.

[568]'Gard. Chron.,' 1843, p. 628.

[569]'Gard. Chron.,' 1867, p. 381.—Art. "Chinese primroses."

[570]See also p. 79, fig. 36. A similar flower is figured in 'Hort. Eystett. Ic. Arb. Vern.,' fol. 5. "Fructus nondum observatus est fortassis alimento uberius in flores refuso, nullus sperari possit."

[571]See De Candolle, 'Plant. Rar. Genev.,' 1829, p. 91; and Alph. de Candolle.' Géog. Bot.,' p. 1080.

[572]See 'Gardeners' Chronicle,' 1868, p. 1113.

[573]Ibid., 1843, p. 628.

[Pg 508]

NOTE.

During the progress of the foregoing pages through the press, several additional illustrations of particular malformations have come under notice. Some of the more important of these may here be recorded.

Fasciation (see p. 11).—The following plants may be added to the list:—*Acer eriocarpum, Arabis albida, Brassica oleracea,* var., *Guarea,* sp.,*Artabotrys* sp. In all, with the exception of the first-named, the fasciation occurred in the inflorescence. In some species of *Artabotrys,* indeed, fasciation and curvation of the inflorescence are common.

Synanthy (p. 39).—Several additional instances of adhesion of two or more flowers in *Calanthe vestita, C. Veitchii,* and other forms of this genus may be cited. These furnish further illustrations of the much greater liability of some plants to particular changes as compared with others.*Scilla bifolia, Gagea arvensis,* and *Viola odorata* may be added to the list of synanthic plants.

Alterations of placentation, &c. (see pp. 98, 483).—M. Casimir De Candolle, in a letter to the author, dated March 8th, 1869, thus writes of the existence of a double row of carpels in *Pyrus spectabilis* and *Cratægus Oxyacantha,* "a longitudinal section of a double flower of *Pyrus spectabilis* shows two rows of carpels, placed one above another. The arrangement of the vascular bundles shows that the upper row is external in relation to the lower series. The carpels of the latter are wholly coalescent as in a pear, while those of the upper verticil are only partially coherent or sometimes quite distinct. The placentation is constantly axile in the inferior row and parietal in the upper one. The number of ovules in each carpel of the superior row varies greatly, and they are often, but not always, inserted in two longitudinal ranks, as is constantly the case in the lower carpels. Double flowers of *Cratægus Oxyacantha* present the same anomalies." For analogous instances in *Digitalis,* see p. 98. See also p. 380, *Saxifraga.*

Prolification, p. 120.—A. P. De Candolle, "Organographie Végétale," tab. 40, figures an instance of suppression of one lobe of the ovary in *Iris chinensis,* and of the presence at the base of the flower of an[Pg 509] adventitious and imperfect flower-bud, as in the *Phlomis,* mentioned at p. 119.

Monœcious Misleto, p. 193.—In this specimen, exhibited at one of the meetings of the Scientific Committee of the Royal Horticultural Society in 1869, there were both male and female flowers on the same bush. The plant was of the male sex, with numerous long

238

slender whip-like, somewhat pendulous, branches bearing comparatively large broad yellowish leaves, and fully developed male flowers at the end. From the side of one of these male branches, near the base, protruded a tuft of short, stiff branches, bearing small, narrow, dark green leaves, ripe berries and immature female flowers. There was no evidence of grafting or parasitism, of the female branch on the male, the bark and the wood being perfectly continuous so that the only tenable supposition is that this was a case of dimorphism.

Adventitious leaflet and pitcher, see pp. 30 and 355. In a species of *Picrasma*, in which the leaves are impari-pinnate and spread horizontally, an adventitious leaflet was observed to project at right angles to the plane of the primary leaf. It emerged at a point nearly corresponding to that at which the normal pinnæ were given off. The appearance presented was thus like that of a whorl of three leaves, except that the shining surface of the adventitious leaflet, corresponding to the upper face of the normal leaflets, was directed towards the axis, *i.e.*, away from the corresponding portion of the neighbouring pinnæ, while the dull surface, corresponding to the lower part of an ordinary leaflet, looked towards the apex of the main leaf, or away from the axis. In one instance, a stalked pitcher was given off from the same point as that from which the supernumerary leaflet emerged, the pitcher being apparently formed from the cohesion (congenital) of the margins of a leaflet.

In the normal leaf of this plant there is between the bases of the pinnæ, a small reddish gland or stipel? attached to, or projecting from, the upper surface of the rachis. It appeared from some transitional forms that the adventitious leaflet, just mentioned, was due to the exaggerated development of this gland, but no clue was afforded as to the origin of the ascidium. It was not practicable to examine the arrangement of the vascular bundles in the rachis.

Additional labella in Phaius.—A flower of *Phaius grandiflorus* was found in the same condition as the *Catasetum*, mentioned at pp. 291 and 382.

Tubular stem.—A species of *Sempervivum*, exhibited by Mr. Salter, of Hammersmith, at one of the summer exhibitions of flowers at the Royal Horticultural Society in 1868, under the name of *S. Bollei*, deserves notice from its bearing on the question of such structures as the calyx-tubes, the hip of the rose and such like, see pp. 394, 482. In this plant[Pg 510] the leaves appeared to be arranged some on the outside, others on the inside, of an erect hollow cylinder, some six inches in height. The oldest leaves were outside, the youngest within, so that the appearance presented was as if the summit of the axis had been pushed or drawn in, much as the finger of a tight glove might be invaginated in withdrawing it from the hand.

The plant in question thus furnishes an actual illustration of the supposititious case mentioned at p. 482.

Double flowers, see pp. 499, et seq.—The following species may be added to those already recorded: *Lychnis coronaria, Hibiscus mutabilis, Lotus major, Pisum sativum, Godetia* sp., *Ipomœa purpurea, Convolvulus minor, Heliotropium peruvianum, Trillium grandiflorum,* and *Phaius grandiflorus.*

www.ingramcontent.com/pod-product-compliance
Lightning Source LLC
Chambersburg PA
CBHW070106290526
45789CB00005B/1940